영어로
논문
쓰기

The Essential
Guide to
Writing Papers
in English

영어로 논문쓰기 최신 개정판

지은이 김상현
펴낸이 임상진
펴낸곳 (주)넥서스

초판 1쇄 발행 2004년 4월 20일
초판 7쇄 발행 2006년 7월 21일

2판 1쇄 발행 2006년 12월 25일
2판 29쇄 발행 2022년 10월 14일

3판 1쇄 발행 2024년 5월 25일
3판 2쇄 발행 2024년 5월 31일

출판신고 1992년 4월 3일 제311-2002-2호
10880 경기도 파주시 지목로 5
Tel (02)330-5500 Fax (02)330-5555

ISBN 979-11-6683-555-1 93740

www.nexusbook.com

영어로 논문 쓰기

김상현
지음

최신 개정판

The Essential Guide to Writing Papers in English

넥서스

저자
약력

김상현

전) 한국노어노문학회 편집장, 부회장
전) 성균관대학교 러시아어문학과 교수 / russianstyle67@hanmail.net
전) Full time lecturer in Dept. of East Asian Lang. and Lit. at the University of Kansas
전) *The Journal of Eurasian Studies* (네덜란드 ELSEVIER 출판) Chief-in-editor

저서
『쟁점으로 보는 러시아 미술』(근간)
『푸쉬킨의 예브게니 오네긴 깊게 읽기』(근간)
『도모스트로이 : 러시아의 풍속과 일상의 문화사』(민속원, 2020)
『러시아 정교회 건축과 예술』(민속원, 2018)
『러시아 문화의 풍경들』(성균관대출판부, 2017)
『레닌묘 : 상징의 건축, 기억의 정치』(민속원, 2017)
『러시아의 전통혼례 문화와 민속』(성균관대출판부, 2014)
『소비에트 러시아의 민속과 사회이야기』(민속원, 2009)

특강 경력
"학문하는 자세와 영어로 논문쓰기 전략" 특강 100회 이상

2001년에 첫 출판된 『영어로 논문쓰기』는 이듬해 2002년에 개정-증보판이, 2006년에는 최종 증보-결정판이 나왔다. 지금의 개정판이 나오기까지 누적 쇄로 하면 38판을 찍었다. 이 분야 도서 중에서 이렇게 스테디셀러로 사랑받는 책도 드물 것이다. 이제 『영어로 논문쓰기 최신 개정판』이라는 이름으로 새롭게 등장한 개정판은 독자 여러분에게 또 다른 자극과 공부에의 동기부여를 줄 것이다. 영미권으로 유학을 준비 중이거나, 이미 현지에서 학업을 이어가는 모든 분에게 신간 출간은 분명 반가운 소식일 것이다.

미국의 MLA Handbook for Writers of Research Papers나 Publication Manual of the American Psychological Association, Chicago Manual of Style 같이 영어 논문 작성의 대표적인 참고서들은 이미 각각 10판을 넘어가면서 세계적인 유명세를 자랑하고 있다. 저자 역시 영어 논문을 저널에 내면서 이러한 책들로부터 많은 도움을 받아 온 것이 사실이다. 그러나 위의 책들은 영어 논문 작성 방식을 설명해 놓은 매뉴얼이지 영어 표현을 외국인에게 소개하고 있는 영작문류의 책은 분명 아니다. 그간 한국에서는 미국의 MLA, APA, CMS 등을 기반으로 한국어 논문 작성법을 설명하는 책은 물론이고 위의 미국 원서들을 번역한 역서들이 생겨나기 시작했다. 그러나 『영어로 논문쓰기』처럼 전 학문에 걸쳐, 특히 인문사회과학 분야의 영어 논문 작성자들을 위한 논문 작성법을 항목별, 주제별로 나누어 상세하게 설명하고 있는 것은 지금껏 전무하다고 해도 과언이 아닐 것이다. 외국의 경우에서도 마찬가지로 학술적 논문의 내용과 형식에 맞는 영어 표현 academic English expressions을 이렇게 집대성한 참고서는 존재하지 않는다. 어학사전 및 백과사전을 만들어 내는 세계적인 출판사들인 Blackwell이나 Random House에서도 저자의 책과 유사한 것을 찾아볼 수 없다. 독자들은 저자의 이 책에서 논문 작성에 필요한 주요 표현들의 예문과 모범적인 학술 영어 표현을 실제로 발견하게 될 것이다. 이 책에는 영어다운 표현의 벽을 넘어, 본인의 영어 논문을 해외 유수 저널에 자신 있게 내놓을 수 있도록 기본적인 수준에서 가장 고급스러운 표현에 이르기까지 많은 종류의 예문들이 실려 있다. 총 3,600개가 넘는 학술 영어 표현은 어떠한 종류의 영어 논문 – essay, term paper, research paper, review, M.A. thesis, Ph.D dissertation – 에 사용되어도 손색이 없을 것이다.

그간 『영어로 논문쓰기』는 영미권으로 유학 가는 학생들, 한국에서 영어로 논문을 써서 해외 저널에 투고할 준비를 하는 분들에게서 각별한 주목을 받았다. 인문사회과학 계열의 관심 독자들에게 매우 유용한 지침서로 자리매김한 이 책은 한국에서 '영어로 논문쓰기' 분야의 '바이블'로 등극한 지 오래다. 유사한 종류와 제목의 책을 뒤로 하고, 『영어로 논문쓰기』는 책의 형태를 한 도서에 그치지 않고, 청중과 만나는 특강의 발판을 만들어 주기도 하였다. 그리하여 탄생한 것이 바로 필자가 100회 이상 해 온 영어 글쓰기 특강이다.

저자는 지난 10년이 넘는 동안 대학가에서 〈학문하는 자세와 영어로 논문쓰기〉 혹은 〈영어 논문 작성법〉이란 제목으로 특강을 해 왔다. 학술적인 영어를 잘 쓰고자 갈망하는 학생들과 교강사들에게 가장 필요하고 실용적인 내용의 강연을 해 왔다고 자부한다. 유학 생활에서 실제로 겪었던 경험담, 학위를 마치고 귀국하여 영문 저널을 창간하고 편집 업무를 담당하는 에디터로 일하면서 알게 된 깨알 같은 정보를 이 책에 담았다. 귀국 후, 저술의 경험과 강연의 현장에서 필자는 한국 학생들에게 무엇이 가장 필요하고, 실질적으로 중요한 것인지를 알게 되었다. '학술적인 영어 표현'이 바로 그것이다. 우리의 생각과 창조적인 아이디어가 아무리 뛰어난들, 이것을 학계에서 실제로 통용되는 영어다운 문체와 표현으로 소개할 수 없다면 우리가 들인 시간과 노력은 사실 무용지물이 될 것이다. 개정판은 이러한 문제를 잘 알고 있는 필자가 오랜 시간 모은 3,600개가 넘는 유용한 학술 표현을 모은 모음집이다.

『영어로 논문쓰기 최신 개정판』은 기존의 책 구성에 대폭 변화를 주었다. 시대의 흐름에 맞게 영어 논문 작성의 실제 현실에서 꼭 필요한 것들만을 선별하여, 그 내용과 예문을 한층 보강하였다. 논문의 일반적인 구조가 서문, 선행 연구, 논문의 목적 기술, 이론적 배경, 실험 처치, 실험 결과, 결론, 논의 등을 포함하고 있다면, 각 챕터에서 실제로 빈번하게 사용되는 학술적인 표현을 모은 것이 이 책의 핵심이다. 따라서 영어로 논문을 쓰는 과정에서 그때그때 막히고 어려워하는 문장의 예를 이 책에서 발견하여 자신이 필요로 하는 곳에 활용한다면 영어 논문을 쉽고도 빠르게 작성할 수 있을 것이다. 『영어로 논문쓰기 최신 개정판』은 이런 점에서 아주 훌륭한 참고서의 역할을 하게 될 것이다. 또한 여기에 나오는 표현들은 관용어구이기 때문에, 자신의 영어 논문에 그대로 가져다 써도 표절의 예가 아니란 점을 알려 주고 싶다.

저자는 초판본을 냈을 때나 지금이나, 자부심에 앞서 전인미답의 분야에 손을 대는 부담감과 책임 의식을 더 느끼는 것이 사실이다. 돌이켜 보면, 지금의 개정판이 나오기까지에는 가장 큰 동기가 있었는데, 그것은 그간 독자들이 보내 준 정성어린 조언과 기대였다. 이에 저자는 이전의 재판보다 내용을 보충·추가하여 새로운 모습으로 독자들의 열정과 관심에 보답할 수 있게 되었다. 더불어 개정판에는 인용 예문들이 풍부해졌고, 도치 구문과 감사의 변이라 할 수 있는 Acknowledgement 부분이 추가되었다. 즉, 문체상의 다양함을 맛볼 수 있도록 유익한 문장 해설과 예문의 번역이 많이 삽입되었는데, 한 예가 바로 도치 구문 항목에서 나타난다. 한글 문장과는 달리, 영어로 글을 쓸 때 자주 느끼는 한계가 바로 이 같은 도치 구문을 자유자재로 쓰지 못함에서 느끼는 문체의 조야함과 나열식 문장의 단순함이 아닐까 한다. 고급스러운 문구에, 복합 문장을 쓴다든가 관계대명사를 삽입어로 쓰면서 문체의 현란함을 보여 주어야 꼭 영어다운 글이 된다는 것을 말하고자 하는 것이 아니다. 도치 구문과 같은 문체 훈련은 다채로우면서도 영어다운 문장을 완성하기 위해서 우리가 겪게 되는 통과 의례인 것이다. 같은 의미를 전달하고 있는 문장이지만 숙어나 단어, 삽입어 등의 쓰임새를 달리함으로써 전혀 다른 느낌의 문체를 만들어내는 예를 많이 실어 놓은 이유가 바로 여기에 있는 것이다. 덧붙여 ', with ~'(with 전치사구)가 들어간 예를 다수 추가하였다. 필자가 생각하기에, 영작문에서 가장 구사하기 힘들어하는 것이 바로 with가 동반된 부사구이다. 반드시 극복하고 실제 영작문에서 활용해야 할 것이기에 이번 개정판에 풍부한 예와 함께 수록하였다.

개정판의 속편이자, 기존에 저자가 공들여 왔던 대면 특강의 책 버전이라 할 수 있는 『영어로 논문쓰기 입문편』은 이 책과 나란히 두고 보아야 그 효과가 극대화될 것이다. 두 책은 상호 보완이 될 뿐만 아니라, 동시에 읽으면 더욱 좋겠다. 단, 이 후속편은 거시적 관점에서 대학원 과정에서 본격적으로 시작될 '자기 학문 이뤄 나가기' 과정을 총체적으로 보여 주는 역할을 하고 있다는 점을 알아야겠다. 『영어로 논문쓰기 최신 개정판』이 주로 표현 위주의 실용성을 강조하고 있다면, 특강 강의노트인 『영어로 논문쓰기 입문편』은 원론적인 의미에서 자신의 학문을 빚어가는 과정에서 필요한 것, 영어 논문 작성 시에 반드시 알아야 하는 요소들을 정리해 두었다는 점이 특징적이다. 요컨대, 영어로 논문을 어떻게 쓰는지, 왜 써야 하는지, 어떠한 과정을 거치는지, 해외 저널에 투고는 어떻게 하는지, 학술적 영어 표현 중에서 우리가 잘못 알고 있거나 오용하여 일명 콩글리시로 알려진 것들은 어떤 것이 있는지 등을 하나의 큰 흐름 가운데 서술하고 있다.

『영어로 논문쓰기 입문편』은 저자가 그간 10년 이상 해 온 〈학문하는 자세와 영어로 논문쓰기 특강〉의 '강의노트 완결판'인 셈이다. 영어로 논문쓰기의 큰 그림을 먼저 설계하고, 독자 자신이 속해 있는 학문의 전공과 분과에서 어떤 자세와 접근 방법으로 학문을 하며 논문을 써야 할지 밑그림을 먼저 설계하는 과정에서 『영어로 논문쓰기 입문편』은 먼저 읽어야 할 첫 단계의 책이나 다름없다. 이 기초 위에서 학술 영어 표현을 필요로 하는 순간순간 『영어로 논문쓰기 최신 개정판』을 참고하여 사용한다면, 두 책을 잘 활용하게 되는 것이다. 이런 과정을 거치면 여러분도 세계 우수 저널에 자신의 논문을 당당히 게재하는 쾌거를 반드시 이룰 수 있을 것이다.

모름지기 학습이나 사업이나 전략에 해당하는 큰 그림을 설계해야 한다. 이것이 가장 먼저 마련되어야 이 목적을 이룰 구체적인 단계별 실행 목표가 설정될 것이고, 체계적인 실천 방법 목록이 작성될 수 있을 것이다. 이 과정에 드는 노력과 시간 투자에서 위 두 책은 좋은 안내자의 역할을 하리라 저자는 자부한다. 강연 현장에서 깨닫고, 다짐하고, 새로 설정한 목표와 전략이 이 두 책에 빠짐없이 담겼다. 동시에 독자의 질정과 제언을 겸허하게 기다린다.

출판사 넥서스 편집부의 개정판 제안과 격려에 깊이 감사드린다. 이 책의 가치를 인정해 주신 넥서스의 장인 정신과 조언이 없었다면 이렇게 좋은 책이 세상의 빛을 볼 수 없었을 것이다. 값진 책을 만들어 주신 그 외 모든 분께도 무한한 감사의 마음을 전한다. 끝으로, 책이 온전히 출판되는 과정에서 저자의 제자 김담정이 큰 몫을 해 주었다. 제자가 청출어람을 이뤄내는 것을, 그 시작부터 스승이 행복한 표정으로 바라보고 있다. 곡진한 말과 사랑스러운 마음으로 제자의 앞날을 기원한다. 애제자 담정이의 열정적인 기여와 헌신을 기억하고자 감사의 말을 꾹꾹 눌러 종이에 새긴다.

2024년 개정판이 완결판으로 기억되기를 희망하는
저자 김상현 책의 영어 제목 The Essential Guide to Writing Papers in English가 잘 나타내고 있듯이 이 책은 한국 내에서 영어로 논문을 쓰기 원하는 독자들을 포함해 영어권으로 유학을 준비 중이거나 이미 현지에서 유학하고 있는 학생들을 대상으로 만들어졌다. 넓은 독자층만큼이나 책이 다루고 있는 내용의 범위 역시 리서치 페이퍼 research paper에서 석 · 박사학위 논문 thesis, dissertation에 이르기까지 실로 넓다 하겠다. 영어권에서 말하는 리서치 페이퍼는 간단히 다음과 같이 정리해 볼 수 있다.

첫째, 자신이 잡은 주제 topic와 관련한 1차 및 2차 자료 primary and secondary sources에 대한 연구 현황이 반드시 들어가야 한다. 즉, 논문의 저자는 기존에 있어 왔던 연구물들에 대해 언급을 해야 하는 것은 물론이고 자신의 견해를 꼭 넣어야 한다.

둘째, 종합적인 개요 comprehensive overview를 포함하여 많은 자료를 인용하기 때문에 각주 혹은 미주를 이용하기 마련이다.

셋째, 간혹 학제 간 연구 interdisciplinary study의 수준을 요구하기도 한다. 다시 말해, 저자가 논문의 요지를 이끌어 나갈 때 다른 학문에서 이용하고 있는 접근 방법을 활용한다든가 자신의 연구 범위를 다른 학문 분야로까지 확장시켜 폭넓게 다루는 것을 interdisciplinary study 또는 interdisciplinary research라고 한다.

이런 이유 때문에 리서치 페이퍼는 '대학원 과정에서 요구하는 비중 있는 연구 논문'을 가리킨다. 석 · 박사학위 논문은 이러한 리서치 페이퍼의 기본 성격을 기반으로 하여 만들어진다. 내용과 형식적인 면 모두에서 리서치 페이퍼보다 상위 수준을 요구하는 학위 논문은 논문의 양에 있어서도 많은 차이가 난다. 리서치 페이퍼가 20~30쪽 정도의 분량이라면 석 · 박사학위 논문은 짧게는 50쪽에서 길게는 350쪽에 이를 정도로 방대하다.

이 책은 크게 **PART 1**과 **PART 2**, 그리고 부록으로 구성되어 있다.

PART 1에서는 논문 작성에 많이 등장하는 주요 표현들을 중심으로 다루었다.

서론, 본론, 결론, 각주 및 미주, 서평에 자주 등장하는 표현이라는 독립된 장에서 다양한 영어 표현을 소개하였다. 영어 논문을 작성해 본 경험이 있는 독자들은 **PART 1**의 영어 표현 예문이 실제로 논문을 쓰는 입장에서 영어다운 다양한 문체를 습득하는 데 많은 도움이 된다는 것을 알게 될 것이다. 그리고 **PART 1** 말미 부분인 〈IX 논문 투고와 요약문 작성의 실례〉에서는 이 단원의 내용을 총정리해 주는 예문을 실어 복습하는 기회를 만들었다.

이 책에 실린 모든 예문들은 영어 극복의 난제를 해결하기 위해 미국 유학 첫 학기부터 해 온 작업으로, 바로 이 책의 기반이 된 저자의 '영어 표현 정리 노트'이다. 저자는 이 과정을 통해 모든 종류의 학술적인 책과 논문에서 자주 발견되는 문체상의 공통된 표현법 common expressions, stock expressions, clichés을 발견하게 되었다. 또한 논문의 저자에 따라 그 글의 맛과 구성, 논지를 이끌어 가는 힘과 균형감이 저마다 다 다르면서도 글 속에는 일정하게 나타나는, '문체상의 공통된 표현법'이 있다는 것을 알게 되었던 것이다.

예를 들어, 서론에서 대부분의 글은 저자가 다루고자 하는 주제에 대한 기존의 연구 현황을 먼저 개괄(view)하는데, 이런 문체상의 특징은 책보다는 적은 분량의 리서치 페이퍼에서 보다 뚜렷하다.

e.g. **Much has been written** in description of Bulgakov's color system in his novels. **Some arguments have been made that** ~.

그리고 논문을 통해서 저자가 말하고자 하는 메시지, 즉 논문의 목적이 본론으로 넘어가기 전에 짤막하게 언급된다.

e.g. **In the present paper we shall see** how this myth is transformed through Tolstoy's text. **The aim of this article is** a stylistic analysis of Nabokov's prose, paying attention to his some controversial novels.

본론에서는 논문의 핵심이 다루어진다.

e.g. In order to understand the nature of the ~, it is necessary to examine first some of ~. In considering our discussion, it may be useful to start out by examining ~.

결론에 가서 저자는 본문을 간략하게 요약하면서 전달하고자 하는 주제를 다시 한 번 간단히 정리해 준다.

e.g. This article has attempted to sketch out the main characteristic of ~. To capitulate briefly, we have shown that two discernable approaches ~.

논문의 이러한 커다란 틀 속을 잘 들여다보면 놀랍게도 반복되어 자주 나타나는 표현들이 있다는 것을 독자들도 알게 될 것이다. 이 책의 **PART 1**에서 모아 놓은 많은 영어 예문들은 바로 저자가 다양한 영어 논문을 읽으면서 발견하여 주제별로 정리해 놓은 것이다.

PART 2에서는 논문 작성의 형식적인 측면들을 자세히 정리하였다.

PART 1이 논문 작성자의 주제를 잘 전달해 주도록 안내하는 역할을 한다면, **PART 2**는 논문을 쓸 때 관행적으로 지켜야 하는 '형식적인 약속'에 대한 중요한 사항들을 다루었다. 논문의 기본 서식, 장

chapter 구성, 구두법, 인용 방법, 각주 및 미주 기재 방법 등의 가장 기본적인 규칙들은 〈I 논문의 기본 형식〉에 나타나 있다. 일례로 논문 작성 시 글자 크기, 글자체, 문단 간격, 정렬 방식, 여백, 쪽수 매기는 방식 등이 다루어져 있다. 이제 처음으로 영어 논문을 작성하기 시작한 사람들은 물론이고 영어 논문에 익숙하다고 자신하는 사람들도 PART 2를 읽어 보기 바란다. 왜냐하면 간단해 보이는 마침표, 쉼표 하나조차도 한국의 논문 작성법과 다르기에 자신이 놓치고 있거나 간과한 부분이 있을 수 있기 때문이다.

마지막으로, 부록에서는 본문에서 미처 다루지 못한 유용한 정보들을 실었다.

먼저 〈1. 논문 작성 방식 소개〉는 현재 학계에서 가장 널리 통용되는 세 가지 방식(MLA, CMS, APA)을 다루고 있다. MLA 방식은 1883년 미국 현대 언어학회 The Modern Language Association of America가 발족된 이후 지금까지 가장 많이, 오래도록 사용되며 인문학계 humanities에서 널리 채용된다. 미국 시카고 대학에서 처음 쓰면서 확산되기 시작한, 일명 시카고 스타일 CMS(The Chicago Manual of Style)와 미국 심리학회 American Psychological Association에서 지정하여 널리 통용되고 있는 APA 방식 모두 인문사회학과 자연과학 분야에서 두루 이용된다. 자료의 인용 방식에 있어 차이점이 있기는 하지만 세 양식은 논문을 쓰는 저자로 하여금 자료의 정확한 출처를 밝히도록 하는 점에서는 다르지 않다.

〈2. 기본 약어 Common Scholarly Abbreviations〉와 〈3. 기본 용어 정의 Glossary〉에서는 논문 작성 시 필요한 각종 약어와 기본 용어에 대한 정의를 정리해 놓았다. 〈4. 주요 어휘〉와 〈5. 이탤릭체로 표현되는 외래어〉는 알아 두면 좋을 주요 고급 단어와 영어에서 상용되는 외래어와, 외국어(주로 라틴어, 독어, 불어에서 파생한 단어들: e.g. "per se" 혹은 "ad hoc")의 목록을 첨가하였다. 부록의 마지막 항목인 〈6. 대학원생들을 위한 조언〉에서 저자가 독자들에게 꼭 들려주고 싶은 얘기들을 정리하였다. 좁게는 미국 대학원 과정에 들어와 이제 막 향학열을 불태우는 학생들, 넓게는 학계에 몸담을 미래의 모든 학생들에게 저자가 지금까지 해 온 학습 과정을 밝혀 놓았다.

이렇듯 이 책은 논문 작성의 내용과 형식으로 대별하여 가능한 많은 정보를 담으려고 노력하였다. 그러나 여기에 실린 예문들을 열심히 창조적으로 모방하고 응용하여 실제 자신의 논문에 대입해도 문제는 곳곳에서 생길 수 있다. 그러므로 이러한 문제들을 스스로 고쳐 나가는 과정을 통해 영어 논문에 대한 자신감을 갖게 될 것이라고 확신한다.

목차

PART 1

Ⅰ 논문의 기본 내용
  1. 전통적인 논문 작성 과정 · 18
  2. 인문사회과학과 자연과학 논문 간의 주요 차이점 · 23

Ⅱ 서론에 자주 등장하는 표현
  1. 문제 제기 · 28
  2. 논문의 범위 설정 · 52
  3. 논문의 목적 / 방향성 / 개요 · 54

Ⅲ 본론에 자주 등장하는 표현
  1. 충만 / 지배 / 일관 / 점철 · 86
  2. 해석 가능성 / 타당성 · 89
  3. 유사점 / 동일시 / 등가물 / 병치 관계 · 91
  4. 차이점 / 대조 · 99
  5. 측면 / 관점 / 입장 / 고려 · 104
  6. 제시 / 제공 / 부여 · 113
  7. 기능 / 역할 · 134
  8. 중심점 / 초점 / 할애 · 138
  9. 언급 / 관계 / 관련성 · 141
  10. 암시 / 예시 / 예견 / 힌트 · 146
  11. 환기 / 상기 / 연상 · 148
  12. 사용 기법 · 153
  13. 화법 / 화자 / 서사 기법 · 158
  14. 작품 구조 · 164
  15. 삽입구 / 부사구 / 접속사 · 168
  16. 텍스트 인용 · 176
  17. It ~ that 구문의 다양한 활용법 · 180
  18. 도치 구문 · 185
  19. 순위, 등수 차지 · 190

Ⅳ 결론에 자주 등장하는 표현
  1. 본론의 요약과 결론 제시 · 192
  2. 질정을 바라는 저자의 희망 / 여전히 남아 있는 문제점 지적 · 201

Ⅴ 챕터 전환 및 문맥 흐름 언급에 자주 등장하는 표현 · 208

Ⅵ 각주 및 미주에 자주 등장하는 표현
　1. 재인용 방법 · 212
　2. 논문에서 이용하는 텍스트의 출처 언급 · 213
　3. 반복되는 주요 텍스트 생략법과 저자의 특별한 언급 · 215
　4. 다른 논문에 대한 언급 · 216
　5. 연구 현황에 대한 언급 · 226
　6. 감사의 표현 · 240
　7. 학회 Conference 등에서 발표된 논문에 대한 언급과 박사학위 논문에 대한 언급 · 245

Ⅶ 서평에 자주 등장하는 표현
　1. 애정 / 열정의 소산 / 관심의 성장 / 결실 · 248
　2. 책의 내용에 대한 구체적인 언급 · 249
　3. 책의 구성과 편집에 대한 언급 · 257
　4. 책의 장단점에 대한 언급 · 267

Ⅷ Acknowledgement
　1. 연구를 하게 된 동기 / 세월 · 284
　2. 연구비 / 장학금 / 도서관 시설 등 각종 혜택 언급 · 287
　3. 특별한 감사의 표현 · 290
　4. 가족과 부모 / 지인 / 스승에 대한 감사의 표현 · 294
　5. 독자 제현에 대한 언급 · 296

Ⅸ 이력 Curriculum vitae 소개에 자주 등장하는 표현 · 298
　RESUME
　Sample-1 Biology Major · 307
　Sample-2 Business Administration Major · 308
　Sample-3 Economics Major · 309
　Sample-4 International Relations Major · 310
　Sample-5 Women's Studies Major · 311
　Sample-6 Communication Major · 312
　Sample-7 English Major · 313

Ⅹ 논문 투고와 요약문 작성의 실례
　ABSTRACT
　Sample-1~4 Political Science · 317
　Sample-5~7 Sociology · 319
　Sample-8~9 International Affairs · 320

Sample-10 Child Education · 321

Sample-11~12 Education · 322

Sample-13 Special Education · 323

Sample-14 International Education · 323

Sample-15~17 Business · 324

Sample-18~20 Economics · 325

Sample-21 Statistics · 327

Sample-22 Accounting · 327

Sample-23 History · 328

Sample-24 Library and Information Science · 328

Sample-25 Asian Studies · 329

Sample-26 Anthropology · 329

Sample-27~28 Sports · 330

Sample-29 Philosophy · 331

Sample-30 Science Philosophy · 331

Sample-31 Literature · 332

Sample-32 Urban Planning · 332

Sample-33~34 Psychology · 333

Sample-35 Ecology · 334

Sample-36 Biology · 335

PART 2

Ⅰ 논문의 기본 형식

　1. 기본 서식 · 340

　2. 기본 구성 · 342

　3. 장 chapter의 구성 · 344

　4. 구두법 Punctuation · 345

부록

　1. 논문 작성 방식 소개 · 360

　2. 기본 약어 Common Scholarly Abbreviations · 365

　3. 기본 용어 정의 Glossary · 367

　4. 이탤릭체로 표현되는 외래어 · 369

　5. ', with ~' 전치사 구문 · 375

　6. 대학원생들을 위한 조언 · 381

PART 1

Ⅰ 논문의 기본 내용
Ⅱ 서론에 자주 등장하는 표현
Ⅲ 본론에 자주 등장하는 표현
Ⅳ 결론에 자주 등장하는 표현
Ⅴ 챕터 전환 및 문맥 흐름 언급에 자주 등장하는 표현
Ⅵ 각주 및 미주에 자주 등장하는 표현
Ⅶ 서평에 자주 등장하는 표현
Ⅷ Acknowledgement
Ⅸ 이력 Curriculum vitae 소개에 자주 등장하는 표현
Ⅹ 논문 투고와 요약문 작성의 실례

The Essential Guide to Writing Papers in English

I 논문의 기본 내용

1. 전통적인 논문 작성 과정
2. 인문사회과학과 자연과학 논문 간의 주요 차이점

01 전통적인 논문 작성 과정

논문이란 자신의 논리로 다른 사람의 주의를 집중시키고, 결국엔 자신의 주장을 다른 사람에게 설득시키는 것이 목적이다. 리서치 페이퍼에서 석·박사학위 논문에 이르기까지 모든 논문은 연구자 당사자의 학문적 성숙 과정 즉, 학업 과정을 거쳐 도달한 연구 결과와 학술적 발견을 보여 주기 위한 것이다. 뿐만 아니라, 자신의 학문적 결실을 보여 주는 무대의 장이자 다른 연구자와 벌이는 지상 토론의 장이기도 하다. 때문에 이러한 목적을 위해서 가장 효과적인 주장법을 익혀야 하는 것은 지극히 당연한 일이라 하겠다. 동시에 우리는 논문이 학문을 하는 사람들 사이에서 통용되는 일정한 관례를 기초로 하여 작성된다는 것을 알아야 한다. 논문을 작성하는 연구자들은 이러한 전통을 따르면서도 혁신적인 학문적 결실을 보여 주는 데 노력해야 한다.

아래에 소개하는 내용은 논문을 작성하는 방법론에 대한 것이다. 이 책을 쓰기 위해 여러 참고 문헌들을 읽고 정보를 얻는 과정에서 저자는 『리서치 방법론』(Bonnie L. Yegidis and Robert W. Weinbach, *Research Methods: for Social Workers*, 4th ed., Boston and London: Allyn and Bacon, 2001)으로부터 많은 도움을 받았다. 실제로도, 이 책은 흔히 사회복지학이라고 불려지는 전공분야에서 리서치의 방법론 교재로 널리 이용되고 있기도 하다. 비록 이 책에서 말하고 있는 내용이 '사회복지학'을 중심으로 한 내용들을 담고 있지만, 모든 분야에 두루 적용될 수 있는 기본적인 원칙들 역시 많이 포함하고 있다는 것을 알게 되었다. 위의 책에 따르면 '전통적인 과학적 리서치 작성 과정' traditional scientific research process을 다음과 같이 제시하고 있다.

1 Problem Identification
2 Research Question Formulation
3 Literature Review
4 Construction of Hypothesis or Refinement of Research Questions
5 Design and Planning
6 Data Collection
7 Sorting and Analysis of Data
8 Specification of Research Findings
9 Interpretation of Research Findings
10 Dissemination of Research Findings

이상의 내용은 10단계 과정을 통해 리서치 작업이 어떻게 이루어지는지 잘 보여 주고 있다. 그런데 본래 방법론 책에서는 총 11단계로 나와 있으나 저자가 보기에 마지막 과정은 우리 책의 내용과 큰 관련이 없어 생략하였다.

구체적인 설명에 들어가기 전에 저자가 강조하고 싶은 것이 있다. 저자는 이 방법론 책에서 제시하고 있는 10단계 과정을 염두에 두면서, 여러 논문들이 실제로 어떻게 쓰여졌는지 그 사례들을 분석해 보았다. 그 결과 저자는 이 방법론 책의 내용이 다른 학문분야의 논문에도 광범위하게 적용된다는 사실을 확인할 수 있었다. 인문사회과학과 자연과학으로 대별해 보더라도 이 방법론이 상당히 유효하다는 것이 증명되었다. 이 부분에 대해서는 PART 2의 〈II 논문 유형의 실례〉에서 각종 그림과 함께 보다 자세하게 다루어질 것이다.

다만, 아래에 소개될 10단계 과정의 일부 내용이 인문과학 분야의 연구 논문 작성 요령과는 약간 다르다는 점을 지적하고 싶다. 비록 많은 분야에서 이 방법론이 통용되고 있는 것이 현실이지만, 특히 어문학, 철학, 역사 등에서는 이공계에서는 아주 일반적인 데이터 분석이나 도표 삽입 같은 내용들을 거의 다루지 않는다는 것이다. 즉, 흔히 발견할 수 있는 각종 도표, 그래프, 수식 분석들이 어문학 계열의 논문에서는 없다는 말이다. 하지만 전체적인 면에서 두 분야의 논문 작성의 주요 단계는 상당히 일치한다. 참고 문헌에 대한 사전 조사 작업, 논문의 주제 설정 방식, 주요 주제들에 대한 적절한 배치 등은 비록 분야가 다르다 해도 논문 작성을 위해 서로 비교해 볼 수 있을 것이다.

아울러 이하의 10단계 내용은 위의 영어 참고 문헌이 보여 주고 있는 것 그대로가 아니며, 원저에서는 매우 간략하게만 서술되어 있는 것에 저자 자신이 보탠 내용이 더 많다는 점을 밝혀둔다.

1 Problem Identification : 논문의 논제에 대한 정확한 진단

논문을 쓰기 위해서는 가장 먼저 어떤 문제를 다룰 것인지를 잘 생각해야 한다. 명확하고 정확한 문제의식 속에 이미 답이 들어있는 경우가 많은 것처럼 논문이 다루게 될 문제 즉, 주제로 발전되는 문제를 잘 설정해야 한다. 막연하게 알고 있거나, 깊게 고민해 오지 않던 문제들은 일단 배제시키는 것이 좋다.

2 Research Question Formulation : 3개 이상의 폭넓은 주제 선별

논문의 주제를 아무리 잘 선택한다고 해도 논문을 써 나가다 보면 참고 자료를 읽으면서 나중에 얻게 된 추가 정보와 자신의 아이디어로 인해 논문의 방향이 바뀌어 애초에 의도했던 주제에서 벗어나는 경우가 종종 있다. 이런 경우 경험이 부족한 연구자들은 당황하여 논문 진척에 상당히 많은 시간을 허비하게 된다. 이러한 좌충우돌의 상황에 대비하고 흔들림 없는 논문의 방향을 위해서 처음부터 논문의 주제 혹은 문제의식의 폭을 넓게 해 둘 필요가 있다.

3 Literature Review: 논문의 주제에 해당하는 참고 문헌 확인 작업

때에 따라서 주제 선정 이전에 기존의 발표 문헌을 보면서 참신한 아이디어가 떠올라 주제를 나중에 정하는 경우도 있을 수 있다. 그러나 대부분은 주제를 정한 후 이에 관련된 참고 문헌 조사 작업에 들어가는 것이 일반적이다. 참고 자료에는 단행본 book, 저널의 논문 article, 박사학위 논문 dissertation, 석사학위 논문 thesis, 서평 review, 학회논문 발표 모음집 proceeding, 참고 문헌 reference 등 다양한 자료들이 포함된다.

이러한 자료 source에는 1차 자료와 2차 자료, 두 가지 유형이 있다. 예를 들어, '아리스토텔레스 철학의 현대적 해석과 그 가치'란 주제로 자료를 모으고 있다고 하자. 이때 이 철학자가 남긴 원저자의 저작물 works or writings에서 직접 찾아낸 자료를 1차 자료 primary source라고 한다. 그렇지 않고 원저작이 아닌 그 외의 모든 자료들, 이를테면 아리스토텔레스의 저작인『시학』,『향연』,『공화국』등에 대해 후에 비평을 하거나 설명을 해 놓은 모든 책들은 따로 2차 자료 secondary source라고 한다. 그리고 참고 문헌을 달 때 사용하는 논문 맨 뒷부분의 표제어는 각각 Reference, Bibliography, Works Cited 등으로 다른 용어가 사용된다.

실제로 논문 작성에 들어갔을 때, 이 단계에서 가장 중요한 것은 기존에 발표된 문헌에 대해 총체적인 개괄 comprehensive overview를 하는 것이다. 자신이 쓰고자 하는 주제에 관련된 자료들을 소개하는 것은 물론, 이것들에 대해 약간의 비평을 다룸으로써 어떤 참고 문헌이 자신의 논문 작성에 실질적으로 도움이 되고 있는지를 밝히는 것이 이 단계의 주된 목적이다.

4 Construction of Hypothesis or Refinement of Research Questions: 참고 문헌에 의거, 주제에 초점이 될 문제와 가설 설정

참고 자료를 찾는 작업에서 우리는 많은 경험을 하게 된다. 전혀 생각지도 못하던 새로운 주제의 자료를 운 좋게 발견하는 경우도 있고, 일단 자료의 제목만 열람하면서도 자기 논문에 보탬이 될 좋은 아이디어를 떠올리기도 하기 때문이다. 때문에 자기 논문의 주제에 잘 맞는 자료를 정확하게 찾아내는 것이 가장 중요하다. 또 하나 염두에 두어야 할 점이 있다. 자료를 찾다 보면 언뜻 제목만 가지고서 그 내용을 유추할 수 없는 것들을 보기도 한다. 때에 따라서는 자기 논문에 딱 맞는 자료의 제목만 얻겠다는 강박관념 때문에 더 좋은 다른 자료들을 놓치기도 한다. 이런 경우를 미연에 방지하기 위해 우리는 3단계에서처럼 주제 범위를 융통성 있게 설정해 놓은 상태에서 참고 자료의 관련 범위를 넓게 잡아 시작하는 것이 많은 도움이 된다.

5 Design and Planning: 주요 용어 정리, 실험 대상 구체화, 데이터 분석 방법론 확립

참고 자료가 어느 정도 준비되고 실제로도 자료를 많이 읽어 논문 작성의 얼개가 잡히는 지금 단계부터 우리는 다음을 주의해야 한다. 자신이 쓸 이론, 주장, 실험, 방법론, 데이터 활용 등에서 자주 쓰게 될 용어 term에 대한 뚜렷한 정의 definition를 해 놓아야 한다는 것이다. 이와 관련해, 어떤 이론이나 방법론을 중점적으로 쓰고자 하는 경우 처음부터 자신이 어떤 접근법 viewpoint, theoretical ground, theoretical approach, methods으로 쓸 지를 분명히 밝혀야 한다. 이에 대한 분명한 설명이 없이는 저자의 논문은 처음부터 독자로 하여금 혼선을 줄 우려가 있다. 그래서 우리는 논문에서 다음과 같은 표현을 자주 보게 된다.

- By the term, post-modernism, I mean that ~.
- With this mind, I will examine the theory from the standpoint of Huntington's arguments.
- In this paper I shall follow the general contour which William presents in his recent study.
- As with the term first suggested by David Gosling, I want to argue with him because his theoretical ground is wrong in that ~.

6 Data Collection : 사전 검토된 방법론에 의거, 데이터 수집

자신이 이용하고자 하는 방법론이 선정되면, 이 분석방식대로 적용할 재료 즉, 데이터가 준비되어야 한다. 자연과학 분야 대부분의 실험 논문, 혹은 사회과학의 사례분석 case study 논문에서 우리는 이러한 데이터 분석 도표와 그래프를 많이 보게 된다. 질적 방법론 qualitative method으로 할 것인지, 양적 방법론 quantitative research을 이용할 것인지, 연역법 deductive method이 아니면 귀납법 inductive method으로 택할 것인지를 먼저 결정한다.

문학 분야에서의 예로 말해 보면, 형식주의에서 말하는 에이헨바움의 플롯 plot 개념으로 어떤 단편 소설을 분석할 것인지, 바흐쩐의 다성음 이론 polyphony으로 단테의 신곡을 해부할지를 선택해야 한다. 심리학인 경우, 칼 융의 아니마 anima와 아니무스 animus로 현대 트랜스젠더의 사회 심리를 분석할 것인지, 프로이드의 오이디푸스 콤플렉스 Oedipus complex 개념으로 한국 정치 사회 풍토를 살펴볼지를 먼저 확인해야 한다는 것이다.

7 Sorting and Analysis of Data : 방법론에 기초하여 데이터 분석, 검토, 요약

자신이 적용하는 방법론으로 수집한 데이터를 분석하는 단계이다. 어문학 계열의 논문에서는 데이터라는 용어보다는 분석 대상이 되는 문학 작품의 구체적인 내용 (작중 인물의 성격, 플롯, 서사기법, 연극의 무대 장치 등)이 적절한 말이 되겠다. 일단 분석이 완료되면 최종적인 결론을 내리기에 앞서 다시 한 번 차근차근 검토하는 훈련을 하도록 하자.

8 Specification of Research Findings : 각종 도표, 그래프 등에 대한 분석 결과 배치

언뜻 보면 이 단계가 왜 들어가야 하며, 왜 중요한지 의문을 가질 수 있을 것이다. 자신이 분석한 데이터의 결과대로 도표나 그래프를 논문 중간 중간에 삽입하면 끝나지 않을까 단순하게 생각할 수 있다는 말이다. 그러나 문제는 간단하지만은 않다. 어떤 종류의 수식이 들어간 그림이 자신이 입증하고자 하는 결과를 가장 효과적으로 나타내 줄 수 있는지를 고민해야 하는 것이다. 다

이어그램 diagram, 단순한 도표 table, 그래프 graph 혹은 그림 figure, 그 밖의 일반적인 형태 standard formats들 가운데 어떤 것을 선택할 것인지 잘 생각해야 한다. 또 하나 잊지 말아야 하는 것은 그림을 말로 설명할 수 있는 것도 굳이 불필요한 도표를 넣어 논문을 읽을 때 흐름의 방해를 줄 수 있는 것은 가급적 피하도록 하자는 것이다. 이번 단계와 관련해서는 PART 2의 〈II 논문 유형의 실례〉에서 각종 예들을 다루어 놓았으니 참고하기 바란다.

아울러, 곁들인 수식, 도표 등을 설명할 때 자주 쓰이는 표현에는 다음과 같은 것들이 있다.

- According to our analysis, the figure 4 illustrates that ~.
- The finding we have presents that ~.
- The result given above strongly supports my earlier assumption that ~.
- Drawing on the general findings, we might be able to conclude that ~.
- It is no doubt that the result can provide a reasonable evidence on the ~.

9 Interpretation of Research Findings: 주제의 가설을 실증하기 위한 결과의 해석

이제 논문 작성은 마지막 단계에 이른다. 자신이 세운 가설이나 분석 대상에 대한 예측에 맞게 결론이 나오면 이것을 간단하게 핵심만 요약해 주면 된다. 본론에 나와 있는 내용을 길게 반복하기 보다는 짧은 문구를 사용하는 것이 좋다. 또는 자연과학 분야의 논문에서처럼 아라비아 숫자를 이용하여 1), 2), 3) 등으로 일목요연하게 정리하는 방법도 있으니 자신이 전공하는 분야에서 사용되는 일반적인 관례를 먼저 검토해 보도록 하자.

10 Dissemination of Research Findings: 논문의 방법론과 결과를 보고할 수단 선정

자신이 예상했던 대로 만족스런 결과가 나왔거나 반응이 좋을 거라고 기대가 되는 논문을 썼다고 가정해 보자. 쓰는 것도 중요하지만 일단 작성이 되었다면 자신의 학술적 결과물을 어떤 방식으로 어디에 발표할 것인지를 선정하는 것은 최종 단계이자 아주 중요한 과정이라고 하겠다. 다시 말해서, 저널 journal에 논문을 응모하거나 학회 conference에서 발표 presentation, paper reading를 함으로써 자신의 공들인 논문을 알릴 수 있다. 대개 저널은 게재 의뢰를 하는 논문 편수가 세계 각지에서 몰려오기 때문에 실제로 저널에 실리기까지 많은 시간이 걸린다. 1년 이상이 소요되는 것이 일반적이며, 논문을 수정해 다시 제출 revision하는 조건으로 기다리면 그 이상 지체될 수도 있다. 학회에서는 매년 정기적으로 논문발표회 annual meeting or conference를 갖는데, 이 역시 미국 전역의 대학교를 대상으로 논문을 응모하기 때문에 관심 있는 자가 있다면 최소 1년 전부터 준비를 해야 한다. 왜냐하면 학회의 소식지 newsletter에 실리는 논문 응모 call for papers 광고는 최소한 4~8개월 이전에 게시되기 때문이다.

02 인문사회과학과 자연과학 논문 간의 주요 차이점

통계 자료, 데이터 분석, 실험 결과 등이 논문의 주된 내용을 이루는 자연과학과 사회과학 분야의 대부분에서는 앞에서와 같이 10단계의 리서치 과정을 따르고 있다. 근소한 차이는 있지만 대체로 논문 작성의 기본 골격은 동일하다. 인문사회과학과 자연과학 논문에서 발견되는 가장 큰 차이점을 정리해 보면 다음과 같다.

1 장 구분의 문제

인문과학 그 중에서도 특히 문학, 철학, 역사학 분야의 논문은 장 chapter 구분을 거의 하지 않는다. 처음부터 끝까지 논문이 끊이지 않고 연결되어 있다. 설령 장 구분이 되어 있다 하더라도, 자연과학 논문에서처럼 분명하고 자세하게 나뉘어져 있지 않고 굵은 글씨체로 표제어를 이용해 눈에 띄게 하는 정도이다. 반면 자연과학의 대부분과 인문사회과학의 일부 분야인 언어학, 심리학, 정치학, 행정학, 교육학, 지리학 등과 같이 분석, 실험, 통계 활용 등이 잦은 분야의 논문에서는 장 구분을 하고 있다. 물론 각 학문의 영역마다 특징적인 관례가 있을 수 있다.
논문에서 비교적 자주 쓰이는 주요 장들의 표제어를 소개하면 다음과 같다.

1 논문의 목적 purpose of the study
2 논문의 논제 research questions
3 참고 문헌 조사와 개괄 literature review
4 방법론 소개 methods (test development + data collection)
5 소결론 results, findings
6 마지막 최종 결론 혹은 이후 가능한 토론 주제 제시
discussion / conclusions and implications / further research

2 문체의 문제

논문 작성 언어의 문체 면에서도 뚜렷한 차이점이 드러난다. 학문의 특성상 자연과학 분야에서는 인문과학 계열에 비해 비교적 간단명료하고 수식어구가 적은 언어 표현을 많이 쓰는 경향이 있다. 예를 들어, 자연과학 분야 논문의 본론이나 결론에서는 아라비아 숫자를 사용하여 핵심 문장을 간단하게 요약하는 경우가 많다.

- **This article has four main findings. First, ~. Second, ~. The third finding is that ~. The fourth finding is that** ~. Each of these findings runs counter to the assumptions of earlier scholars that ~.
- The principal finding of my study is important for **three reasons**. (1) it demonstrates that ~. (2) it suggests that ~ , and (3) this finding provides that ~.

인문과학 계열의 논문이라도 심리학이나 교육공학 같이 실험과 데이터 분석을 이용한 논문을 쓰는 분야에서도 위와 같은 스타일의 문장이 많이 사용된다.

- **Taking into account** the theory of interactive vision and the studies carried out by cognitive psychologists and their importance of the objectivity of science on the other hand, **we can conclude that**: (1), (2), and (3).

서론의 마지막 부분 즉, 서론에서 본론으로 넘어가면서 이후 전개될 논문의 전체적인 윤곽을 설명하는 방식에서도 이러한 차이점이 나타난다.

- **I shall proceed in the following way**: **first**, I will examine the function of teaching and learning through dialogue as it is conveyed by these three figures; **second**, I will be able to describe the different ways of empathic imitation they require; **and third**, I will conclude by broaching the difficult problems of the political involvements of inter-personal transmission.

3 어휘 선택의 문제

어휘 선택에 있어서도 자연과학과 인문과학 두 분야의 차이점이 잘 나타난다. 어문계열에서는 시적이고 비유적인 표현이 많이 사용되는 것에 반해서 자연과학의 논문들은 비교적 쉽고 명료한 언어를 선호한다. 예를 들어, A란 사람은 B라는 사람의 성격과 많이 닮아 있어 A의 어느 한 구석을 설명해 줄 수 있는 단서가 B에 들어 있다는 것을 표현한다고 하자. 이때 문학 논문에서는 전형적으로 echo, foil, mirror, resonate 등을 쓰며, 다수의 문학 논문이 사실 이같은 동사를 많이 활용한다. 엄연히 reflect같은 단어가 있음에도 말이다.

다음 예문을 비교해 보자.
- There are obvious **echoes** of the relationship between A and B.
- There are numerous **echoes** of A in B which attest to the fact that they are interrelated.
- The character A and B, **each is a foil to the other**.
- Many of B's sentiments exactly **mirror** those of A.

그럼 보다 구체적으로 알아보자.
다음의 예들은 인문과학과 자연과학에서의 단어 사용이 얼마나 다른지를 잘 보여 준다.

a considerable amount of	much
a majority of	most
a number of	many
are of the same opinion	agree
at this point in time	now
based on the fact that	because
despite the fact that	although
due to the fact that	because
first of all	first
for the purpose of	for
has the capability of	can
in many cases	often
in my opinion that	I think
in order to	to
in the even that	note that
it is worth pointing out in this context	if
it may, however, be noted that	but
lacked the ability to	could not
of great theoretical and practical importance	useful
on a daily basis	daily
perform	do
take into consideration	consider
the question as to whether	whether
through the use of	by
with a view to	to

왼쪽에 열거된 단어들은 일반적으로 인문과학 논문에서 빈번하게 나타난다. 반면 오른쪽에 정리된 단어들은 왼쪽의 단어들을 일컬어 장황하고 불필요한 표현 및 단어 wordy expression and redundant words로 규정하면서 예로 든 대안이다. 그리고 실제로 이러한 단어들은 자연과학 분야의 논문 작성법에서 추천하는 예이며, 다음의 책에서 참고하였음을 밝혀둔다. Robert A. Day, Scientific English: *A Guide for Scientists and Other Professionals* (Phoenix: Oryx Press, 1992): 86-87.

마지막으로, 일부 용어에 관련해서도 그 특징은 잘 나타난다. 자연과학 계열 전체, 혹은 실험을 많이 이용하는 분야의 논문에서는 결과란 단어를 표현할 때 results보다는 findings를 더 많이 쓰고 있다. 구체적인 실험에 들어가기 전에 설정하는 가설 hypothesis과 분석의 예로부터 나온 결과물을 통칭해 findings라고 한다. 논문의 맨 끝에 나오는 결론이란 항목도 인문과학에서는

conclusion이라고 쓰는 것과는 달리 자연과학 분야에서는 이 단어와 concluding remarks 혹은 discussion을 비슷한 비율로 쓰고 있다.

The Essential Guide to Writing Papers in English

II 서론에 자주 등장하는 표현

1. 문제 제기
2. 논문의 범위 설정
3. 논문의 목적 / 방향성 / 개요

01 문제 제기

~하기 힘든 개념

■ Victorian feminism is **a difficult concept to analyze** (or deal with, cope with, tackle with, figure out).

동사 analyze는 '분석하다'란 뜻으로 쓰이는 가장 대표적인 단어 중 하나이다. 굵은 글씨 부분은 '분석하기 어려운 개념'이란 뜻이다. 괄호 안의 deal with, cope with, tackle with는 모두 '~한 문제를 다루다'란 뜻이며, figure out은 '파악하다, 이해하다'란 뜻이다. '붙잡기 어려운' 이란 뜻으로 가장 대표적인 형용사는 slippery(difficult to hold)가 있다. slippery는 본래 susceptible, allowing, admitting으로 대체될 수 있다. 다음의 문장 하나를 더 확인해 보자. "Creolization is a slippery concept." 또는 "Defining politics is a tricky business. Like all fundamental concepts it is not susceptible to easy characterization."

■ The historical origin of folklore is **a very complex issue which has not yet definitely resolved.**

'지금까지 확실하게, 분명하게 해결되지 않은 매우 복잡한 현안, 혹은 문제'란 의미의 문장이다. 과거 어느 때부터인가에서 지금까지의 지속적인 문제를 언급하는 대목이기 때문에 동사의 시제는 당연히 현재완료시제, 즉 has not yet resolved를 사용하고 있다는 점도 눈여겨보자. 이처럼 해당 분야의 연구 현황을 언급하는 자리에서는 거의 대부분 현재완료시제를 사용한다.

~을 먼저 해야 하겠다 / ~을 먼저 분명히 하고자 한다

■ **At the outset, it is imperative to** clarify what we mean when we talk about ~.

imperative는 necessary와 동일어이다. at the outset이란 표현은 논문의 시작 부분에서 자신의 본격적인 논지를 밝히기 전에 필요한 개념 정의, 이론 설명 등 중요한 담론을 전개시키기 전에 시작하는 말로 많이 쓰인다. 다음 밑줄 친 부분도 유사한 의미로 썼다. Beginning with an overview of women's position in the peasant women, the author first discusses ~. 즉, 위의 문장은 '~에 대한 문제를 개괄하면서, ~에 대한 개괄로 시작하면서 저자는 먼저 ~을 논쟁한다'로 보면 된다. The first, preliminary question which must be set is whether ~. 이 문장은

'선행되어야 할 문제점은 ~에 대한 ~의 관련 여부이다'란 의미다. 앞의 예문들과 다소 다른 의미이긴 해도 같이 알아 두자.

- As such the approach is wholly theoretical and **it must be stated at the outset** that it tries to overcome the arbitrary distinction of issues as ~.
  ~라는 점이 초반에(처음에) 언급되어야 한다.

~의 신호탄이다 / ~의 처음을 장식한다

- This divergence of views in the early 1970s **signals** both the complex origins of second wave feminism and its internal divisions. At the 2003 MLA Annual Convention, the Publishing and Tenure Crises Forum signaled that important changes had taken place in how scholars disseminate and evaluate research.

- The second Bush administration **signaled** a more positive outlook on Yucca.
  반면 지금까지 어떤 학자의 업적 (책, 논문)이 해당 분야에서 독보적인 위치를 차지할 정도로 확고한 경우엔 다음과 같은 표현도 알아 두자. 핵심적인 뜻은 '어떤 분야의 주제에 있어서 가장 잘 알려진 연구는 ~이다.' The best-known source in English on this subject in general is still Rinda's monograph on ~. 위 예문에서 명사 outlook이 사용된 예를 하나 보자. Humans are always on the lookout for something better, bigger, tastier.

~이 논문의 중심이다

- Thompson's 2001 article **placed** sexual difference **at its analytic center**:
  ~의 논문은 성별상의 차이점을 분석의 중심에 두었다. 즉, ~의 논문은 ~을 중심으로 분석하였다.

- **My point will be that** such investigations beg question about ~.
  저자의 요지(핵심)는 ~라는 점이다.

- The essential debate **revolves around** the differentiation of the executive and the legislature.

- **Central to this paper** are two ideas: ~.
  위의 뜻은 '본 논문의 중심은 ~이다'란 의미로 다음의 유사 표현도 같이 알아 두자. '주도적, 본질적인 것은 ~이다' 또는 '~에 본질적인 것은 ~이다,' '~에 있어 ~는 매우 중요하다'란 의미로 폭넓게 사용해 보도록 하자. Case-study projects observations are vital to testing and reformulating the hypothetical development process through practical experience. / Central to the development process hypothesis is the theory that unethical, self-interested

cartels operate a culture at the institutional in such as ~. / <u>Fundamental to</u> these efforts are the clear self-understanding and articulation of a firm's distinctive competence and the value it brings to clients. / <u>What is evident is that</u> a new social space has opened up where the constraints of everyday life ~. / Political support and legal expertise has also <u>been crucial for</u> the adaptation of more liberal media legislation.

■ Credit was crucial to early market exchanges because it enabled buyers and sellers to conduct transactions without fully payment.

■ Essential to the notion of the market is the existence of calculative agency.
~에 대한 언급의 본질적인(중요한) 것은 ~이다.

■ More elaborate rituals were directed toward ancestors who were seen to inhabit the supernatural realm.

■ From the time of Gregory VII to the middle of the thirteenth century, European history centers around the struggle for power between the Church and the lay monarchs.
~를 중심으로 전개되다

대두되다 / 나타나다

■ The present research question emerged from the question: "Did you experience feelings of being treated differently from others in either school/outside in America?"
흔히 논문의 서론에 자주 등장하는 표현으로서, '저자의 논문은 ~ 문제(의식)에서 비롯한다, 비롯된 것이다'란 것을 밝히고자 할 때 사용한다.

■ These activities emerge as a consequence of the selection in the pursuit of resources.
~의 결과로 나타나다.

■ The second wave of feminism emerged in the late 1950s in the form of a sustained women's movements.
1950년대에 출현한, 나타난 제2의 페미니즘 물결(운동)

■ Communibiology has emerged recently as a new paradigm for the study of communication.

- The environment has recently emerged as an important dimension of the public debate over international trade.

- Korean emerged as one of the fastest-growing foreign languages in the world.

- In Russia, interest in the people and in folk life glimmered in the 18th century and then emerged during the first half of the 19th century.

  emerge는 '본격적으로 나타났다'는 의미이고, glimmer는 말 그대로 '명멸, 나타났다가는 이내 죽어가는'이란 뜻으로 잠시 나타났지만 큰 영향이나 반향을 불러일으키지 못한 경우란 의미이다.

- Concern about becoming a magnet for the high-level nuclear waste of other nations has not surfaced as a serious issue in the United States.

  동사 surface는 '표면으로 드러나다, 가시화 되다, 나타나다'(bring to the surface; cause to appear openly)란 의미를 모두 포함한다. 즉, '~한 이슈가 공론화 되고, 논쟁의 대상이 되기 시작했다'는 의미이다.

- Intense criticism of the auditing standards-setting process has surfaced periodically over the last 20 years.

- The major myth of Chinese national identity was born out of symbolic cultural discourse between ~ and ~.

  ~로부터 생성, 비롯되었다.

납득할 만한 / 설득력 있는 답변을 제공한다

- Prof. Norman Saul's recent studies give convincing answers to many questions in regard to ~.

  '~에 대한, 대하여, 관하여'란 의미의 숙어를 우리는 잘 알고 있다. 이 자리에서 한 번 정리해 보도록 하자. 위에서 예로 든 in (with) regard to 외에도 in terms of, in light of (~의 입장에서 혹은 ~의 측면에서), regarding, pertaining to, germane to, as to, as for, as with (~에 대하여, ~에 관한 한) 등의 다양한 표현이 있다. 다음 예문을 참고해 보자.

  - Top-down decision-making with regard to public investment allocation has slowly shifted toward a more bottom-up conception of policy-making.
  - Differences between the two countries with respect to financing pension systems have been much more evident.
  - With respect to the nature of man, Hobbes takes the position that man is selfish.
  - Being born female ensures double jeopardy with respect to access to these basics.

- The position of both major historians <u>with respect to</u> the historical tradition in their respective countries suggest ~.
- Russian history is usually told <u>in terms of</u> how this people concentrated power and extended it beyond preexisting boundaries.
- The story is told in this book, rather, <u>in terms of</u> how they created art and drove it beyond previous limits.
- <u>In</u> institutional <u>terms</u>, there is an additional reason for this difficulty.
- <u>In general terms</u>, this book has theory, new concepts, policy evaluations and some microstudies of cities and progress while implementing the recommendations from the 1992 UN Conference on Environment.
- <u>In very general terms</u>, Russian female folk costume existed in two main variants, the male costume being everywhere virtually the same.
- <u>In terms of whether</u> the reforms would tend towards cooperation or contest, the government had acted perceptively in issuing its GO.

■ Both works **give convincing answers to** many questions **in regard to** the ~.

■ Emerson **proves convincingly** that ~. 설득력 있게 증명하다.

■ Annales methods **proved** to be particularly applicable to relatively stable societies in which ~.
(프랑스) 아날 학파의 접근 방법들은 비교적 안정된 사회들(의 연구에)에 특별히 적용 가능한 것으로 증명되었다.

■ Hosking **has convincingly argued** that ~.

■ The explanatory power of this theory **has been convincingly demonstrated** in several surveys conducted by Locke (1976).

■ The cascade of financial crises that pummeled one East Asian economy after another beginning in the second half of 1997 **has called into question** the much-vaunted East Asian miracle.
call in(to) question은 dispute, challenge 등과 같은 뜻으로 '~에 반기를 들다, 논쟁하다, 반대하다'란 의미로 아주 많이 쓰인다.

■ The problem of orientation **has been given a considerable attention in** recent theoretical literature on planning and architecture.
~에 대한 문제가 ~에서 상당한 관심(주의)을 받았다.

■ In recent years the terminology of ~ **has been given scholarly considerable attention**, with the emphasis on ~.

■ The researcher provides **considerable insight into** this complex issue.
상당한 통찰력을 보여 주다.

■ The author of this paper **acquaints the reader with** the definitions of parody and satire in Soviet literary criticism.
acquaint A with B란 표현은 'A에게 B를 제공하다, 알게끔 하다'의 의미이다. 즉, to make aware; to furnish with knowledge; inform이다. 따라서 위의 문장은 '이 논문의 저자는 독자에게 ~의 정의가 무엇인지를 말해 준다, 제공한다'로 해석할 수 있다.

■ Two recent studies of the poem **illuminate the question of** ~.
~의 문제를 조명하고 있다.

■ **What I try to do in this paper is to confront** Levi-Strauss and question the adequacy of his concepts.
본 논문을 통해 저자가 하고자 하는 것은 ~에 반박하는 것이다.

■ For the first time, the study **presents** a clearly explained and richly illustrated survey of the formal features of French verse.

■ In many early Buddhist texts, the Buddha **presents** various moral standards.

■ Historians have generally **described** ~.

■ This essay suggests a different approach to the Dulle Griet (1562), which **sheds new light on** Brugel's moral lesson.

■ This article describes the methods of a study of grain markets in Bangladesh, which set out to **shed light on** three concerns: (1) ~, (2) ~, and (3) ~.

■ The author **does not give clear evidence as to** why ~.
저자는 ~에 대해서 왜 그런지 그 이유를 분명히 밝히고 있지 않다.

■ This article **uses** the IHS **model to** illustrate one approach to training injury prevention practitioners.

'~을 설명하기 위해 ~한 모델을 논문에서 사용하고 있다.' 다음의 문장은 '본 논문의 가장 중요한 이론적 틀은 ~의 ~이다[인용한 저자의 ~한 개념]'란 뜻으로 널리 쓰이는 패턴 중에 하나이다. Symbolic Interactionism (Blumer, 1986; Mead, 1934) is <u>the primary theoretical frame</u> supporting this research.

■ The political elements analyzed in this article **bear testimony** to the presence of shamanic features at the ~.
~은 ~에 대한 증거(입증)를 보여 준다, ~을 입증해 준다.

~의 문제를 조명하고 있다 / 다루고 있다 / 제기하고 있다

■ Robert Jackson **addresses the question of** Western European influence on Russian poetry.
반대로 '~에 대해 무시하다, 간과하다, 언급하지 않다'는 말을 표현하고자 할 때는 다음 예문을 참고하자. Prof. Pachmus's bibliography <u>makes no mention of</u> the existing studies on emigre writing in the English language. 여기에서 동사 address는 다른 말로 discuss, deal with와 대체될 수 있다.

■ The book **addresses** issues which are of great interest to Japanese scholars who ~.

■ For while his essay **ostensibly addresses** the vexed question relation between pure science and vocational training.
~한 문제를 표면적으로 다루다.

■ Both Bretell and Tony **address** themselves **directly to this question** and both conclude that ~.
~에 대한 문제를 직접적으로 다루다, 언급하다.

■ This paper **calls attention to** the central problem **as to** ~.
~에 대한 문제를 환기시킨다, 관심을 촉구하고 있다.

■ The author **calls in question** the meaning of ~.
■ Given the uncertainties, the scientific soundness of ecosystem restoration **has** also **been brought into question**.

■ Kohn's loyalty to the Czech nation **was** further **brought into question** following the anti-German and anti-Jewish violence.

- Moreover, the author **gives plausible explanations for** the ~.

  이 밖에도 형용사 plausible은 '설득할 만한'이란 뜻과는 약간 거리가 있지만 '그럴듯한' 혹은 '설명이 잘 된'(having an appearance of truth or reason, credible, believable; well-spoken and apparently worthy of confidence)이란 의미를 표현하고자 할 때 아주 유용하다. 다음의 문장도 살펴보자. It is not implausible to suggest in this context that ~. 또는 Kirk proposes certain plausible modifications: that ~.

- The theory has been convincingly **expounded** by Slavists outside Russia.

  동사 expound는 특히 '학술적인 이론 등을 내놓다, 공표하다'(to set forth in detail; to explain)란 의미이다. 다음의 문장도 알아 두자. The basic concepts underlying the ~ will be expounded below. 여기에 사용된 동사 expound와 같이 알아 두면 좋은 것은 work out이란 구동사이다. Democritus worked out his theories in considerable detail, and some of the working-out is interesting. 여기서 구동사 work out(v. find the solution to; a problem or question)은 '짜내다, 생각해 내다'의 의미로, 이 문장은 "철학자 데모 크리토스는 자신의 이론을 상당히 자세하게 고안해 냈고, 그 결과의 일부는 흥미롭다."로 해석할 수 있다.

- Victor Terras presents **absorbing account of** Tolstoy's complex system of esthetics and his assessment of Turgenev's creative process. **In the course of the piece,** Terras **provides several useful comments about** Dostoevsky: The tragic conflict in Dostoevsky deals with man's attempts to assert his freedom through affirmation of his Self, to ascend to the regions of the metaphysical as an individual, and to realize the ideal without God.

  형용사 absorbing은 말 그대로 '~을 빨아들이는, 흡수하는'의 뜻으로 사전적인 의미는 '흥미 있게 만드는', '흡입력 있는'이다. '설득력 있는'이란 뜻의 plausible과 같이 알아 두었다가 활용하면 유식하고 고급한 문장을 만들고자 할 때 매우 유용할 것이다 (The paper does an excellent job of weaving together a wide range of absorbing material.). 그리고 이렇게 긴 문장 전문을 다 인용한 이유는 먼저 흡입력 있다는 저자의 진술 이후에 어떤 방식으로 그 뒷받침을 하고 있는지 문체론적인 입장에서 도움이 되었으면 하는 마음에서이다.

- Greenwillow has failed to **give persuasive evidence that** ~.

  '설득력 있는 증거를 제시하다.' 참고로, 직접적인 증거가 없다는 뜻을 나타내고자 할 때는 다음 표현을 알아 두자. Unfortunately, direct evidence to answer this question (problem) is nonexistent; but it is nonetheless plausible to assume. (~의 문제에 답할 직접적인 증거는 존재하지 않지만 그럼에도 ~을 추측할 수는 있다.)

- Morris's **account of** the main hero as a productive type in German literature is pervasive and thought provoking.

  ~에 대한 설명이 설득력 있다.

- Clearly, these simple arguments cannot **account for** the variation of market reactions to different political events.

  '~을 설명하다'란 의미로 가장 일반적인 동사 표현인 account for를 알아 두자. It may appear problematic in accounting for those cases of more or less solid canonized items ~.

- On the eve of World War II, Japan had **accounted for** 5 percent of world industrial production.

  ~한 수치에 다다르다, 이르다

- This climate zone **accounts for** around 10.8 percent of the land area of Eurasia and was home to a somewhat larger proportion of the population: around 15.1 percent in 3000 BCE and 14.5 percent in 1000 BCE.

- The deaths from AIDS quickly **mounted into** the tens of millions, with vast attendant suffering.

  ~한 수치에 다다르다, 이르다

- The book, nevertheless, is highly informed and **persuasively argued against** the ~.

- Hosking's study does **make no attempt to answer** the silent questions of the reader.

  ~에 대해 답하려 하지 않는다. 즉, ~에 대한 문제를 간과하고 있다.

- Balin, in his book, **touches upon** the very important theme of dual culture, ~.

  touch upon (on)은 '~을 다루다, 처리하다'란 의미로 흔히 deal with와 같은 뜻으로 많이 쓰인다.

- The king's finance ministry **wrestled with the problem** but met with resistance.

  ~한 문제와 씨름하다

- Sex was a complicated topic throughout Look's history because it **touched on** strongly held values, longstanding norms, and intimate behaviors.

- This study **establishes** the contours of argument ~.

  동사 establish는 '~ 문제를 제기, 야기하다 (to bring about)'란 의미이다.

- **This paper is predicated on the notion that** privacy is the right to be let alone, physically, morally, and intellectually.

  본 논문은 ~라는 언급에 입각해 있다.

  여기에서 동사 predicate는 '~에 입각, 기반해 있다'란 뜻으로 to found or derive (a statement, action, etc.)를 의미한다.

- **To put the question of** American soft power hegemony **in perspective**, it helps to look at China.
  ~의 문제를 고찰해 보기 위해서는, 고찰해 보자면

  "문제를 야기하다, 생각해 내다"란 의미를 원할 때는 다음의 예문이 있다. This <u>brings up a question</u> which is half ethical, half political. "야기하다, 발생시키다"를 의미하는 대표적인 동사에는 cause 가 있다. Although curiosity is one of the most celebrated human attributes, it can cause problems when it fosters technology that we have not yet learned how to manage wisely. "give rise to"란 관용어구도 있다. Each age of globalization has given rise to new tensions and wars.

관심을 끌어 왔다

- Great **attention has been shown to the question of** ~.
  ~의 문제에 대해 많은 관심이 쏠렸다.

- Belknap's study **has attracted** a fair amount of **critical attention**.
  ~의 연구는 상당한 비평적 관심을 끌어 왔다.

- The "cultures of remembrance" in east central Europe is an important research topic that has recently **attracted the attention of scholars**.
  학자들의 주목을 끌었다

- Over the years this book **has received much attention** in the critical literature.
  수년 동안 이 저서는 많은 관심을 받아 왔다.

- The fame of this play **has generated** scores **of studies**, **ranging from** biographies of the writer's life to more formal analyses of the play's poetics.

- The iconography of medieval romance **is far less fully studied and catalogued than** that of sacred manuscripts.
  수동태를 이용해 A is less studied than B, 즉 'A는 B보다 연구가 덜 되어 있다'는 뜻이다.

- In his short but very useful introduction, the author **calls to the reader's attention various facets of** the changing dynamics of the Russian literary scene.

- Cronin's work **draws valuable attention to** the tension between US domestic policy and US foreign policy.

관심과 주목을 끌지 못했다 / ~에 무관심을 보이다

- **It has been too little observed that** the iconoclasm of the Protestant north was part of a larger program to rid the church not only of images but of the entire material culture of luxury that had grown up around the liturgy and to redirect that wealth to the poor.

- The play **has attracted(paid) little attention** as an object of critical observation.

- Unfortunately, this debate **has shed little light on** the origins of these family arrangements while making the task of uncovering them seem more hopeless than is warranted.

- The researcher **pays scant attention to** the ~. ~에 무관심하다, 주의를 기울이지 않다.

- The economic foundations of civilization **received scant acknowledgment** in the ancient world.
  덜 인지되다 = 충분하게 인정받지 못하다

- The author **pays** relatively **little attention to** the epiphany in Dostoevsky's text.

- The story **has never been a favorite of** the critics even in Russia.

- The novel **has largely been ignored.** 대체로(일반적으로) 무시되어 왔다.

- Historians **have generally slighted** Kolpakov's fiction and focused instead on his non-fictional works.

- Russian emigre literature is much **neglected branch of** Russian literature.
  등한시 된 분야, 관심 밖의 영역

- This paper **provides** both **long-neglected study of** ~, thereby overcoming the tendency of many historians to ignore ~.

- This field **has received only minimal attention.**

■ The culture of the Spanish peasant **has received relatively little attention from** Western scholarship in general and American scholarship in particular in comparison with such fields of the ~.
~은 ~의 학계로부터 상대적으로 적은 관심을 받아 왔다.

■ It apparently **has not been addressed elsewhere** in the critical literature on Zamiatin.

■ Daniel's monumental work, ~, **was not much studied** until the end of World War II.
많이 연구되지 않은

■ Mexican ethnographic sources **are** discreetly **silent about** peasant excretory arrangements.
~에 대한 문제에 침묵을 지키다, 관심을 보이지 않다.

■ Yet within the vast territory of studies of the classical tradition, **there remains a large piece of uncharted terrain.**
아직 연구되지 않은 영역이 남아 있다.

~에 대한 연구(논란, 논쟁)가 많다 / 주목받을 만하다

■ In recent years, **numerous studies have attempted to find and explore** Joyce's place on the Hispanic cultural map.

■ In recent years, **there have been several accounts that point to** the increasing [issue or trend]
최근 점증하는 ~을 지적하는 몇몇 설명들이 있어 왔다.

■ **Some arguments have been made** that [specific argument].
지금까지 ~와 같은 주장(논쟁)들이 있었다.

■ Ever since the publication of *War and Peace*, critics **have argued over** the text of it.

■ **Enough has been said to** demonstrate how thoroughly Pasternak revives the Hamlet myth.

■ **Much has been said about** the similarities between [subject1] and [subject2].

- **Much has been written in** description of Wilons's color system.

- **Much** scholarly **work has been done on the topics of** civil society and ethnic conflict, but no systemic attempt has yet been made to connect the two.
  이처럼 much로 시작되는 문장 유형에 익숙해지면 영어 표현이 보다 수월해질 것이다.

- From among the interdisciplinary group representing anthropology, psychology, and sociology, special community studies **are increasingly abundant** in both published and unpublished works.
  위 문장에서 interdisciplinary는 말 그대로 학제 간, 즉 '타학문들 간의'란 뜻으로 여러 인접 학문들을 두루 연결 지어 연구하는 경향을 말할 때 쓰이는 형용사이다. 굵은 글씨 부분은 '~가 점점 풍부해지고 있다'로 보면 되겠다.

- The **question has** also **been raised as to** whether ~, and if so, to what extent this view present the views of Chekhov.
  지금까지 ~에 대한 문제가 대두(제기) 되었다.

- Studies by other historians of the Russian literature **stress** development ~.

- Lexington's works **were published in wide of journals,** including ~.

- Recent years **have witnessed** the appearance of several interesting regional newspaper source and historical studies, as well as bibliographies.
  위의 예문을 직역하면 '최근 여러 해들은 ~의 출현을 목격해 왔다'란 어색한 문장이 된다. 이처럼 무생물 주어 다음에 동사 witness를 사용하는 문장 유형을 잘 익혀두자. 대표적인 또 다른 예로 우리는 어떤 '시대'가 문장의 주어가 되는 경우를 많이 보게 된다 (The 1990s have witnessed ~.). 이 경우 우리는 '1990년대는 ~를 목격했다'고 단순히 직역하기보다는 '~는 1990년대에 발생했다'로 의역해 보는 것이 좋을 듯하다. 이 밖에 동사 see도 똑같은 역할을 하여, The second half of the 20th century had seen the increase of ~.와 같은 문장을 우리는 흔하게 발견할 수 있다.

- **Recent years have seen a rapid boom** and bust cycle surrounding the automotive telematics market in the United States.

- To be sure, **there have been studies concerned** specifically **with** this problem, **but** ~.
  동사 concern은 전치사 with와 결합되어 매우 자주 쓰이는 표현이다. 여기에서 알아 두어야 할 것은 To be sure, ~, but ~이란 표현이다. 이 구문은 '물론 ~하다. 그러나 사실은 ~하다'를 뜻하는 고정된 표현법으로서 거의 예외 없이 but이 뒤따른다는 것을 꼭 기억해두자. 때에 따라서는 Of course, ~, but ~으로도 사용된다.

■ Our **concern is not with** the recovery of original meaning **but with** the network of representation that is configured by readings of *Ulyses*.

■ Gerald Mikkelson's studies are **deserving of the scholarly attention** they have received, especially as regards two problems: ~.

■ The importance of Hong Kong as an international trade entrepot in the 19 century **is widely researched**.

■ There is a **growing body of evidence** that ~.
~에 대한 증거 자료가 늘어가고 있다.

보다 정확하게 얘기하자면 body 다음에 bibliography 또는 문헌을 뜻하는 literature를 넣으면 좋겠다. growing은 '점차 증가하는, 성장해 가는'이란 뜻으로 특히 최근 연구 동향을 분석할 때 빈번하게 나타나는 형용사이다. 다음 예문들을 통해 익숙해지도록 해 두자 (In recent years there has been growing public recognition that sexual and domestic violence overlap and are interrelated. 또는 Increasingly prevalent in the past two decades, anorexia nervosa and bulimia have emerged as major health and social problems. literature가 들어간 예는 다음과 같다. The literature on violence against women has expanded steadily over recent decade.). 한편, growing과 유사한 의미로 burgeoning이 있으며 (In recent years, there has been a burgeoning interest in looking at women in quite another light.), '전례 없는, 비할 바 없는'이란 의미를 나타내고자 할 때는 형용사 unprecedented를 사용해 보자 (In the 20th century, there has been an unprecedented interest not only in the written remains of the music of previous generations.).

■ Gender differences in school achievement **have been studied extensively** during the past two decades.
~가 광범위하게 연구되어 왔다.

■ This fact has been **extensively** commented by critics. Laviton notes: "~."
extensive를 이용한 표현의 보다 전형적인 예를 알아보자.
There is already an extensive literature devoted to ~. 이 문장은 '~을 다루고 있는 (~에 대한) 문헌이 이미 광범위하게 있다'란 뜻이다.

■ The Institute for International Economics (IIE) **has done extensive research on** ~.

■ The work of female medical missionaries **has** so far **been studied mainly within this context**, that is, as one aspect of the history of Western women missionaries seeking opportunities and funding fulfillment by doing women's work for women.
~한 맥락에서 상당히 연구되어 왔다.

■ The role of Hong Kong as a financial center since the 1970s **has been vigorously researched** by Jao.

'매우 왕성하게, 활발하게 연구되다'란 의미를 나타내고자 할 때, be vigorously researched란 표현을 이용해 보자. 이 외에 학술 경향을 지적하고자 할 때는 다음과 같은 평범하면서도 정석적인 표현들이 있으니 잘 알아 두자 (In the early 1970s, under the lead of Lucas, new classical economics <u>appeared on the scene</u>. 또는 <u>Significant changes have been taking place</u> in the structure and organization of economic life during the past three decades.). 여기에서 동사 appear는 '~의 결과로 나타나다'라는 뜻의 동사 ensure와 대체될 수 있다. 다음 문장을 확인해 두자. This algorithmic structure <u>ensures</u> that it does not really matter who is the receptionist, nurse or doctor on duty.

An interesting debate <u>has ensured</u> between two competing perspectives on organizational change.

연구가 미비하다 / 자료가 거의 없다

■ There is **no comprehensive** monograph.
~을 다루고 있는 포괄적인(전체적으로 다룬) 단행본이 없다.

■ There is **no study of** ~ in English, except for the ~.

■ There is, to my knowledge, **no serious study** in any language of the woman question in African women.

■ So far, **no definitive answer has been given to** this question.
지금까지 ~에 대한 문제에 결정적인, 분명한 답이 제시된 적이 없다.

■ So far, very **little has been done** in this direction.
지금까지 이런 방향에서 (문제가) 다루어진 적은 거의 없다.

■ **Little is known of** the original copy of ~.
~에 대해 알려진 바가 거의 없다.

■ To date, **there has been minimal research regarding** ~.
~에 대한 연구가 극소수였다.

■ **Relatively few studies have been devoted to** an analytic, detailed examination of the language of Leskov's works.

- **Relatively little attention was paid to** differences in male and female personality about behavior.
  비교적 적은 관심이 ~에 쏠렸다, 주목을 거의 받지 못했다.

- **Relatively little research has been carried out on ~.**

- **Fewer studies have attempted to construct** a systematic political explanation of Fund behavior.

- Curiously, despite the rise of cultural studies as an academic discipline, **few have attempted to address ~.**
  ~의 상승, 늘어남에도 불구하고, ~을 다루는 시도는 그간 거의 없었다.

- **While there has been little research into** female tribal police officers, **some have been done on** the problems faced by female officers.

- **Although** general information about these programs is available on the Internet and through campus-based materials, **little research has been conducted on** the effects of these projects.
  여기에서 사용된 동사 conduct를 눈여겨보자. research, field work, expedition, exploration 등의 명사에는 거의 예외 없이 이 동사를 사용한다. 즉, 현장 답사, 탐험 등을 수행한다는 의미로 가장 고급하면서도 널리 쓰이는 이 동사를 반드시 알아 두자. 숙어인 carry out ~는 위의 동사를 대체할 수 있는 것으로 가장 적합하다. 예를 들어, I have previously <u>carried out</u> research at ~ over 8 months. 또는 That summer, in the village where Rachel lived several years earlier, I <u>carried out the fieldwork</u> on which this study is based.

- The strategy of the comic and the devices of satire **are hardly discussed at all.**

- This **has recently received the least close critical attention.**
  지금까지 가장 밀접한, 면밀한 비평적 관심을 받지 못했다. 즉, 거의 외면되고 주목을 받지 못했다.

- This area still remains **far from fully answered.**
  우리가 잘 아는 숙어 far from은 '~과는 거리가 먼, 그래서 결코 ~가 아닌'이란 의미이니, 이 문장은 '여전히 해결되지 않은 문제로 남아 있다. 즉, 해답이 필요하다.'는 말이다.

- **Considerable doubt has been cast over** the literal existence of ~:
  ~에 대한 문헌의 존재에 대해 의구심(회의적 반응)이 많았다. 즉, ~에 대한 자료가 있는지에 대해 사람들은 믿지 않고 있다.

■ Nevertheless there remains an **unexplained aspect**.
그럼에도 불구하고 설명되지 않은 측면이 여전히 남아 있다.

■ But the fundamental importance of the ~ **has never been examined**.
그러나 ~의 근본적인 중요성은 지금껏 한 번도 점검되지 않고 있다.

■ Leskov's satire **has not been examined to date**.
레스코프의 풍자는 지금껏(오늘날까지) 연구, 조사, 점검되지 않았다.

■ But there is **little evidence to** support his assumption. 입증 자료가 거의 없다.

■ There is **no evidence as to** who actually titled the poem.
~에 대한 증거가 부족하다.

■ Unfortunately, **direct evidence to answer this question is nonexistent**, but it is nonetheless plausible to assume that ~.
evidence가 들어간 다양한 예문을 살펴보자. Horticulturalists also evidenced a more explicit court structure and, in many causes, a system of courts. The evidence is too fragmentary to trace the introduction and spread of Buddhist images across China with any precision. Evidence for sacred icons in China before the entrance of Buddhism is as sketchy as it is for sacred icons in pre-Buddhist India. 한편, evidence가 동사로 사용되어 '~을 증명하다'로 쓰일 경우 bear out과도 상호 교환되어 사용된다. Data from bone sites in Ohio and Indiana do not bear this out. Medieval vernacular romance is assumed to bear the stamp of the class to which it was first directed. 또 다른 숙어로는 '~의 증거로'란 뜻의 by token of, as a token of가 있다. As tokens of friendship or esteem, monks and laypeople exchanged gifts of tea, rosaries, and other objects.

■ The rich multiethnic dimensions of life in the 19th century of France **are still vastly underexplored**.

■ **No mention of the ~ is made in** the account of ~.
~에 대한 설명 속에는 ~에 대한 언급이 전혀 없다.

■ **No further accounts are** either **rendered** or forthcoming.

■ Surprisingly, this important lyric is **often noted but rarely studied** in the vast literature on Pushkin.
~이 자주 언급은 되었어도 막상 연구는 되어 있지 않다.

■ Scholars of early French culture and history **rarely pause in their studies to consider** the ~.

~을 연구하는(~분야) 학자들은 ~에 대한 문제를 거의 문제삼지 않는다, 관심을 기울이지 않는다.

■ These questions **have not**, so far, **been noticed, nor have** they **been studied in detail**.

~의 문제들은 지금껏 주목받지 못했을 뿐만 아니라, 자세하게 연구되지도 않았다.

■ John Steinback's preoccupation with visual images in his fictions has been widely noted, **yet little studied**.

■ Surprisingly, though, critics **have not extensively researched** this topic either in the West and Russia.

놀랍게도, 이 분야에 대해 비평가들은 광범위한 연구를 해 오지 않고 있다.

■ The international political aspects of IMF lending **have received far less rigorous analysis**.

정확한, 혹은 정밀한 분석을 받아본 적이 없다. 즉, 주목받지 못해 왔다, 또는 연구되지 않았다.

■ **Though** highly popular and **much received** in recent years, the concept of civil society **also needs to be subjected** to critical scrutiny.

위의 두 문장에서처럼 동사 receive는 '어떤 반응 등을 받다'와 같은 의미를 나타내고자 할 때 많이 사용된다.

■ These arguments **have not been yet developed** conceptually **nor thoroughly tested** empirically.

■ The novel **was never analyzed by** Rozanov scholars.

로자노프의 소설은 그를 연구하는 학자들로부터 한 번도 분석된 바 없다. 즉, 그의 소설은 거의 연구되지 않았다.

■ With a few significant exceptions like ~, peasant studies **passed into an oblivion** which lasted for thirty years.

주목할 만한 일부 예외가 있긴 하지만, ~ 연구는 오랜 동안 망각 속에 빠져 들어갔다. 즉, 연구되지 않고 사장되어 왔다.

■ **In contrast to the voluminous scholarship on ~, there have been few general studies on ~.**

~에 대한 엄청나게 두터운 학계(학문적 결실이 많다는 의미에서)에 비해 ~에 대한 일반적인 연구는 매우 적었다, 거의 없었다.

~에 대한 의견의 일치 / 공통된 견해 또는 반대 / 불일치가 있어 왔다

- According to **common consensus**, ~. 공통된 견해, 일치점, 일치된 견해에 따르면

- All evidence from Indo-European countries **has** one **characteristic in common**: a marriage cannot be contracted and celebrated without at least one bridesman.
  공통된 특징을 지니다.

- Throughout these studies runs a **common theme**: that language is understood in context. 이 연구들을 통틀어 하나의 공통된 주제는 ~이다
  이때 that절 이하의 내용을 콜론(:)을 이용해 표현한 위의 예문은 사실 그렇게 권장할 만한 것이 아니니 사용에 주의를 바란다. 대신 영어의 다양한 문체를 경험하는 정도에서만 알아 두자.

- In no case, however, has anything resembling a **consensus** been reached.

- At a fundamental level, **there is a similar consensus on** the nature of understanding.

- Organizational justice researchers have **reached nearly universal consensus** that fairness can be divided into at least two types.
  보편적인, 공통된 일치점에 이르다.

- There was absolutely **no consensus as to** the word's meaning.
  ~에 관한 일치된 견해는 전혀 없었다.

- One problem is the **lack of consensus regarding** the meaning or measurement of the three most important aspects of politics that ~.

- **There is no overall agreement as to** Euripides' intent in *Troades*, but there is little doubt that this tragedy most movingly presents the suffering caused by war.
  ~에 대한 전반적인 동의는 없다.

- J. Le Goff **is not fully in agreement with** John's position and thinks that the latter has suggested ~.
  ~과 완벽하게, 충분하게 동의하고 있지 않은

- **There is no general agreement about** what the term religion means.

- Although there is no definitive explanation as to why and how capitalist crises occur, **there is general agreement** that crisis does periodically occur.

- While there is **general agreement about** the ~, there is continuing discussion over the ~.

- Although there is **no universally accepted** definition, the social insurance approach is usually based on the following characteristics: ~.
  보편적으로 인정된, 받아들여진

- The relationship between religion and the state is always **problematic.**
  ~간의 관계는 늘상 문젯거리이다, 문제가 많다.

~에 대한 시각 / 의견의 인정과 그 반대

- **As has been noted by** virtually every commentators, ~.
  실질적으로 모든 논평자들에 의해서 언급되어 왔듯이, ~

- Gosling's view of ~ **has not been acclaimed.**

- I looked at these themes **with an anthropologist's eye for** myths of city.
  ~(문화인류학자)의 견해로, 눈으로 ~의 주제를 바라보다.

- I have some **reservations as to** certain details, e.g. ~에 대한 이견, 다른 생각

- It is **generally acknowledged** that ~.

- It is **generally agreed that** ~.

- The majority of critics **agree that** ~.

- I **cannot subscribe to** Sheley's opinion.
  동사 subscribe to는 agree with와 동일한 의미로 '~에 동의하다'라는 말이다.

~에 대한 연구는 아직 걸음마 / 초보 단계이다

- **Research on ~ is still in its early stage**, as the brevity of the bibliography attests. There are currently only two monographs on the subjects: one is ~, and one ~.
  소량의 참고 문헌으로도 나타나듯이 ~에 대한 연구는 여전히 초보 단계에 있다. 최근 두 편의 단행본 연구 목록을 열거하면 다음과 같다.

사실 이같은 언급은 서론에서 얘기할 수도 있겠지만 논문의 흐름에 큰 방해가 되지 않는다면 가급적 각주 footnote 혹은 미주 endnote에 넣어 간단히 설명하면 좋을 듯하다. Computer support for collaborative design is still in the early stages of development.

■ In the embryonic tradition of modernist prose, the incursion of this alternative interpretation was rather limited.
embryo는 임신 과정에서 가장 초기의 배아 상태를 뜻하기도 하고 이런 의미에서 어떤 발달 단계의 시초나 시작 단계를 말해 주는 비유적인 의미로 많이 쓰인다.
In the introductory part, I present two vignettes that contains, in embryonic outline, the reconstructed Soviet woman of the 1930s.

■ The field of tourism studies is relatively young and, as such, is still establishing its basic tenets. In addition, gender analysis within tourism studies is even younger and the integration of the two bodies of tourism and gender research is, in fact, almost never seen.
~의 영역, 연구 분야는 아직 초보 상태이다.

■ Divorce and property rights were only a beginning for the women's movement.
~에 있어서 단지 시작일 뿐이다

~을 유념해야 한다

■ On further consideration, however, it becomes evident that a definition of "power" so broad that it encompasses the objectives both of states trying to grow smaller, as well as of those using violence and aggressions to enlarge their territorial domains has lost its descriptive or analytical value.
더 숙고하다 보면
'논의가 더 필요한' 경우의 표현은 다음의 경우에서처럼 고급화 한 예가 또 있다.

■ Various stages have to be traversed before we can state this problem in modern times.
이 문제를 진술(설명)할 수 있으려면 여러 다양한 단계들이 검토되어야(살펴져야) 할 것이다.

■ But these new manifestations of nationalism must be put into the proper perspective.
보다 적절한 관점에서 살펴져야 한다

■ This new career **put me in close touch with** most of the AI pioneers, and over the decades I rode with them on waves of enthusiasm, and into valleys of disappointment.

전치사 put이 들어가면 뭔가 정확하고, 분명한 의미가 형성되는 효과를 보여 준다. 예를 들어, 앞선 문장에서 조동사 must/should를 쓰지 않고도 '~을 해야 한다, 혹은 하는 것이 좋겠다'의 의미를 살릴 수 있는 방법이 있다. 다음의 문장은 그 좋은 예가 된다.

■ It would **be foolish**, however, **to overlook** the fact that ~
~를 간과, 무시하면 어리석은 일이다

■ There is a **further problem with** universal recognition, summed up in the question, "Who esteems?"
~한 문제가 더 있다

■ Poverty **was a highly visible problem** in the 18 th century, both in cities and in the countryside.
~는 분명하게 드러나는 문제이다

■ When answering this question, we should(have to) **bear in mind** that ~.
이것과 유사한 표현으로 keep in mind가 있다.

■ In evaluating the data and conclusions of this paper, it is important to **bear in mind** that ~.

■ In regard to this problem, we **have to remember(have not to forget)** ~.

■ **With these considerations in mind**, let us now draw some distinctions among the postsocialist regimes with respect to ~.
이같은 생각들을 염두에 두면서

■ **With these purposes in mind**, I should like to use the first chapter of my dissertation to survey recent historical and literary critical approaches to ~, and to sketch briefly some of the development in ~. The second chapter is intended to demonstrate the resonance of some of these new ideas about ~.
이같은 목적(의도)을 염두에 두면서 저자는 ~을 하고자 한다.

■ **With** these insights of network theory **in mind**, we can now revisit the history of the Illuminati.
~를 염두에 두고, ~를 고려해 본다면

- **With this** complex structure of political and historical moments **in mind**, let us turn to recent history itself.

- **With this body of date at hand**, we may return to the proposed model to examine ~.

- One of the best vantage point <u>from which to consider</u> the dynamics of intertechnic and interconfessional relations in the late China empire is provided by the associational life within the empire's largest cities.
가장 고려해야 할 포인트는 ~이다.

~에 대한 연구는 주로 ~을 중심으로 이루어져 왔다

- For the most part, recent critical debates about Tolstoy's *Resurrection* have **tended to center around** the question of ~.

- **My approach in this paper is based on** the concepts of the Prague School as exemplified in the works of Roman Jakobson and particularly the work of C. H. Schooneveld.
본 연구에서 저자의 접근 방법은 ~에 기초되어 있다(~을 기반으로 한다).

- I see a three-**pronged approach for** the near future. It also requires more energy and effort, but the payoff is that it attracts more students and gives them a wider perspective.
가닥진 / 본인은 ~에 대한 세 가지 측면의 접근 방법을 살펴본다. 그러나 ~의 장점(이로운 점은) ~이다.

- From the point of view of method **the author** of the book **owes a great deal to** German philosophy.
'~에 빚지고 있다'란 말 그대로, 위의 문장에서 굵은 글씨로 표현된 숙어는 '~에 의존하다, 기초를 두고 있다'로 이해하면 좋을 것이다. 참고로, 이와 유사한 의미에는 rely on(upon)이 있다. 한편, depend on은 그 의미가 약간 달라, '~에 달려 있다, ~ 때문에 좌우된다'란 뜻으로 사용된다 (The sound <u>depends on</u> the position of the bow and the width of the hair brought into operation.).

- **The discussion here is informed by** recent feminist theoretical works on women and culture, such as ~. These are texts which have productively engaged with recent literary-critical and historiographical debates on the relation between text and context.

- The **premise which underpins a good deal of my subsequent argument** is ~

이하 저자가 보여 주고자 할 토론의 상당 부분을 뒷받침해 주는 전제는 ~이다.

동사 underpin은 매우 중요한 동사이니 그 활용도를 잘 알아 두자. 여기에서 동사 underpin과 동일한 의미의 다른 말에는 undergird가 있다. 다음 예문을 비교해 보자. The central insight that <u>undergirds</u> any interregional research on skills-based wage inequality is that ~. 또는 The research and travel <u>undergirding</u> this lengthy project have been funded at times by grants from the Davis Postdoctoral Fund of Princeton University.

premise는 논문의 시작 부분에 나타나는 전제나 가설의 의미(a basis, stated or assumed, on which reasoning proceeds)로 쓰이는 일반적인 단어이다. 이 단어가 들어간 문장을 살펴보자. The basic <u>premises</u> of the approach to the ~ can be reduced to the following: 1), 2), and 3)...

흥미로운 점은 / 눈여겨볼 만한 것은 ~이다

- **Especially interesting from our point of view is** ~.

우리의 시각에서 볼 때 한 가지 매우 흥미로운 점은 ~이다.

- **One of the outstanding features employed in this device is** that ~.

- **Of special interest is** ~.

특별히 흥미로운 것은 ~이다.

- **Of particular important in this regard is his insistence on** ~.

이 점에 있어서 특히 중요한 것은 ~이다.

- **Considerable doubt has been cast over** the literal existence of ~.

~에 대한 문헌의 존재에 대해 의구심 (회의적 반응)이 많았다, 즉 ~에 대한 자료가 있는지에 대해 사람들은 믿지를 않아 왔다.

02 논문의 범위 설정

~에(만) 한정할 것이다

- We(I) will **limit ourselves (myself) to** outlining a few of the novels' major thematic configurations.

- In exploring the questions of ~, **this paper will be limited to consideration of ~.**
  ~한 문제를 다루면서 본 논문은 ~만을 다루는 데 그칠 것이다.

- For the most part we shall **limit ourselves to** Jakobson's major theories.

- **Rather than confining myself to the story's** socio-political **context**, I shall focus on(upon) the psychological nature of the author's fantasies. Here my attention will be focused principally on documentary materials, specially the private acts which have survived.
  rather than은 '~하기보다는 차라리 ~'을 의미한다. 간혹 둘을 떨어뜨려 rather A ~, than B (A 보다는 차라리 B이다)로 표현하기도 한다.

- In order to avoid this, **I have limited the main body of this study to** a number of texts belonging to ~.
  지금까지 본 연구의 중심을 ~에 한정해 왔다.

- **The span of time I hope to cover includes** the centuries between 500 and 1500, the conventional Middle Ages.
  (본 논문에서) 저자가 다루고자 하는 시대 범위는 ~이다(~을 포함한다).

- Such considerations **are** merely **beyond the scope of the present study**.
  그같은 생각들은 본 연구의 범위를 벗어나 있다.

- The discussion **is beyond the scope of the present paper**.
  본 연구의 범위를 벗어나 있다.

- **It is not within the scope of this study to outline** all ~.
  ~개괄하는 것은 본 연구의 범위를 벗어나는 일이다.

- Many of the concerns that I formulated above **remained outside the scope of** Mead's considerations.

- This is a complex theoretical issue, however, it **goes beyond the bounds of the present paper**.

- A fuller examination of this issue is **beyond the scope of** the present essay.

- It **seems appropriate to limit** this study of ~ **to** the tenth century.
  ~에 대한 본 연구(의 범위)를 10세기에 한정하는 것이 타당해 보인다.

~하지는 않을 것이다

- However, here we will **neglect** to pursue any arguments **as to** the ~.
  동사 neglect는 말 그대로 '~을 소홀히 하다, 게을리 하다'란 의미로 이 예문에서는 '~을 하지 않겠다'는 말의 완곡한 표현이다.

- I **shall not dwell** here **on** Ermolaev's critical remarks about ~.
  숙고하다

- I **shall not polemicize** here **on** this subject with ~.
  ~을 논쟁으로 삼지는 않겠다.

- **Because the present paper is primarily** historical and thematic **in scope, I am choosing to ignore** here the interesting question of the psychological function of fantasy.
  본 논문의 범위는 기본적으로 ~이기 때문에 본인은 ~을 무시하겠다.

- **While this paper does include a brief sketch of** ~, **it does not attempt to provide** ~. There are a number of excellent texts which readers can turn to for that.

03 논문의 목적 / 방향성 / 개요

본 논문에서 우리는 ~할 것이다 / 살필 것이다 / 시도해 볼 생각이다

아래의 예들을 잘 보면 자주 반복되어 사용되는 동사와 기본 구문이 있다는 것을 알게 된다. 예를 들어, '본 논문은 ~을 살필 것이다' 혹은 '점검할 것이다, 밝히고자 한다, 다루고자 한다' 등과 같은 표현인 경우 거의 대부분 동사 examine, demonstrate, deal with, explore, present, describe, reveal, disclose, consider, offer, provide, argue, pursue, exhibit, expound 등을 사용하고, 때에 따라서는 treat, tackle, approach, take a look at을 사용하기도 한다. '~을 하겠다'는 의미에서 will이나 shall과 같은 미래시제를 쓰기도 하지만 대부분의 상황에서는 현재시제를 쓰기도 한다. 한가지 더 우리가 잘 아는 표현으로 '~하는 것이 목적이다'고 할 때, be to용법을 활용한다는 것을 상기하자.

서론에서 '~의 주제를 다루고자 한다' 혹은 '~을 하고자 한다'고 하는 저자의 의사를 표현할 때, 대부분의 영어 논문은 도식적인 표현법, 이를테면 첫째, 둘째, 셋째 대신에 1), 2), and 3)와 같은 나열 방법을 삼가는 경향이 있지만, 다음과 같이 그 반대의 경우와 같은 예도 있을 수 있다. 참고해 보도록 하자.

In order to present such a reading this paper will (1) offer a general outline of the problem of self-interest in 18th century thought, (2) indicate the problematic approaches to the problem developed by Derzhavin in a number of poems of various genres throughout his literary career; and (3) offer a reading of ~. 또는 I proceed by examining 1) the novel's conscious investigation of the general relationship between words, deeds, and truth, and 2) the way in which this verbal text's liner axis simultaneously proves and disproves its own particular truth.

shall see / to consider

- In the present paper(article) **we shall see how this myth is transformed** through Tolstoy's text.

- We **will see** in this article(paper) **how this theme is being unveiled**.
  이 논문에서 우리는 주제가 어떻게 드러나고 있는지를 살펴보게 될 것이다.

- In our discussion, **we shall first consider** ~, **then**, and **finally** ~; a few remarks will also be made ~.

to examine

- This paper **examines** the problem of moral law, particularly of ~.
  본 논문은 도덕률, 특히 ~의 문제를 점검하고(살피고) 있다.

- The paper **will be examined** with reference to the writer's subject, character, setting, theme and style.

- **To facilitate understanding of** this paper, and thus as an introduction to the questions themselves, **it seems necessary to examine** the different meanings and evaluations assigned to the concept of civilization in Germany.
  본 논문의 이해를 돕기 위해서 ~을 점검할 필요가 있다.

to aim / aim

- **My aim is to highlight** several aspects of ~.
  ~에 대한 다양한 측면을 강조하는 것이 (본 논문) 저자의 목적이다. 저자의 목적은 ~을 강조하는 것이다.

- **My aim is to provide an alternative framework for** evaluating them.
  저자의 목적은 ~을 평가할 대안의 프레임웍을 제시하는 것이다.

- **My aim is to add a new perspective to this debate** by ~.
  본인의 목적은 ~을 함으로써 이 토론에 새로운 시각을 보여 주는 것이다.

- This paper **aims to** synthesize the insights of these two critics ~.

- Theoretically, **this paper aims to** continue to the interdisciplinary discourse centering around the concept of ~.

- **The aim of this article is** a stylistic analysis of Nabokov's prose, **with an emphasis on** ~.
  본 논문의 목적은 ~이고, ~에 특별한 강조점을 두고 있다. 즉, ~을 특히 강조하고 있는 본 논문의 목적은 ~이다.

- **The aim of this study is to provide an overview of** the recent development of childcare policy in the UK.
  본 연구의 목적은 ~에 대한 전체적인 개괄을 보여 주는 것이다.

■ **The aim here is to challenge** built-in assumptions that ~.

본 논문의 목적은 이미 정착되어 확고하게 받아들여진 가정(가설)들에 대한 도전, 반박이다.

built-in은 '붙박이'란 뜻(built-in bookcases)이 있지만, existing as a natural or characteristic part; inherent란 의미로 통용되기도 한다. 즉, '~의 자연스러운, 혹은 특징적인 부분으로 존재하는; 고유의, 본래의'란 뜻도 갖고 있다.

■ **The aim of this first section is to explore the ways in which** some of the best-known writers on nationalism and national identity, namely ~, have considered the cultural and its relationship with the ~.

본 장의 목적은 민족주의와 민족 주체성 분야에서 가장 잘 알려진 연구자들이 ~에 대해 어떠한 관심을 기울여 왔는지를 살펴보는 것이다.

■ **In this paper I aim to** begin to reconstruct the context and meaning of Sumarokov's adaptation of "Hamlet" in two ways.

■ I have two broader **aims. The first is to** encourage scholars to incorporate ~. My **second aim is to** address the literature on the ~.

■ **My aim accordingly is not to examine** specific rituals, **but,** firstly to make clear what follows from ~, **then to indicate** where criticism might be offered, **and finally to suggest how** in principle these rituals might be understood ~.

■ **It is the aim of the present paper to** rectify this situation in small measure by presenting to the interested scholar of German history.

여기에서 동사 rectify는 '개정, 개작, 수정하다'라는 뜻으로, '어떠한 입장, 논리, 주장, 근거 등을 바꾸다, 수정하다'란 의미의 가장 고전적인 단어라고 할 수 있다.

to attempt

■ In this paper, **I will attempt to** ~. 이 논문에서 나는 ~을 시도하고자 한다.

■ This paper thus **attempts to** outline an alternative reading of ~.

이 논문은 ~에 대한 대안적 해석(또 다른 해석)을 시도해 보는 것이다.

흔히 reading이라 하는 표현 속에는 어떤 작품이나 글, 책, 또는 읽는 대상의 모든 것에 대해 읽은 사람이 이해하는 방식, 즉 해석, 읽은 관점, 반복 등의 폭넓은 의미를 두루 포함한다. 따라서 위 문장에서 우리는 전치사 of 다음에 이어지는 것이 무엇이든 간에, 논문의 저자가 ~에 대해 저자 나름대로 또 다른 해석의 방식을 선보이고자 한다는 취지를 알아낼 수 있는 것이다.

■ This introduction will attempt to outline some of these issues in order to set the papers into a broader context of discourse.

■ My arguments will attempt to identify certain principles behind Plato's philosophical assimilation of poetry.

■ This paper attempts to fill some of those gaps in the literature and proposes answers to those questions by developing and testing statistically a political explanation of IMF lending patterns.

■ This study does not attempt a fully-fledged account of these concerns, but simply points to their importance when considering the way in which state theories are constructed.
여기에서 fully-fledged account란 '~에 대한 총체적인(entire, whole) 설명'을 말한다.

■ What is offered here is by no means a definitive account of recent excavations in Dublin but rather an attempt to draw together the bulk of the published summaries and see what can be gleaned from them.

■ With the aid of recent scholarly exploration of available sources, this book will attempt to show the main lines of development of marriage and the family through the thousand years of the Middle Ages (A.D. 500 to 1500).
굵은 글씨 부분은 '최근 학계의 [연구 성과] 연구 결과에 힘입어[~의 도움으로]'란 뜻이며, 다음 부분은 '본 저서는 ~ 연구의 주류를 보여 주고자 한다'로 이해하면 좋겠다.

■ My article, after briefly outlining the background and nature of ~, will attempt to examine the ~, exploring questions as how the ~.
본인의 논문은 ~의 문제를 파헤치면서 ~을 점검할 것이다.

purpose

■ My purpose is to discuss some of the main theme of the play.
저자의 목적은 본 연극의 주요 몇몇 주제를 토론하는 것이다.

■ The most immediate purpose of my paper is to furnish an interpretation of ~.

■ The purpose of this article will be to predicate that ~.

- **The purpose of this article** is not to argue for ~, but to explore through ~.

- **The purpose of the present paper is to offer** an analysis of the novel's characters and organization.
본 논문의 목적은 ~에 대한 분석을 보여 주는 것이다.

- The author of this book **offers the possibility of wide cross-cultural comparisons**.
저자는 광범위한 문화간 비교의 가능성을 보여 준다.

- My account of ~ **offers** a subjective view of ~.
~에 대한 본인의 설명은 주관적인 견해를 보여 준다.
No account of the 2016 US presidential election will be complete without a discussion of the roles played by media networks. (~ 논의 없이는 ~에 대한 설명은 완결될 수 없다. 즉, ~을 반드시 설명해야 한다). 부정비교급이 사용된, 거의 유사한 같은 유형의 구문 하나를 더 보도록 하자. Nothing better illustrates the simultaneous efficacy but illegitimacy of the emergent networked order than the career of Henry Kissinger.

- This study will **offer further evidence of** the authenticity of the texts ~.
본 연구는 ~에 대한 충분한(더 많은) 증거를 보여 줄 것이다.

- The purpose of this paper **is to describe** the families of sexually abused children **within the context of** the child victim's experience.

- The purpose of this paper **is to gain insight into** the ambiguity surrounding the dual categorization of women.
유사한 문장으로 '~로 인해서 연구의 신선한 바람을 불러 일으켰다'란 의미를 나타내고자 할 때엔 다음의 문장을 잘 익혀두자. Milton's essays gave fresh impetus to the debate about the male gaze and voyeurism, power and subordination(~의 에세이가 ~에 대한 토론에 신선한 자극제를 부여했다). 마찬가지로 다음의 문장도 살펴보도록 하자. Lacan's ideas opened up the field for ~.

- This is an **investigation into** the relationship between perceived parental physical availability and child sexual abuse.

- This essay is **an investigation into how** the ~.

- **The purpose of this paper is to provide** a quantitative analysis for the claims that ~.

- In this essay, **I hope to provide an assessment of** the practical and scholarly theoretical value of the ~.
  이 글에서 본인은 ~에 대한 평가를 보여 주고 싶다.

- **The purpose of this paper is to redirect** the discussion of the ~.

- **The purpose of my paper is to take a closer look at** ~.
  저자 논문의 목적은 ~을 자세히 살펴보는 것이다.

- **The purpose of this paper is to analyze** ~ **as to how** ~.
  본 논문의 목적은 어떻게 ~한지를 분석하는 것이다.

- **The purpose of this section is to examine** ~ **and to suggest thereby** that ~.
  본 장의 목적은 ~을 점검함으로써 ~을 제시하는 것이다.

- **The goal of this example is to test hypotheses about** the extent to which the CRADA network demonstrates a structural tendency toward mutuality.
  이같은 예의 목적은 ~에 대한 가설을 검증해 보이는 것이다.

- **The purpose of this paper is to relate** the concept "understanding" to process of language use in education.

- **The purpose of this article is to outline and elaborate main features of** the institutionalization at Community level.

- **The major purpose of the present study is to gauge** the general applicability of theories of ~ to ~, and **to test** the comparative validity of different social-psychological theories.
  본 연구의 주요 목적은 ~한 이론의 적용 가능성(유용성)을 점검하고, ~을 테스트하는 일이다.

- **The purpose of my paper is to use an alternative approach** which might present evidence useful in addressing this question.
  저자 논문의 목적은 ~을 보여 줄 수 있는 대안을 이용해 보는 것이다.

- **My goal** in this paper **is to take a** panoramic **view of** the institutional basis of human societies.

■ **It will be our purpose here to consider ~.**

영어 논문을 읽다 보면 우리는 지금의 예문에서처럼 here를 습관적으로 많이 쓰고 있는 것을 발견한다. 물론 here는 저자가 쓰는 자신의 논문 내에서란 의미이지만 사용에 각별한 주의가 요망된다. 왜냐하면 전후 맥락이 확실하지 않으면 이 말이 지칭하는 것이 명확하지 않게 해석될 수 있기 때문이다.

■ **A prime example for the purposes of this study is** how a psychoanalytic approach to films of the Stalin era can probe beneath the overt heroics of their leading men. In this study we shall **treat** ~.

■ This paradox will **find its place in the course of our discussion.**

■ A research for Dostoevsky's answer in *The Brothers Karamazov* **forms the core of this paper.** ~이 본 논문의 중심, 핵심을 이룬다.

core가 들어간 문장을 점검해 보자. At its core, evolutionary theory is fundamentally a theory of change. 같은 의미로 In essence, ~. 또는 At the heart of the neo-liberal view is the notion that ~.이 있다.

위의 예문에서 쓰인 동사 form은 formulate와 동의어로 사용될 수 있다. 다음의 예문을 통해 그 용례를 알아 두자. If you have not yet formulated a clear research question, you will have to spend some time reading around just looking for a topic that you can narrow down and question.

to consist

■ **The present paper consists of** an interpretative analysis of specific occurrence of subtextual allusion ~.

본 논문은 ~에 대한 해석적 분석으로 구성되어 있다, ~을 구성하고 있다.

■ **The present study is an analysis of** two cases operating within the structural systems of light and color in Andrei Belyi's *Petersburg*.

to design / to intend / intent

■ The present paper **is designed to test** the hypothesis that ~.

■ I **designed my research to** evaluate two schools of thought concerning the impact of ~.

- The present paper is intended to serve as an introduction to the topic of ~.
  본 논문은 ~ 주제의 서론 격으로 의도되었다.

- It is intended to broaden our horizons of understanding the tale.
  (본 논문의 의도는) ~ 이해의 지평을 넓히는 것에 있다.

- This book is intended in part to refute that persistent claim by showing that ~.
  이 책은 ~을 보여 줌으로써 ~라는 주장을 반박하기 위한 것이다.

- This article is intended to provide a catalyst for such a debate.
  이 논문은 그같은 논쟁에 한편의 촉매제를 제공하는 것에 있다. 즉, ~의 논쟁에 불을 당기고자 하는 것이 이 논문의 목적이다.

- This study is intended to provide a description of the peasant way of life under normal condition around 1998.

- In this article, it is my intention, on the basis of recorded data, to demonstrate the ~.

- It is my intention to address the problem of ~.
  ~에 대한 문제를 언급하는 것이 본인의 의도이다, 의도하는 바이다.
  동사 address는 to direct to the attention, to deal with or discuss의 의미를 모두 포함한다. 흔히 '어떤 문제를 환기시키거나 또는 문제를 다루다'란 뜻으로 널리 쓰인다.

- My intent here is merely to review briefly one aspect, a not unimportant one.

- My intention, then, is to offer a new methodological framework for analyzing the full range of ~.
  저자가 하고자 하는 바는 ~의 분석을 위한 방법론상의 새 틀거리를 보여 주는 것이다.

- This brief study is intended as a prologue to my forthcoming work on ~.
  이 짧은 연구는 곧 있을 ~에 대한 연구의 초석(서막)으로 의도되었다.

기타

- My paper presents empirical evidence to support that ~.
  저자의 논문은 ~을 뒷받침할 경험적 증거를 보여 준다.
  동사 present와 유사한 의미의 표현을 다음 문장들을 통해서 알아보자.
  She presents a detailed discussion of ~ (그녀는 ~에 대한 자세한 토론, 논쟁을 펼쳐 보인다).

She represents a very different avenue of approach (그녀는 매우 상반된 접근 방법을 선보인다). One of the most profitable avenues for exploring the meanings and uses of objects has been via actor network theory (~을 밝혀 내기 위한 수단, 방법, 방식).

■ This expression **encapsulates** a theory which views ~.
이 표현은 ~을 바라보는 이론을 잘 함축하고 있다, 잘 담고 있다.
'~한 주제를 함축, 잘 표현하고 있는'이란 뜻으로 다음의 예문을 알아보자.
This book's title, *Social Insecurity in the New Millennium*, encapsulates the worldwide concern in general.

■ The present study **suggests an approach to** the delineation of the major attitudes and patterns common to ~.
본 연구는 ~에 일반적인 주요 입장과 유형들의 설명에 대한 한 가지 접근 방법을 제시하고 있다.

■ The **object of this paper is to revisit** the themes originally explored in ~.

■ The **main objective of this paper is to investigate** the validity of the ~ to identify ~.
~의 유용성을 검토하는 것이 본 논문의 주요 과제(목적)이다.
여기에서 동사 investigate를 활용한 문장 하나를 예로 들어 보자.
An accurate study of a demographic crisis is an excellent way to investigate social structures, because social groups behaved differently during crises.

■ The **main objective of this dissertation is to study of the presentation of** death in the prose fiction of one of the great nineteenth-century Russian writers: Tolstoy, Dostoevsky and Chekhov.

■ The present paper **takes it as focal point** ~.
본 논문의 초점을 ~으로 한다. 본 논문의 초점은 ~이다.

■ The **basic framework for this study is** a chronological sequence, which is as important in cultural history as in economic or political history.

■ The **emphasis of this paper is on** the elusive world of ideas and ideals which Russians refer to as *sobornost'*.
이 논문의 강조(점)은 ~에 있다.
이때 emphasis 다음엔 전치사 on이 항상 쓰인다는 점을 기억해 두자. 물론 저자에 따라서는 upon을 쓰기도 한다.

- **It is the purpose of this paper to demonstrate** the essential point of ~, and to indicate some of devices by which the total effect of the story is achieved.

- **The purpose of this article is to initiate a discussion of** the ~.
  여기에서 initiate는 '야기시키다, 불러일으키다, 생겨나게 하다'란 의미로 광범위하게 사용되고 있는데, 이 동사의 쓰임새를 다음 예문을 통해서 알아 두자. Other archival changes <u>initiated</u> during the reign of Catherine the Great included the creation in Moscow of the Razriad-Senate Archive. 또는 Ernest Boyer's book <u>initiated a profound shift in</u> the ways professionals in higher education thought about ~ (~에서의 뚜렷한, 커다란 변화를 일으키다).

- Therefore, the present study primarily **sets out to investigate whether** ~.

- This article has a double **goal**: to discuss ~, and then to take a new look at ~.

- It is my **goal** to **familiarize the reader with** ~.
  저자의 목적은 독자들에게 ~을 친숙하게 하는 것이다, 소개하는 것이다.

- **The ultimate goal of this paper will be to investigate** how ~.
  본 논문의 궁극적 목적은 ~가 어떻게 이루어지는지를 관찰해 보는 것이다.

- This paper **has** two central **goals**: 1) **to determine** the degree to which ~; and 2) **to develop** and **test** a more precise and more general explanation of how ~.
  이처럼 저자가 쓰고자 하는 논문의 목적을 서술하는 방법에는 그 내용을 풀어쓰지 않고 아라비아 숫자를 이용해 간단히 나열하는 방식도 있을 수 있다. 대체로 이같은 형식은 사회과학 혹은 자연계의 실험보고 논문 등에서 자주 사용된다.

- The study **purports to** reveal ~.
  원래 이 동사는 '~을 취지로 하다' 또는 '~을 목적으로 하다'란 의미이다. 사전적인 의미는 to present, especially deliberately, the appearance of being; profess or claim; to convey, express이다.

- **In exploring** our questions, **this paper will be** ~.

- **In connection with this issue, I wish to address** newly created myth surrounding Macha.
  이 문제와 관련지어 저자는 ~을 언급하고자 한다, 다루고자 한다.

- In this paper, I will endeavor to infer and elucidate Epshtein's assumption on the basis of my readings of his work.
  이 논문에서 저자는 ~을 하는 것에 진력할 것이다. ~을 하고자 노력할 것이다.

- In this paper, I will introduce a crucial layer of analysis in investigating the underlying premise that ~.

- I will discuss these problems in greater length in Chapter 3, but I want to take issue with some of the implicit cultural assumptions in Wilson's account.
  ~의 문제들을 ~에서 보다 자세하게 다루겠다.

- In this paper, I focus only on the issue of point mutations with a basis in quantum indeterminism. This is an important and relatively unappreciated topic.
  focus를 이용한 또 다른 문장을 알아보자. This will be my focus throughout the paper: What negotiations were involved in making Buddhist objects? 이처럼 콜론을 이용해 다루고자 하는 토론 주제를 부각시키는 문체를 잘 익혀두자. 이때 전혀 새로운 독립 문장이 나올 때, 즉 이 자체가 콜론(:)을 쓸 수 있는 예가 될 때 지금처럼 콜론 다음에 대문자로 시작한다는 점에 유의하자.

- This article is concerned with the formal classification of ~.
  이 논문은 ~을 주로 다룰 것이다. ~을 주된 초점으로 한다.
  이 숙어가 들어간 문장을 예로 들어보자. On a purely materialist level, feminism is crucially concerned with the ways in which women's bodies are controlled within a patriarchal system. Business cycle theory is concerned with why economics do not grow smoothly, but show recurrent fluctuations. Social research is concerned with the definition and assessment of social phenomena. On a purely materialist level, feminism is crucially concerned with the ways in which women's bodies are controlled within a patriarchal system.

- This article employs an explicitly institutional approach to explaining the linkages between supranational policy and domestic outcomes.
  동사 employ는 use와 같은 의미로 '~을 설명하기 위해 ~한 접근 방법을 사용하고자 한다'는 뜻이다. 다음의 문장을 통해서 동사 employ를 응용해 보자. Contemporary feminism has employed deconstructive strategies in order to destabilize a binary model inscribed in the masculine /feminine dyad. 또는 This article employs the methods of discourse analysis to analyze the International Criminal Tribunal for the former Yugoslavia's precedent-setting ruling.

- I am using the concept of model here in a triple sense: 1) ~; 2) ~; 3) ~.

- **In what follows, I explore ~.** 이어지는 부분에서(이하의 내용에서) 저자는 ~을 밝히고자 한다.

- **By exploring** some key signifying structures in Tolstoy's *Resurrection*, **I hope to show** that ~.
  몇몇 주요 핵심을 파헤침으로써 저자는 ~을 보여 주고자 한다.

- **By applying this challenging conceptual approach to his subject, Prof. Raeff manages to illuminate** familiar problems from a new angle, to pose provocative questions, to demonstrate the limits of our knowledge, and to make us reconsider what had hitherto seemed to be incontrovertible truths.
  이같은 매우 도전적인 개념을 적용하면서 ~의 설명을 시도

- **In dealing with** this issue, **I will not speak of** issues of deep structure, nor will I **address the issue** in terms of ~.
  동사 address와 관련하여 다음의 문장을 참고해 보자. 모두 '~의 주제를 다루다' 혹은 '~한 주제를 상정하다'란 개념으로 모두 유사하다. In the introductory essay, the author sets forth his two central issues. 마찬가지 의미에서 동사 take가 이용된 다음과 같은 문장을 기억해 두자. This article takes issue with the conceptual and analytical underpinnings of the ~.

- In my comparison of the prose and the film, **I will look most closely at** this shift and examine how it is produced.

- It is within the framework of his conception that **I shall take a look at** Chekhov's realism.

- Assuming general acquaintance with current readings of the *agon*, **I shall start with** a section-by-section discussion of the old queen's speech and its immediate effect, with an emphasis on significant motifs.

- In this paper, **we shall start by an attempt to define** ~.
  ~을 정의 내리는 것으로 본 논문을 시작하고자 한다.

- In order to focus my discussion, **I will concentrate on** the central problem.

- In order to **ferret out** these key points, **we will explore** fundamentally comparative questions about ~.
  ferret out은 explore, search out, bright to light과 같은 뜻으로 '~을 탐색하다, 밝혀내다'란 의미이다. explore가 들어간 문장을 살펴보자. In this book, Mary Evans explores the extent to

which social theory has engaged with and illuminated the question of relations between genders and the social world.

■ I will use Lacanian theory **as a framework against** which to understand ~.
~에 반대되는 이론적 틀로서

■ In my paper, I **propose a completely new and more rational way to solve** the puzzle of ~.

■ I **propose** in this essay **to address a set of questions about** how Plato invokes, confronts, and absorbs poetic texts within his own philosophical writing.
예로 들다, 언급하다

■ I **propose an alternative investigation of** ~. ~에 대한 대안적 연구를 제시한다.

■ **What I propose to do here is to** examine a series of textual documents ~ and to see ~.
여기에서(본 논문에서) 저자가 제시하고자 하는 것은 ~을 점검하는 것이다.

■ This paper will **seek to broach an aspect of** ~.
꺼내다

■ This study **seeks to open up a new perspective, based on** the thematic and structural importance of reading, from which to evaluate Nabokov's novels in the light of major existing interpretations.

■ I **offer a new interpretation of** this text as a philosophical commentary on ~.
~에 대한 새로운 해석을 내려 본다, 제공한다.

■ This paper **offers the possibility of** wide cross-cultural comparisons.

■ The author's study **offers an impressive case for** how particular visual images have made their way into an immensely popular brand and film genre.

■ In this paper, I **would like to argue** for the importance if a model of frame ~.
~을(논의, 연구, 토론 등을) 하고자 한다.

■ In the light of ~, **I would like to call attention to** the criticism of Gogol.
   ~에 대해 문제를 환기시키고자 한다.

■ **I would like to approach** the theme of exile from a point of view which ~.

■ **This essay will approach** Dostoevsky's *Crime and Punishment* through an examination of each of the three aspects mentioned above: ~, ~, and ~.

■ In this paper, I will **apply an interdisciplinary approach to** analyze ~.
   interdisciplinary란 뜻은 말 그대로 학문간의 제휴, 협동이란 말로 학제간 연구를 의미한다. 즉, 다른 학문과의 교류를 말하는 것으로 이 문장에서는 '~을 분석함에 있어서 문학 연구 방법론 이외에 다른 분석 방법까지도 이용하겠다'라는 뜻이 담겨 있다. William Emile's book is an interdisciplinary work engaging such important dimensions of Chinese culture and civilization as sociology, psychology, literary history and criticism. His interdisciplinary inquiry into landscape aesthetics opens a rich vein of cultural history that other researchers will want to explore further. My interdisciplinary project drew on the resources of both the humanities and the social sciences.
   한편, 이와 가장 유사한 말로는 multifaceted study란 표현이 있다 (This is an extremely well produced and multifaceted study, which makes use of an impressively wide range of source materials, including ~.).

■ In this paper I **suggest a new approach to the problem of** ~.
   ~라고 하는 문제점에 대한 새로운 접근 방법을 제시한다.

■ The present study **suggests an approach to** the delineation of the major attitudes and patterns common to ~.

■ This essay **takes a highly microscopic approach to the question of** ~.
   ~에 대한 문제를 상당히 구체적이고, 자세하게 다루고자 한다.

■ The proposed paper **will combine the two approaches.**

■ I **take as my point of departure a passage from** that great work of ~.
   ~로부터의 인용문으로 논의의 출발점을 삼겠다.

■ **To help start us thinking about** the needs and benefits for students as well as for faculty members of working at teaching-oriented institutions, **I begin with a quotation from** ~.
   ~에 대한 토론의 이해를 돕고자 저자는 ~의 인용으로 시작하고자 한다.

- With respect to the nature of man, Hobbes **takes the position** that man is selfish.
  ~한 입장을 취하다.

- The researcher **takes** a systemic and comprehensive **approach**, with new methods of management.
  동사 tailor는 '~에 맞추다'란 뜻으로 연구 현황을 서술하는 논문의 서론에서 자주 나타난다. 특히 take the position, take approach of ~란 저자의 분명한 입장을 드러내기 전에 반대 진영의 비판 혹은 미비한 점을 드러내고자 할 때 유용하게 쓰인다. 다음의 두 예문을 참고하면서 읽어 보자.
  To maximize success, approaches should be <u>tailored</u> to meet unique community needs.
  The community-based approach to injury prevention <u>fits in well with</u> the public health priority of improving the health of population groups.

- **In examining** the State-women relationship, I **take up** Georgi Waylen's **conception of** the State as a site of struggle.
  ~라고 하는 ~의 개념을 준거로 삼는다, ~의 입장을 취하고자 한다.

- **This study is informed by** the theorizing prompted by Michel Foucault's suggestive observations on ~.
  본 연구는 ~의 이론화 작업으로부터 도움을, 영향을 받았다, 연구의 아이디어를 얻었다.

- This research is partially **animated by** a curiosity about ~.
  본 연구는 ~을 알고 싶은 호기심으로부터 촉발되었다.

- In my paper I am **fleshing out** my thesis that ~.
  flesh out은 '~을 더욱 충실하게 하다, 현실성 있게 만들다 (to give dimension or substance to, or to become more substantial)'란 의미로 고급한 표현이다. To <u>flesh out</u> what is distinctively political in it we now turn to the experience of the political actor. Archeological evidence helps us to <u>flesh out</u> this picture of monks roaming the countryside soliciting funds and overseeing the construction of monasteries.

- Certain **further implications will be pointed out** at the end of the paper.

- **The point of this paper is to problematize** rather than challenge the status of ~.

- The technological complexity of the sector requires us to **set out** certain issues in greater detail, such as interconnection and universal service, to allow us to comment on the recent and future challenges in the regulation of the sector.
  동사 set out은 '~을 시도하다'란 의미의 attempt 외에도 describe, define과 같은 뜻으로 많이 쓰인다. This book <u>sets out to examine</u> the more obscure and puzzling aspects of ~.

■ Aspiring to comprehensiveness and synthesis, the author **sets out to present the range of ways** in which fields of knowledge have come to relate to each other.

■ This study returns to some of the larger unresolved issues, and it **sets out** a new explanation of how and why modern Western societies developed in some peculiar and still puzzling ways.

■ The article is divided into two parts. One **scans** a conceptual framework ~. The second part **discusses** specific areas of ~.

■ The essay will seek to **locate** the term "courtly love" more broadly **as** a series of questions which are debated across large numbers of texts.
'용어 ~을 어떠한 담론 차원에서 사용하고 있는지를 자리 매김하는 것이 본 논문의 목적이다' 로 의역해 보자. 다음의 문장은 '~한 용어는 본 논문을 통해서 어떠한 정의로 사용된다'란 의 미이다. The term "heritage" is used here with a specific definition that distinguishes it from preservation and not ~. 또는 The term peasant movement is surely merited for this period. 이와 유사한 문장을 더 알아보자. Here the term popular culture will be taken to apply to what has been called, in very general terms, an ~ (여기에서 대중 문화란 용어는 매 우 일반적인 의미에서 ~라고 불려지는 의미에 적용될 것이다). The term ritual has been used in a wide set of contexts in various disciplines (의례란 용어는 다른 학문과의 광범위한 문맥 속에서 사용되어 왔다).

■ **Drawing from** the macrocomparative method, **I analyze** variation across more than five hundred labor markets in the United States in 1990 to determine whether ~.
~한 방법론에 의거하여(기초하여) 저자는 ~을 분석하고자 한다. 한편, 동사 draw on (upon)은 '~에 의거, 의존한다'는 뜻으로 rely on(upon)이나 dwell on과 같은 뜻으로 매우 많이 사용된다. 아래 예문을 참고하자. 한편, build on도 아주 많이 쓰이는 표현이니 아래의 예문과 함께 익혀두 자.
  • Drawing on traditional knowledge for ideas on cosmological referents of presumed long history, researchers evaluate the ~.
  우리가 알고 있는 ~에 대한 전통적 지식에 의거하여
  • This paper draws on a number of statistical and survey sources to explore recent changes in the sexual division of labor in three European countries.
  본 논문은 ~에 대한 통계 자료를 바탕으로 한다.
  • This discussion draws on a growing literature offering theoretical and empirical insights into the differences and similarities between countries in the contemporary development of gender relations.
  본 논의는 ~에 대한 이론적, 경험적 관찰을 보여 주고 있는, 최근 늘어가는 문헌 자료들을 바탕으로 한다.

- In this section we will <u>draw on</u> the work of Dubet in order to develop a theoretical framework for the analysis of gender and occupational feminization.
  본 장은 ~의 연구에 기초할 것이다.
- The essays gathered here not only <u>draw on</u> research from several provinces but also illustrate a variety of methodologies and academic styles that can be used to explore our topic.
  본 에세이는 여러 지방에서 실시된 리서치를 바탕으로 함은 물론 ~.
- More often than not, the historian <u>relies on</u> the first-hand accounts of those who are no longer living and <u>builds on</u> the work of other historians, living and dead.
  자주 사학자들은 다른 사학자들의 연구물에 기초하기도 한다.
- This <u>builds on</u> Marx Weber's conviction that democratic institutions function between when perceived as legitimate by much of the population.
  ~은 ~의 신념에 기초한다.
- A responsible research and policy agenda that <u>build on</u> the evidence currently available about ~.
  최근에 들어 이용 가능하게 된 증거를 바탕으로 하는 믿을 만한 리서치와 정책 현안
- Following the lead of the scholars reviewed above, my analysis <u>builds on</u> their insights by attempting to determine ~.
  저자의 분석은 ~을 시도함으로써 ~의 관찰에 기초해 있다.
- Ritual landscape studies <u>build on</u> traditional archeological examinations of patterns in the spatial distributions of ritual features.
  전통적인 고고학적 탐사들에 기초하는
- By <u>dwelling upon</u> historical and dialectal data from Ukrainian, <u>I will explore</u> well-phenomena in a different way.
  ~을 바탕으로 저자는 ~을 파헤치고자 한다.
- Contemporary governmental practice <u>relies on</u> statistical knowledge of the objects to be governed.
  ~은 통계적 수치, 지식에 의존한다.
- Throughout this study I have <u>relied</u> as much as possible <u>on</u> data from a variety of sources to facilitate ~.
  본 연구를 통해 저자는 가능한 한 ~로부터의 데이터에 많이 의존해 왔다.
- My analysis <u>rests on</u> a comparison of rights revolutions in the United States in the period of 1960-1990.
  저자의 분석은 ~의 비교 연구에 의존한다.
- My analysis of ~ for this article <u>rests upon</u> the primary materials in a number of archives in both Moscow and Paris.

■ **Drawing on a wealth of historical literature,** Janet's book **provides an example** of this position.
  풍부한 역사 문헌을 바탕으로 ~의 책은 ~의 예를 보여 준다.

70

■ Based upon a reading of existing literature, this paper **maps out** a series of ways in which within the relationship between globalization and the process at work within the EU might be understood.

동사 map은 out과 결합하여 present, sketch (In this chapter we have <u>sketched out</u> a model for the social context of joint reading. The following pages <u>sketch</u> the common and diverse features of the ethnic world view.)에서와 같이 plan 등의 뜻으로 쓰인다. 이 문장은 '기존에 존재하는 문헌들을 읽는 것을 바탕으로 하여 이 논문은 ~ 방식을 보여 주려 한다'로 이해하면 좋겠다.

유사한 다음 문장을 참고해 보자.

- We shall <u>map out</u> a theory of transformation that defines globalization as a new social architecture of cross-border human interactions.
- This series of articles intend to <u>map out</u> the ways in which social theory is being transformed and how contemporary issues have emerged.
- In this section I will dedicate considerable space to <u>mapping out</u> the specific historical and political contexts of violence against women.
- The task is to <u>map out</u> knowledge readily available, to identify the collection of works, and to devise a conceptual framework organizing this collection.
- In <u>mapping out</u> the forms of violence in contemporary India, I am particularly interested in ~.

이번 장에서 배운 모든 것을 종합적으로 점검할 수 있는 다음의 원문 전문을 잘 익혀두기 바란다. 영어 논문의 서론에서 자주 볼 수 있는 매우 전형적인 문장으로서 문제 제기와 저자가 하고자 하는 내용이 쉽고도 일목요연하게 잘 나타나 있다.

a) **I first examine** Henry Fielding's reactions to some of the conservative eighteenth-century ideologies concerning women and wives as they were presented in conduct books, didactic fiction, and the covert-baron laws, **and how** his theme of feminine absence develops from his conventional use of the ideal woman motif in his early miscellaneous poetry, to his major novel. **I then endeavor to demonstrate** that feminine absence in Fielding's works points to his concern that women were being figuratively erased from society to the detriment of its spiritual and moral values.

b) **This study explores some of the ways in which** the experience if was on such a large scale may have affected the dominant myths of Stalinist masculinity on screen, and is **underpinned by** two **theoretical strands. For a start**, the wholesale introduction of women into the traditionally male workplace **called into question** the hitherto accepted notion of male physical superiority. **The second of my theoretical strands,** as I have earlier concentrates on the model of the male ego as a prototype for the bourgeois state. The first point that needs be made here is that ~.

c) I begin with some brief and necessarily superficial observations on the characters of turn-of-the-century French symbolism, and I then look in more detail at three areas of women's writing.

d) The article is organized as follows. The first section clarifies three key terms whose meanings are not self-evident. The second section deals with the puzzle that led me to discover the relevance of civil society for ethnic conflict. The third section summarizes how the puzzle was resolved and presents arguments that can link ethnic conflict and civil society. The fourth section presents empirical evidence in support of the arguments made. The fifth section considers causation and endogeneity. The final section summarizes the implications of the project for studies of civil society.

e) Listed below are a few proposals, some ambitious than others, but all of which are deserving of serious considerations: ~.

f) The paper seeks to introduce a more comprehensive method of analysis involving a number of different ways of thinking about democracy. In particular, it seeks to judge the process of democratization not so much in relation to universal standards but to the way in which institutional structures and practices are grounded in local realities and the extent to which these respond to people's needs and expectations.

g) I shall proceed in the following way: first, I will examine the function of teaching and learning through dialogue as it is conveyed by these three figures; second, I will be able to describe the different ways of empathic imitation they require; and third, I will conclude by broaching the difficult problems of the political involvements of inter-personal transmission.

h) The structure of the paper is as follows: I first document ~. I then consider why ~.

i) The focus of this paper is global politics and in particular the arena of global political evolution. The first part recapitulates the essence of ~. The second part briefly lays out the theoretical and methodological grounding of our ~.

j) Chapter 1 develops the theoretical framework for this study, critiquing previous conceptions of ~, proposing an approach to the key concepts of ~. Chapter 2 examines the different levels through which ~. I first look at ~, moving on to consider ~. Chapter 3 focuses on ~. Commencing with an assessment of the contemporary effect of ~, I move on to examine ~. Chapter 4 considers how we might conceive ~. After a theoretical outline of the ways in which ~, I will develop and exemplary analysis of the ~. Chapter 5 investigates the ways in which ~. Taking the example of ~, I consider how ~. Chapter 6 acts as a conclusion by summarizing the points I have made throughout the book by assessing the representation of ~

논문은 ~을 중심으로 전개될 것이다

■ **Discussion** in this article(paper) **will center around** finding the key scene to ~.

■ **My discussion** will have three points **on** the moral level: ~.

■ **The discussion of** these issues here will be from a pedagogical **point of view.**

■ **In treating** the theme of the novel, I will **be concerned with** ~.
이런 표현은 일반적으로 자주 쓰이는 예이긴 하지만 동사 treat는 고급한 학술 논문에서는 사용에 가급적 주의를 기울이기 바란다. 좀 casual한 분위기를 만들어 내기 때문에 학술 논문에서는 적절치 못하다고 생각한다. 그리고 동사 사용에 있어서 능동태 (즉, 저자가 '~하겠다'는 표현)뿐만 아니라, 수동태 (즉, '본 논문의 주제, 논쟁점, 핵심은 ~이 될 것이다'와 같은)도 빈번하게 사용되고 있는 것도 주의하자.

■ The **focal point of our discussion will be** ~.
focal point는 말 그대로 중심 되는 대상 즉, 중점 혹은 쟁점으로 이해하면 좋겠다. 이 문장에서 처럼 수동태로 사용되는 경우가 많으며, 의역하면 '저자는 본 논문에서 ~을 중점적으로 다루고자 한다'가 되겠다.

■ The **focus will be directed at** selected instances of ~.
초점은 ~을, ~에 겨냥될 것이다.

■ This **paper will focus on the** ~, giving most attention to its most provocative, and perhaps problematic in Orwell's works.

■ This point of view **will be argued in connection with** three of the main structural features of the text.
이 관점은 ~과 관련하여 논의될 것이다.

■ **The method of this paper will** consist primarily in a comparison of selected passages in the novel.

■ Starting from the concept of ~, **this paper will identify** ~.

■ From our perspective, **the key question to be asked is how** policy-making is affected.
우리의 관점으로 볼 때, 탐구되어야 할 핵심 문제는 ~에 대한 것이다.

■ **The first part of the article comprises** a discussion of examples from seven of Nabokov's novels; **in the second part some conclusions are** drawn from this material.

■ The **central question that I intended to examine** is ~.
저자가 알아보고자 했던 중심 문제는 ~이다.

■ The approach adopted seeks **to privilege** a consideration of the historical inheritance and the way in which the past affects the present.
동사 privilege는 말 그대로 ~에게 특별한 권한을 부여하는 것으로 '~을 중심으로, ~에게 큰 의미를 부여한다'로 의역해서 이해하면 좋을 것이다.
여기에서 동사 adopt는 말 그대로 '무엇인가를 수용, 받아들이다'란 뜻이다. 다음의 문장을 통해서 그 쓰임새를 알아 두자. This paper seeks to adopt a position closer to ~. 즉, 이 문장은 '본 논문은 ~에 가까운 한 입장을 수용하고자 한다'라는 의미이다. 또는 It is this theoretical perspective that I have adopted in the present study of death rituals in rural Greece.

본론에 들어가기에 앞서 우리는 ~해야 한다 / ~을 다루면서 ~하는 것이 필요하다

■ **Before we embark upon** an analysis of Chekhov's work, **we will briefly examine** the general feature employed by the writer.

■ **Before working out this aspect of** the story, we need to analyze ~.

■ **Before going on with the question of** ~, it should be pointed out(mentioned, stated, considered, stressed) that ~.
이런 표현들이야말로 가장 대표적인 예라 할 수 있다. 즉, 본론에서의 본격적인 분석으로 들어가기에 앞서 일반적으로 서론에서는 이같은 표현을 자주 쓰면서 앞으로 얘기할 주제나 문제 제기를 하곤 한다. 이때 강조하고자 하는 내용을 It ~ that을 이용한 가주어, 진주어의 구문을 일반적으로 많이 사용한다는 점 주의하기 바란다. 또한 It should be considered that ~. It should be mentioned that ~. It should be taken into consideration that ~ 등과 같은 동일한 표현이 있으니 같이 기억해 두면 실제 작문에 많은 도움이 될 것이다. 마지막으로 이런 표현들 다음에 흔히 '그럼 다음의 본론에서 보다 자세하게 살펴보도록 하자'란 의미를 말하고 싶은 경우엔 We shall now examine in more detail. 또는 The present study will first examine. In the following, I will try to show that. We can begin by examining the main hero's name in the text.라고 하면 좋다.

■ **Before** we can **undertake** this task, **it is necessary to consider that** ~.

- Before looking more closely at ~, it might be useful to briefly consider ~.

- Before looking into the body of ~, I should say a few words about the ~.

- Before examining Pechorin's character, something should be said about the ~.

- Before we can examine ~, however, we need to consider ~.

- Before examining the ethnical foundations of European citizenship, it is useful to draw out more clearly ~.

- Before we can accept the argument about ~, two more questions must be explored.

- Before delving into my analysis, I would like to briefly explain how and why the research presents ~.

- Before entering into the main analysis of the text, I shall briefly address the problem of the early version of it ~.

- Before moving to the central part of my argument, I shall briefly discuss the question of the episode's historicity.
  저자가 주장하는 논점의 핵심으로 옮겨가기 전에 잠시 ~을 토의해 보고자 한다.

- Before developing this argument, it is worth identifying some of the major forms of ~.
  저자의 논점을 개진시키기에 앞서 ~을 확인할 필요가 있다.

- Before I turn to the film itself, however, it is worth taking a quick look at Eisenstein's previous features.

- Before turning to the realist account of scientific activity, I will deal at greater length with the idealist approaches.
  ~의 (주제, 항목, 장으로), ~로 넘어가기 전에 저자는 ~을 자세하게 다루고자 한다.
  동사 turn이 들어간 전형적인 표현을 알아 두자.
  To answer these questions, I turn to some examples drawn from classroom experiences, for it is in the material details of a classroom that ~, (이같은 문제들에 답하기 위해 본인은 ~로부터 몇몇 예에 주목한다). After considering the ~, I turn to the question of ~, (~을 고려한 후 본인은 ~의 문제로 돌아간다, 살펴보고자 한다). 또는 In view of this fact, one must

turn to the basic aspect of the question ~, (이같은 점을 볼 때, 이같은 사실로 볼 때, 혹자는 ~ 의 기본적인 측면에 눈을 돌려야 한다, ~을 살펴보아야 한다, ~에 주목해야 한다).

- **Before passing** an analysis of these visions, **we must consider** the possible hypothesis that ~.

- **Before I expand on** this, **it is necessary to discuss** what ~.
  ~로 확대, 확장하기 전에 ~을 논의할 필요가 있다.

- **Before we close this section, let us pause to note** that ~.
  본 장을 끝내기에 앞서, (여기에서) 잠시 ~을 지적하도록 하자.

- **Before pursuing** a systematic response to the ~ problem, we should be clear about what it is ~.
  선행될 문제점은: The first, preliminary question which must be set is whether the Annales are in fact a single or multiple entity.

- **Before seeking an answer to** Yali's question, **we should pause to consider** some objections to discussing it at all.
  ~에 대해 답을 하기에 앞서, ~를 고려해야 한다

- **Before we look at** America's domestic problems, **it is important to ask about** relative decline and which other states might challenge the United States.
  유사한 예문을 더 보도록 하자. Western culture posits a dichotomy between mind and body, subject and object, and between male and female. (상정하다, 받아들이다

- To begin to answer these questions **we must first recall some essential facts about** ~.
  ~에 대한 몇몇 본질적인 사실들을 먼저 환기해야 할 것이다.

- **To see how this formula works in practice, let us** calculate the separate components separately in the example I just discussed.
  ~하기 위해 ~를 해 보도록 하자

- Some preliminary observations have to be made first.
  몇몇 사전적 관찰이 선행되어야 한다.
  보통 본론 혹은 구체적인 논의로 들어가기 전에 ~에 대한 개념 혹은 이론을 설명하는 부분에서 이같은 표현을 많이 쓰는데, 다음을 통해 그 용법을 알아보자.

The first, <u>preliminary question which must be set</u> is whether *the Annales* are in fact a single or multiple entities.

- Those **preliminary comments seem necessary** in order to provide a proper setting for what I have to say.
  저자가 해야 할 말의 적절한 배경을 위해서 그와 같은 사전적 언급들이 필요해 보인다.

- **It may be useful to start out by examining** separately the three components of the narrative structure of the writer.
  ~을 점검하는 것으로써 시작해 봄직하다, 시작할 수 있다, ~을 시작하는 것이 필요하다.

- In our discussion, **we shall first consider** ~.

- **A clear understanding of** the arguments of contained in Engel's writings of 1858 **requires** a brief examination of some of the currents of the feminist debate in Europe during the 1850's.
  ~에 대한 분명한 이해는 ~을 필요로 한다, ~을 요구한다.

- **To understand** the extent to which this increasingly contradictory image of the Soviet woman diverged from the theoretical understanding of woman's position under socialism, **we will need to look briefly at** some of the key Marxist writings of the late 19th century on the causes of female inequality.

- **To understand** that framework in regard to ~, **we need to consider** the relationship between ~.
  ~을 이해하기 위해서 우리는 ~을 고려하여야 한다, 고려할 필요가 있다.

- **To explain** this transition, **one must consider** ~.
  동사 explain은 spell out과 동의어로 사용될 수 있다. 특히 spell out은 어떤 것의 규칙, 수칙 등을 설명한다는 뜻으로 널리 쓰이는 동사이다. 한편, 동사 recount도 동의어로 자주 나타난다.
  The framework of biographical romance, which <u>recounts</u> the extraordinary history of an individual, served to tell the stories of exemplary national heroes.

- The author does not **spell out** all the implications of her position, but her thesis suggests that ~.

- **To get to the heart of questions** relating to the theme, therefore, **we must answer the question of** how ~.

- To deal with these objections, I turn my survey, first of all, into a way of collecting brief and histories on special questions.

- To state this same argument in a series of ~ we may say that: (1) ~, (2) ~, (3) ~.
  일련의 ~ 속에서 이와 유사한 논의를 설명하기 위해서 우리는 ~을 말해야겠다.

- To address the problem of poverty, we need to understand better its causes and extent.

- To provide a framework for our analysis of the ~, we will first review a body of literature that addresses the concepts of ~.
  ~의 분석을 위한 틀거리를 제공하기 위해 우리는 ~에 대한 참고 문헌을 먼저 살펴보아야 한다.
  이와 유사한 내용의 다른 예문을 살펴보자.
  Development plans provide the framework and establish the criteria within which local authorities make land-use planning decisions. 또는 This paper develops an analysis framework for the assessment of public participation in EIA based on the underlying principles of Harbermas's TCA idea. / This paper develops a simple framework to analyze various pollution control strategies that have been used or are proposed in the urban passenger transport sector.

- To understand the apparent strangeness and durability of the Soviet system we need to know about Russia's past: not just the decades that immediately preceded the Revolution of 1917, but the distant epoch that saw the emergence and consolidation of the empire of the tsars.

- As we will see in a moment, ~.

- As will become obvious from the continued discussion below, ~.

- The first part of this paper will be initiated with a brief summary of ~.

- Our starting point for the first question may well be the Lotman's affirmations concerning the cultural self-model.
  우리가 다룰 첫 문제의 요점은 ~에 대한 것이다.

- Clearly, our starting point must be the ~. Only afterwards can we talk about ~.
  우리의 논의 출발점은 분명히 ~이다. 그런 연후에야 ~에 대한 토론이 가능할 수 있다.

- **Having discussed ~, it is now time to** focus on the ~, particularly insofar as it is articulated with ideas about ~.

지금과 같은 분사구문도 아주 일반적인 장 전환 방법이 된다. 즉, '이전까지 ~을 해 왔으니, 이제는 ~을 하고자 한다(~할 때이다)'란 표현은 아주 새로운 독립장을 열기 전에 할 수 있는 좋은 소개 방법이다. 또는 The forthcoming chapter will exemplify this in greater detail.란 표현도 깔끔해 보인다. '이어질 장은 이것을(지금까지 논의해 온 것을) 보다 자세하게 살펴볼 것이다'로 해석할 수 있다.

~함에 있어 ~은 ~하다

- **In defining ~, it may be useful to** begin with the suggestion that ~.

  ~을 정의함에 있어 ~을 제시하는 것으로 시작하는 것이 유용해 보인다.

- **In considering ~, it may be useful to** start out by examining ~.

  ~을 고려할 때, ~을 점검하는 것으로 출발하는 것이 좋아 보인다.

- **In presenting** this argument, **I begin with** the historical angle because it provides the necessary background for discussing ~.

  이같은 논의를 제시함에 있어 저자는 ~로 시작하고자 한다.

  위의 예문에서 '배경(background)'과 동일한 의미로 많이 쓰이는 명사를 알아 두자. 바로 backdrop란 단어이다. The agrarian revolts served as a backdrop to the Great Fear, a vast panic that spread like wildfire through France between July 20 and August 6. (~의 배경 역할을 하다)

- Largely **in response to** this undercurrent of radicalism, U.S. industrialists developed innovative employees under their control.

- **In tracing** the ~, **it will be necessary to** consider two points: ~ and ~.

- **In writing** about the comic/serious line in Gogol, **critics have noted that** Gogol's initial alternation of the serious and the comic gradually gave way to a stylistic fusion of the two.

- **In developing our methodology and testing** the hypothesis of market efficiency, **we start from** the restricted assumption that ~.

- **In developing this analysis, I put forward two themes** that appear to prevail in much recent discourse about the Islamic revolt: ~.
  이 분석을 발전시키면서 본인은 다음과 같은 두 가지 주제를 상정하고자 한다.

- **Addressing the question of** the emergence of human sciences in the course of the 19th century, Michel Foucault **argues** that ~.
  ~의 문제의 대두를 다루면서 미셸 푸코는 ~을 주장한다.

- **Elaborating** further on the issue of differences ~, Emerson **remarks** that ~.

서론에서 본론으로 넘어갈 때, 또는 장이 전환될 때의 다양한 표현

- We shall **now examine in more detail**.

- The present study **will first examine**.

- The paper **begins by posing** problems of definition first ~.
  동사 pose는 assert, state, or put forward와 같은 뜻으로 '~을 주장, 진술, 제시하다'란 의미이다. 즉, 위의 예문에는 저자의 논지가 본격적으로 나타나기 시작하는 본론 처음 부분에서 지금처럼 용어나 이론의 정의를 먼저 언급하면서 문제를 풀어가겠다는 의미가 담겨 있다.
  동사 pose가 들어간 예문들을 아래에서 확인해 보자.
  - Posing key questions about a text and then answering them to the best of your ability are a helpful means of understanding more cogently an essay's substance and structure.
  - Disciplines are nothing more than conceptual clusters, ways of posing questions and propelling the development of those questions with ever greater precision.

- **Let us** examine the two instances in the following.
  기본적인 얘기이겠지만 학술 논문은 물론이고 모든 공식 문건, 서류 등에서는 일체의 축약 형태를 사용하지 않는다는 점을 기억해두자. 위의 경우 Let's라고 표기하지 않는다. 다시 말하면, don't 대신에 do not, doesn't 대신에 does not, haven't 대신에 have not, hadn't 대신에 had not, can't 대신에 cannot, wouldn't 대신 would not으로 반드시 써야 한다.

- **Let us begin our survey of** postsocialism with the economic side of the equation.

- I **now** return to the problem of ~.

- With this body of date at hand, **we may return to** the proposed model to examine ~.

- I **now intend to** focus more closely on the implications of the ~.

- **Let us now** consider ~.

- **Now I want to address the problem** posed by ~, and then I will ~.

- Our investigation now **stands in need of two things**. First, we require ~. Secondly, we need to clarify ~.

- **Returning to ~, we will first discuss** ~.
  ~로 되돌아가서, 우리는 먼저 ~을 논의할 것이다.

- **To begin with**, I would like to examine ~ in some detail.
  일단, 우선 ~을 먼저 점검하고자 한다.

- **Next**, we should note that ~.

- **Next, we move to** three specific questions that are informed by our empirical study

- **In the next section**, we clarify the findings ~.

- At this point, therefore, **let us return to** ~.

- **In the following**, I will try to show that ~.
  다음에서(이하) ~을 보여 주고자 한다.

- **In the following section, I will carry out** a cross-national **analysis of** ~.
  다음 중에서 저자는 ~에 대한 분석을 해 보일 것이다.

- **In the following**, we will give a brief general survey of ~.

- **In the following page** I would like to discuss the context ~.

- **In the pages which follow, we shall develop** such a view based on ~.
  이어질 장에서 우리는 ~을 바탕으로 ~에 대한 의견을 발전시켜 볼 생각이다.

- **In the preceding pages,** we have given an introduction to the concept ~.
  이전 장에서 우리는 ~에 대한 개념의 기본(서론)을 살펴보았다.

- **In order to understand the nature of the ~, it is necessary to examine first** some of the ~.
  ~의 성격(본질)을 이해하기 위해서 ~을 우선 살펴보는 것이 필요하다.

- **In order to provide a framework for** more detailed consideration of the ~, **it will be helpful to** summarize ~.
  보다 자세한 프레임웍을 보여 주기 위해서는 ~하는 것이 필요하다.

- **We shall now proceed to examine more closely the plotline,** in order to determine how it expresses the scheme which has been outlined.
  이제 우리는 ~을 보다 자세하게 살펴보게 될 것이다.

- **In the discussion of themes below,** works embodying particular themes will be listed in each case.

- **Now that** we know something of ~, **we may better** understand how ~.
  이제 ~을 알았으니(~을 살펴본 바) 우리는 ~을 이해하는 것이 나을 것이다.

- **Now that** we have established the structure of inequality associated with any given place is a unique intersection of gender, class, and racial inequality, **the next step is to determine** the conditions that foster each ~.
  ~을 한 이상(~을 해 왔으니까), 다음 순서는 ~을 결정하는 것이다.

- **What follows is** ~ that examines the conceptual basis of **ongoing discussions of** ~.
  ongoing (현재 한창 진행 중인 토론 주제, 이슈 등)이 들어간 문장 하나를 검토해 보자.
  In the United States abortion has been an ongoing controversy for more than a quarter-century, (미국에서의 낙태 문제는 25여년 이상 진행 중인 쟁점이다).

- **The remainder of this paper will illustrate** the foregoing remarks by considering the ~.
  이하에서 우리는 ~을 살펴보고자 한다.

- **What I wish to do in the reminder of this paper is** examining some ways in which ~.

82

- **The remainder of the study is organized as follows**: Section 2 provides the background for the study, and Section 3 develops ~. Section 4 describes the data, Section 5 presents and discusses the results, and Section 6 concludes.

  이하 책의 구성은 다음과 같이 이루어져 있다.

- **We now begin with a discussion of** the historical context of ~, and **then turn to** the ~. Following this, we shall examine ~.

- **Having framed** the context of the crisis in the political economy of Jamaica, **I will now turn to** frame this study in more detail by providing a contextual analysis of ~.

  위의 예에서처럼, 새로운 내용의 시작을 미리 알리면서 문단을 바꿀 때 흔히 분사구문의 형태를 많이 사용한다. 즉, '~했기 때문에, 이제 우리는 ~하고자 한다' 혹은 '지금까지 우리는 ~을 해 왔기 때문에(현재완료), 이제부터는 ~을 한다'로 이해하면 가장 좋겠다.

- **Having outlined** the institutional context of transforming workplace relations **the discussion now turns to** the salient characteristics of the evolving workplace relations.

- **Having discussed** the social and ethnic conditions of responsibility, **we will now proceed to describe** the relevance of responsibility to the politics of civility in two specific related ways.

- **Having extended the concept** ~ in certain respects, **let us now venture some delimiting comments**.

  더 나아가/설명을 더 해 보도록 하자.

The Essential Guide to Writing Papers in English

III 본론에 자주 등장하는 표현

1. 충만 / 지배 / 일관 / 점철
2. 해석 가능성 / 타당성
3. 유사점 / 동일시 / 등가물 / 병치 관계
4. 차이점 / 대조
5. 측면 / 관점 / 입장 / 고려
6. 제시 / 제공 / 부여
7. 기능 / 역할
8. 중심점 / 초점 / 할애
9. 언급 / 관계 / 관련성
10. 암시 / 예시 / 예견 / 힌트
11. 환기 / 상기 / 연상
12. 사용 기법
13. 화법 / 화자 / 서사 기법
14. 작품 구조
15. 삽입구 / 부사구 / 접속사
16. 텍스트 인용
17. It ~ that 구문의 다양한 활용법
18. 도치 구문
19. 순위, 등수 차지

01 충만 / 지배 / 일관 / 점철

~으로 가득 찬 / 지배적인 / 표현된

- Pushkin's text **is imbued with** ~. 시인 뿌쉬낀의 텍스트는 ~으로 가득 차 있다.

- Belyi's novel **is invested with** eschatological significance.
  벨르이의 소설은 묵시록적인 의미로 가득하다, 충만되어 있다.

- The other worlds of romance **are invested with** the erotic desire of their audiences as well as their acquisitive and utopian ones.

- In fact, Gogol's work **is saturated with** metonymy, symbols and metaphors.

- On the level of style, the work **is saturated with** similes, metaphors and metonymies.
  문체의 입장에서 볼 때, 본 작품은 직유와 메타포, 환유법 등으로 가득 차 있다.

- Briusov's poems **are saturated with** a feeling of excess; his passerby is not as fleeting as the title suggests.

- Japan today **is saturated with** shrines, temples, festivals, rituals, prayers, and other religious practices.

- Style **encrusted with** symbols and similes usually carries ~.
  유사한 표현에 be larded with가 있다.

- Some articles **are enriched with** meticulously complied bibliographies covering ~.

■ Lawrence's works **are permeated by** ~.
  동사 permeate를 써서 다른 표현을 예로 들면, The irrational in *Crime and Punishment* permeates the work in many ways (in certain significant ways).

■ The poem **is permeated with** water imagery. 이 시는 물의 이미지로 관철되어 있다.

■ The metaphor of the moon **permeates** the poem and forms an expressive reference to the poet's frame of mind.

■ The entire play **is pervaded with** forebodings.
  연극은 시종일관 예시로 점철되어 있다. 연극 전체가 예시로 가득하다.
  foreboding은 예감, 전조를 의미하며 prediction, portent와 유사한 뜻이다.

■ Plant imagery **pervades** the short story in a network of associations that link many of its main hero.
  식물 이미지가 이 이야기를 관통하고 있다.

■ Gogol's text **is dominated by** evocations of vulgarity and banality.

■ The second line **is dominated by** a fourfold repetition of the sound ~ and ~ .

■ The thrush **is** also **prominent** in the works of two major Western poets.
  ~이 두드러지다.

■ In this prose, the equation literature=cityscape **is quite prominent**.

■ Mayakovsky's plays **are full of** metaphors of life and death.

■ Leskov's comic linguistic tropes **are** often **filled with** folk resonance.

■ The images **are filled with** sadness, coldness, and nostalgia, semantic components powerfully intensified and broadened by the use of parallelisms.

■ The text of Lev Tolstoy's novella **is filled with** depictions of human bodies.

■ The description **is heavily charged with** symbolic implications.
  동사 charge는 '~으로 충만, 충전시키다'란 뜻으로 be charged with와 같이 전치사 with를 결합시켜 수동태 문장으로 많이 쓰이는데, 아주 고급하고 잘 다듬어진 문장에서 자주 나타난다. 예를 들면, emotionally charged, sexually charged 등의 표현이 있다. 다음을 참고해 보자.
In a poetic text, it may heighten the emotional charge.
charge가 동사 외에 명사로 사용될 때에는 전혀 다른 의미로도 사용된다. 학술적인 표현으로 자주 사용되니 꼭 알아 두자. This aspect of Hegel's thought has led to the charge that he was a militarist.(판단의 이유, 혐의)

- Pushkin's lyric **abounds in** descriptions of the Russian countryside.

- The everyday life of the Romans **abounded in** songs concerned with all subjects.

- Zoshchenko's stories **abound with** Gogolian elements.

- The **abundance** of folklore traits in Dostoevsky's works contains ~.
'~의 풍부함, 다량'을 의미하는 말에는 고급한 표현으로 plethora가 있다.

- Briusov's novel is itself **a rich assembly of** quotations from various literary models.
~의 풍부한 결합들

- The description **is replete with** similar examples: ~.

- His account **is replete with** detailed descriptions of the fortification and the garrisons of the cities he visited.

- The history of science **is replete with** instances in which improved observational tools produce unanticipated theoretical breakthroughs.

- Gay culture **is replete with** symbols.

- History **is replete with** paradoxes—and few have a finer sense of them than the author of this volume.

- The story **is salted with** repeated phonetic clusters.

- The diary **bristles with** descriptions of sexual acts in this spirit.
'~으로 꽉 차다'란 의미이다.

02 해석 가능성 / 타당성

■ **It is highly probable that** ~.
~은 상당히 타당해 보인다.

■ **There are also some hints**, which might be interpreted **as suggesting** the possibility of ~.
또 다른 해석의 가능성을 제시하고 있는 힌트

■ **There is one further argument(possibility) that might be considered.**
고려해 볼 만한 또 다른 가능성, 토론의 여지

■ This may all **the more possible** because ~.
~은 더욱, 한층 가능해 보인다.

■ This reading seems **plausible**, yet it requires further examination.
이같이 읽어 내는 방식은(해석은) 그럴싸해 보이지만 검증이 보다 필요하다.

■ This description **may be seen as** representing her dream ~.

■ Given these interpretations, **it appears likely to us that** the many stereotypes represent intellectual rigidity ~.
~인 것 같다
'be likely to'가 들어간 문장을 더 살펴보자. His theories help us to identify the foreign policy issues that <u>are likely to</u> have the greatest effect on American political life. 또 는 Politicians' environmental agendas <u>are likely to</u> get in the way within each of the countries. 반대로 '그럴 것 같지 않은'의 예로는 다음을 참고한다.
And while Tolstoy is one of the <u>less likely candidates to</u> appear in a volume on humor, the author emphasizes the ironies between life as it is and life as it should be in exploring the ~.

■ There is somewhat the **likelihood**, however, that the problems associated with ~ will continue.
~가능한 것이 있다, 가능해 보인다.

03 유사점 / 동일시 / 등가물 / 병치 관계

parallel

■ Ieshua is an obvious **parallel to** the Master.
'~와의 패러렐' 즉, 비교하고자 하는 대상이 비교되고 있는 상대와 등가의 무게 중심을 가지고 있으면서 반대/역접/모순/상대측 진영에 서 있는 경우를 일컫는 가장 모범적인 예문이라 할 수 있다. 여기에서 긴 문장 하나를 예로 들어 보자.
Bulgakov established a system of <u>parallel</u> by which the three parts of the novel are further united and by which each character's delineation is enhanced and reinforced.

■ Alesha's role **parallels** that of Natasha.

■ There is the same **parallel between** the artist and the priest.
~간에(예술가와 사제 사이에는) 병렬 관계가 있다.

■ Orwell too used the **parallel between** pigs and humans as a leitmotif in his political allegory.

■ These two sets of ideas **stand in parallel**.
이같은 두 생각들에는 서로 양립하는 병렬 관계가 있다.

■ Other **parallels** may be drawn.

■ Other characters **act as parallel**: Judas is to Jeshua as ~ is to ~.

■ The Russian village and the Russian city **appeared as parallels, rather than as antipodes**: both were represented as places of infection and corruption in such writings.
대척점, 정반대(antipod)

■ Trends in swimwear **have run parallel to** fashions in underwear as well as with other sportswear such as bike pants.

■ The uncertainties in European intellectual and cultural life **were paralleled by** growing anxieties in European political life.
~과 병행하였다, ~과 나란하게 진행되어 갔다

to juxtapose / juxtaposition

■ In this scene, the tree's image **is juxtaposed to** (with) the image of ~.
위의 패러렐과 함께 가장 많이 사용되는 것으로 의미는 거의 동일하다. 명사는 juxtaposition. 그러나 이 문장에서처럼 주로 수동태로 쓰여지며 전치사는 to나 with를 동반한다. The actual events are juxtaposed with (to) legends created by the retelling of history over the generations.

■ The **juxtaposition of** two worlds **is closely related to** the antithetic worlds.

■ **In the juxtaposition of** Pugachev-Grinev, Pushkin broke with the romantic notion that ~.
~의 병치 관계를 통해서

■ Gogol bases his story **on the juxtaposition of** a series of contrasts.

resemblance

■ The motif **bears (a striking, a clear) resemblance to** ~.
(놀랄 정도로, 뚜렷한) ~와의 유사성을 지니다.
동사 bear의 쓰임새를 알아보자. This volume brings together papers from a variety of scholars bearing on the topic of the historical content with oral tradition. 이 문장에서 나타나듯이 bear는 take, carry, have와 같은 뜻으로 '~한 의미를 지니고 있는, 함유, 담지하고 있는'의 뜻에 아주 가깝다.
The work bears the stamp of laments for the dead. 여기에서는 '~의 흔적을 지니고 있는'의 뜻에 가깝다. 한편, 엄청난 차이점을 나타내고자 할 때는 profound difference, marked difference 를 써 보자. 다음과 같이 구어적 표현도 자주 쓰인다. Clearly this is a far cry from ~.

■ The White Domino also **bears a curious likeness to** the pagan Belobog who aided travelers who had lost their way.
~은 ~과 흥미로운 유사점을 지니고 있다.

92

be analogous / analogy

■ The fire and sword can be seen **as analogous to ~**.

■ In many ways, outer space is directly **analogous to** the oceans.
~은 ~과 등가이다, 닮아 있다.

■ Weddings and funerals **are structurally analogous to each other**.
구조적으로 유사하다, 비슷하다, 상동이다.

■ The tale has many **analogues** in ~.

■ There is **a striking analogy between** ~.

■ The **analogy** of structure **between** the controller and the controlled was central to the cybernetic perspective.

■ An interesting **analogy** in this case can be made to the ~.
흥미 있는 유사점(성)이 ~에서도 이루어 질 수 있다, 즉 ~에서도 이같은 유사성이 나타난다.

■ Jasinsky **drew an analogy between** the use of words on the one hand and the use of shapes in plastic art on the other.
~간의 유사성을 이끌어내다

참고로, draw on(upon)은 '~에 의존, 의지하다'란 뜻이다.
• Stephen Baker has produced a work of remarkable erudition and scholarship, <u>drawing on</u> an extensive corpus of primary materials and secondary sources from ancient to modern times.
• Chekhov drew on techniques developed in his earlier fictional work.
• Richardson's discussion of the psychological process <u>draws heavily upon</u> Freud's theory of culture.
같은 뜻으로 rely on(upon), rest on이 있다.
• Frazer's arguments as to the origins of the myth of a royal victim <u>rest on</u> doubtful foundations.
• In presenting this pattern Tolstoy <u>relies on</u> the ~.
• Her entire argument <u>rests on</u> the assumption that ~.
• The soft power of a country <u>rests heavily on</u> three basic resources: its culture, its political values, and its foreign policies.
• By <u>relying on</u> the folklore tradition, she has succeeded in creating a modern tale of horror.
• The first argument <u>rests on</u> two premises: (1) and (2).

- Every scientific investigation <u>rests on</u> basic assumptions.
- Although he seems to be <u>leaning towards</u> Alison's approach to Romanticism ~.

to equate / equivalent

■ In this poem, the poet **is equated with** the priest.
동등하게 취급, 간주되다.

■ ~ **have an equivalent of** ~. ~과의 등가물을 갖다, ~과 동등한 ~을 지니다.

■ Petrushka is the Russian **equivalent of** Punch.
~과 같은 것이다, ~과 등가이다.

■ In many ways, outer space may be regarded as **equivalent to** the high seas.

■ The European Court of Justice is perhaps the closest **equivalent to** its counterpart in federal states like Germany or the USA.

■ In its broadest sense, intelligentsia is still used in the USSR as a rough **equivalent for** white-collar workers.

be identical with / to

■ Much of Peter's characterization **is identical with** that of ~. ~과 동일하다.

■ Lara's views and feelings **are (virtually) identical with** those of Zhivago.
~과 실질적으로 동일시, 유사하다.

■ The terms and terminology of Trediakovsky's analysis **are virtually identical to** those Sumarokov uses in his tragedies.
~과 실질적으로 동일하다.

to compare

■ Dostoevsky **uses the comparison with** a spider to suggest something that is morally unhealthy.
~과 비교하다.

- The poet **is compared to** an awakened eagle.
  ~에 비유되다.

- **In comparison**, the analytic work on civil society in the more empirical fields of the social sciences has not been as voluminous.

- **By comparison with** the Scandinavian economies, the three countries examined here all have relatively underdeveloped social and domestic services sectors.
  ~과 비교했을 때, ~은 ~하다.

- **By comparison with** their Western counterparts, Japanese teenagers indeed appear much less sexually active.

- **By drawing comparisons between** the techniques themselves and their place in the practice of self-expression, diverse techniques of dress and decoration can be seen as purposeful and constructive.

- The history and culture of the French peasantry have received relatively little attention from Western scholarship in general and American scholarship in particular **in comparison with** such fields of study as French intellectual history.
  ~과 비교했을 때, ~과 비교할 때

- In fact, Rotengurg **pursues a number of comparisons between** ~.
  ~과 ~ 사이에서 여러 차례의 비교를 시도해 보다, 비교를 한다.

- **Compared with** the national traditions, the EU stands out through a number of unique features of interest articulation.
  ~과 비교했을 때, ~에 비해서

기타

- **~ be tantamount to** ~.
  ~과 대등하다, ~에 필적하다

- It retains **a great similarity**.
  be similar to와 가장 유사한 표현으로 be akin to가 있다. 다음 문장을 통해 알아보자.
  Brown's paradigm of the development of European civilization <u>is also akin to</u> that of Marx in the long-range trend it discerns. 또는 Elias's paradigm of the development of European civilization <u>is also akin to</u> that of Aries in the long-range trend it discerns.

- **Have** great **affinity with** the ~.
  이것과는 반대로 '공통점이 거의 없다'는 표현은 ~ have little common with the ~이 주로 쓰인다.

- The history of mentalities **has obvious affinities with** approaches to intellectual history developed before the arrival of the French school.
  ~의 접근 방법과 뚜렷한, 명백한 유사성을 지니고 있다.

- The ~ **is very much like that of** ~.
  ~과 매우 유사하다.

- **Much the same can be said of** ~.
  ~ 역시 상당 부분 동일하다고 말할 수 있다, ~도 상당히 유사하다.

- **The same is true of** the ~.
  ~도 마찬가지이다.
  The same question can be asked of the effect of networks on the international system: for better or for worse? (~에 대하여 같은 질문을 던질 수 있다)
  The same went for the health system. (~의 경우에도 마찬가지였다, 마찬가지로 말할 수 있다)

- On the whole, **this is also the case with** fiction.

- **As in the case of** Japan and Korea, a variety of studies have been carried out on the effectiveness of policies.
  ~에서와 마찬가지로

- **And the converse is also true.**
  그 역도 마찬가지이다.

- **The same held true for** women, whom the Soviet system boasted of having liberated.
  ~의 경우에도 마찬가지이다.

- This **holds particularly true for** ~, which remains considerably understudied in comparison to ~.
  이것은 ~과 관련지어 특히 들어맞는다. 그리고 이것은 ~과 비교해서 지금껏 거의 연구되어 있지 않다.

- This **holds true** irrespective of whether they admit to the heuristic nature of their presuppositions or not.

- **Just as** the internal plan of the text is complex and multi-leveled, **so** do the material building blocks of the text reflect the complexity of the world outside of the text.
  숙어 just as A, so B는 'A와 마찬가지로 B도 그러하다'란 의미이다.

- **Just as** sexuality has become a more salient issue in recent times, **so** too has there been a marked increase within Europe in awareness of, and debate on, gender.

- **Just as** normal ideas were interpretive in approximating the archetypes of natural species, **so** aesthetic ideas are interpretive in approximating rational ideas.

- Much of what Onegin says in the course of the poem is **in accord with** Pushkin's own views.
  동사 accord는 to be in agreement or harmony의 의미로서 '~과 일치하여'를 뜻한다. 한편, '~과 잘 조응된다, 어울린다'의 의미를 나타내고자 할 때에는 be in (well) tune with를 알아 두자. Revolutionary culture history <u>is in tune with</u> the Christian conception of culture as a whole. 반대로 '~과 일치하지 않는'의 뜻으로는 be at odds with가 있다. It <u>is at odds with</u> his earlier exposition.
  Historians of Homo Sapiens such as Yuval Noah Harari and Steven Mithen <u>are in general agreement that</u> the decisive ingredient that gave our ancestors the ability to achieve global dominion about forty thousand years was their ability to create and store a mental representation of their environment, interrogate that representation, distort it by mental acts of imagination, and finally answer the "What if". (일반적으로 ~라는 점에 동의하고 있다) 혹은 More recently, <u>a consensus has emerged around the idea</u> of a rational agent that perceives, and acts in order to maximize, its expected utility. (~에 대한 생각에 공통의 의견이 수렴되고 있다, 공통된 의견이 나타나고 있다) 컨센서스와 반대는 당연히 반대 의견, 반대 의사일 것이다. 다음의 예문도 함께 알아 두자. <u>Objections have been raised to these arguments</u>, primarily by researchers within the AI community.

- **In accord with** the introductory rationale, these findings suggest that ~.

- Such a view **accords well with** the ~.

- Clearly, this image of the Soviet woman **did not accord with** the Marxist theoretical writings about women under socialism.

■ The effect of these three components **in concert with** the image of the dove is very telling, indeed.

말 그대로 '~과 협주를 하고 있는'이란 뜻으로 '~과 잘 조화를 이루고 있는' 정도로 이해하면 좋겠다. 이와 유사한 표현으로 in consonance with가 있다. In consonance with the content of these stanzas, the style and imagery are romantic throughout.

■ Some gestures and movements occur **in concert with** verbal noise.

■ **Consistent with** the trend since Tito's death, democratic elections in the region have tended to reinforce separatism rather than encourage multiethnicity.

~과 일치하여

■ Some of the patterns outlined above are **consistent with** the hypotheses outlined at the beginning part of this section.

consistent with는 accordant with와 같은 뜻으로 '~에 일치하는, 일관되어, 마찬가지로'란 의미이다.

■ **Concurrent with** the adoption of specific educational programmes in the second half of the 1980s, the Council passed resolutions on the educational co-operation.

■ While contemporary research has expanded, **concurrent with** the development of activism and NGO support for women, the expansion largely reflects the degree to which countries have been willing to nurture open research and interventions.

concurrent 역시 위 문장의 accord, consistent 등과 거의 비슷한 의미(accordant, agreeing)로 많이 쓰인다. 형용사 compliant도 곁들여 알아 두자. Compliant with the fiscal criteria, it can be limited in scope and consequences.

■ The author **assimilates** the actual historical personage **with** an ideal or model.

~과 ~을 동일시하다.

■ Most of these words do not fully **coincide** in French and English.

완벽하게 일치하지 않는다.

■ Franklin Roosevelt's United Nations had one thing **in common with** Theodore Roosevelt's hopes for a 'realized Utopia.'

~와 공통되는, 유사한

04 차이점 / 대조

contrast

- This image **brings about a sharp contrast between** ~.
  양자 사이의 대조, 대립을 의미하는 가장 대표적인 표현이다. 문장 가운데의 sharp은 말 그대로 날카롭다는 뜻으로, '뚜렷한 대조 혹은 극단의 대조'로 번역하면 좋을 듯 싶다.

- The **sharp contrast between** ~ **and** ~ **is enhanced by** ~.
  ~과 ~ 사이의 대조가 ~에 의해서 강조되다.

- The **contrast between** ~ **and** ~ illustrates two thematic oppositions.
  ~과 ~ 사이의 대조점이 ~을 설명해 준다.

- Gerald's image **is in sharp contrast with** that of ~.
  ~이 ~과 극단의 대조를 이룬다, 정면으로 상반된다.

- The new-essentialist feminism **stands in sharp contrast to** post-structuralist feminism, with its emphasis upon ~.

- **A sharp contrast** is drawn between ~.

- The scene provides **a strong contrast to** ~.

- It is presented in **stark contrast to** the ~.
  ~은 ~과 극단적인 대조로 나타나 있다, ~은 ~과 극단적으로 대조적이다.

- There is **a marked contrast between** ~.
  ~간의 뚜렷한 대조, 차이점이 나타나 있다.

- Bunin **contrasts** his character **with** ~.

- Yet the Americans also **contrasted greatly with** their overseas counterparts.

- The neglect of financial history **contrasts sharply with** the increasing interest in Hong Kong as a manufacturing center.

- The **contrast** is as much as in their mental ~ as their physical.

- In both novels the narrator **establishes a contrast between** narrative reality and the reported delusions of the main character.

- **In contrast to** man-made Petersburg, the founding of Moscow ~.
  ~과는 대조적으로

- **In contrast to** the calculated response of anti-Communist leaders, popular reactions were overwhelmingly enthusiastic.

- **In contrast to** the American, British workers had a decidedly class-biased world view.

- **In contrast to** the agricultural sector, the financial sector is oriented towards general regulations to strengthen market stability and efficiency.

- **In contrast to** the infighting and ideological nature of the Regan administration, President Bush became a hands-on administrator who authorized a stronger NSC system.

- **In responding to** this objection, we should acknowledge an important truth that it contains.

- **A strong contrast** is drawn between the venality in ordinary civilian affairs and the behavior of the political police.

- That degree of geographical and jurisdictional certainty in Mexico **is in vivid contrast to** the American case.

be opposite / opposition

■ **~ stand in sharp opposition to** the ~.
위의 contrast와 함께 가장 많이 쓰이는 opposition을 넣어 쓰는 대표적인 문장으로 동사는 stand를 활용한다. 다음 문장을 참고해 보자. Both in subject and style, the story <u>stands apart from</u> Bulgakov's other early works.

■ **The** very **opposite** may be observed in ~.

■ **The opposition of** the two characters also illustrates the ~.

■ **In opposition to** the ~.
~과 반대로, 대조적으로

■ Gentrification stands **in opposition to** both the rigid separation between city and suburb.

■ **~ be diametrically opposed to** ~.
극단적으로 대조를 이루다

■ In manners, they **are diametrically opposed**: Pavel's reversed formality **is contrasted** to Bazarov's off-hand casualness.
명사 counterpoise를 써서 대조의 의미를 표현하면 다음과 같다. He acts as a counterpoise to ~.

■ The two characters **are diametrically opposed** in their ways of thinking.

disparity / distinction

■ There is a significant **disparity between** ~.
~간의 뚜렷한 차이

■ Solzhenitsyn **made a distinction between** secular society and the virtually religious service of the writer-priest in *The Cancer Ward*.
make a distinction between은 '~간의 뚜렷한 구별을 짓다'란 의미이다.

- In his work, the author **drew the distinction between** republican and imperial China.
  ~간의 차이점을 나타내다, 보여 주다

- In his remarks at the hearing, Dorson **drew a sharp distinction between** academic and public or applied folklore.

- Mobile communication can **be distinguished from** online communities according to social scope and formation.

counterpoint

- **In counterpoint to** the preceding passage discussed, ~ .
  ~과 대조적으로

- Emerson's story **provides a strong counterpoint to** Lena's.

기타

- These two characters are **poles apart** ideologically.
  완전히 다른 두 진영

- Here are two worlds **in antithesis.** 상반된 두 세계
  antithesis는 두 가지 서로 다른 것이 완벽하게 반대의 의미를 지닐 때 쓰이는 것으로 A is antithesis to B의 형태로 많이 쓰인다. 다음 예문을 참고해 보자.
  Prince Myshkin represented the antithesis to Rakhmetov.

- Several words are completely **at variance with** his former convictions.
  ~과 일치하지 않는, ~과 모순되는

- These data are utterly **at variance with** the perception that ~.

- Mounting empirical evidence **is at odds with** traditional economic theories of underdevelopment which blame deficiencies in the momentary policy.
  ~와 어울리지 않은, 부조화인, ~와 다른

- What decisively **marks off A ~ from B is** ~.

  A와 B가 현격하게 구별되는 것은 ~이다.

- There is **a fundamental difference between** individual woman's anorexia and anorexia when applied to Soviet society under NEP.

  ~ 사이의 근본적인 차이점

- These two poems **are vastly different to** those metrical and stanzaic forms.

- Approaches to the secondary economic effects of railroads **differ markedly**.

  현격하게 다르다, 차이가 나다

- All the same, there was some **difference in** style and content between the ~.

  all the same은 notwithstanding과 흡사한 뜻으로 '~임에도 불구하고 여전히'란 의미이다. 이 표현을 쓰려면 당연히 앞 문장 어딘가에서 유사점을 설명하는 내용이 나와야 한다.

- The status of Latin American issues in political science does not **differ greatly from** that in anthropology.

- Opinions as to the actual help offered by the midwife during childbirth are **contradictory**.

  ~한 의견은 상호 모순적

- This requirement can **come into contradiction with** our ideas of social justice.

05 측면 / 관점 / 입장 / 고려

■ **In this overall perspective**, then, Gerasim may be viewed as the true of the story.
이같은 전반적인 측면에서

■ **this perspective (= in this reading),**
이같은 측면에서, 이런 식으로 작품을 읽다 보면, 해석하다 보면

■ **In the light of the above illustrations, one can say that ~.**
위에서 예로든 입장에서 볼 때 혹자는 ~라고 얘기할 수 있을 것이다.

■ **In the light of these considerations, ~.**

■ **In the light of this**, we are able to identify instances of resistance which we can legitimately identify as feminist in nature.
이같은 입장에서 우리는 ~할 수 있다.

■ **In terms of the story's linear surface, ~.**
겉으로 쉽게 드러나 파악되는 스토리 즉, '스토리의 표면적 의미에서 볼 때'란 의미로, 이와는 반대로 스토리의 깊은 이면에 존재하는 또 다른 줄기의 스토리를 흔히 sub-text라고 부른다.

■ **In this sense**, the novel's message goes far beyond the ~.
이런 의미에서 ~은
in a sense는 전혀 다른 뜻으로, '한편으로, 어떤 점에선'으로 보면 좋다.

■ **With this in mind**, we are not so surprised to hear that ~.
~을 고려하면 ~라는 것에 그리 놀라지 않는다

■ **With this in mind**, Kasold divides the cannon into three types.

- **With this minimal detail**, we can speculate that ~.

- **With regard to** ~, the novel is situated on some meta level.
  ~한 측면에서, ~과 관련하여

- The same point can be made **with regard to** ~.
  ~과 관련하여도 같은 입장(핵심, 요소)이 나타난다, 이루어진다, 생성된다.

- It is important in **two regards**: ~. 두 가지 입장에서 ~은 중요하다.

- **In this regard**, we should remember ~. 이점에 있어서, 이렇게 볼 때

- Bush also faced significant domestic cross-pressures **in regard to** the growing economic interdependence with China.

- The analysis of the interesting statement and the chess-game is similar **in the respect that** they are both activities which proceed according to certain rules of an institutional nature.
  ~란 점에서 유사하다.

- Landscape as a cultural medium thus has a double role **with respect to** something like ideology.

- **With** this range of characteristics Pechorin presents an impressive and most unusual combination of thinker and man of artist.
  성격의 여러 측면들로 볼 때, ~는 ~을 보여 준다.

- **As with** the United States Supreme Court, its role is generally recognized as one of law clarification rather than error correction.
  as with는 '~로 말하면, ~인 경우'의 의미로 같은 표현으로는 when it comes to ~가 있다.

- **Seen from this point of view**, ~. 이 같은 입장에서 보면(볼 때), ~

- **Seen in this perspective**, ~.

- **Viewed in this light**, ~.

- **Judging from** the ~, it is clear that ~. ~로 판단해 봤을 때(보면), ~은 분명하다.

- All this **considered**, ~. 이 모든 것이 고려될 때, 이 모든 것을 생각해 볼 때, ~

- **Considered** in this framework, ~.

- **From another point of view**, it reveals that ~.

- **From the point of view of** the novel's structure, ~.

- **From** the biographical **sketches of the characters we learn that** ~.

- **Looking from the point of view of** eternity, ~.

- **From what we have seen of** the description, we might expect the ~.
  지금까지 우리가 보아 온 묘사를 통해서 우리는 ~을 기대할 수 있다.

- **From all this** it should be clear that ~. 이 모든 것들로 보았을 때, ~은 분명할 것이다, 명백하다.

- **To judge from his writings**, Anna felt a great affinity for the formal emphasis of ~.
  ~의 작품집으로 판단해 보았을 때

- **On the surface**, the story is about ~. 표면적으로 볼 때 스토리는 ~에 관한 것이다.

- **On the surface**, this case could be an excellent typifying example of what critics men when they say that ~.

- **On the surface**, the title could refer to ~.

- **On the metaphorical level**, it may be associated with ~. 메타포의 측면에서 볼 때
  level이 들어간 기본적인 문장들을 점검해 보자: On the federal level, Canada has been better able to impose losses on business through regulation. At the level of constitutional developments the state appears ~. At the most fundamental level, human social institutions cannot exist without people. At the symbolic level, government must enjoy a diffuse legitimacy in the eyes of the population.

- **In a symbolic sense**, ~. **In a metaphorical sense** ~.
  상징적인 의미에서, ~. 메타포의 의미에서 볼 때, ~.

- **In symbolic terms** words represent the ongoing and positive nature of human identity.

- In other words, ~ **are in certain significant respects** both like and unlike wedding-songs.
  몇몇 의미있는 부분에 있어서

- **More to the immediate point**, a lament in Greek is ~.
  보다 직접적인 의미에서

- **In immediate sense**, this outlook counseled acceptance for life-energy.

- **Given** the difficult situation of Soviet libraries, universities and research institutes, it will take some time and effort to overcome the ~.
  흔히, '~란 점을 감안할 때' 혹은 '~한 이상 ~은 ~하다'란 의미로 given이 많이 쓰인다. 문법적으로 given that은 본래 미래에 있을 어떠한 가능성을 예측해 볼 때 주로 사용되는 표현이다. 따라서 supposing that 혹은 if로 대체될 수 있다. 뿐만 아니라, given은 문장 뒤에서(주절 뒤의 종속절에서)도 많이 사용된다. 아래의 모든 예문들을 잘 살펴보자.

- The European Council is more problematic in comparative politics terms, **given** its similarity to more traditional intergovernmental bodies.

- This should hardly be surprising in the case of the Commission, **given** its mandate of impartiality.

- **Given** these interpretations, **it appears likely to us that** the many stereotypes represent intellectual rigidity ~.
  이 같은 해석을 생각해 보면, ~은 ~인 것 같다.

- **Given** these cultural processes, it should not surprise us to discover manifold appreciations of the border in Soviet literature.
  이 같은 문화 과정을 고려해 보면, ~은 결코 놀랍지 않다.

- **Given** the paucity of material on Japanese culture written by non-Japanese citizens, this collection of essential monographs is certainly welcome.
  ~에 대한 자료의 부족을 감안해 보면,

- **Given** this combination of spectral unreality, the most pertinent symbol for the border in the novel turns out to be the mirror.

■ **Given** the precedents of Russian culture, however, one suspects consciousness of the border will not disappear; it will simply be redrawn.

■ **Given** the very genuine popularity of the film, attested to not only by staggering ticket sales but also by the ensuing semi-legendary status accorded the figure of Freedman himself, **it is certainly worth inquiring into the reasons** behind its apparent fascination.

■ **Given that** violence marks many multiethnic societies, our research may well have great practical meaning if we can sort out some key relationships.
위 예문에서 Given이 사용된 주절은 "폭력은 여러 다민족 사회를 나타낸다는 점을 고려할 때 (감안할 때)"로 번역할 수 있다. 여기에 사용된 단어 mark의 다양한 용법을 알아보자. 1)The Industrial Age <u>marks</u> a distinct and remarkable phase in the history of globalization. 2) AIDS <u>marked</u> another major event of globalization, at both its most devastating and its most inspiring. 3) Recent U.S. presidential elections have thus <u>been marked by</u> the aggressive application of big data analytics to the voter rolls in ways that raise big questions about the integrity of democracy itself. 4) Our use of the phrase 'the Dark Ages' to cover the period from 600 to 1000 <u>marks</u> our undue concentration on Western Europe.

■ **Given the fact that** almost all environmental regimes are implemented by these domestic actors, the ultimate effects of these new forms of governance can be ascertained only through such implementation studies.

■ **Given** the glaring lack of normative data regarding ~, this study can be seen as the first in a needed stream of research investigating ~.
토대가 될 만한, 규범적인 데이터가 없는 실정을 고려했을 때, 이 연구는 가장 요구되는 첫 번째 시도이다.

■ **Given** the undeveloped state of the European economy at the time, this building nourished the roots of artisan traditions in the production of the liturgical apparatus, even though much of the building and furnishing of rural churches remained modest.

■ **Given** how common creepiness has become as a way of thinking about privacy, it should be no surprise that creepiness has entered privacy law.

■ The novels are polyphonic **in the sense that** there are frequent shifts from one dominant viewpoint to another.
~라는 점에서

■ **Accepted at face value** and taken in isolation from the novel itself, these words convey ~.
액면 그대로 받아들일 때

■ **Approached from a purely semiotic perspective**, the novel differs considerably from the urban oral story.
순전히 기호학적 측면에서 보면, ~로 접근해 볼 때,

■ The question above, **when approached from the perspective of** the individual looking outward, calls to mind issues of free expression.

■ **In relation to** what I have previously said ~. 이전에 언급한 것과 관련하여

■ **In relation to** the devils, Margarita ~.

■ Especially **with respect to** ~, it is unusually rich in interpretative possibilities.

■ **As far as** the novel's plot **is concerned**, ~.
'~에 관한 한, ~을 말해 보자면'의 뜻으로 as for ~, as to ~, regarding ~ 등과 같은 말이다. 예를 들어, As to the nature of the fusion of the text, Bakhtin distinguishes between a clearly parodistic relationship to the text ~. As to the European position in the international economic structure, different indicators pointed to different conclusions.

■ But **as far as** the main point of the play **is concerned**, ~.

■ **Insofar as** the theme **is concerned**, ~. 주제에 관련한, 주제가 관련되는 한

■ **So far as** the global view of history **is concerned**, one of the most remarkable examples centers on the ~.

■ **As far as** the major part of the interview **was concerned**, the method of choosing my informants was both selective and systematic.

■ Such work is important, **inasmuch as** it demonstrates prevailing attitudes toward ~.
~하는 한

■ **If we take into account** ~.
take into account는 '~을 고려하다'란 숙어로, 동사 consider와 동일한 의미를 갖는다.
If we <u>consider</u> the motifs, we will see that ~.

■ **Such a reading of the story**, however, is also fraught with problems.

■ **Such an approach** helps elucidate the essentially symbolic and poetic character of the novel.

■ **This analytic approach** is as ingenious ~.
(= Ingenious as this approach to the insane is, we must be guided by ~.)

■ **A closer look at** the structure **gives** a different answer; ~.
위의 문장을 의역하면, '보다 자세히(비교급으로 주로 쓰임) 들여다보면 우리는 ~임을 알게 된다' 혹은 '보다 치밀하게 분석할 때, 우리는 ~한 것을 알게 된다'의 의미가 된다. 위의 예문은 매우 빈번하게 나타나는 구문으로서 잘 기억해두어 실제에 활용하면 좋을 것이다.

■ **A look into** the genre and distinguishing specifics for each of the two poems involved will precede the discussion of Anna's poem, "Stansy."

■ **A look at** these later stories could result in some new insights.

■ **A closer reading of** the text reveals ~.

■ **A close reading of** the literary process makes it clear that ~.

■ **A brief survey of** the first scene entries illustrates this recurring structure.

■ **An understanding of** the critic's use of the dialectic similarity explains ~.

■ **A thoughtful comparison of** Annensky's poem with the Mallarme text shows a significant thematic difference which are revealing ~.

■ But, **on closer examination, it reveals** ~.

■ However, **on closer inspection,** ~ the description **reveals that** ~.

- **By closely examination** this newly available manuscript, **we are able to** observe ~.

- **By taking a closer look at** the ~, I wish to illuminate the compositional significance of ~.

- **Taking a current look at** the Scandinavian countries, we will examine the progress of the processes and their impacts on the market participants.

- The allegorical **reading** can be refined and deepened **through a closer look at** the process of the narrative of the novel.
  다음 문장을 참고하여 reading의 사용법을 알아 두자. One must distinguish two main readings of *The Queen of Spades*. The first treats the story as realistic and tries to demystify all the instances of the mystic and fantastic. The second reading is most explicitly presented in Marry's study(article, paper).

- An allegoric **reading of** *The Idiot* is supported by ~.
  '~한 작품을 우화적으로 이해한다'는 의미로 어떤 수단에 대한 설명을 문장의 주어로 사용하여 맨 앞에 위치시키는 예문으로 매우 자주 쓰인다. 유사한 문장을 예로 들어보자.
  A psychological reading of the novel has been attempted.

- **Attention to** the dialectic, however, **reveals** ~.

- **Careful attention to** Belinsky's interpretation of ~ **resolves** ~.

- **In applying** Zemskaia's theory to Pasternak's prose **one notices** some fundamental differences.
  ~함에 있어서 즉, ~의 이론을 ~에 적용시키다보면 혹자는 ~을 발견하게 된다.

- **In constructing her argument**, Robin has **relied on** an extensive list of works, both primary and secondary.
  ~을 주장함에 있어서, ~에 의존하다.

- **In an attempt to** clarify a particular point, the author **resorts to** an unending list of ~.
  '~에 의존, 의지하다'란 뜻의 숙어 resort to와 유사한 것으로 have recourse to가 있다.
  Belinsky had recourse to this type of argument in ~.

■ This claim will seem considerably less far-fetched **if we pause to consider** Gogol's attitude towards religion.

■ Two questions in particular arise **as one** contemplates a literary phenomenon of this nature.
위의 두 문장 모두 도치된 구문으로, 후자는 '혹 누군가, 만약 우리가 ~하다 보면 두 가지 문제가 제기된다'란 의미이다.

■ **As such,** ~ is by no means idealized; rather, it exemplifies that combination of dark and light and evil and good.
as such는 '그 자체로는'이란 의미로 as itself와 같은 뜻이다. As such, the chapters, in spite of repetitive and common themes, are a bit disjointed.

■ **As such,** the law posits that education be universal, obligatory, free, participatory, intercultural, multilingual and equitable.

■ One problem might be **put** like this:
한 가지 문제를 우리는 다음과 같이 달리 얘기해 볼 수 있다.
동사 put은 위의 예에서처럼 '~으로 표현하다, 다른 말로 하다' 등으로 쓰인다. 일상 대화체에서도 매우 유용하게 사용되는데, 다음과 같은 표현('그렇다면 이렇게 얘기해 보죠')도 put을 사용한다.
Let me put it this way ~.

■ **At this point,** it may be useful to give the full context of the remark from Plato ~.

■ **At this point,** we have to rely on ~.

06 제시 / 제공 / 부여

이 항목에 예로 들어 있는 문장을 잘 살펴보면 주로 수동태의 표현이 많다는 것을 알게 된다. 특히 동사 find → be found, detect → be detected, represent → be represented, view → be viewed, construe → be construed, read → be read, present → be presented가 실제로 많이 등장한다.

to find

- The image of ~ **finds its fullest expression in** his character, who ~.
  '~에서 가장 잘 표현되어 있다'는 의미로 보편적인 표현이다. 이와 유사한 표현으로 다음 문장을 잘 살펴보자. The poetic idealization of Peter the Great <u>received its amplest expression in</u> the odes of Lomonosov, in his poem. 즉, '~에서 가장 풍부한 표현이 나타난다'로 이해하면 좋 겠다.

- In its Byronic form, the myth of ~ **found its most powerful expression in** Lermontov's *Demon*.

- The narrative focus, steadily narrowing since Part III, **reaches its finest concentration** at the ending.

to present

- This can **be presented** schematically as follows: ~.

- All **are presented with** in a high concentration of negative traits.
  부정적으로 나타나 있다, 처리되어 있다.

- The passage **is presented in highly figural discourse** conveying ~.
  고도로 비유적인 담론으로 제시되어 있다, 드러나 있다.

- Characters **are presented in** a laconic manner.
  등장 인물, 혹은 주제가 '작품에 나타난다 혹은 그려지고 있다'란 의미를 표현하고자 할 때 매우 유용한 예문이다. 동사 present의 수동태를 이용한 이 구문을 독자들은 실제 영어 논문에서 자주 발견할 것이다.

■ The image **is presented in a twofold manner**. First of all, ~.
두 가지 방식으로 나타나 있다.

이에 관련한 유사한 문장을 예로 들어보자. <u>His aim is twofold</u>: to demonstrate first that ~, and second that ~. 또는 The course of argument followed in this article is <u>as follows</u>: Part I is a general consideration of ~(본 논문에서 나타난 논점은 다음과 같다).

■ *The Brothers Karamazov* **presents** Dostoevsky's most famous and **scathing** portrait of the jury trial.
형용사 scathing은 '가차없는, 신랄한'이란 뜻이다.

■ Makar's opinions **are presented in the form of** a lengthy monologue.
~한 방식을 통해서 드러나다, ~의 형태로 나타나다.

■ The passage **presents a crescendo of** grotesque. ~의 극치, 절정을 보여 준다.

to portray / portrait

■ Their relationships **are portrayed in considerable detail**.
상당히 자세하게 묘사되다, 그려져 있다.

■ Pushkin gives the following **portrait of** Anna.
~에 대해서 다음과 같은 묘사를 하고 있다.

명사 portrait는 동사 portray에서 나온 것으로 '~에 대한 묘사, 기술'의 뜻이며, 위의 문장은 Pushkin <u>portrays</u> the figure of Anna.로 옮길 수 있다. 이 단어와 가장 유사한 것으로는 describe가 있다.

■ In the novel's early chapter, where the writer **creates his detailed portrait of** the self-deceiving poet in action ~.
~에 대한 묘사

to provide / to offer

■ An initial **clue to** such an interpretation **is provided by** the novel's epigraph.
여기에서 '~을 위한 핵심, 단서, 해결점' 등의 의미를 표현하고자 할 때, 전치사는 for나 of가 아니라 to라는 점을 기억해두자. 즉 a <u>key to</u> ~, a <u>solution to</u> ~, a <u>guide to</u>에서와 같다. The <u>key to</u> developing such a theoretical understanding is to see how ~. International cooperation and amalgamation was the logical <u>solution to</u> the problems facing merchant sailors in the Second World War.

- No indication is **provided as to** where the sacred rite is to be performed.
  ~에 대한 지적이 없다.

- Towngend's letter **provides** unique **evidence to help us is to be performed understand** the precise terms in which the issues are framed in Sumarokov's plays.

- This paper **provides an update on** records of mammoth localities.

- This investigative system **provides an in-depth view of** the families of sexually abused children.

- As Joseph Bradley has shown, civil society and voluntary associations **provide a key with which to unlock many of the riddles** of imperial Russian society.
  ~의 수수께끼를 풀 열쇠/단초를 제시하는

- This approach **provides an umbrella under which we see each other as working within the same paradigm**, but in different ways.
  통합적 패러다임 (안목)을 제시하는

- The second chapter **provides** a context **within which** the study is situated.

- **No explanation is offered**.
  어떠한 설명도 나타나 있지 않다, 설명을 전혀 하고 있지 않다.

- The writer **offers unique insights** and can provide a much more vivid **portrayal of** society's political and moral problems.

- Recent work by Western scholars **has offered refreshing new insights into** the workings of the ~.
  ~에 대한 신선한 안목, 식견을 보여 주어 왔다.

- Lermontov's poem **offers an insight into** the destructive sides of nature.
  ~에 대한 통찰력을 보여 주다.

- Individual-level strategies can be **offered** in varied settings such as homes, residential institutions and work sites.

- Democratic politics also **provides an outlet for** ambitious natures.
  ~를 위한 방법, 수단을 제공하다

거의 같은 개념과 의미로 통하는 예문들을 더 보자. The twentieth-century German historian and philosopher Karl Jaspers <u>offered a crucial insight into</u> this era with his concept of the Axial Age. 혹은 Correspondence networks <u>allow</u> us <u>a deeper insight into</u> the evolution of the Scientific Revolution. (서신왕래는 우리로 하여금 ~ 속으로 더욱 깊게 들어가도록 해 준다). But military power <u>needs a closer look</u>. (자세히 들여다볼 필요가 있다).

to display

■ The narrator's comments on the events **display** a comparable attitude towards ~.
화자의 ~은 이중적, 양립적 태도를 보인다.
여기에서 동사 display는 exhibit, show, give, reveal, uncover, deliver 등으로 대체될 수 있다. 모두 빈번하게 쓰이는 중요한 동사들이다.

■ The description **displays** Chekhov's customary stylistic mastery.

■ Belikov **displays** a number of characteristics of typical of Gogloian figure: ~.

■ Most kinship systems **display** clusters of norms concerning family activities.

■ Their texts **display** a **coherent** structural and compositional organization, a distinctive narrative voice.
형용사 coherent는 '처음부터 끝까지 일관하는 즉, 계속되어 일정한'이란 뜻으로 작품 구조를 논하는 문학 논문이나 논문에서 말하는 논지의 흐름을 얘기할 때에도 많이 사용되는 단어이다.

to impart

■ Chekhov **imparted** his works **with** mood of ~.
impart something with는 '~에 어떠한 것을 부여하다'라는 뜻으로, 문학 논문에서는 '~작가가 자신의 작품에 ~한 (종교적, 묵시적, 신비적 등등) 분위기, 무드를 부여한다, 보여 준다'는 의미를 표현할 때 이런 문장이 자주 쓰인다.

■ Set in this order, these actions in the poem **impart** a sense of determinate action.

■ The magazine **imparted** the idea that home ownership was a great investment and key to prosperity.

to acquire

■ The universal tree **acquires** obvious Biblical and **religious overtones**.

위의 예에서처럼 동사 acquire는 본래 '~을 획득하다'란 뜻이지만 문학 논문에서는 '암시, 함축적인 의미, ~한 성격을 갖는다'란 의미로 널리 쓰인다. 유사한 의미에서 또 다른 문장을 적어 보면 다음과 같다. The candle acquires a religious connotation.

여기에서도 동사 acquire는 '~한 의미를 갖는다'란 말로 아주 고급한 표현으로 자주 사용되니 잘 기억해두면 유용할 것이다. connotation이 들어간 문장을 확인해 두자.

Globalization carries less precise, yet nevertheless important, connotations related to loss of national control, sovereignty, or identity in the organization of economics and cultural life.

■ This motif **acquires** unpleasant and unnatural, even supernatural effects.

■ The plot of the novel **acquires** a wholly different dimension.

'양상을 띠다, 성격을 띠다, 성격을 획득하다'라는 의미로 문학 논문에서 매우 빈번하게 나타난다. 꼭 알아 두기 바란다.

■ The poem thus **acquires** unmistakable eschatological overtones.

시는 묵시록적 함축들을 담고 있다.

■ Culture has indeed **acquired** a central position within late capitalist consumer society and a growing proportion of economic activity.

to lend

■ Nadia's youth **lends** the story an optimistic note.

스토리에 ~을 부여한다.

동사 lend는 앞장의 impart처럼 '~에 더하다, 보태다, 부여하다'의 의미이며 전치사 to를 동반하기도 한다. Certain kinds of documents lend themselves to a quantitative approach to the problem. The concept of culture lends itself easily to a dichotomy definition as general and particular in two ways.

The Kluckhohn model lends itself well to cultural analysis of a theme, whether in literature of a popular medium such as folk song, for example (~의 모델은 ~에 잘 부합함을 보여 준다, 즉 ~에 잘 부합된다.) Such indicators lend themselves more readily to oral communication than to writing, and the improvisational use of creole speech is generally negotiated more readily orally than in writing. 또는 These results lend support to those who argue that democratic politics still matter in a world of global capital.

- The third line **lends** a sense of definite, dynastic and purposeful action.

- In so doing, Rusanov is **lend**ing his narrative an appropriate air of antiquity.

- The importance of bells in **lend**ing color and solemnity to church proceedings was heightened by the general prohibition on the use of musical instruments in Orthodox services.

- Finally, a number of issues simply do not **lend themselves to** forceful solutions.
  ~에 적합하다

to create

- All of this **creates** the sense that ~.
  동사 create는 위의 예에서처럼 '~을 창조해 내다, 만들어 내다'란 의미이며, 이와 유사한 의미로 yield를 사용한다. This stanza <u>yields</u> a balanced structure with two alternating quatrains on either side of the third. 또는 A closer examination of the novel <u>yields</u> startling evidence concerning ~. A close look at Japanese peasant art <u>yields</u> two divergent impressions.

- Zhukovsky's ballad **creates** something of the excitement in Russia.

- A special tension **is created** in the description, in which the narrator ~.

- Tension **is** also **created by** the dramatic contrast of the poet's states of mind.
  위의 경우에서처럼 '긴장감이 발생한다, 나타난다'란 의미를 쓰고자 할 때, 흔히 동사 take place 혹은 occur, appear 등이 주로 쓰인다. 다음 예를 참고하자. The tension between two components <u>occurs</u> in ~.

to construe / be construed

- In a critical context Moscow **is construed** as a mythologized city.
  동사 construe 이외에도 같은 의미로 즉, '~으로 해석된다' 혹은 '~으로 이해된다, 받아들여질 수 있다'로 쓰이는 동사 중 가장 대표적인 것이 바로 read이다. 다음 예문을 통해서 알아보자. The introduction can largely <u>be read</u> as a ~ (서문은 대체로 ~로 이해될 수 있다). The text of *The Idiot* may <u>be read</u> as ~. The novel <u>is read</u> like an avant-garde account of ~. 그리고 실제 영작문을 할 때 주의할 점은, 이 표현이 거의 수동태로 사용되고 있다는 점이다. 다른 동사를 써서 비슷한 의미를 지니는 다른 예를 들어보면 다음과 같다. This description <u>may be seen</u> as representing her dream ~. 즉 '이 묘사 부분은 ~을 나타나고 있는 것으로 볼 수 있다'라는 의미이다.

■ The passage can **be construed** in such a way that ~.

to read / be read

■ The novel **can be read** in the context of the preceding two stories.

■ The story **has been read as** an allegory of the revolutionary transformation of Russian society.
~으로 받아들여지다, 해석되다.

■ Sokolov's fiction should **be read in the context of** political events in the early 1920s.
~한 맥락에서 이해되어야 한다, 살펴져야 한다.

to interpret / be interpreted / to render / be rendered

■ The novel has **been interpreted** variously. 다양하게 해석되다.
이처럼 '~으로 해석, 이해, 풀이된다'란 의미에는 동사 construe, interpret가 있다. 이외에도 be rendered(= to be translated into another language)란 표현이 있는데, 이 역시 마찬가지의 의미로 빈번하게 쓰인다. 예를 들어, Raskolnikov's dream <u>is rendered</u> in one long paragraph toward the end of the novel. 혹은 Tvardovsky not only omitted certain details from the prose <u>in his rendering</u> of the original story, but also added much to it; in doing so he provided his work with a richly developed Christian subtext. 이 문장에서 in his rendering 을 우리는 원작에 대한 저자 뜨바르돕스끼 자신의 이해 즉, '그가 소화한 원작'이란 의미로 이해하면 좋겠다. 이렇게 동사 render 는 understand 혹은 interpret와 유사한 의미로 사용된다. 그러나 다음의 예문에서는 to cause to be or become, make의 의미로 쓰였다. 그 차이점을 비교해 보자. In this paper, the author argues that rapid political changes <u>have rendered</u> it necessary to consider models of democracy and citizenship. The following passage is a perfect <u>rendering</u> of the author's distinction.

■ Typically this type **is rendered** inaccessible to the reader through a variety of narrative devices.

- This argument **can be rendered in** more abstract language and separated from transcendental truth claims without damaging its force.
  이같은 논의는 ~ 속에 나타날 수 있다, 담겨져 있을 수 있다.

- Shakespeare's innovation in *Henry V* is to **render** historiography as affective labor, linked to the labor of conception.

to begin / to conclude

- Chapter III **commences with** ~. (= begins with)
  ~한 장면으로 시작되다.

- The story **closes with** a description of a magnificent sunset.
  ~한 장면으로 대단원이 종결된다, 끝난다.

- The story **ends on the note of** optimism which is so characteristic of Chekhov's late plays.
  ~의 메시지를 끝으로 스토리가 끝난다.

- The tale **concludes on a pessimistic note**-in the end he rejects the polarities of the tragic life for a virtual nonexistence on earth.
  이야기는 염세적인, 비관적인 메시지로 끝나고 있다.

- This chapter **concludes with the author's verdict**: "Everyone is guilty."
  이 장은 저자의 ~한 신념으로 끝맺고 있다.

to decode

- These works constitute a good case study for **decoding** for several reasons.

- The word-play effect **is achieved through the decoding** of all these elements.

- The artistic significance of all of Gogol's dream sequences **is enhanced by decoding** the symbolism of their settings, events, and characters.

- The narrator **decodes** the message that may lie hidden.
  ~의 코드를 풀다, 풀어가다.

동사 decode와 같은 의미로 decipher(암호, 수수께끼를 풀다) 역시 자주 쓰인다. 다음 예문과 비교해 보자. Stalin's presence <u>is coded for</u> obvious political and artistic reasons.

기타

- The term "human nature" generally **connotes** stable biological and psychological traits beyond social control.
  동사 connote는 to signify or suggest (certain meanings, ideas, etc) in addition to the explicit or primary meaning을 의미한다.

- It now **proceeds** to its comic **climax in** the scene in which ~.   ~에서 절정에 이른다.

- The influence of ~ **is most noticeable in** the description of the event.
  ~에서 가장 눈에 띈다, 가장 뚜렷하다.

- The meaning **is apparent** from the very opening lines; **it is described in** minute detail.
  ~이 뚜렷하다, ~한 방식으로 묘사되어 있다.

- As my work progressed it **became apparent** that ~.

- Ivanov **exhibits** the characteristics of key figures in the literature of this period.

- For each character, we(the reader) learn **in meticulous detail** his age, his height, the color of his hair, and even even in many cases the color of his eyes.
  매우 자세한 세부 묘사를 통해

- His **views are conveyed** for the most part in a series of aphoristic statements.
  견해가 드러난다, 입장이 전달된다.

- The apocalyptic dimension **is exploited by** the poet in a macabre way ~.
  ~에 의해서 이용, 사용되다.

- Physical description gives one **clue as to** how the characterization of Lara in *Doctor Zhivago* moves beyond national epic patterns.   ~에 대한 단서를 제공하다.

- The author **lays the groundwork for** a major component of its imagery.
  ~의 기반, 토대를 마련하다.

- Iurii Tynianov **laid much of the theoretical basis of** Formalism.

- The theme of the indifference to nature is also **met with** in the story *The Hope*.
  ~이 ~에서 목격된다, 나타난다.
  '신속한, 즉각적인 반응, 논평을 받다, 얻다'란 뜻을 나타낼 때 be met with를 자주 사용한다. 다음 예문을 통해 잘 알아 두자. William's own articles and his views of ~ <u>met with</u> immediate response. 또는 The *Annales* school left its most controversial imprint and <u>met with</u> the most opposition abroad (가장 논쟁적인 흔적, 인상을 남겨 놓았고 가장 강한 반대에 직면하였다).

- The unity of structure in Part II **is** thus **given by** the repetition of the contrast of ~.

- This short passage **tells the reader** more about the ~ than it appears to do on the surface.

- This description of ~ **sums up** the meaning of the whole story.
  sum up은 '~을 정리, 요약하다'란 의미로 '~을 잘 표현해 준다'로 확대 해석할 수 있다.

- The significance of this motif **is confirmed by** ~.

- The final chapter **implies** a connection between ~ and ~.
  동사 imply는 '의미, 암시, 제시하다'는 의미이다.

- The opening section of *What is to be done* **reveals** the general tone of the novel.
  ~을 드러내 보이다, 보여 주다.

- But the most important stylistic jolt **is delivered by** the changed rhyme structure.
  ~을 통해서 나타나다, ~에 의해서 전달된다.

- **Such an underlying** concrete situation or setting **can be uncovered**(**or deciphered**) in the poem "The Poet."

- The epigraph from a playwright, therefore, **projects a theme** which is central to the novel.
  ~한 주제를 드러내다, 나타내다.

- Dostoevsky **took up the theme of** guilt and redemption in *Crime and Punishment*.
  ~한 주제를 다루다, 선택하다.

- The title, *The Cave*, **poses** the central metaphor which extends throughout the story and transforms ~ into a ~.
  ~한 의미를 획득하다, 지니다, 갖다.

- Explaining such divergence **poses** a momentous task for social science, and many analysts have taken up the challenge ~.

- Bakhtin's monograph does not **take up** this question.
  take up은 '~한 주제를 선택하다'란 뜻으로 deal with, tackle, treat 등과 같은 의미로 많이 사용된다. 다음 문장과 비교해 보자. From this vintage point, the paradoxes in American public opinion <u>take on</u> a different cast.

- Gogol **goes to some lengths** to establish his character's dignity.
  숙어 go to some lengths (~ all lengths, great lengths)는 '~을 철저하게 다루다'란 의미이다.

- It **bears the imprint of** Western tradition. ~의 흔적, 인상을 풍기다.

- The street **bore the imprint of** aggressive assertion, then, it was the space left over after people asserted their rights and powers.

- Adamovich is a character in the novel who **partakes of** the sexuality.
  partake는 특히 문학 논문에서 자주 쓰이는 동사로서 '~의 기미를 띠다, ~한 성격을 갖다'(to have the nature or character)란 의미이다.

- Sholokhov **gives a sad picture of** a man in a period of physical and spiritual dislocation of war and revolution.
  다분히 시적인 표현으로서, '~한 내용을 펼쳐 보인다, 묘사한다' 정도로 이해하면 좋을 듯 싶다.

- The play has **bequeathed to** the Russian culture a number of archetypes: ~.
  ~에 ~을 넘겨 주다, 후세에 전하다.

- The motif of trees **recurs** frequently in Chekhov's plays.
  동사 recur는 '~이 자주 반복된다, 반복되어 나타난다'는 의미이다. 형용사는 recurrent이며 알아 두면 매우 유용하게 쓸 수 있다 (<u>recurrent</u> motifs in Tolstoy's works). Recurrent와 비슷한 의미로 '변함없이, 끊임없이, 영속적으로'란 표현을 원할 때는 persistent가 유용하다. 다음의 예를 참고하자. It is thus natural that ~ also <u>serves as a persistent theme</u> through much of Russian literature. 또는 That women virtually everywhere play a subordinate role is a <u>recurrent</u> implicit or explicit assumption in anthropological literature.

■ This primary concern with the upper classes **recurs** in Febvre's later works in his study of ~ and especially in his great works on ~.

■ The satirical short story **traces** the fate of the main hero. ~을 추적하다, 치밀하게 다루다.

■ The novel's title *War and Peace*, in this context, has a more **inclusive meaning** of rites of passage.
inclusive는 포괄적, 종합적(including everything, comprehensive)이라는 의미이다.
My goal is to be <u>inclusive</u> in thinking about information and privacy so that we don't leave out of our definition important ways human information can be used.

■ Pasternak appears to have **attached great importance to** his *Doctor Zhivago*: it is alluded to twice in the course of the novel.
'~에 특별한 중요성을 부여하다' 혹은 '~을 특히 강조하다'로 보면 좋을 것이다.

■ He **adapted** an archetypal folklore figure **to** his own original purposes by giving him the moral attributes which he most cherished.
~에 ~을 가미하다, 부여하다.

■ In addition to the dense literary aura, both author **lace** his prose **with** references to other arts.
lace A with B는 'A를 B와 엮다'란 의미로 이 문장에서는 '자신의 산문을 다른 예술에다 연관짓고 있다'로 보면 좋겠다.

■ Belyi **throw** some **light on** the novel's philosophical significance.
~에 조명을 비추다. 즉, ~을 강조하다, ~에 ~한 분위기, 색채를 부여하다.

■ In this respect, ~ fully **corresponds to** the ~. 부합, 조응, 일치한다.
이 동사와 유사한 의미로 쓰이는 다른 예를 들면 다음과 같다.
Bogodul in many ways <u>fits the patterns of</u> the God's fool.

■ But the ending of the story **adds** a new note, quite unlike all that has gone before.
~을 부여하다, 더하다, 추가하다.

■ Chekhov's short stories **bear** throughout **the traits of** literary impressionism.
~의 흔적을 갖고 있다, 보유한다.

■ The portrayal of Smerdiakov has its own **significant overtones**.
overtone은 implicit meaning or quality 즉, '함축적이거나 암시적인 의미'로 문학 논문에서 매우 빈번하게 사용되는 단어이다. 따라서 have overtones는 '~의미심장한 암시를 지닌다'로 보면 된다. 비슷한 예로, take on symbolic overtones는 '상징적인 암시를 내포한다', 혹은 의역하여 달리 표현하면 '상징적 색채를 띤다'가 어울리는 해석이다.

■ The passage **has strong overtones** of an act of his religious fanaticism.
이 인용구는 ~에 대한 강한 암시를 띠고 있다.

■ The author **holds** extraordinary opposing **views of** nature.
~한 견해를 가지다.

■ It can **be explained in** terms of the common Leskovian heritage.
~한 입장에서 설명될 수 있다.

■ The backbone of women's fiction before 1880 had been a narrative that might **be termed for convenience's sake** the "escape plot": it depicted an exceptional women who managed to break out of her provincial fastness and elude the cultural imperative of marriage.
여기에서 for convenience's sake는 '편의상, 그냥 쉽게 말해서'란 뜻이다.

■ His reaction **is cast in the** rhetoric of Tolstoyan argumentation that ~.
~에 나타나 있다, 비추어진다.

■ Something similar may **be observed in** connection with ~.

■ This view may **be found in** the works of Tolstoy.

■ The clearest proof of ~ **is found in** the fact that ~.

■ These examples **are observable** elsewhere in the novel. 도처에서 발견된다.

■ Yermakov **gives a unique reading of the story** in Freudian terms as a castration fantasy.
독특한 해석, 이해를 보여 준다.

- Mulvey's essays **gave fresh impetus to the debate about** the male gaze and voyeurism, power and subordination.

  ~의 에세이가 ~에 대한 토론에 신선한 자극제를 부여했다, 즉 ~로 인해서 연구의 신선한 바람을 불러일으켰다.

  이와 유사한 표현으로 다음의 예문도 알아 두자. Lacan's ideas opened up the field for ~ . (라깡의 생각은 ~에 대한 분야 여지를 열어 놓았다.)

- The structure could best **be described as** ~. 기술되다, 설명되다.

- It can be significantly **deduced from** a scene. ~로부터 유추하다.

- **Further evidence** to support this view could **be adduced from** the passage of the novel.

  '~로부터 예증된다, 찾아볼 수 있다'란 의미. 반대로 '~에 대한 증거가 없다'는 표현은 다음을 참고하자. Apart from this, there is no evidence as to who actually titled the poem.

- Similar examples **are** readily **adduced from** Dostoevsky's other works.

- From this it might **be deduced** that ~. ~로부터 ~을 유추할 수 있다.

- Much of it undoubtedly **came from** ~. 상당 부분은 필시 ~에서 비롯되었다.

- The poet's conflict with his society can **be ascribed to** his inspiration, given that he is a docile citizen.

  본래, 동사 ascribe to는 '원인, 동기, 기원 등을 ~ 탓으로 돌리다'란 뜻이다. 이 문장은 수동태로 쓰여졌기 때문에 즉, '~의 원인은 ~에서 기인한다'로 이해하는 것이 자연스럽겠다.

- The theological debate, which **is carried on** throughout the whole novel, has been suggested among numerous scholars.

  '~을 통해서 견지되어 온, 전달되는'이란 의미. 다음의 문장과 비교해 보라. Figurative expressions carry more weight than they do in everyday language. 여기에서 carry는 '비중, 무게감을 갖는다, 전달한다'는 의미로 take, hold와 유사한 의미를 보여 주고 있다. 동사 hold는 이외에도 '~한 견해를 지니다 hold the view that ~' 혹은 '~한 모델, 대표적인 예로 정착, 받아들여지다'란 의미로도 쓰여진다. 다음의 문장을 확인해 보자. Free love was held up as the model of the progressive way of life in the 1920s in the Soviet. This view of the history of Chinese Buddhism does not hold up to closer scrutiny.

- This chapter **carries implications for** the novel's moral import.

  ~에 대한 함축적인 의미를 담고 있는, 전달하고 있는

- In Canada, the abrupt fiscal swings of the 1990s **had important implications for** the dynamics of health care policymaking.

- This may in part **be due to** its ~. 이것의 일부는 ~ 때문에
  due to가 들어간 문장과 '~때문에'란 뜻의 다른 표현도 같이 알아 두자.
  At first sight, this cleavage in space appears to be <u>due to</u> the opposition between an inhabited and organized territory and the unknown space. 한편 "by virtue of," "owing to" 역시 마찬가지 표현이다. <u>By virtue of</u> its geographical size and vital resource provisioning, Russia looms largest. <u>Owing to</u> the status of research universities as flagship institutions, their leaders are frequently called on to speak for higher education as a whole.

- **There can be little doubt that** ~. 의심할 나위가 하나도 없다, 거의 없다.

- The more recent studies of congressional voters **leave no doubt that** ~.

- A similar presence of submerged Biblical motifs has **been detected** in the story of *The Bishop*.
  여기에서 submerged는 '숨겨진, 감추어진'이란 뜻이다. 동사 detect는 흔히 '무엇인가를 찾다'인데, 주로 수동태로 쓰여 '발견된다' 혹은 '찾아진다, 나타난다'란 의미로 사용된다.

- Within this semiotic system, Petersburg **was conceived of** as artificial ~.
  ~로 간주된다, ~로 이해된다.

- Although the author **conceives of** Pasternak's texts as cryptograms hiding and displacing their own semantic coherence, these ciphers turn out to be suspiciously accessible to a methodical unraveling.

- The ambivalent attitude toward Peter and Petersburg is further **underlined in** ~.
  ~ 강조된다.
  '강조하다'란 의미로 많이 쓰이는 또 다른 동사는 enhance, underscore, reinforce, intensify 가 있다. 주로 수동태로 사용되어 ~ is further enhanced by ~ 등으로 표현된다. 예를 들어, The syntactic ambiguity <u>is intensified by</u> the typographic devices. 혹은 The realistic setting <u>is reinforced by</u> the meticulous accumulation of details of everyday life.

- All of these figures **are emphasized by** contrasting ~.
  ~에 의해서 강조된다.

■ This **is emphasized** from the very first paragraph.

■ The descriptions are repeatedly **stressed by** the author.　재차 강조된다.

■ Vincent **lays heavy emphasis on** ~.　~을 매우 강조하다.
'~을 강조하다'라는 숙어로는 lay stress on이 있다. 이때 동사는 place를 써도 무방하다.
Feminist sociologists have, therefore, very firmly placed the discussion of women and
gender on the sociological agenda. 혹은 The work ethic placed emphasis on the virtue of
work.

■ The love-making scene is further metonymically **elaborated** in the next ~.
상세히 부연되고 있다.

■ The candle image **is fully developed** later in *Doctor Zhivago*, where it becomes a
metaphor of ~.
~이 아주 정교하고 충분히 전개되어 잘 나타나 있다.

■ ~, which is the **figurative expression** of his ultimate recovery.
비유적인 표현

■ In this chapter, there is a poetic **articulation**.
'명확한 표현'이란 뜻으로 작품 분석을 다루는 논문에서 빈번하게 나오는 단어이다.

■ Kelly's work **is governed by** a new dominant.

■ The irony of this passage **is occasioned by** the events which ~.
~에 의해서 야기되다, ~로부터 생겨나다.

■ Many features of oral narration **are retained** throughout the story.
~을 통해서 유지된다, 관류한다.
사전적인 의미에서 동사 retain은 to continue to use, to continue to have or hold를 뜻한다.

■ The novel **retains** some of the mythic, ritualistic elements of this imagery.

■ Most studies of policy-making have **retained** a national bias, and this is true even in
the case of comparative studies.

■ Even more **remarkable** is the treatment of ~.　~보다 뚜렷한 예는 ~이다.

- Even more **conspicuous** than ~, however, is ~.

- **Of particular significance is** ~. 특별히 의미심장한 것은 ~이다.

- Such considerations are **of particular importance** to the South-East Asian region for two main reasons.

- **It is much more significant that** ~. ~은 한층 더 의미 있는

- Thus **it becomes apparent that** ~. ~이 점점 뚜렷해진다.

- This **is** especially **true of** something.
  be true of는 뒤에 딸려오는 명사가 '맞다, 사실이다, 그렇다, 참으로 그러하다'란 뜻으로 사용된다. 따라서 the same is true of A라는 문장은 'A도 마찬가지다'로 해석하면 된다.

- **As important as** death itself **is** ~. ~만큼이나 ~한 것은 ~ 이다.

- Many more instances **might be enumerated** (=listed) here: ~.
  빈번한 예를 처음으로 들고 난 후 그 밖의 무수한 예를 더 들 수 있다. 즉, 많은 예가 있다는 표현이다. 이것 말고도, The list of those examples <u>can be listed here</u>도 무난한 문장이다. 혹은 Further, such connections may <u>be drawn</u>. Many other examples could <u>be cited</u>.

- This metaphorical relationship between the ~ and ~ **underlies** the whole of *Anna Karenina.* ~의 기초가 된다.

- Zhukovsky's epithet **laid the foundation for** the vocabulary of Russian romantic poetry.
  ~의 기초를 놓다, 마련하다.
  유사한 표현으로 다음 예문을 참고해 보자. In its thicker form, this kind of analysis readily <u>forms the basis for</u> arguing that ~.

- Much of Gogol's writing **is grounded in** what Bakhtin calls "the culture of folk humor."
  위의 문장과 유사한 표현이지만 수동태가 사용된 것으로 '~에 기반하다, 뿌리를 두고 있다'로 해석하면 가장 적합하다. The use of multiple strategies <u>grounded in a theory</u> of behavior change is critical. Much of what follows <u>is grounded on</u> Angus Taylor's *Magpies, Monkeys and Morals* (1999). Scientific urban animal ecology is <u>grounded in</u>

instrumental rationality and oriented toward environmental control. The theory has been criticized on several grounds. 또는 This theory <u>is grounded in the idea of</u> progress, which holds it as axiomatic that ~.

■ The mission of a comprehensive community college **is grounded in** the commitment to give the opportunity to pursue higher education to all citizens who ~.

■ Pomerantsev's concept came to **set the tone for** most of Soviet literary criticism in the late 1940s. ~에 초석을 만들어 놓다, 기반을 이루다.

■ The ambivalence which **is incorporated into** the character's name.
작중인물의 이름은 많은 경우에 작가 자신이 의도적으로 숨겨놓은 깊은 뜻이 있기 마련이다. 이때 이런 뜻을 표현하기에 동사 incorporate는 아주 고급하면서도 유용한 단어이다.

■ Such moments **are purposefully incorporated into** the communicative act of dialogue.
~ 속에 의도적으로, 은밀하게 삽입되어 있다.

■ The character's name **betrays** his nature.
작중인물의 이름이 ~한 성격을 드러내 보이게 이용될 때 쓰는 말이다. 동사 betray가 들어간 다른 문장을 예로 들어 보자. Russian Futurism <u>betrays</u> a desire for the presence and totality of meaning which remains visible in its gestures of denial and negativity.

■ The opening lines of Pushkin's poem **reverberate** in Briusov's title: ~.
동사 reverberate는 본래 '반향되다'란 뜻이지만 문맥으로 보면 '재등장한다' 혹은 '상기된다'라는 뜻으로 해석이 모두 가능하다. 선대의 한 작가의 작품 혹은 유명한 구절이 후대의 다른 작가의 작품에서 그대로 사용되거나 유사한 느낌을 야기시킬 때를 일컫는다. 이와 비슷한 예로 가령 '~에서/~로부터 작가의 상당 부분 ~이 발견된다 즉, 전기적 요소라든가, 아니면 작가 생애의 실제 ~와 같은 많은 것들이 발견된다'고 하는 내용을 표현하고자 하면 다음의 예문을 참고하자.
In St. George, there is doubtless <u>much of</u> Zhivago <u>himself</u>.

■ The hunting scene is **a classical illustration of** what ~. ~의 전형적인, 고전적인 예이다.

■ ~, **characteristic of** the poetics of folklore. ~에 특징적인

■ Narrative poetry is essentially a form **characteristic of** the oral phase of literature.

■ It **is characteristic of** Cornwell to investigate ~.
~에게서 나타나는 특징 즉, ~은 ~의 특징이다.

■ The widespread use of metaphors **was** also **characteristic of** other Polish Futurists.
이때 '두드러지다'란 의미를 넣고 싶을 때 가장 많이 쓰이는 말은 형용사 salient가 있다.
즉, one of the <u>salient characteristics of</u> <u>Gogol</u>

■ The following is an outline of the main **characteristics of** the theory of interactive vision, as proposed by William and Robert: ~.

■ Philosophers **have some characteristic ways of** helping us forget that their notions of ethical improvement must themselves be drawn from human experience.
~하는 특징을 지니고 있다.

■ The tourism industry **is characterized by** further divisions between the workers themselves, notably in the form of gender and race.
~에 의해서 특징적이다 즉, ~은 ~가 특징이다.

■ There exist various branches of science **characterized by** scientific theories that are on the same level.

■ It **is typical of** Chekhov's characters to yearn for a new life and for a happier future.

■ Shamanic religions **are typical of** simple horticultural populations of hunter-gathers.

■ The narrative has some traits that are **peculiarly** Gogolian.
작가 고골 특유의 독특한 특징을 지닌

■ By the late nineteenth century, the demographics **peculiar to** international expositions had given rise to a class of petty entrepreneurs.

■ **No** discovery could be **more** Gogolian **than** that of the uncanny tendency of domestic places and prosaic passages to harbor aliens.
직역하면 '~보다도 더 고골 같은 것이 발견되지 않는다'이다. 즉, 이 문장은 '~한 점에 있어서 작가 고골의 가장 특징적인 면이 발견된다'란 의미이다. 이처럼 영어 문장에는 강조를 위해 부정어 구를 문두에 위치시켜 쓰는 표현이 많이 있으니 익숙할 정도로 실제 논문 작성에 많이 사용하면 좋겠다.

■ Russian language **possesses some features** exclusively its own.
~한 특징을 갖다, 소유하다.

■ Karmazinov **has been given certain of** Turgenev's physical and moral **characteristics**: ~.
어떤 인물의 형상 속에 비춰진 다른 인물의 확실한 특징적인 요소를 말할 때 자주 쓰이는 표현이다. 이와 유사한 표현으로 Karmazinov is presented as trying to ~.는 '까르마지노프란 인물이 ~하는 인물로 그려지고 있다'는 의미이다.

■ ~ **arise** a lyrical response, as if they are part of a life.
동사 arise는 말 그대로 '나타나다' 혹은 '생기다, 일어나다'란 뜻으로 '서정적 감흥이 생겨난다'로 보면 좋을 듯하다. 마찬가지로 '~을 불러일으키다', '초래하다'는 의미를 표현하고자 할 때는 bring about 혹은 cause를 사용하면 무난하다.

■ This **requires** some explanation, since ~. ~은 설명을 필요로 한다.
유사한 의미의 문장을 알아보자. The idea that ~ needs some explanation for those who are unfamiliar with ~ (~에 친숙하지 않은(잘 모르는) 자들을 위해 ~은 설명이 필요하다).

■ *The Possessed* **invites a reading** on several levels of understanding.
어떤 작품이 '다각적인 이해의 수준을 요구한다'는 의미, 혹은 '~의 작품 이해를 위해서는 다각적인 측면이 요망된다'는 의미이다. 유사한 의미의 문장을 하나 더 알아보자. In the short story, we are invited to accept, as the characters themselves unquestionably do, a set of totally absurd situations as real ones. 또는 At first glance, the image invites a sexual interpretation.
위 예문에서와 같이 '~을 요구, 요청하다'의 개념으로 call for가 매우 많이 쓰인다. In the period with which we are concerned, three of the activities of the Church call for special notice: first, ~ (call for: 각별한 주의를 요구한다)

■ Many of the other characters in the novel **have prototypes in real life.**
이같은 작중인물의 실제 배경이 있는 원형적 인물을 말할 때 사용한다.

■ Romantic aesthetic **makes use of** the concept of "genius."
이 표현과 유사한 것에는 take use of, utilize가 있다.
Akhmadulina's novella makes no use of religious context, and her readers find no reference to any of the churches which figures so prominently in Bykov's film.

■ The author **makes a stab at** extending his analysis to ~. ~을 시도하다.

- At no time does Karlinsky **try to** bring any evidence of ~.

- Area studies and development projects have **exerted** little discernable impact on the enhancement of students.

- The fiscal policy **exerted a strong influence on** equilibrium aggregate production.
  동사 exert는 '~을 끼치다, 행사하다'의 의미로 exhibit과도 호응한다.

- Tylor's views **have an enormous impact on** subsequent schools of religion.

07 기능 / 역할

- The bird imagery **serves to** indicate that ~.

- Such a system **served as** a functional equivalent of bureaucracy.
  동사 serve가 들어간 유사한 문장을 더 살펴보자. 보통 serve는 serve as와 같이 as가 결합되어 자주 쓰인다. In its various embodiments, this symbol may simultaneously serve as a ~.

- ~ **serve as a catalyst for** Ivan's emotional objections. ~을 위한 촉매 역할

- The legacy of the gulag **serves as a linchpin in our understanding of** Stalinism, for the labor camps formed a defining feature of Soviet life until the mid 1950s.
  ~의 이해를 위한 연결고리(꼭 필요한 것 something that holds the various elements of a complicated structure together) 역할을 한다.

- Scientific theories **serve** multiple roles, for explanations, for descriptions, and for predictions.

- Romantic irony **serves as** the main structural/structuring principle in the narrative of *The Queen of Spades*.

- Akhmatova's "Requiem" **serves as** the voice of all the women who waited outside prison walls.

- These two characters **serve as models for** the kind of personal growth the author would like to encourage in his readers.

- At the end of the century, literature in language teaching **served** many causes but it was used mostly as an authentic window on a foreign culture and society, not as the unique expression of an artist's vision of the world.

- Bird imagery **is used to** convey positive attributes.

- The narrative technique of the dream **fulfills** three functions in the nineteenth-century Russian literature.

- These dreams in the novel **fulfill** a dual role.

- Sometimes metaphor **is used to** intensify the expression of a character's emotions.

- The role of God as Spirit **takes on** a much **greater role** than on ~.

- It here **takes on** a very special **function**.

- The theme of "blood" has **played a dominant(an important) role** so far in the novel.
  ~한 역할을 하다.

- Margarita **is cast in** several **roles of** ~.
  연극이나 문학 작품에서 등장인물의 성격이 ~어떠하다, 어떤 역할을 한다고 얘기할 때 동사 cast 의 수동태로 자주 쓰이는 표현이다.

- Stephan casts **himself in the role of** the knight true to his lady.
  ~한 역할로 등장한다, ~한 역할을 맡는다.

- The positive hero inherited from the classical period of Socialist Realism **embodied** a certain set of psychological attributes-spontaneous energy, willpower, stamina, etc.
  동사 embody는 특히 작중인물의 성격을 분석할 때 많이 사용되는 단어이다. 인물의 내면에 대한 성격, 특징이 구현되어 있음을 나타낼 때 이 동사를 쓰며, 위의 예문에서처럼 능동태로 쓰이기도 하며, 수동태로도 많이 쓰인다. 참고로, 작중인물이 어떤 신체적 특징으로 구별되는 즉, '~한 점에서 특징적으로 나타나는 점'을 표현하고자 할 경우엔 동사 identify를 사용하면 무난하다.
  다음 문장을 참고하자.
  - Kuragin in Tolstoy's *War and Peace* is identified by his broad, white shoulders which suggests at most the coldness of his personality.
  - The researcher identifies globalization as a process from which a nation cannotabstain involving the flow of technology, economy, knowledge, people, and ideas across borders.
  - The relation between sociology and economics has been identified as the most complex and problematic of disciplinary differentiations.

뿐만 아니라, embody는 '~한 주제를 구체적으로 표현하다, ~한 이념을 구현하다'의 의미를 포함하기도 한다.

- Kustodiev's characters are archetypal and <u>embody</u> traditional folk conceptions of beauty, wealth, and fertility.
- This drama <u>embodies</u> the author's view of the revolution of 1917.

유사한 의미로 incarnation(육화, 화신)이란 단어를 알아 두자.

This will be the real <u>incarnation</u> of a complex, integrated, systematic approach to the problem of the education, particularly for mastery of this field for medieval China.

■ Parchment, ink, writing, seals, and the like **embody** not just a representation, but also an imagination of a society's culture.

■ Every idea **is embodied in** words, and every word reflects some reality.

■ These two events **contribute to** a more total understanding of Ivan's character.

'~에 공헌하다, 그래서 도움이 된다, 기여한다'의 의미로 널리 쓰이는 동사이다. 같은 의미로 help를 써도 무방하다. 한편, be instrumental to란 표현은 '~에 도움이 되는, 기여되는'이란 뜻으로 contribute과 유사한 의미로 사용된다. 다음의 문장을 통해 그 쓰임새를 알아보자.

An interest in novelty, that driving force of modernity, can <u>be an instrument of</u> renewal, an historical agent (새로운 것에의 관심, 즉 모더니티의 추진력은 역사를 만들어 내는 구심체 이른바 역사 갱생에 도움이 될 수 있다). 또는 Thomas lists eight basic negative emotions <u>instrumental</u> in the shaping of the Japanese attitude toward the world, though he admits the list to be far from exhaustive.

■ Many of Dostoevsky's characters thus **vacillate between** the two spheres of reality and fantasy or ecstasy.

■ The **protagonist** of the novel **is inspired by** the European values of individualism and chivalric honor.

■ The main hero **undergoes** a spiritual transformation.

'~을 경험하다'란 의미를 사용하고자 할 때, 특히 문학 논문에서는 experience보다는 지금과 같이 undergo를 보다 빈번하게 쓰곤 한다. <u>undergo</u> a symbolic death(상징적인 죽음을 경험하다)

■ Futurism **is** seldom **given credit for** its contribution to the development of 20th century Polish poetry.

숙어 give something / someone credit for는 '~을 / 누구를 ~한 것으로 당연히 보다, ~을 누구의 공로로 돌리다'란 의미이다. 따라서 위 문장은 '미래파는 20세기 폴란드 시 발전에 아무런 공헌을 하지 않았다고 받아들여진다' 정도로 이해하면 좋을 듯 싶다. 비슷한 예를 점검해 보자.

• Futurism should also <u>be given credit for</u> the development of free verse. No doubt Karl Marx <u>is credited with</u> being the founder of modern political science. Modernism <u>is credited with</u> the destruction of the traditional city and its older neighborhood culture. The Chicago Fair <u>was credited with</u> stimulating the "City Beautiful" movement which spread nationwide through the organization of local municipal arts societies.

08 중심점 / 초점 / 할애

■ The events **are structured around** ~.

■ A great deal of his poetry **is devoted to** ~.
단순히 직역해서 '~에 바쳐져 있다'는 말로 이해하지 말고, '~을 다루고 있다'로 의역하면 좋을 듯
싶다. 주로 이렇게 수동태로 사용되기도 하지만 다음의 예처럼 능동의 의미를 강조해 이용하는 표
현도 간혹 나타난다. <u>Gorky occupies himself with</u> matters less examined in this novel.(~에
전념하다, 몰입하다, 바치다)

■ The central place of the novel **is devoted to** an account of Douglas.

■ Gorky **devotes** an entire harrowing chapter to a description of the ~.

■ In the discussion of the three poetic modes, the author **devotes the most space to**
intertextual relationships.
말 그대로 '가장 많은 지면을 ~에 대한 설명 혹은 언급에 할애하고 있다'는 의미이다.

■ Hertz **devoted** his analysis to ~, **with only passing comments on** ~.
~에는 지나가는 식의 짧은 평만을 남기면서 ~의 분석에 전념하다, ~에 초점을 기울이다.

■ The story **is concerned with** the inner world of the main character.
'~을 다루다, ~에 주로 관심을 쏟다'란 의미로 be devoted to와 같은 의미로 자주 쓰인다.

■ The narrator **is oriented to** the natural harmony of peasant life.

■ The text **affords** much evidence to show that ~.
동사 afford는 give와 거의 같은 뜻으로 사용된다. 위의 문장으로 예를 들면 '~을 보여 주고 있는
증거들을 많이 가지고 있다'로 해석하면 좋을 듯 싶다.

■ **Attention was directed to** the language of folk literature.
~에 초점이 맞추어져 있다.

■ **Much attention is given to** the fate of the main hero.

■ The debate has **centered on** the question of whether ~.
논쟁이 ~을 중심으로
Political observers <u>have long debated whether</u> economic power or military power is more fundamental. (~한지 오랫동안 토론해 왔다) '논쟁/논의'가 들어간 문장을 더 살펴 보자. One of the most <u>heated debates on</u> the Industrial Revolution <u>concerns</u> the standard of living. (~에 대한 가장 열띤 논쟁은). A seemingly <u>compelling argument</u> goes as follows. ~ (외견상 매우 설득력 있는 주장은 다음과 같다)
Political scientist Andrew Moravcsik <u>makes</u> a similar <u>argument</u> that European nations are the only states other than the United States able to "exert global influence across the full spectrum from 'hard' to 'soft' power. (유사한 주장을 펼치다) 반대로 주장이 받아들여지지 않는 경우에는 다음과 같은 예문을 쓴다. This argument has <u>never been accepted by</u> theologians. (이 같은 주장은 신학자들에 의해 단 한 번도 수용된 적이 없었다).

■ The novel **centers on** the figure of Saladin.

■ Over the past decade, a new term has **entered discussions of** men and clothing—the New Man.

■ Smart power **goes to the heart of** the problem of power convention.
~의 중심 속으로 들어가다, 중심이 되다
반면, 주요한 단어를 알아 두자. Economic growth thus becomes the crucial <u>juncture</u> where almost all modern religions, ideologies, and movements meet. (집합 장소, 교착점)

■ The broader economic context **is pivotal** in interpreting the causes and consequences of gender inequality in immigrant labor markets.
여기에서 형용사 pivotal은 of vital or critical importance의 의미이다. 즉, '남녀 불공평의 원인과 결과를 해석함에 있어 광범위한 경제 여건은 매우 중요하다'란 뜻이다. 그러나 pivot around 는 은유적으로 '~을 중심으로 전개되다, 나아가다'를 의미하는 것으로 (revolve around와 동일한 의미로 쓰임) 자주 사용되는 표현이다. Social Security policy discussions often <u>revolve around</u> issues concerning its financial and economic effects.

■ Such is the semantic **core** of Pushkin's lyrical masterpiece, "The Poet."

■ The author **adds a great deal to** the characterization of the protagonist by subtly comparing her to a bird.

09 언급 / 관계 / 관련성

■ The text contains several **allusions to** the ~.
'~에 대한 언급'이란 의미로 reference to와 함께 가장 대표적으로 쓰이는 말이다.

■ There are frequent **references** in *Eugene Onegin* **to** the folkloric elements.

■ There are three specific **references to** ~ in the text: ~.
'~에 대한 언급'이라는 의미로 가장 대표적인 예이다. 동사 refer는 아래의 예에서처럼 수동태, 능동태 모두 고루 사용된다. 동사 state의 명사형 statement를 넣어 make a statement about, regarding ~을 써도 유용한 표현이 된다. 다음의 예를 참고하자. Clark makes a curious statement regarding bilingual writers and their linguistic choices.

■ ~ can be **referred to** as a paradise.

■ ~ **be intimately linked with** ~.
~과 직접적으로 관련되어 있다.

■ The emergence of interdisciplinarity as an explicit problem of knowledge **is linked with** the rise of modernity.
위의 뜻과 유사한 표현으로 be bound with가 있다. This chapter intends to show that in Japan the concept of nature is so intimately bound with the idea of beauty.

■ ~ **be directly, consistently linked to** ~.
~과 직접적으로 관련된다, 항상 ~과 연관된다.

■ Both events **are linked to** each other.

■ In this poem, the poet **is linked to** a prophet.

■ Solomon's scornful grin **is coupled with** ~.
~과 관련되어 있다.

■ Hope **is fairly associated with** the hours of daylight, and despair with darkness.
'~과 관련, 연관된다'란 표현에 거의 따라붙는 부사가 바로 fairly이다. 말 그대로 '언제나, 늘, 변함없이'란 의미로 be associated with란 숙어에 항상 따라다닌다. 이것 외에도 consistently 와 invariably도 자주 쓰인다. They are almost <u>invariably</u> associated with ~. 그리고 이 숙어와 동일한 의미로 사용되면서 많이 쓰이는 표현에 be coupled with와 be aligned to가 있다. 다음의 예문을 참고하자. This approach to his characters <u>is coupled with</u> his method of presenting important events and seemingly irrelevant details together. Gogol's technique of focusing on a single feature or detailed, producing a distorting, unrealistic, caricature effect <u>is closely aligned to</u> folk methods of characterization. As a result of financial openness <u>coupled with</u> computerization, international financial markets have also become much more volatile. 한편, '~에 아주 밀접하게 관련되어 있다'란 뜻으로 유용한 표현은 be wedded to (직역하면, ~와 결혼해 있다)이 있다. Robertson's writings <u>are firmly wedded to</u> a conventional mainstream sociological theory of society as a social system. 한편, 이것과 반대말은 dissociate from이 된다 (It is almost an impossibility to <u>dissociate</u> the writer <u>from</u> his works.).

■ The word **provokes an association with** the Russian word for ~.

■ His name **suggests an association with** ~.

■ Italy **is associated with** youth in the poem.

■ In Western Europe oral literature **is associated** only **with** the poorest and most backward elements in the population.

■ In civilized countries, we are inclined to **associate** literature **with** writing.

■ Evaluating texts is an important activity **associated with** teaching statistics.

■ The passage **has a strong association** which underlines the connection between the ~.
~과의 강력한, 뚜렷한 연관 관계를 갖다.

■ More generally, the postmodernist trend in social theories **has been associated with** a turning-away from the grand theories and metanarratives of modernity, whether of Marxism or liberalism.

■ The motif of mirror **permits association with** the episodes of ~.

위에서 동사 permit은 '~을 하도록 해 주다, 가능케 하다'란 의미로 보는 것이 적절하며, 때문에 '~한 결과로 나아간다, ~을 가능케 한다'의 의미로 사용된다. 같은 뜻으로 allow를 사용하기도 한다. 다음과 비교해 보자.

- The concept of viability at least <u>allows</u> us <u>to</u> explore the extent to which such a variant of democratization may be able to reproduce and defend itself.
- Computers <u>allow</u> collection managers <u>to</u> inventory and describe huge numbers of items and related records.
- A more radical exploration of ~ <u>allows consideration to be given to</u> the possibility that ~.
- Through careful analysis of their contents, however, manuscripts can <u>allow us to approach</u>, at least, the earliest textual versions that lie behind the surviving copies.
- Standard literary approaches have <u>permitted</u> the belief in two antithetical ideas.
- Quantitative social scientific history <u>permits</u> new directions <u>to</u> be taken, new questions to be asked, new methods to be used to answer both new and old questions, and new perspectives to be added that often cannot be obtained in any other fashion.
- This vies <u>led</u> the critic <u>to</u> examine reality of ~.
- As mentioned earlier, empirical data <u>allow</u> analysis of a number of issues that are difficult to deal with in hypothetical studies.

한편, 동사 lend의 쓰임새도 눈여겨보아야 한다. '~한 도움을 주다, 허용하다, 알맞도록 하다, 적합하다 (to adapt [itself or oneself] something; be suitable for)' 등으로 사용되는 이 동사는 때에 따라서 permit, allow와 동일한 의미로 쓰인다. 다음의 예문을 통해 lend의 정확한 뜻을 알아 두자. Our data do not <u>lend</u> much support <u>to</u> the self-selection hypothesis as an explanation of occupational differences. 즉, 이 문장에서 lend는 '~에 적합하지 않다'는 뜻으로 사용되었다. 해석을 하면, '우리가 갖고 있는 데이터는 직업상의 변별성을 설명해 줄 하나의 선택적 가설을 뒷받침하기엔 부족하다'가 된다. The building <u>lends</u> itself <u>to</u> inexpensive remodeling.에서 lend는 '그 건물은 개조 비용이 많이 들지 않는다'로 이해하면 된다.

■ The juxtaposition of these episodes in turn **calls on an association with** the ~.

■ There can be no doubt **as to** the identification of the Master with Bulgakov himself.
~에 대한

■ **Have (particular) relevance to ~.**
~과 특별한 관련을 갖고 있다.

- The first main feature of Japanese literary development with direct relevance to Japanese nation-building is the ~.
  ~과의 직접적인 관계(관련)하에

- The concept of a virtual world (VW) is relevant to the VDS because the same software environment that supports VWs provides support for the participants in a VDS.

- Such conventions pertain to the kind of instruments used, the process measures that seem most germane to assessing adult-child interactions, and the need for direct observations of children's behavior toward peers and adults.

- Sociologists have made a wide variety of typologies pertaining to the organization of religious activity.

- The following list is intended to help you start searching for other helpful information pertinent to your needs.

- Something similar may be observed in connection with ~.
  ~과 관련지어

- Another device borrowed from folklore by Gogol is connected more specifically with the influence of vertep.
  ~과 연관되다.

- The nature of kinship is very much connected to the type of economy.

- In conjunction with this universal picture of the bestial devil in Western art, literature, and folklore, a curious visual component of the demonic body began to appear during the late Middle Ages.
  '~과 관련된 것으로'란 뜻으로 conjunction은 being associated with의 개념으로 보면 좋다.
  Followers of Karl Marx were especially eager to argue that imperialism was economically motivated because they associated imperialism with the ultimate demise of the capitalist system. (~과 ~을 관련 짓다)

- Aggressive behavior often occurs in conjunction with other antisocial behaviors such as the use of harmful substances, truanting, and stealing.

■ In many regions, university anthropology departments, sometimes **in conjunction with** university museums, conducted large field projects.

■ These are texts which have productively **engaged with** recent literary-critical debates on the ~.

■ **In the** Tolstoyan(Chekhovian, Gogolian) **vein** ~.
~의 풍에서, ~식 스타일로 보면

■ **In a similar(different) vein,** ~.

■ **In a slightly different vein,** ~.

■ **In the same breath,** ~.

10 암시 / 예시 / 예견 / 힌트

- Chapter VII **brings** the first **hint of** the possibility of ~.

- It **contains a hint of** something that is typical of Gogol's writing.

- One of the symbolic **referents** of this image is certainly death.

- This direction is already **intimated** in the first chapter with ~.
  암시, 예견되어 있다.

- The scene **is** directly **prefigured by** the opening line of the novel ~.
  ~에 의해서 직접적으로 암시, 예견되어 있다.

- This reversal of roles **presages** Ivan's fate.
  ~의 예견

- The event **foreboded** his destiny.
  예시, 전조가 되다.

- There is a passage that **foreshadows** ~.

- The motif of the mirror in the street **was foreshadowed** at the very beginning.

- The description also functions as **foreshadowing**; ~.

- The opening paragraph of the novel is **a foretaste of what is to come.**
  다음에 나타날 내용의 예견

- The theme of death moreover has been **anticipated** in ~.

동사 anticipate는 '~을 예견하다'란 대표적인 단어이다. 즉, ~이전에 선행하는 것이 다음에 올 것을 예견하고 준비하게 하는 것을 말한다.

■ **Implied** in this statement are two notions ~: first, ~, and second, ~.
~이 함축된, 내포된

■ The narrator of *The Petty Demon* **makes explicit statements about** Peredonov's delusions.
~에 대한 명백한 설명을 가하다.

■ There are also some **hints**, which might be interpreted as suggesting the possibility of ~.
또 다른 해석의 가능성을 제시하고 있는 힌트

11 환기 / 상기 / 연상

■ Birds by and large **conjure up** the image of freedom.
동사 conjure up은 '~을 생각나게 한다, 연상시킨다'는 의미의 고급한 표현으로 문학 작품을 대상으로 하는 논문에서 빈번하게 쓰인다.

■ Burning candle is one of **the symbolical centers of** meaning around which *Doctor Zhivago* is constructed.
symbol이 들어간 문장을 하나 더 들어 보자. The song's old clock is <u>a symbol for</u> the traditions and values which the main protagonist cherishes.

■ This image **is evoked** twice with reference to the author.
~이 환기되어 있다.
동사 evoke는 사전적인 풀이로 볼 때, to suggest through artistry and imagination, to call up or produce memories, feelings란 의미를 지닌다. Structures and spaces <u>evoke</u> not just their designers, but all those who bring the built environment into being. 참고로, invoke는 '마음에 떠오르게 하다,' 또는 '사고 등을 야기시키다, 불러일으키다'란 뜻으로 쓰인다.
Most growth accounting implicitly <u>invokes</u> a number of restrictive assumptions.

■ The narrative images **are evoked** within a complex network of complementary, symbolic, and abstract gestures and movements.

■ **~ is (an) evocative of ~.** ~은 ~에 대한 환기

■ A smell of pine-one of the sadly **evocative images of** decay in Chekhov's work.

■ The final scene in which both characters meet **evoke the idea of** life ~.
동사 형태로도 많이 쓰이는데, 이런 경우 '~을 환기시키다, 불러일으키다'란 의미로 이해하면 좋을 듯하고, 때로는 bring about의 의미를 내포하기도 한다.

- Chekhov employs this method in order to **evoke** a feeling of immediate experiences in the reader.

- These lines **evoke** the ambiguous registers associated with the relationship between clothing and bodies.

- The second part of the novel is dominated by **evocations of** vulgarity and banality.

- Matryona **recalls** the Russian **for** mother.
  A recall B for C는 'A는 B에게 C를 상기시킨다, 생각나게 한다'는 의미이며, 동의어엔 conjure up이란 표현이 있다. The passage in which the two characters encounter <u>conjures up</u> their fate to come. 유사한 표현으로 put somebody in mind of가 있다. 즉, The phrase <u>puts us in mind of</u> Luke's songs, which are beeweed by tears.

- Gogol's troika, **calling forth** the apocalypse and motioning for other nations to stand aside, is not representative of Stolypin's Russia.
  위의 예에서처럼 이 역시 '~을 환기시키다, 야기시키다, 생각나게 하다'의 의미이다.

- The phrase "slanting rays of the setting sun" **calls forth** various associations with pivotal scenes in many of Dostoevsky's tales and novels.

- The image of the forest **resonates with** both everyday and folkloric motifs.
  '~이 반향되다, 상기되다'란 의미로 자주 쓰이는 표현이며, 특히 시 장르를 논하는 논문에서 자주 발견된다.

- It should be clear that the view I am criticizing here **resonates** in the conceptions offered by Smith discussed above.

- Marx and Engeles's dictum that "the working men have no country" **resonated deeply with** one part of the union's experience.

- There are obvious **echoes** of the relationship between ~.
  말 그대로 '울림, 반향'이란 뜻으로 '~을 상기시키는 (매개체, 혹은 그 대상)'의 의미이다. 동의어에는 resound (~ with)가 있다.
  The brass motif <u>resounds with</u> the arrival and the departure of the boat.

- There are numerous **echoes of** *Eugene Onegin* in *A Hero of Our Time* which attest to the fact that they are interrelated.

■ In many ways, moreover, Akhmatova's poem constitutes a contemporary compressed echo of Pushkin's text in terms of content and idea.

■ It also strongly echoes the description of the ~.

■ The sense of male-female as an oscillation of sexual energy is echoed in peasant designs.
~ 속에 반향되어 있다.

■ The secrecy paradigm echoes throughout American law as well.

■ In many ways, *The Bishop* reminds the reader of Turgenev's ~: ~.
'~을 상기시켜 주다'란 의미로 아주 많이 쓰이는 표현이다.

■ Remizov's sentences are reminiscent of the common Leskovian heritage.
형용사 reminiscent는 '~을 상기, 회상하는'이란 뜻으로 위의 문장은 '레미조프의 문장들은 레스코프의 [언어상의] 유산을 떠올리게 해 준다'로 의역하면 좋겠다. 다음과 같은 예를 추가로 알아 두자.
Sokolov's corset image is reminiscent of that evoked by Karolina Pavlova in her novel.

■ Margarita is strongly reminiscent of Solovyov's all-embracing feminine principle.

■ Brodsky's statement here is strikingly reminiscent of one of Nabokov's which appeared in his 1970 interview with the journal *Vremia*.

■ Akhmatova's lyrical persona is reminiscent of the strong woman character of the nineteenth-century novel.

■ The image of the woman in her icy coffin brings to mind sleeping princesses in fairy tales.

■ This is itself emblematic of ~.
~의 표상이다.

■ The outer world is a metaphor for the inner.

- These phrases "green ears" become a fixed epithet and even **stand as synecdoche for** Apollon.

  synecdoche는 일명 제유법으로 일부로써 전체를 표현하는 비유법(a figure in which a part is used for the whole or the whole for a part, the special for the general or the general for the special) 가운데 하나이다. metaphor for의 경우에서처럼 '~에 대한 표현'이란 의미가 들어가기 때문에 전치사 for를 쓴다는 점 기억해 두자. 다음의 경우도 일반적인 표현이다.

- In this passage, the repetition of green ears <u>creates a stock phrase for</u> the atmosphere of city Petersburg with dank greenness seeping from the rivers.

- The history of Hong Kong's financial institution **is tightly bound up with** the development of the colony as a whole.

- Romance history **is bound up with** the creation of elite lay culture in courts and wealthy households throughout the European Middle Ages.

- Music **is** intimately **bound up with** important events in all our lives.

- The differences in interpretation of the grotesque principle in medieval culture are also undoubtedly **bound up with** the conditions of our materials' origin and existence.

  위의 네 표현은 모두 '~과 밀접한 관계에 있다'란 표현이다.

- In the post-Cold War era, science will **be** increasingly **tied to** the demand for economic innovations

  이 밖에도 '~과 긴밀하게 연관되어 있다'는 뜻으로 같은 뜻으로는 be related to(with)가 있다. 마찬가지로 connection을 이용한 표현도 익혀 두자. <u>In connection with</u> the issue of integration, substantial work has been put into defining what the agreement embraces, and what is no longer applicable. 한편, be related with와 같은 의미로는 dovetail with와 be likened to가 있다. 다음의 문장을 살펴보자. These observations <u>dovetail with</u> a number of studies that compare American reward allocation preferences against those in other countries. 또는 He has <u>been likened to</u> an anatomist of the soul.

- It is symbolically **relevant** that ~.

  ~은 상징적인 면에 있어서 관련있다.

  이 밖에도 비슷한 표현에는 be allied with가 있다. It is worth noting that Petrovich <u>is allied with</u> the image of the tsar Peter I. 반대로, 아무런 관련이 없다는 말은 <u>bear(have) no relation to</u> ~ 즉, The events <u>bear no relation to</u> one another.처럼 사용하면 된다. 혹은 다음 문장과 같은 표현을 알아 두면 좋다. There is no further detail to be added to these facts.

- This concept appears to **be** especially **relevant to** the Asia-Pacific region, which is experiencing immense structural changes.

- This approach **is** broadly **relevant to** society as a whole.

- This theory **has relevance to** reducing adverse child labor.

- Many social theories are based on generative mechanisms that **are** directly **relevant to** the emergence and co-evolution of human network.

- Many foreign area-related programs today at least encourage the study of one or more languages **relevant to** the area of specialization.

12 사용 기법

■ *Resurrection* is, among other things, an interesting **example of the application of such a technique**.
~과 같은 기법이 적용된 흥미 있는 예

■ The **novelty** of Pasternak's **technique** of characterization is to show this private development in the few characters capable of surpassing the roles assigned to them by historical necessity.
어떤 작가가 보여 주는 기법상의 특이점, 획기적인 내용을 언급하는 문장이다. 이럴 때 흔히 technique와 novelty를 많이 사용한다.

■ The word may be regarded as a **metonymy for** ~.
예문은 말 그대로 '~에 대한 환유로 간주될 수 있다'의 의미이다. 이처럼 ~에 대한 은유, 직유, 메타포, 상징 등의 표현을 쓰고자 할 때, 그 대상은 반드시 전치사 for라는 사실을 상기하자.

■ Gorky **employs** the device ~.
흔히 작가가 작품 속에서 사용하고 있는 여러 기법을 논할 때 동사 employ 혹은 exploit를 쓴다.

■ Other devices frequently **employed** by Bulgakov are similes.

■ The basic rhetorical figure **employed** in all these examples is obviously ~.

■ In order to illustrate the moral and spiritual truths, Lermontov **employs** a variety of exotic images.

■ Ian Hacking **employs** the concept of dynamic nominalism to accentuate the interplay between experience and classification.

- We **employ** the analytical tools of comparative politics, focusing mostly on meso-level policy-making.

- The theories and concepts **deployed** in the analysis of markets are male-biased or gender neutral and in need of gendering.

  동사 deploy는 arrange, place, put forward 등의 뜻으로 '~을 전개시키다'로 해석하면 가장 무리가 없을 것이다. 위의 문장에서는 '~ 분석에 사용된, 나타난'이란 의미로 사용되었다. 다음의 예문과 함께 참고해 보자. Cox <u>deploys</u> the concept of historical structure to examine how and why ~.

- Pasternak **relies on** the juxtaposition of apparently disparate ideas.

  ~한 기법에 의존한다, ~을 주로 사용한다.

- In the tradition of Gogol, the author **relies** heavily, largely **upon** ~.

  ~에 의존하다, 기반을 두다.

- Often the leitmotif **is camouflaged** under a form of ~. ~로 위장되어 있다.

- The **black-and-white grouping of** characters.

  '흑백의 뚜렷한 이분법으로 구분된 등장인물군'을 말한다. 이같이 뚜렷한 이분법을 dichotomy라 한다.

- **By means of** a variety of linguistic and structural **devices**, Solzhenitsyn points to ~.

  ~한 기법으로 작가는 ~을 보여 준다, 지적한다.

- This **device** can **be traced to** Gogol. ~ 기법이 ~로부터 연유, 기원한다.

  지금처럼 '~로부터 연유, 기원을 찾을 수 있다'는 표현을 원하고자 할 때는, 이것 외에도 다음의 두 숙어를 참고해 보자. 하나는 hark back to이고, 또 하나는 derive from이다. 후자는 특히, '어떤 단어의 기원이 ~로부터 파생한다'는 의미로 많이 쓰인다. 주로 수동태의 의미로 사용되는 것이 대부분임을 기억해 두자. The Homeric version of men's transformation into pigs is itself probably <u>derived from</u> folklore sources. <u>Derived from</u> all available written sources, her analysis is completely reliable. 혹은 유사한 의미로 evolve from(~로부터 전개, 진화, 발달되다)도 있다. It also <u>evolved from</u> Russian medieval and Classical sources where dreams were used for quite different purposes.

  이 외에도 동사 proceed도 from과 동반하여 같은 의미를 만들어 낸다. Both the *Annales* and the Marxist traditions <u>proceed from</u> the assumption that the realm of conscious human actions. 또는 The monological model of inquiry <u>proceeds from a conception of</u> science which assumes that the logic of scientific inquiry is one for the cultural as well as the

154

natural sciences.(~한 개념에서 비롯된다). 이 밖에도 arise, come into being / existence(생성되다, 나타나다)의 표현을 알아 두자. "Likewise the idea of the family <u>came into being</u> to serve the needs of a newly recognized childhood. Brass bands <u>came into existence</u> in England and Wales in the 1830s as a result of the philanthropic efforts of factory owners to enrich the lives of their work forces.

- The grotesque **has** obvious Romantic **roots**. ~한 기원, 근원을 지니다.

- Both terms **have a long pedigree in** German intellectual history.
  ~에서 오랜 기원 (계보, 족보; lineage, a genealogical record, derivation, history)을 지니다.

- The earliest archeological evidence of the use of musical instruments **dates from** about 3000 BC.

- The tradition **goes back well over** a thousand years.

- The word 'orchestra' **comes from** Greek, and originally meant the place where the Greek chorus sang and danced.

- The **dominating structural device of** his short story lies in the fact that ~.

- Full realization of a dream's satiric potential **is achieved through** decoding all these elements.

- The sound effect of the third stanza **is achieved by** the help of the metaphoric repetition.

- The comic effect **is achieved through** devaluation.
  위의 세 예문에서 나타나듯이 동사 achieve는 주로 수동태로 사용되어 '문학 기법 등이 어떠한 방식으로 획득된다' 즉, '~한 효과가 생겨난다'의 의미로 활용된다. 때문에 문맥상 be created by 와 비슷한 의미를 갖는다. The narrator <u>creates comic effect</u>, mocking tone to the another character's speeches.

- Cost savings in both countries **were achieved through** highly technical changes.

- The transmission of national identity and ideology **is typically achieved through** ~.
  ~은 ~을 통해서 전형적으로 나타난다, 얻어진다, 획득된다.

- **In the figure of** Ivan, Tolstoy **creates a character who** is completely at variance with the traditional ~.

  ~의 형상, 인물을 통해 ~을 창조한다.

  인물의 성격을 얘기할 때, ~한 스타일 혹은 ~의 부류를 표상하다, 대표한다고 할 때, 흔히 stand for를 많이 쓴다. 일례로 Ivan Denisovich <u>stands for</u> all those who ~.

- Pushkin **places** a type of positive and indisputable beauty **in the person(figure) of** the Russian woman, Tat'iana.

- Ivanov **exhibits** the characteristics of key figures in the literature of this period.

  동사 exhibit는 reveal, show, unfold, disclose 등과 동일한 의미로 사용된다. 다음 문장과 비교해 보자. This article looks at student misconceptions <u>exhibited</u> in an evaluation of an instructional software package. 또는 The definition of folklorism as a form of self-cognition of folklore helps to <u>disclose</u> a variety of folklore appearances."

- The apocalyptic dimension **is exploited by** the poet in a macabre way ~.

  ~에 의해서 이용, 사용되다.

- These relationships are the **medium through which the theme** represented by the title is developed.

  작품의 주제가 ~한 관계들을 통해서 즉, 매개가 되어 나타난다.

- Joseph Conrad **handles** the images of the raven and the dove.

  동사 treat와 같이 '~을 다루다, 처리하다'를 뜻하지만 학술적인 논문에서는 되도록 사용을 금하고 대신 deal with 같은 표현을 쓰는 것이 좋다.

- Mallarme's poem **treats the theme of** the poet's inability to create, represented by the allegory of a swan looking in the ice.

- Norman Ingham **treats** the underlying theme of Leskov's works as a satire of political corruption and conspiracy.

- This motif **operates** most strongly at the end of the novel.

  작용한다.

  동사 operate가 들어간 또 다른 예를 들면, There are at least two levels of <u>operation</u> for color and light symbols, one which obtains most noticeably in characterization and mood and another which represents a literary function employed by the author.

- The presentation of these compositions **is effected in such a way that** Arkady and Bazarov are the organizational focus of the novel.
작품 구조, 혹은 기법을 얘기하면서 자주 나타나는 표현이다. '~하는 방식으로 ~한 기법이 효과적으로 나타난다, 이루어진다'는 의미이다.

- The themes of ~ **are presented in such a way as to** carry general reminiscences of *The Bronze Horseman*.

- The description **is done in such a way as to** instill in the reader a feeling of irony toward ~.

- *The Idiot* uses the device of symbolic **foreshadowing**.

- This idea we have already met before **in the mouth of** Myshkin.
작중인물인 ~의 입을 통해서

- The Onegin-type hero **was labeled** the "superfluous man."
~로 불려지다, ~한 타입으로 정착되다.

- Belinsky **was enshrined as** the official creed in the Soviet Union.
~로 기려지다, 모셔지다, 숭앙되다.

- Tat'iana **was elevated to** sainthood.
~로 기려지다, 숭앙되다.

- The play **is devoid of** any moral message.
~이 없는, 결여된

- There is a general **absence of** didacticism.

- There is also a serious **intention behind** the word-play.
이면에 숨겨진 의도

- The epigraph to the novel no doubt is **a microcosm replica of** the ~.
~은 ~의 축소판, 축소된 세계의 복사판, 축소된 세계

13 화법 / 화자 / 서사 기법

■ Essentially, there are three narrative modes **employed** here: ~.
작가가 작품을 통해서 보여 주고 있는 서사 기법을 얘기할 때, 가장 빈번하게 쓰이는 동사가 바로 employ이다. 때에 따라서 이 동사는 사람을 주어로 하여 능동태로도 많이 쓰인다. 예를 들어, Lermontov employs very unique narrative mode in his novel. 물론 use, utilize, take use of를 활용할 수도 있지만 적어도 저자가 아는 한 employ가 가장 많이 쓰인다는 점, 그리고 학술적인 논문에서 특히 애용되고 있다는 점을 알아 두자. 또 다른 예문을 들어 보면, Other devices frequently employed by Bulgakov(불가코프가 빈번하게 사용하고 있는 그 밖의 다른 기법들은 ~). 또 다른 표현에는 Belyi avails himself of much of the complex mythology.가 있다. Contemporary feminism has employed deconstructive strategies in order to destabilize a binary model inscribed in the masculine/feminine dyad.

■ Throughout Gogol's fantastic works, he **draws** much of his imagery **from** the animal kingdom.
~로부터 ~을 이용하다, 끌어오다.

■ **As the story continues**, ~.
'스토리가 전개되면서 ~은 ~하다'를 표현할 때 대표적으로 사용되는 구문이다. 마찬가지의 의미로 as the story unfolds 혹은 as the narrator unfolds his story가 있다.

■ The whole **story develops** on three levels: ~.

■ This **motif develops into** the episode of the poignant sensations experienced by the protagonist.

■ **As the novel moves**, Ivolgin **was displaced to the fringes of the plot**.
'스토리가 전개되면서 차차 ~하다'의 의미이고, 그다음 문장은 '플롯의 가장자리, 주변으로 밀려난다'란 뜻이다. 즉, 소설의 플롯 전개상 비중 있는 인물이 아닌 관계로 갈수록 중심에서 벗어난다는 뜻

■ The entire **story proceeds** under the sign of ~.

■ **In the course of the narration**, we are not aware of the presence of the narrator.
서사가 진행되는 동안 즉, 작품을 읽다 보면

■ **During the course of the novel**, the narrator ~.

■ Natasha **is introduced offstage** in the first chapter, then her portrait is shown in chapter III, and in chapter VIII she finally **appears in person**.
작중인물이 소설에서 어떻게 등장하는지에 대한 아주 구체적인 설명을 하고 있는데, 여기에서 눈여겨볼 것은 등장인물이 흔히 어떤 chapter에서 처음으로, 그리고 실제적으로 몸을 드러낼 때 우리는 이것을 appear in person이라고 하고, 남의 입을 통해서 간접적으로 소개되는 경우는 전자의 예에서처럼 be introduced offstage라고 한다.

■ At the beginning **the reader is given** ~.
문학 작품을 논하는 논문에서 가장 흔하게 볼 수 있는 표현이다. 즉, 작중 화자가 독자에게 자신의 이야기를 들려주는 것을 표현하는 문장으로서, 우리말로 의역하자면 '독자는 ~한 장면을 알게 된다, ~한 장면이 펼쳐진다, ~을 통해서 독자는 ~을 알게 된다' 등이 적절하다. 이와 비슷한 예를 열거하면 다음과 같다. The reader is <u>informed</u> that ~. 또는 The reader is <u>told</u> that ~.

■ **The reader is presented** it all in dramatic detail as the novel opens.
'독자에게 제시된다, 나타난다'란 의미로 독자는 소설이 시작되면서 '~을 알게 된다'란 뜻

■ As this passage shows, the reader **is presented with ample evidence** that ~.

■ **The reader is left** intrigued ~, / **The reader is** initially **left uninformed**.
두 문장 모두 수동태로 사용된 예로서 작품을 읽으면서 '우리는(독자는) ~하게 된다'라는 의미이다. 첫 번째는 '우리는 여전히 어리둥절한 채로 남게 된다,' 또는 '작품은 여전히 풀리지 않는 매력을 갖고 있다'로 의역해 보면 좋을 듯 싶다. 두 번째 문장은 독자에게 정보가 제시되지 않은 것을 말하기 때문에, '우리는 처음부터 알고 있지 못하다' 즉, '화자 혹은 작가가 보여 주지 않는 부분을 우리는 알지 못한다'로 해석하면 좋겠다.

■ In fact, **the reader is not certain** until Sonia's story is narrated at the end of ~.

■ The reader is completely **deprived of information on** ~.

■ The reader **is still mystified by** the ~.

- The narrator **makes** his **reader privy to** information which had previously been withheld.

  privy to는 '~을 은밀하게 알고 있는'이란 뜻이다. 따라서 위 문장은 '독자는 ~한 사실을 은밀하게 알게 된다' 혹은 '화자는 독자에게 ~한 사실, 정보를 은밀하게 제공한다'는 의미

- In a few instances **the narrator makes his presence felt by referring to** the ~.

  '화자가 자신의 존재를 ~에 대한 언급을 통해서 전면으로 드러낸다'란 의미로 '~에 대한 말을 함으로써 화자가 자신의 목소리를 드러낸다'로 이해하면 좋을 것이다.

- The **action begins with** the narrator.

  소설의 줄거리가 화자에 의해서 시작된다.

- The narrator **proceeds to follow** the character's every move as if he were reading his mind.

- The narrator **constructs** the main hero of the novel **as** a Byronic character at the beginning.

- The **narrator** of the story **makes** this connection unmistakably **clear** when he notes that ~.

- The author **is present in the guise of** omniscient interpreter.

  ~로 가장하고, ~인 것처럼 나타나다, 제시하다.

- The events **are** thus **reported to the reader**.

- **The reader is informed of** specific incidents.

- The story **is told from** Anna's **point of view**.

  작품의 화자 혹은 작품이 어떻게 서술되고 있는지를 말할 때 가장 보편적으로 사용되는 예문이다. 즉, '스토리는 작중 화자인 Anna의 시점에서 얘기된다, 전개된다, 펼쳐진다'란 의미

- The story **is told in the first(third) person narrator**.

- The story **is written in the form of** a third-person **narration**.

- The story **is told in terms of** mental reaction to the realities of his situation.

■ The story **is narrated in** the third person from a dog's point of view.

■ The reader knows it from the **omniscient narrator**. 전지적 작가 시점

■ The entire **narrative is presented through the eyes of** one or another of the character narrators.
'~의 눈으로 본, 비춰진 대로 스토리가 전개되는 상황'에 대한 표현으로 아주 많이 쓰인다.

■ The first half of the story in the text **is told in the form of an extended flashback** as Lena explains why ~.
회상의 형태 속에서 서사가 진행된다.

■ The narrative **conveys** the opposition between ~.

■ **Through his narrator** Nelson comments: ~.
위의 예들이 모두 작품이 어떤 화법으로 전개된다는 의미에서 주로 수동태로 쓰이고 있는 반면에 이 예문은 작가가 작중 화자를 통해서 얘기를 하는 상황을 말하고 있다.

■ Step by step, from chapter to chapter, we **learn** to understand that ~.
흔히 논문에서 we 혹은 the reader는 같은 대상을 지칭하는 말이다. 즉, 글을 읽는 사람을 염두에 둔 말투로서 일인칭의 I보다는 더 일반적으로 많이 쓰인다. 그리고 '~을 알게 된다'란 의미를 표현하고자 할 때, 이처럼 동사 learn이나 know, notice (we have noticed that ~.)로 대체해도 좋은 문장이 된다. 참고로 '독자는 ~만을 알 뿐이다,' '~만이 제시되어 ~만을 알 수 있는 것이 고작이다'란 의미를 말하고자 하면 간단히 the reader(we) learn only that ~. 하면 무리가 없을 것이다.

■ Solzhenitsyn commonly **calls up** omniscient **narrator for** the purpose of nature descriptions and certain type of ~.
call up은 말 그대로 '~을 불러내다, 상기시키다'란 뜻으로 이 문장에서는 '전지적 시점의 화자를 이용한다'로 의역하면 좋을 듯 하다.

■ The passage **prepares** us for what is to happen.
'독자에게 ~을 준비시킨다'는 뜻으로 독자는 인용문을 통해서 이후에 벌어질 일에 대해 미리 알게 된다는 뜻으로 이해하면 좋을 것이다.

■ The narrator **puts** these **words into Sonia's mouth**.
'~의 입 속에 화자가 그같은 말을 넣었다'는 말로 작중인물 '~를 통해서 들려주는 화자의 말'로 이해하면 좋겠다.

- Dostoevsky **adopts** a wide range of viewpoints.

- Attention then shifts **from** the problem of whether Makar is a poor civil clerk or not to the idea that ~.

- The narrative **moves(shifts) from the ~ to** ~.
  서사의 초점, 중심이 ~에서 ~로 옮겨지는 상황을 얘기할 때 이렇게 move 혹은 shift 동사를 사용한다.

- **The narrative is** often **interrupted by** lyrical outbursts reflecting the narrator's emotional reaction to the misery he depicts.
  이 말은 소설이 진행되면서 화자의 서술이 간혹 갑작스러운 회상이나, 감정적인 논외의 이야기 등의 삽입으로 줄거리의 큰 흐름이 방해되는 것을 말한다. 흔히 digression이라고도 한다. 다음 예문을 참고하자. Frequent lyrical digressions are the most characteristic feature of Levitov's prose.

- **The narrator's intrusions into the text** are often introduced by the phrase "I remember."
  작품을 분석할 때, 작중 화자 character narrator와 작품의 실제 작가의 목소리를 구분하며, 때로는 이 화자가 작가의 목소리(즉, 작가의 메시지 혹은 하고 싶은 얘기 등을)를 그냥 여과 없이 늘어놓는 경우가 있다. 이 경우 화자의 목소리가 작가의 것과 동일 author narrator하다고 보는데, 위의 예문은 바로 이같은 경우와 혼돈될 수 있으나 엄밀히 말해서 작중 화자와 작가는 언제나 구분하여 작품을 이해하는 것이 일반적이다.

- In this tale, **the intrusion of** the supernatural **into** the real world creates an effect of shock and horror. The reader totally bewildered by the strange events and made unsure how to interpret and respond to the tale.

- **On the surface**, the story is about ~. 표면적으로 볼 때 스토리는 ~에 관한 것이다.

- But this mood is soon **toned down**. ~한 분위기는 이내 잠잠해진다.

- The **changes in the tone of narration** can be interpreted in terms of alternation between the two narrative modes: ~.

- Monologue, dramatically **rendered** in narrated speech. 드라마틱하게 나타난, 표현된

■ This **is accompanied by** the startling shift on the point of view.
~에 의해서 동반되다, 즉 ~가 뒤따르다, 수반되다.

■ The twentieth-century evolution of English as a supranational language **has been accompanied by** significant cultural changes.

■ This episode also **parodies** a Romantic motif whereby corpses visit the living in order to inflict guilt.
~을 패러디하다.

■ The last episode of this story line is Maria's **interior monologue upon** realizing what had really happened in her absence.
~에 대한 내적 독백

■ The motif **harks back to** the circumstances of the original Shakesperean heroine's drowning.
hark back to는 '생각이나 이야기 서술이 ~로 되돌아가다'란 뜻이다. 넓게 해석하면 '~의 기원, 유래가 ~에서 비롯된다'로 이해해도 무방하다. 따라서 result from과도 비슷한 의미를 띠기도 한다. 한편, 이 숙어는 be traced (back) to나 stem from, result from 등의 표현과도 잘 조응한다. 다음 문장과 비교해 보자. A final link to Stalin can be traced through the fact that ~. 즉, '~로 거슬러 올라간다, ~의 기원이 ~에로 소급된다'란 의미까지 내포한다. 그 밖에, The image of wailing wife stems from Musorgsky's opera ~.
'~에 기인한다'란 뜻으로 대표적인 숙어는 be attributed to이다. The contrasts can be largely attributed to various economic and social policies(그같은 모순 혹은 대립들은 다양한 경제, 사회-정치적 정책들에 기인할 수 있다).

14 작품 구조

■ The entire story has been turned into a **mirror-image structure**.

거울-이미지 구조 혹은 거울 구조란 문학 작품에 사용되는 한 서술 방법으로 거울의 반영이라는 특성을 살려 작품을 구성하는 것을 말한다. 예를 들어, 총 6장으로 구성된 소설의 제 1장이 맨 마지막 장과, 제 2장은 5장, 3장은 4장과 내용과 구조가 서로 연결되는 식으로, 마치 거울 앞에 반영시키거나 서로 포개어 놓은 듯이 장을 배열하는 것이 이런 구조에 포함될 수 있다. 뿐만 아니라, 인물 분석에도 이러한 mirroring이 적용되는데, 어느 한 인물의 모든 것 이를테면 성격, 주요 신체적 특징을 거의 꼭 닮은 또 다른 인물을 설정하여 그 인물의 내면을 보다 깊이 있게 드러내 보이는 기법으로 이용되기도 한다. 러시아 문학으로 얘기하면 도스토옙스키나 고골 같은 작품이 이런 구조를 많이 사용한다. 중요한 단어 한 가지를 더 소개하면 foil이 있다. 주방에서 많이 쓰이는 알루미늄 호일이 그것인데, mirroring image처럼 같은 의미로 빈번하게 이용된다. 다음 예문을 참고해 보자.

The characters Bazarov and Puganov, <u>each is a foil to the other</u>.

■ Many of Razumikhin's sentiments exactly **mirror** those of *The Underground Man*.

이 문장과 다음 예문을 비교해 보자.

Svidrigailov, a figure deliberately <u>paralleling</u> that of the main character Raskolnikov ~.

여기에서 패러렐은 서로 다른 두 인물이 평행을 이루듯이, 한 인물의 내부에 상대 인물의 유사한 속성이 들어가 있는 경우를 말한다. 문학 작품 분석에 특히 빈번하게 나오는 개념이니 잘 기억해 두자.

■ **Characters are played off against** each other or are **used as mirror images of each other**.

■ To an extent, this trend has been **mirrored** by the security problems in Eastern Europe.

■ This deteriorating political relationship **was mirrored** in the economic realm.

- The principles of good governance in the developmental state **mirror** those of the People's Action Party.

- Social delusions and epidemics of hysteria contain powerful symbolic messages that **mirror** prevailing beliefs, attitudes, and stereotypes that we should carefully heed.

- The characters **are** realistically **observed**. 작중인물이 사실적으로 그려져 있다.

- Chapter V could **be transposed to** the end.
  '제 5장이 맨 마지막 장으로 옮겨질 수 있다'는 것도 위에서 말한 거울 구조에서 잘 쓰이는 한 예이다.

- Roughly speaking, **the chapters are organized in a pattern of** ~.

- We must consider the text in the light of **several sub-texts embedded** within it.
  동사 embed와 관련된 다음 예문을 참고해 보자.
  Sometimes Grosmann <u>embeds</u> soliloquies into the narrative. 또는 Though survivals of past custom and belief may be <u>embedded</u> in the various genres of lore ~, New Testament episodes <u>embedded</u> into the main narrative and the appearance of Christ in them reflect the influence of Dostoevky's Legend of the Grand Inquisitor.
  Although the government controls policy, culture and values <u>are embedded</u> in civil societies.

- Identity is a consequence of self-consciousness within particular social networks **embedded** within a particular language.

- The whole of *Doctor Zhivago* **is structured on the** "contrapuntal" **principle of** ~.
  ~의 원칙 위에 기초하여 짜여진 ~ 작품이다.

- The novel **is structured on** a symmetrical principle.

- The novel **is structured by** a network of polarizations on many levels.

- **The whole story**, in Lotman's view, **is constructed** not according to the principles of logical speech, but according to the principle of expressive speech.

- We can **consider** *War and Peace* **as constructed of** three parts, each of which demonstrates ~.
  ~로 구성되어, 짜여있는 것으로 이해하다.

- The writer **constructs** an entirely different set of associations around the image of the ice hole.

- The story **is built on** a series of polarities. ~ 위에 구성되어 있다, ~을 기반으로 짜여져 있다.

- *The Nose* **is founded on** contrast.

- The whole story **is marked by** contradictions.
  전체 스토리는 대립에 의해서 특징적으로 드러난다.

- The tale **is marked by** the dominance of narration over description.

- The novel **achieves** a certain symmetry of structure. ~한 구조를 가지고 있다.

- The story **is set** in 1990.
  be set은 '~한 범위, 시대 배경에 설정되어 있다' 혹은 '~을 배경으로 한다'는 의미이다.

- The novel, written in early 1925, **is set in** the Moscow of the immediate past, December, at the height of the NEP period.

- As Gogol **sets the scene**, there is action going on simultaneously at three levels: ~.

- The main hero **is placed at the vortex of** ~. ~의 한 중심에 놓여져 있다.

- The scenes during which Ippolit **attains the central place** ~. 중심 위치를 차지한다.
  동사 attain은 애초에 '~을 이루다, 달성하다'의 의미이다. 다른 예를 알아보자.
  Gogol's artistic vision eventually <u>attained</u> a dynamic blend of the two lines, with the serious being submerged into the comic and serving only to heighten the comic effect.

- The passage time **is indicated by the alternation** of day and night.
  밤낮의 교체로 시간 경과 처리

- The central narrative **covers** just three days.
  소설의 줄거리가 다루고 있는 시간의 범위를 얘기할 때 주로 cover란 동사를 쓴다.

- We can **consider** the novel **as constructed of** three parts, each of which demonstrates a phase of the main character's development.
  ~로 구성된 소설로 이해할 수 있다.

- The plot **hinges on** a series of ~.   ~에 따라 결정되다, 정해지다(to be dependent), ~에 달려 있다

- The question ultimately **hinges on** which of Sokolov's ideas are understood to be parodied.

- The structure of Akhmatova's poem **hinges on** the pattern of balladic poems.

- The main **plot-development** in *The Portrait* **traces** Pozniakov's growing estrangement from both his past life and his projected future.
  플롯의 전개가 ~을 따라 펼쳐진다.

- For most readers the novel **crumbles into** vignettes. But freed from the discipline of plot, these isolated scenes are often brilliant, revealing ~.
  crumble into는 '산산조각이 되어 ~하다'라는 의미

- *Catapult* is a **complex, multi-strata novella** which **presents** a paradoxical contrast between people's images of their own lives and their real form.
  ~한 구조를 보여 주는 복잡한 다층 구조의 노벨라

- Blok's **satire was directed against** ~.
  흔히 풍자가 '~의 공격을 목표로 하고 있다' 혹은 '~에 반대하고 있다'는 의미를 표현하고자 할 때 이런 문장이 많이 쓰인다.

15 삽입구 / 부사구 / 접속사

보다 정확히 말하자면, 구체적으로 말하면,	~, to be exact, ~. ~, more exactly, ~. ~, to put it more concretely, ~. ~, to put it more accurately, ~. To put it bluntly, ~.
저자가 아는 한	As far as I know, ~. To my knowledge, ~.
이미 지적되었듯이, 살펴보았듯이	~, as has been noted earlier(above), ~. ~, as has been mentioned in the previous chapter, ~. ~, as observed(noted) earlier, ~. ~, as was suggested above, ~. ~, as discussed above, ~. ~, Terras tells us, ~. As we have seen, ~. As the author shrewdly observes, ~. * shrewdly 날카롭게, 통찰력 있게
나중에, 이후에 논의되고 있듯이	~, as will be argued later ~. ~, as we shall see later ~.
누가 언급하고, 분석하고, 주장하고, 지적하고 있듯이	As Slonim observes, ~. As Shklovsky points out, ~. ~, as Pusso states, ~. Clark has pointed out, ~. ~, as Thomas Winner has aptly observed, ~. * aptly 적절하게

~, as Victor Terras pointedly, poignantly stated, ~.

* pointedly, poignantly 날카롭게, 매섭게, 신랄하게

~의 표현을 빌자면, ~에 의하면	~ to borrow Nabokov's ironic phrase, ~. ~ to use Klemora's terminology, ~. To speak in Hegelian context, ~. ~, to use Schmid's words, ~. In Nabokov's estimate, ~. According to Lotman, ~. In Uspensky's view, ~. In Parker's understanding, ~. In Pushkin's phrase, ~. In McCullough's paradigm, ~. In the words of Victor Erlich, ~. In Lotman's argument, ~.
좌우간, 여하튼, 하여튼	At all events, ~. In any events, ~. At the very least, ~.
유감스럽게도	Regrettably, ~. Unfortunately, ~. Regretfully, ~.
때때로	Sometimes, ~. Occasionally, ~. On occasion, ~.
자주, 빈번히	Time and again, ~. More often than not, ~.
의미심장하게도, 두드러진 것은	Notably, ~. Significantly, ~. Especially important is ~. Remarkably, ~. / Conspicuously, ~.
결론적으로, 따라서	As a consequence, ~. Consequently, ~. As a result, ~.

	Accordingly, ~.
	Therefore, ~.
	In sum, ~. / Summing up, ~. / In short, ~. / In conclusion, ~.
	Subsequently, ~.
주지하다시피, 알려져 있듯이	As is well known, ~.
표면적으로, 표면상, 언뜻 보기에	Ostensibly, ~.
	On the surface, ~.
	~, on the face of it, ~.
	~, at first sight(= glance), ~.
~이 결코 아닌, 최소한의 ~도 아닌	There is not the least wind today.
	Not the least of these is its mixture of styles.
상당 정도, 상당히 ~할 정도로	~, to some extent~, ~.
	To some extent the theme of the story might be interpreted as a story about ~.
	To a great extent ~.
	~, to a large extent, ~.
	~, to a certain extent, ~. 어느 정도
	To a considerable degree ~.
~을 예외로 하고	With the exception of ~, ~.
	With one single exception, ~.
	Except for ~, there is nothing ~.
어떤 측면에서 보면, 한편으론	For one thing, ~.
	On the one hand, ~.
	On the other hand, ~.
흔히 그렇듯이, ~에서 빈번하게 나타나듯이	~, as happens so often in Chekhov's works, ~.
	As in the case of Russian, ~.
	~, as often happens with Leskov, ~.
	~, as is often the case with Dostoevsky, ~.
	As is frequently the case in Rasputin, there are affinities with other elements of traditional Russian life.
	~, as is also the case with Tolstoy, ~.
	As was the case in most British colonies, ~.

As is common in the 19th century novel, ~.

In common with most Western Europe, tourism-related employment ~.

In common with other contemporary environmental agreements, reservations are specifically not allowed.

As is usual for Gogol's stories, ~.

~, as is typically the case in an East Slavic folkloric context, ~.

이같은 이유에서	For that reason, ~ / For these reasons, ~.

가장 ~한 것은	Most obviously, ~.
	Most importantly, ~.
	Most prominent at the beginning of the story is ~.
	Of special important, ~.
	Of particular value is the ~.

분명히,	Admittedly, ~
확실하게,	No doubt, ~.
의심할 나위 없이	Doubtless, ~.
	Without a doubt, ~.
	Undoubtedly, ~.
	It is needless to say that ~.
	Needless to say, ~.
	Clearly, ~.
	Clearly, there is no question of ~.
	Decidedly, ~.
	Unquestionably, ~.
	Obviously, ~.
	Indisputably, ~.
	Evidently, ~.
	Apparently, ~.
	Certainly, ~.
	Surely, ~.

줄잡아 말하더라도	~, to say the least, ~.

일반적으로,	By and large, ~.
대체로	Generally, ~.
	In general, ~.

	As a rule, ~.
	All in all, ~.
	On the whole, ~.
	Overall, ~.
마찬가지 이유에서	~, by the same token, ~.
아마도, 추측컨대	~, in all probability, ~. (= probably) Possibly, ~. / Supposedly, ~. Presumably, ~.
더욱이, 게다가, 동시에, 마찬가지로	Moreover, ~. In addition, ~. Additionally, ~. Besides, ~. Furthermore, ~. At the same time, ~. Simultaneously, ~. Likewise, ~. Similarly, ~. Analogously, ~.
~임에도 불구하고	Notwithstanding, ~. All the same, ~. In spite of ~. Despite ~. Nonetheless, ~.
반면에 ~은, ~과는 반대로, 대조적으로	While A ~, B ~. / Whereas A ~, B ~. On the contrary, ~. By contrast, ~. In contrast to ~. Conversely, ~.
~라고 하면 충분하다, 간단히 ~라고 해두자.	Suffice it to say that ~. It suffices to say that ~.
즉, 달리 말해서,	~, as it were, ~. Namely, ~.

간단히 말해서	In other words, ~.
	That is to say, ~.
	~, to put it another way, ~.
	~, to put it as briefly as possible, ~.
	To put it differently, ~.
	Put otherwise, ~
	Simply put, ~.
	Or, better put, ~.
	To put the point another way, ~.
	To put it plainly, ~.
	In brief, ~.
	Briefly, ~.
~의 의미에서, ~한 관점, 용어로	Note that China's overtaking of the United States us in aggregate terms. (모든 지표에서, 종합적 의미에서)
	In United Nations parlance, it is "to leave no one behind." (~의 용어로, 어법으로)
	In the broadest sense, a person's quest for understanding is indeed a search problem, in an abstract space of ideas far too large to be searched exhaustively.
솔직히 말해서	To be frank, science knows surprisingly little about mind and consciousness.

강조는 저자의 것

흔히 논문을 쓰다 보면 인용하는 원문 텍스트에서는 없는 것을 저자가 자신의 논지를 강조하기 위해 이탤릭체로 고쳐 표현하는 경우를 보게 된다. 이럴 때 쓰는 표현이 바로 '강조 이탤릭체는 저자의 것' 혹은 '강조 표시는 저자의 것'이다. 때에 따라서는 인용 후 저자의 이니셜을 괄호 속에 삽입하여 표기하기도 한다.
(원문 인용 italics mine)

"I feel that I am *alive* (ital. mine-E. F. Steve)."

(원문 인용 Ivan smiled suddenly *"quite like a little gentle child"*: emphasis added)
"My reasoning about that scenario was that it would be a disaster for our society and a dead end, that it would turn the country back and ruin everything we now have [emphasis added]."

(원문 내에서 대문자 표시를 통한 강조 "the FIRST book-length study of the subject in any language": 27, my capitalization)
위의 경우와 마찬가지로, 원문에는 없지만 저자의 강조를 위해서 이렇게 모두 대문자 표시를 한 후 괄호 안에 '대문자 표시는 저자가 한 것임'이라고 써 넣는다.

원본 인용시 인용자의 임의적 수정 〔sic〕

원본 인용을 하다보면 독자들의 입장에서 볼 때 불분명하여 인용자가 임의로 수정을 가하거나 어떤 특별한 설명이 필요한 문장이 있을 수 있다. 다시 말해 원본에서 철자가 잘못되었거나, 문법적으로 바르지 못한 부분, 부적절한 표현이 생기면 바로 다음에 아래와 같이 괄호 속에 sic이란 말을 넣어 주거나 예외적으로 인용자의 수정을 첨가함으로써 독자의 이해를 돕도록 해 준다. 라틴어로 thus, so란 뜻의 sic은 사용에 각별한 주의가 필요하다.[1] 다음의 문장을 통해서 그 쓰임새를 알아보자.

Or on a Sunday afternoon. If I chanced to be at home, I heard the cronching [sic] of the snow made by the step of a long-headed farmer, who from far through the woods sought my house, to have a social "crack."

---

1) 이 부분에 대해서 본인은 다음의 두 책을 참고했으며 이 자리에 원본의 영어 설명을 그대로 옮겨 놓는다.
    "...you may decide that a quotation will be unclear or confusing to your reader unless you provide supplementary informations. For example, you may need to insert material missing from the original, to add sic to assure readers that the quotation is accurate even though the spelling or logic might make them think otherwise..." Joseph Gibaldi, MLA Handbook for Writers of Research Papers, 6th edition (New York: The Modern Language Association of America, 2003), p. 118. Or "...sic may be inserted in braskets following a word misspelled or wrongly used in the original." The Chicago Manual of Style: The Essential Guide for Writers, Editors, and Publishers, 15th edition (Chicago and London: The University of Chicago, 2003), p. 464.

위의 문장에서 인용자는 cronching이 '눈을 밟을 때 나는 바스락 소리'를 뜻하는 crunching의 잘못된 원저자 인용, 즉 원저자의 철자법 실수임을 보여 주기 위해 괄호 속에 sic을 넣어 독자들의 혼선을 피하고 있다.

He claimed he could provide "hundreds of examples [of court decisions] to illustrate the historical tension between church and state."
Milton's Satan speaks of his "study [pursuit] of revenge."
위의 두 예문들은 문장의 의미가 보다 분명하게 전달되도록 인용자가 임의로 표현과 단어를 삽입한 경우이다.

The cupolas were immediately thrown down [zrocone-sic], several holes were made in the ceiling, the roof was ripped down-in a word, what could be destroyed was destroyed so that there could be no return [to the earlier situation].
여기에서 sic의 쓰임새는 외국어의 번역과 관련된다. 즉, 인용자는 원본의 *zrocone*를 다른 표현으로 번역할 수도 있었던 것을 thrown down으로 번역하여 강조한 것을 괄호 속에 sic으로 나타내 주고 있는 것이다. 두 번째의 용례는 독자들의 이해를 돕기 위해 인용자가 추가로 문구를 넣어 준 것에 해당한다.

16 텍스트 인용

이하의 예문들은 흔히 논문에서 작품을 인용할 때 주로 쓰이는 대표적인 것들이다. 쌍따옴표(" ")는 인용문장 전체를 의미한다. 예문들을 잘 들여다보면 우리는 화자 문제를 얘기하는 문장에서 수동태가 주로 쓰인다는 점을 알 수 있다. 즉, the reader is told 혹은 we are told 같은 예들이 일반적으로 발견되는 문장이다. 그리고 인용문장이 '~하게 기술되어 있다'는 내용에서 동사는 read 혹은 run을 주로 쓴다.

- Throughout the novel, **we(the reader) find** hundreds of passages such as the following: "……."
  독자는 다음과 같은 대사를 수없이 목격한다.

- **We are** immediately **told**: "……." 독자는 곧바로, 이내 다음과 같은 문장에 접하게 된다.

- The opening line of the novel **reads**: "……."

- **Here is the beginning of** Anatol Stern's short story, "The Cave": "……."

- In the same page, one also **reads**: "……."

- Jennifer's estrangement **is evident from the story's opening lines**: "……."
  이미 작품의 첫 줄에서부터 ~이 뚜렷하다.

- The beginning of the chapter **runs**: "……."

- The novel **opens** with a description of ~: "……."

- The **ensuing paragraph** embodies ~. 다음에 올, 이어질 문단은 ~을 하다.

- In describing the ~, Sholokhov **makes the following comment**: "……."
- Later we **read** the following: "……."

- The first paragraph of ~ **reads as follows**: "……."

- The conversation between ~ and is following: "……."

- A lyrical passage follows the ~: "……."

- The passage below contains ~: "……."

- There is a telling passage early in the novel: "……."

- To exemplify this and much of the preceding, let cite a single illustrative passage from *Resurrection*.

- Gerasim, the main hero of the story even goes so far as to say: "……."

- The author writes the following: "……."

- In the excerpts below, ~.

- Consider, for example, the following passage from the story "The Nose."

- Schematically, they can be represented as shown in Table 4.
  scheme는 '계획, 구도, 구성' 등의 의미로 흔히 논문이나 학술적인 글 내에서는 그림 혹은 도표를 이용한 '도식'(an analytical or tabular statement)으로 가장 널리 쓰이는 용어이다.

- Specifically in this study ethnography included: 1), 2), and 3).

- Several questions related to determining the boundaries of the event were considered. Among them are the following: ~.

다음의 예들은 작품 인용, 도표, 그림 등을 먼저 보여 준 후 이에 대한 설명을 하고 있는 표현이다.
- Here is an explicitly metaphorical statement, ~.

- Here the satirical theme is given an explicit.

- This passage illustrates ~.

- This passage is echoed near the end of the novel when ~.

- The pine tree **is echoed by** a similar image in the narrator's first person account of his own childhood experiences.

- **This passage might be construed as** one of ~.

- **This passage yields** insights into the character of Katiusha.

- It becomes evident that the psychoanalytic approach **yields** insights that are necessary but not sufficient in the decoding process.

- **This passage serves** well **to point out**.

- **This passage follows** immediately on from the description of ~.

- Dostoevsky is referring directly to the Christian value **in the passage quoted above**.

- **This passage interests us for** two reasons. First, ~, and second, ~.

- **This passage is crucial in** the development of the theme of memory.

- **This passage encourages the reader to look upon** water as a further metaphor for the meandering journeys of *Ulyses*.

- The above quotation is **a telling summary** of Wolf's agenda, for in its drawing of ~, she exhibits a subtle and self-conscious approach.

- In this way, Alexander Blok **gave extended quotations from** the poetry in question.

- The author's **ideas in this passage are not stated** in it but have to be deduced.

- I have **divided this long sentence into numbered segments**, to facilitate a close scrutiny of each.
  이 표현은 긴 인용문을 저자가 강조할 목적으로 필요에 따라 번호를 붙여 낱개로 구분하여 쪼개 놓을 때 사용되는 문장법이다.

- Insofar as the **evidence allows**, three distinct social groupings can be distinguished within it: ~.

evidence가 들어간 문장들을 예로 들어 보자. Although the <u>evidence</u> is somewhat <u>scanty</u>, ~ (예증, 증거가 다소 불충분, 빈약하지만). There are several solidly documented cases of high incidence. The <u>available evidence</u>, scant though it is, indicates that ~. The most <u>solid body of evidence</u> concerning ~ is provided by ~(~과 관련하여 가장 확실한, 분명한 증거는 ~에 의해서 제공된다, ~가 보여 준다). There is sufficient <u>textual evidence</u> to believe that ~(~을 믿게 할 만한 문헌상의 충분한 증거가 있다).

■ The system of evaluations in the ~ can be conceptualized according to Table 1.
흔히 도표나 그림을 인용한 후에 이런 식으로 그에 대한 설명을 할 수 있다.

■ What are the consequences from this statement then? And can we take this text at face value?
여기에서 at face value는 '액면 그대로 받아들이다'란 뜻이다.

■ This precept calls for special attention to the sense that ~.

17 It ~ that 구문의 다양한 활용법

■ **It would not be an overstatement to say that ~.**
~라고 얘기하는 것은 결코 과장이 아니다 즉, 그럴 법한 일이다.

■ **It does not seem to rash to suggest that ~.**
~라고 제시하는 것은 얼토당토, 무분별, 말도 안 되는 것 같지 않다, 즉 ~라고 충분히 말할 수 있어 보인다.
rash는 acting too hastily or without due consideration의 뜻으로 신중한 생각이나 고려 없이 덜 익은 생각에서 행동하는 것을 말한다.

■ **It is generally taken for granted that ~.** ~이 당연시되고 있다.

■ **It should be pointed out that ~.** ~은 강조되어야 한다.
같은 의미로 달리 표현하면, It must not be overlooked that ~.이 좋다.

■ **It should be added that ~.**

■ At this point, **it should be mentioned that ~.**

■ **It should be reiterated that ~.** ~은 반복되어야 한다. 즉, 강조되어야 한다.

■ **It is worth nothing that ~.** ~은 부연, 설명할 필요가 있다.
be worth +-ing는 '~할 가치가 있다'이란 뜻이다. 마찬가지로 다음의 문장을 보자. This point is worth mentioning for the sake of anthropological perspective; but it is also important for understanding the significance of love. 위 문장은 '이 점은 문화인류학적 입장에서 언급될 만하다'로 해석하면 좋겠다.

■ **It is necessary** for me to explain here **that ~.**

■ **It must be admitted that ~** ~은 받아들여져야 한다, 인정되어야 한다.

- **It is** very important **that** ~.

  (=It is of importance that ~. = **Of great importance is that** ~.)

- **No less significant** is the fact **that** ~.

  ~에 못지 않게 의미 있는 것은 즉, ~은 매우 중요하다, 의미가 있다.

- **No less important** than humor is **that** ~.

- **It is no less dubious** to connect **that** ~.

  ~은 결코 의심스럽지 않다. 즉, 자명하다, 분명하다.

- **It is of special interest**, since ~. (= It is very interesting that ~.)

- **It seems reasonable to assume that** ~.

  ~라고 가정하는 것은 이치에 맞다, ~라고 생각하는 것은 자연스럽다.

- **It** indeed **may be said with safety that** ~.

  '~라고 말하는 것은 안전할 수 있다', 즉 '~라고 말하는 것은 비교적 논쟁거리가 되지 않고 쉽게 받아들여질 수 있다'는 말의 우회적인 표현이다.

- **It would not be unreasonable** to say, therefore, **that** ~.

- **It is not unreasonable** to postulate **that** ~.

  ~라고 가정하는 것은 비약적이지 않다. 즉, 그럴 듯 하다, 무리가 없다.

- **It is a quite logical conclusion that** ~.

- **It stands to reason** that ~. ~은 합당하다, 합리적이다.

- **It is justifiable to conclude that** ~.

- **As for ~ itself, it seems reasonable to conclude that** ~.

  ~ 자체만 보면 ~라고 결론 짓는 것은 합당해 보인다.

- **It is hard to escape the conclusions that** ~.

  ~라는 결론을 내리지 않을 수 없다.

- **It is difficult to avoid the conclusion** that ~.

■ It has been frequently noted that ~.

■ It is of course not to say that ~. ~을 의미하는 것은 물론 아니다.

■ It is far from my intention to suggest that ~. ~을 제안하고자 하는 것이 아니다.

■ It is highly probable that ~. ~은 상당히 타당해 보인다.

■ It would be scarcely possible that ~. ~은 거의 가능해 보이지 않는다. 즉, 거의 불가능해 보인다.
scarcely는 부정의 뜻을 자체에 담고 있는 부사로 사용에 주의하자. 즉, not을 넣어 이중 부정을
만드는 실수를 피해야 한다(However, his view is scarcely correct).

■ It is completely absent from *On the Eve*.

■ It has often been observed that ~. 자주 언급된다.

■ It should be viewed with reservation. 재고되어야 한다.

■ It is no wonder that ~. ~은 놀랄 만한 일이 아니다, ~은 당연하다, 자연스럽다.
위와 같은 의미에는 다음과 같은 표현이 있다. It is not surprising that ~. / So it is not really
surprising that ~. / Not surprisingly, ~. / Hardly surprisingly, ~. / It comes as no surprise
that ~.

■ It is not by chance that ~.
~은 우연이 아니다. 즉, 매우 당연해 보인다, 이치에 닿는다.

■ It is probably not incidental, therefore, that ~.

■ It scarcely(= hardly, seldom) seems accidental that ~.

■ It is obviously no coincidence that ~.
The new understandings of the body coincided with the birth of modern capitalism. (~과
일치하다) = If one defines it in terms of being the country with the largest economy, the
American century roughly coincides with the twentieth century.

■ It is by no means a coincidence that ~.
~은 결코 우연이 아니다.

■ It is **natural enough** that ~.
natural은 말 그대로 '~한 생각, 추론, 주장 등이 자연스럽다'란 의미이다. 이 말이 들어간 문장 하나를 더 알아보자. It is natural to extend this explanation to the ~.

■ **It may** therefore **be appropriate** to end our analysis of the ~.

■ **It** is **not difficult** to see **that** ~.
어렵지 않게 찾아볼 수 있다.

■ **It is not hard** to guess **that** ~.

■ **It is hard** to exaggerate **that** ~.
~을 과장하기는 어렵다. 즉, 너무나 당연하다, 자연스럽다.

■ **It is** difficult to conceive **of** ~.
~을 상상하기란, 생각하기란 어렵다.

■ **It is** really no more outrageous to say **that** ~.

■ **It** would be **difficult** to overemphasize the importance of ~.

■ **It goes without saying that** ~.
~은 말할 나위도 없다, 당연하다.

■ **It is** quite clear **that** ~.
~은 꽤 분명하다, 매우 뚜렷하다.

■ **It is clear from the above that** ~.
위에서 언급된 것으로 볼 때 ~은 분명하다.

■ **It** is true **that** ~.
'~은 사실이다'란 의미의 가장 단순한 표현으로 그냥 True, ~. 로도 사용된다.

■ **It is precisely because that** ~. ~은 정확하게 바로 ~ 때문이다.
거의 같은 의미의 다음 예문과 비교해 보자. This is due to the fact that ~.

■ It would **be interesting to see that** ~.
~을 살펴보는 것은 흥미롭다.

■ It would **be tempting to see that** ~.

■ It is thus **tempting to conclude** that ~.

■ It should **be mindful** of the fact that ~.

■ It **is quite understandable** if ~.

■ It would **be absurd to argue** that ~.
~라고 주장하는 것은 무모하다, 불합리하다.

■ **It would be erroneous** to perceive **that** ~.
~라고 생각하는 것은 실수, 잘못이다.

■ **It would be a misconception**, however, to argue **that** ~.
~라고 주장하는 것은 오해, 그른 판단이다.

18 도치 구문

단순 도치 구문

- **Not only did** they **fail to** find correlations significantly different from zero, **but** most of the correlations were negative.

- **Not only was** the amount of archeological fieldwork increasing in the 1960s, **but also**, the discipline of archeology was changing in ways that resulted in the collection of more materials.

- **Not only are** younger people unwilling to do the work connected with large parties; they **also** see family parties in terms of obligation and constraint.
  위의 세 예문들은 모두 'not only A, but also B' 숙어의 변형이다. 세미콜론(;)을 이용한 세 번째 문장의 응용도 눈여겨보기 바란다.

- **Had** the U.S. health system responded to the demand for legal abortions, **it would** have been very difficult for pro-life forces to orchestrate a campaign of harrassment against the thousands of hospitals in this country.

- **Had** Buddhist monasteries remained aloof from the rest of Chinese society, then none of this **would** have made much difference.
  위의 두 예문들은 조건법 conditional의 하나로 '과거에 A가 ~했었다면, B가 ~했었을 텐데'(If A had + past participle, B would have + past participle)란 구문의 If절에서 had와 동사의 과거분사가 서로 도치 변형된 꼴이다. 즉, If A had + p.p.에서 If가 생략되면 Had가 문두로 나가면서 Had + A + p.p.의 형태가 되는 것이다.

- **No sooner** has the Cold War seemingly ended **than** we have come to recognize the danger of localized wars among ethnic groups spilling over into wider, global conflict.

■ **No sooner** is the exploitation of the laborer by the manufacturer, so far, **than** he is set upon by the other portions of the bourgeoisie.

No sooner A than B는 'A가 하자마자 B가 ~하다'는 뜻으로 쓰이는 중요한 숙어이다. 문장 중간에 특별한 삽입어가 없는 한, 중간에 콤마(,)를 쓰지 않는다는 것을 알아 두자.

■ **Only** in the United States **does** a large private sector of education exist.

■ **Only when** universal education is mandated by the state and when it is seen to increase economic opportunities **is** this tension between schools and kinship reduced.

■ **Only** in the 1950s **did** the historians of the Sixth Section begin to work seriously with quantitative methods.

위와 같은 도치 문장은 It ~ that 구문을 사용해 다시 쓴다면 다음과 같다.

It was only in the 1950s that the historians of the Sixth Section began to ~.

■ **Only in this way can** the modern reader be given access to the text.

only로 시작되는 문장에서는 위와 같이 '주어 + 술어'의 어순이 바뀐다는 것을 기억해 두자.

■ **That** Old French courtly romances portray gender relations as fraught with tension **is** not surprising.

위의 문장은 It is not surprising that ~(~은 결코 놀랄 만한 것이 아니다).이 도치된 형태이다.

도치 부정문

■ **Nowhere** is this more evident **than** within domestic technologies.

■ **Nowhere** is this more evident **than** in recent scholarship concerned with the ~.

■ **Nowhere** is the spirit of victory more pronounced **than** on the ice of the hockey rink.

■ **Nowhere** is the impact of science more apparent **than** in medicine and health.

■ **Nowhere** is the drive for athletic, cultural, and academic excellence more apparent **than** in the awards, honors, and prizes that are given to outstanding teams or students at the end of each year.

다섯 문장 모두 Nowhere A than B(B에서 만큼 혹은 B만큼 A가 한 것은 어디에도 없다)의 기본 형태를 취하고 있다. 'B에서 A가 가장 ~하다'란 뜻으로 이해하면 좋겠다.

■ **Nowhere** does this range become more apparent **than** when individuals attempt to synthesize ecological information to form an urban ecological restoration plan.

■ **Nowhere** more **than** in Russia did modern journalism stand in such sharp contrast to a system of outmoded absolutistic controls.

■ **Not everywhere** was this custom observed although it was inspired by the Church authorities.

■ **Not that** such structures are not invoked.

■ **Nor** should it be forgotten that ~.
either A or B는 'A이거나 혹은 B이다'이며, neither A nor B는 'A도 B도 아니다'란 의미의 부정을 나타낸다. 그런데 유독 neither A nor B란 표현은 위의 문장에서처럼 부정의 뜻을 나타내는 문장을 앞 문장에서 사용한 후, Nor를 문두에 위치시켜 '뒤에 소개되는 것 (즉, 독립 문장으로 다음에 이어지는) 역시 아니다'란 뜻의 부정을 나타내고자 할 때 자주 쓰인다. 다시 말해서, not only A but also B (A뿐만 아니라 B이기도 하다)란 표현을 한 문장 안에 쓰지 않고 마치 It is not only A. It is also B. 이렇게 독립시켜 두 문장으로 만드는 것처럼 Nor should it be forgotten that ~.는 그 문체로 볼 때, 이미 바로 앞 문장에서 부정의 뜻을 담고 있는 표현이 사용되었음을 말해 주는 것이다.
다음 문장을 잘 살펴보면 그 용례가 보다 확실해질 것이다.
  • Such attributes are <u>not</u> repeated to remind us of something we may have forgotten. <u>Nor</u> are they generalizations like the epithets ~.
  • The character Anna is <u>not</u> merely the wife of a high bureaucrats who falls in love with a rich army officer. <u>Nor</u> is her story a mere tale of adultery.
  • Shanghai is evidently <u>not</u> a typical city in China. <u>Nor</u>, indeed, is it typical of cities in other developing countries.
  • <u>Neither</u> the United States <u>nor</u> Germany has opened any facilities to manage high-level nuclear wastes.

■ **Not until** children had been involved in book reading routines for a long time **did** they reach the more advanced levels of internalization.

■ **Not until** the last half of the sixteenth century did the first press in all of Russia reach Moscow.

■ **Not so clear**, however, **is** the concept of urban design, what we mean by the term, what constitutes "design," and ~.

- **Not so simple is** the assertion that ~.

- **Not all** men who work in these occupations **are** supervised by men.
  ~이 모두 ~한 것은 아니다.

- **Not all** of the pioneering work in the history of mentalities **has** been done by French historians.

- **No book is** solely the product of its authors, and this one is no exception.

- **No** theoretical approach since the end of W.W.II **has** been as important as that of Claude Levi-Strauss.
  세계 2차 대전 이래로 레비-스트로스(프랑스 구조주의 철학자)의 이론적 접근 방법만큼이나 중요했던 것은 없었다. 즉, 레비-스트로스의 이론적 접근 방법이 전후 이후로 가장 중요했다.

- **No** unified historical science or paradigm **has** emerged to dominate the field as did the "paradigm" which emerged from Ranke's seminars.

- **No society** can function without certain forms of social control.

- **No single explanation** can **account for** the apparent change in attitude to ~.
  어떠한 하나의 설명도 ~을 설명할 수 없다.

- **No single answer** will quite suffice.
  어떠한 답변도 충분하지 않을 것이다.

- **No Zeitgeist rule** can describe how culture and aesthetics interrelate in all circumstances, not even for one time and place.

- **No contemporary public squares** have been laid out which could be compared with urban squares like the Grande Place in Brussels.

- The curtain crisis did **not** happen overnight, **nor** will it quickly be resolved.

- The antiquity of the archeological record in the Americas was **not** yet known, **nor** was the existence of the eastern Archaic or Paleoindian fully recognized.

- **In neither case did they feel** a particular empathy with the *Annales* school which did not gain unanimous support from French medievalists either.

- **By no means am I suggesting** that such work does not go on at all types of ~.
  본인은 ~을 제의하는 것이 결코 아니다.

19 순위, 등수 차지

순위, 등수를 차지하다, 위치에 올라 있다

■ A survey of global entrepreneurship **ranked** the United States ahead of other countries.
순위, 위치, 등수를 표현할 때 rank를 동사로 많이 사용한다.

■ In terms of soft power, while Europe has 27 universities **ranked** in the top 100 (compared to 52 for the United States), the United States spends 2.7 percent of GDP on universities and research and development.

■ A few hours of blank-slate **bested** 600 years of learning of chess play by all of the chess experts in history.
best가 동사로 사용될 때도 역시 "1등을 차지하다"를 의미한다.

■ The growth rate of GDP per capita of the developing countries has generally **outpaced** that of the developed countries by 1-5 percentage points per year, though by a diminished margin in the 2010s.

■ Measured at purchasing-power-adjusted prices, China is now the world's largest economy, **surpassing** the United States (on the IMF's measure) in the year 2013, with the gap in favor of China continuing in recent years.
~를 앞서 누르다, 제치다

■ With a population of 1.2 billion people, India is four times larger than the United States, and likely to **surpass** China in population by 2025.
2025년 경에는 인구면에서 중국을 능가할 것으로 보인다

IV 결론에 자주 등장하는 표현

1. 본론의 요약과 결론 제시
2. 질정을 바라는 저자의 희망 / 여전히 남아 있는 문제점 지적

01 본론의 요약과 결론 제시

■ This article **has attempted to establish** ~.
결론에서 가장 널리 쓰이는 표현은 뭐니뭐니해도 현재완료시제(present perfect)이다. 즉, 서론에서 본론을 지나 결론에 이르기까지 논문이 ~한 것을 살피고, 밝히고, 검증하면서 저자의 견해를 보여 주어 왔기 때문에 과거 어떤 시점에서 시작하여 현재까지 쭉 계속되는 시간 상태를 말하는 이 표현법이 많이 쓰인다. 그러나 서론에서 흔히 사용하는 논문의 목적 (aim of the paper)을 결론에 사용하면서 대신 시제를 단순 과거시제를 사용하는 예도 있다. 다음의 예를 참고해 보자. My aim in this article was in no way ~, but rather to place it in a wide perspective ~. 또는 My purpose thus far has been to construct an image of an establishment, or, to use the metaphor of my title, a ~.

■ This article **has attempted to sketch out** the main characteristics of ~.

■ This study **has shown that** ~.

■ **Up to now,** we **have looked at** ~. 지금까지 우리는 ~을 살펴보았다.

■ This paper **reviews** the various components of the online education process and **points out** ~.

■ In general terms, **what all this shows is that** the way we interpret ~.
전체적으로 볼 때, 우리가 이 논문에서 보여 준 것은 ~을 해석하는 방식이다.

■ In this study **we asked whether data on** child-care quality obtained from a telephone interview with the provider **can serve as an adequate** proxy for data obtained from direct observation.

■ In this paper **we have reported findings** from a large cross-sectional study involving ~.

■ **The conclusion to be drawn here is that** ~. 여기에서 나오는 결론은 ~이다.

■ **Some of** her **conclusions are well attention**.
그녀의 일부 결론들은 주목을 잘 받는다, 주목의 훌륭한 대상이다.

■ **The conclusion** which **can be drawn from this study** of ~ are these: 1) ~, 2) ~, and 3) ~.
이 연구로부터 맺어질 수 있는 결론은 다음과 같다.

■ **In concluding, it is worth reiterating** the proposition presented earlier in this paper that ~. 결론을 지으면서 ~을 다시 설명할 필요가 있다.

■ I **tentatively conclude that** ~.
잠정적으로 다음과 같은 결론을 내린다.

■ **To conclude**, we can make the following four observations: ~.

■ We may therefore **come to the conclusion that** ~.

■ **The paper concludes by** mentioning some of the further problems raised by this approach to ~.
본 논문은 ~을 언급함으로써 결론을 맺고자 한다.

■ **Having come to the end of our discussion of** the content and rigour of ~ Kim's major concept in ~, **it is time to recall the conclusions of** each of the three principal divisions of the ~.
우리의 토론이 막바지에 온 이상 이제 ~의 결론을 말할 때이다.

■ **Now having provided a basic summary of** the content of each of the main parts of the paper, **there is an opportunity to highlight one particular aspect of** ~.
~의 내용에 대한 기본적인 요약을 해 온 이상 (지금까지 ~에 대한 요약을 해 왔기 때문에) 이젠 ~의 특별한 측면을 강조할 때이다.

■ **Having made these brief points**, **it is time to bring this paper to a close and to end** with comment from ~.
이같은 짧은(간단한) 요점을 얘기한 이상 이젠 본 논문의 끝을 맺을 때이다.

■ **Proceeding from what has been said above**, it should be concluded that ~.
지금까지 위에서 살펴본 것으로부터 다음과 같은 결론이 도출된다.

- **Proceeding from** this fact, **one could** logically **assume that** ~.
  이같은 사실로 볼 때, 혹자는 ~라고 생각할 수 있을 것이다.

- **To capitulate** briefly, we have shown that two discernable approaches ~.

- **In sum**, these findings add more support to the conclusion that ~.

- To **sum up**, the following conclusions can be made: ~.

- **To sum up, the following kinds of research materials were used**: (1) archival research for historical periods on which ~; (2) documentary research for ~; (3) purposive and focused interviews with ~ and (4) a reading of ~.

- **Summing up** all of the preceding reasoning and returning to the question posed at the outset of this paper, it seems appropriate to state that ~.

- **Summing up**, the present paper shows that how ~.

- **In summary**, ~.

- **In summary**, our discussion of feminist and recent social theory has developed five main points: (1) ~, (2) ~, (3) ~, (4) ~, and (5) ~.

- **To summarize**: the research framework, and associated research methods, were as follows: ~.
  위의 두 예문들은 사회과학과 자연과학의 데이터 분석 논문 등에서 자주 쓰이는 형태이다. 즉, 결론에서 저자는 본론에서 살핀 내용들을 요약하고 최종적인 결론을 내리면서, 아라비아 숫자를 이용하여 (1), (2), (3)식으로 매우 간단하게 정리한다.

- **To summarize**, in the present paper, two questions were explored.

- **In the long run**, the growing use of educational credentials by employers in the economy overcomes the threats experienced by parents.
  결국, 마침내

- We are consequently made to see ~.

■ **In short**, we see ~. 간단히 말해서, ~

■ **In a nutshell**, one of the main challenges of this paper is ~.
요약하자면, 이 논문이 보여 준 주요 반박들 가운데 하나는 ~이다.

■ **Our conclusion could be stated** thus: ~.
따라서 우리의 결론은 이렇게 설명될 수 있다.

■ **I would like to close by proposing that** ~.
~을 제시함으로써 저자는 결론을 맺고자 한다.

■ **I would like to close the discussion by** pointing out that ~.
~을 지적하면서(지적함으로써) 본인은 우리의 논의를 끝내고자 한다.

■ **I want to close by considering** once again Herr's emphasis on the ~.

■ Thus, **it has to be reiterated** that ~.
이리하여, ~은 자세히 설명되어야(반복되어야) 한다.

■ Thus, **it seems reasonable to conclude that** ~.

■ From this evidence at hand I conclude that ~.
우리가 삼고 있는(우리 손에 있는) 이같은 증거로 볼 때 우리는 ~라고 결론을 맺는다.

■ I therefore **found it reasonable to assume that** ~.

■ **It may therefore be appropriate to end** our analysis of the ~.

■ It is **hard to avoid the conclusion that** ~.

■ We **cannot**, therefore, **avoid the claim that** ~.
우리가 위의 두 예문에서 공통적으로 사용된 동사 avoid는 '~을 피하다'란 의미로 '~라는 결론을 내리지 않을 수 없다'로 의역하는 것이 가장 좋겠다.

■ It would be **serious oversight to conclude that** ~.
~라고 결론을 내리는 것은 중대한 실수이다. 즉, 결론을 내릴 수는 없다.

■ One further matter must be considered before closing the present discussion.

- **One conclusion we can draw from this discussion** is that ~.
  이같은 논의에서 우리가 이끌어낼 수 있는 한 가지 결론은 ~이다.

- **The conclusion provided above** can be briefly stated as follows.
  위에서 언급된 결론은 다음과 같이 간단히 설명될 수 있다.

- **As we have seen, the main purpose of this article has been to explore** the role played by the women's magazines ~.
  지금까지 보아왔듯이, 본 논문의 주목적은 ~을 밝혀 보이는 것이었다.

- **Our case study has examined** the crucial points **by seeking to explain** the ~.

- This study **lays the foundation for future work on** ~.
  본 연구는 ~에 대한 이후 연구의 초석을 다지는 연구

- **The key founding of this survey** was that ~.

- **Central to this study have been the questions of** ~.
  ~의 문제들은 본 연구의 핵심(중심)이었다.

- From the above, it is apparent that ~.
  위에서 말한 것으로 미루어 보면, ~은 아주 분명, 뚜렷하다.

- From the above evidence, **some conclusions may be drawn** about the ~.
  위의 증거로부터 몇몇 결론들이 나타난다.

- As may be ascertained from the above discussion, ~.

- Based on the empirical cases in this paper, I have **offered several observations**.

- This analysis **has led to the following** general **observations**: ~.
  동사 lead to는 '결과적으로 ~로 나아가다, 연결되다'란 뜻이다. 따라서 이 문장은 '본론에서 우리가 한 분석은 다음과 같은 결과(결론)가 나온다'란 의미이다. 다음 예문과 비교해 보자. The world economic crisis that began in the 1970s has led to a restructuring of the world economy. 또는 Any serious inquiry into another culture leads to a greater understanding of one's own culture.

- This observation **leads us**, necessarily, **to** a related debate: the role of long-term versus short-term influences on democratization.

- Inequality will almost always **lead to** the centralization of power, particularly its coercive and administrative bases.

- In the Lucas (1973) model, unanticipated money **leads to** unanticipated inflation.

- Evidence of a complex widespread and multiform pattern of rising inequality **leads** Castells **to** argue that ~.

- The history of scholarship provides many examples of similar situations, **leading to** unfortunate results.

- **Taking into account** the theory of interactive vision and the studies carried out by cognitive psychologists and their importance of the objectivity of science on the other hand, **we can conclude that**: (1) ~, (2) ~, and (3) ~.
  ~ 이론을 고려하면서(생각해 볼 때) 우리는 다음과 같은 결론을 내릴 수 있다.

- **For all the reasons** given previously, **I am convinced that** ~.
  이 모든 이유들 때문에 본인은 ~라고 생각한다.

- **For all these reasons**, the courtesans had nothing to gain by being isolated or marked, and so resisted segregation with every means at their disposal.
  이 모든 이유에서(이유 때문에)

- The **evidence** which I have assembled **seems to indicate** that ~.

- Other **evidence confirms** the fact that ~ .
  명사 evidence(증거, 증명)가 사용된 예문은 다음과 같이 많이 사용되며, 동의어로는 'attest to'라는 표현이 있다. Again, I can attest to the truth of these findings from my own professional experience.

- Coupled with evidence that ~, **our results** also **provide support for the view** that ~.
  '우리가 내린 결론은 ~한 견해를 뒷받침해 주고 있다'로 보면 좋겠다. 여기에서 coupled with는 '~와 함께 관련시켜 볼 때' 혹은 '~란 점을 감안해 볼 때'로 해석하면 무리가 없을 것이다.

- The **results of this study provide** empirical **evidence to** substantiate the multidimensional ~ paradigm.

■ Therefore, the result provides a useful ground to test the theories' cross-cultural applicability.

위의 두 예문에서처럼 서론과 결론에서 저자의 이론이나 생각을 표현할 때, 이같이 동사 provide 를 많이 사용한다. 특히 어떤 방법론이 자신이 증명하거나 살펴본 내용과 어떤 관련이 있어서 그 영향 관계를 언급할 땐 더 빈번하게 쓰여지니 잘 알아 두면 편리할 것이다.

■ The results of my study point to several promising applications for future research.

저자가 내린 결론은 이후 연구에 잘 적용될 수 있는 것들(적용 가능성)을 지적해 준다.

■ The foregoing analysis has demonstrated the validity of the hypothesis that ~.

지금까지 선행 분석은 ~한 가설의 진위(유용성)를 살펴보았다.

■ This article has four main findings. First, ~. Second, ~. The third finding is that ~. The fourth finding is that ~. Each of these findings runs counter to the assumptions of earlier scholars that ~.

명사 finding은 흔히 result와 같은 의미이지만 그 쓰임새가 약간 다르다. 즉, finding은 객관적 인 data collection and analysis를 추구하는 사회과학 혹은 자연과학 논문에서 사용되는 용어 이다. 그 외 분야에서 결과란 뜻으로 사용하는 result와 구별해 알아 두자. This conclusion runs counter to current mainstream(논문의 결론이 현재 주류를 이루는 논리에 반대된다.).

■ Findings have provided scholars with a wealth of information concerning ~.

■ Three major findings from the above discussion should be highlighted.

■ The current research and its findings should be considered an initial step.

■ More specifically, the findings from the clothing industry confirm the conclusion of previous studies of overall harmonious ~.

~한 결과물(결론)이 논문의 결론을 확실하게 해 주다.

■ The principal finding of my study is important for three reasons. First, it demonstrates that ~. Second, it suggests that ~ and third this finding provides that ~.

■ As an outcome, this microanalysis offers a more optimistic evaluation of the ongoing transformation of workplace relations in East Germany.

■ While our effort in this paper is only a first step, we believe it **offers** some insight into the problem. In particular, it is important to recognize that ~.

위의 문장에서처럼 간혹 논문의 결론 말미에 가서 우리는 저자 자신의 논문에 대한 자평에 가까운 발언을 보게 된다. 지금처럼 자신의 논문이 '~한 점에 대해 최초로 ~을 보여 준 시도'라는 평 자체가 바로 그 예인데, 가급적 이런 표현은 쓰지 않도록 하자. 마찬가지 맥락에서 다음 예문을 비교해 보자. The present paper <u>expands upon previous research</u> in several ways. The present study also <u>goes beyond previous work</u> in including an analysis of the actual choices of type and quality of ~. Overall, the present study <u>adds to the exiting literature on</u> ~.

■ This study **addressed** two research questions: First, using instruments ~. And second, ~. We began by reviewing the ~. Therefore, we **concluded by describing** the strengths and shortcomings of our criteria and instruments, and proposals for future work.

위의 예문에서처럼 첫째, 둘째, 셋째 순서를 정하면서 간단하게 정리하는 문장 형식은 자연과학 혹은 사회과학 등의 분야에서 통계 분석이 들어간 실험 논문 등에서 자주 사용된다. 한편, 동사 address는 to deal with 또는 to discuss와 같은 뜻이다.

■ There were two major targets to be **addressed** in the analysis. First, it was of interest to distinguish ~. Second, we intended to evaluate ~.

■ The two paths traced here were not entirely mutually exclusive.

■ This article, therefore, **provides a stepping stone for** developing an account of ~.

~을 위한 초석을 제공하다.

■ Two sets of **concluding observations**-one of civil society and one on ethnic conflict-**are in order**.

■ A few additional comments may be **in order**: ~.

■ A few essential conclusions about the ~ may be stated more simply: ~.

■ There are three wide conclusions to be drawn. First, ~, second, ~, third, ~.

■ In an attempt to understand why ~, I have explored ~.

■ What **stands out** most from this study is the ~.

이 연구로부터 가장 분명하게 드러나는 것은 ~이다.

- All of this leads to a straightforward conclusion.

  직역하면 '직접적인(direct) 결론'이란 뜻으로, '이 모든 내용들이 다음과 같은 뚜렷한 결론으로 이어진다' 혹은 '이상 우리는 다음과 같은 확실한 결론에 다다른다' 정도로 이해하면 좋겠다.

- This article has been written with three purposes in mind: to survey the economic and political landscape of ~, to develop an explanation of ~, and to use these observations to address ~.

- We have now traced in some details ~.

- This study has concerned itself with attitudes toward authority, with the conduct models which are officially presented in the Soviet Union.

- So far, I have been discussing the function of ideas in reflective interpretation by considering ~.

- What emerges from this brief discussion is that ~.

  이같은 간단한 토론(논의)에서 나타나는 것은 ~이다.

- The present study was the first to investigate and yield supportive evidence for ~.

  본 연구는 ~에 대한 증거를 검증하고 입증함에 있어 최초이다.

- At the end of this assessment, it only remains for me to express a hope. I hope that there will be ~.

  이같은 평가의 말미에서 본인은 ~의 희망을 말하는 것만이 남았다.

- This brings us to a final set of comments: ~.

  우리의(저자의) 마지막 촌평은 ~이다.

- An implication of this negative finding is that both parties pursue disputed lands with equal degrees of zeal.

  이같은 부정적 결론이 지니는 함축적 의미는 ~이다.

- Other studies reach similar conclusions.

  ~한 결과에 이르다, 다다르다

  동사 reach는 '절정에 달하다'라는 의미로도 많이 사용된다. In the thirteenth century, the Middle Ages reached a culmination.

02 질정을 바라는 저자의 희망 / 여전히 남아 있는 문제점 지적

■ These tentative conclusions await further refinement and correction in the light of further research.

tentative란 말은 unsure, not definite or positive(불확실하고, 긍정적이지 못할 뿐만 아니라 시험적인, 한시적인, 임시의)한 의미를 모두 갖는다. 따라서 이 예문을 직역하면 '이같은 잠정적인 결론은 향후 리서치에서 보다 나은 개선과 수정을 기다린다'가 된다. 즉, 의역하면 '차후에 이어질 연구에서 이같은 불충분한 결론이 개선되고 수정되기를 기대해 본다'로 보면 무리가 없겠다.

■ Further research should be directed at determining how ~.

■ In general, it is believed that further experimentation with the methods outlined is worthwhile.

이 모델을 가지고 더 많은 실험이 필요하다.

■ It remains to be seen whether ~. ~ 인지 아닌지를 살펴보아야 할 것이다.

■ Results of this study leave more to be investigated and answered, but they do throw some doubt on claims of ~.

본 연구의 결과들은 더 많은 검토와 답변을 필요로 한다.

동사 answer는 여기에서 '~에 대한 답을 하다'의 의미로 사용되었다. 같은 의미로 exhaust는 1) 다 써 버리다, 2) 지치게 하다란 대표적인 뜻으로 우리가 많이 알고 있는데, 이 동사엔 중요한 또 다른 뜻, 즉 to draw out all that is essential in (a subject, topic, etc.) 연구 과제 등에 중요한 것을 속속들이 규명하다, 말하다란 의미가 담겨 있다. 한편, 형용사인 exhaustive는 thorough, comprehensive의 의미로 '전체적인, 포괄적인, 철저한'이란 뜻을 의미한다. 다음 예문을 통해 알아 두자.

• This does not mean, however, that the question has been exhausted.
• This article does not provide an exhaustive analysis of romantic irony in the novel.
• The author's interests are by no means exhaustively theoretical.
  (저자의 관심들은 아주 철저할 정도로 이론적이지는 않다.)

- Clark's conclusions are open to serious question.

- The question of how Blok viewed Solov'ev and his ideas remain open.

- There are, however, a number of problems that remain to be explored.
  일단의 문제들이 여전히 풀려야 할 채로 남아 있다.

- One additional problem remains to be explained, ~.
  해결되어야 할 한 가지 문제가 더 있다.

- There remains a range of problems to be tackled.

- Notwithstanding these changes in focus, issues in the area of inclusion and attitudes to disability remain the same and many research questions remain unanswered.

- This point of view still leaves unanswered several crucial question: why ~.

- Although the present study offered an initial contribution to the literature concerning ~, more research is needed.

- Clearly, more research is needed to illuminate the diversity of literacy practices in homes and schools.

- A further point that requires emphasis involves the concept of "state-building" itself.

- It remains to be seen how applicable they are to social situations involving children with and without disabilities.
  동사 remain을 이용해 어떤 미비점이나 향후 연구가 더 필요한 점을 지적하는 문장이 상당히 많다는 것에 주목하자. 다음 예문들은 전부 논문 저자의 이러한 결론적 메시지를 담고 있는 것들이다.
  The question remains as to whether or not feminist theory has transformed social theory. For sociology, and social theory, gender remains deeply problematic in that its impact can vary between the minimal and the absolute. It remains to be seen whether the Internet will remain a communication medium of the middle and upper classes. This leaves the serious problems of ~. The themes of female sexuality and fidelity are equally problematic in Jean Renart's recent book ~.

■ **What remains to be determined by future research is** the ~.

■ Nonetheless, I believe that there **remain fundamental questions**, as yet **unresolved**, about the theoretical feasibility of ~.
저자는 ~에 대한 이론적 적용 가능성(실효성)에 대한 문제들이 여전히 잔존한다고 본다.

■ Despite these findings, **there remain** two basic **limitations** inherent in this approach.

■ **There is still much to be learned** about ~ in a more general sense to include questions such as (1) ~, (2) ~, and (3) ~.

■ **There needs to be a continuing exchange** across these two sociological sub-fields.

■ **A further point needs to be made** with regard to ~.

■ The results of this study call attention to several topics **in need of further investigation**.

■ These observations suggest further questions that **must be reserved for a more extensive study**.

■ **To reach a fuller understanding** of the problem, historians **need to look more closely at** this.
이에 대한 문제에 답하기 위해서 역사학자들은 이 문제를 보다 면밀하게 검토해야 할 것이다.

■ **The paper concludes that** the characteristics of both domestic and supranational institutions **need to be taken into account to fully explain** the ~.
take into account는 '~을 고려하다, 참작하다'란 의미로 consider에 해당한다.

■ This hypothesis **needs to be** substantiated by **additional research**.

■ Certainly, the present paper **was limited in scope. Further studies on** different large-scale assessments **are needed**.
본 논문은 그 범위에 있어서 한정되어 있다. 때문에 보다 큰 규모의 차후 연구가 요망된다.

■ To be sure, this study begins with limited factual data, which some might characterize as insufficiently reliable.
물론, 이 연구는 충분할 정도로 믿을 만한 것은 못되는 한정된 데이터로 시작된다.

■ Clearly, this interpretation is speculative, and considerable work needs to be done ~.
많은 연구가 필요하다.

■ With so many problems to deal with, women's equality was hardly going to be the Bolsheviks' main priority.

■ For this theory to be complete, more is needed than what can reasonably be included in this paper.

■ Continuing deficiencies in the book are, of course, due entirely to me and not them.
이 책의 문제점은 순전히, 고스란히 저자의 몫이다.

■ Any inaccuracies which remain are, of course, my own.
논문 말미에서 간혹 나타나는 이러한 문장은 저자의 겸손한 속마음을 말해 주기도 한다. 우리말로 옮기면 '남아있는 문제는 고스란히 저자의 몫이다' 또는 '~은 저자의 책임이다'로 이해하면 좋겠다.

■ It is to be hoped that this paper will contribute to the rereading of a novel that, in my view, has been unjustifiably neglected.
'~이 기대된다, ~을 바란다'란 의미로 논문의 마지막 결론에서 가장 빈번하게 쓰이는 표현 중의 하나이다.

■ It is to be hoped that the second book will avoid the shortcomings of the first.

■ It is to be hoped that this paper will yield general insights into American history.

■ Now that the project is complete, it is hoped that the contribution included will help to orient our understanding of an area remarkably lacking in studies in English.

■ It is also hoped that this book will serve as a platform from which studies of greater depth and specificity may be undertaken.
본 저서가 ~의 주춧돌이 되기를 바라마지 않는다.

- We **hope** this article is able to **provide an impetus for** strengthening the ~.
  ~하도록 자극을 줄 수 있는 책이길 희망한다.

- **I hope** the outcome of the present paper **will be a step toward a richer and more inclusive understanding of** the reality of ~.

- **It is my hope that these argument will serve as a platform for** communication between doers and thinkers on a subject that is profoundly difficult and profoundly important.

- But several questions **merit discussion**.
  그러나 논의되어야 할 것이 많이 남아 있다.

- At the very least, this ~ **should be pursued to the point** where it links up with ~.
  좌우간 (어쨌든) ~은 ~ 정도로까지 추구되어야 (향후의 연구를 의미) 한다.

V 챕터 전환 및 문맥 흐름 언급에 자주 등장하는 표현

- This chapter **offers a quick tour** of the horizon of these quirkier and lighter features and stories.

  ~ 빠르게 훑어보다

- **The argument of Chapter 1 was that** fashion is a body technique.

- **As indicated in earlier chapters** (especially Chapters 2 and 7), ~

  이전 장에서 언급되었듯

- **In light of our discussion in** Chapter 3 of the ways in which asymmetrical interdependence helps to produce power, it is worth noting that individual actors in the cyberdomain benefit from asymmetrical vulnerability compared to governments and large organizations.

  ~에서 논의한 견지(입장)에서 볼 때

- Chapter 7 **sketched** the immediate factors behind Europe's conquest of Native Americas.

- Chapter 8 **returns to the problem** introduced in Chapter 4, the ~.

- The previous two chapters **offered** a definition of what I mean by "privacy" in this book.

- That **illustrates an issue** that will recur throughout this book.

- **So far, we have** no good answer to this problem.

- So far the **net result of** the struggle was that ~.

  net result는 '최종 결과'라는 뜻이다.

- **So far, I have been speaking of** theoretical science, which is an attempt to understand the world.

  여기서 공통적인 시점은 '현재완료'이다. 그래서 "So far"라는 시간 부사구가 들어 가는데, 이것을 대체할 수 있는 또 다른 부사는 바로 'hitherto'이다. 다음의 예문이 잘 보여 준다. I have hitherto said nothing of the advances in pure mathematics, but these were very great indeed. 또는 From what has been said hitherto about John Locke's views on property, it might seem ~.

- All of these **arguments on** sexual ethics, **it is to be observed**, appeal to purely rational considerations, not to divine commands and prohibitions.
  향후 살펴져야 할 테지만, ~에 대한 이 모든 논의들은

- We **have already seen a number of problems with** this position, but the ~.

- **As argued previously**, the first step in designing a smart power strategy is clarity about objectives.

- **A more sophisticated version of the argument says that** there are different levels of self-consciousness.

- **Now that** we have a better understanding of religion, we can go back to examining the relationship between religion and science.
  ~한 이상, ~했기 때문에

- We should also **be concerned that** an ecological apocalypse might have different consequences for different human castes.

- This question can be **carried a step further**.
  이 문제는 다음 단계로 나아갈 수 있다.

- The **optimal solution to** this problem is not, as one might hope, to ~.
  ~에 대한 최적의 해결책은

- **Let me summarize the argument**. From two strongly supported hypotheses, we have drawn a straightforward conclusion: ~ .

- **Let us sum up where we are**. = **Let us try to make synthesis of** the ~.
  ~를 종합해 보도록 하자

- **Let us keep our eye on** five big questions. First, ~ . = **Let me be clear at this point**: I am not arguing that ~.
  ~의 문제를 주목해 보자, 예의 주시해 보자

- **In the next** two **chapters**, I will say much more about the critical importance of these ~.
  다음 장에서는 ~를 논하고자 한다

■ **It is time now to turn to** Occam's purely philosophical doctrines.
~의 문제로 넘어갈, 다룰 때가 되었다

■ But we **are still left with** the fundamental question why ~.
~한 문제는 여전히 남아 있다

■ **No solution of this problem has hitherto been found,** although ~.
지금까지 이 문제의 해결책은 나타나지, 발견되지 않았다

■ **The finding of argument for a conclusion is** ~.
결론으로 맺어질 논의에서 발견된 것은 다음과 같다

■ In the **remainder** of this chapter I shall try to state briefly the philosophical beliefs which appeared to follow from seventeenth-century science.
본 장의 나머지 부분에서

■ There is, however, **a further point**, which is very curious.
논의가 더 필요한 점은

■ Some **further** quotations will make John Locke's meaning clearer.

■ Catholic philosophy, **in the sense in which I shall use the term**, is that which dominated European thought from Augustine to the Renaissance.
필자가 사용하는 용어의 의미로 볼 때, 의미에서

The Essential Guide to Writing Papers in English

VI 각주 및 미주에 자주 등장하는 표현

1. 재인용 방법
2. 논문에서 이용하는 텍스트의 출처 언급
3. 반복되는 주요 텍스트 생략법과 저자의 특별한 언급
4. 다른 논문에 대한 언급
5. 연구 현황에 대한 언급
6. 감사의 표현
7. 학회 Conference 등에서 발표된 논문에 대한 언급과
박사학위 논문에 대한 언급

01 재인용 방법

■ N. Kostomarov, *Drevnaia Russkaia Literatura* (Moskva: Nauka, 1902), p. 308,
quoted from Katerina Clark, *The Soviet Novel: History as Ritual* (Chicago
University Press, 1985), p. 113.

필자가 인용하고자 하는 부분이 다른 저자의 논문에서 이미 나와 있거나 혹은 그 원본 책을 구할
수 없어 직접 인용을 하지 못할 경우 이렇게 간접인용을 한다.

이때 인용하고자 하는 내용의 원본 출처를 먼저 밝힌 후, 이 내용을 인용한 다른 저자(필자 자신
이 발견한)의 출처를 나중에 (quoted from) 부기한다.

02 논문에서 이용하는 텍스트의 출처 언급

■ All subsequent quotations from this volume are indicated in the text with the page number in parentheses. All translations are mine.

논문의 본문에서 인용을 처음으로 할 때, 주로 이같은 표현을 자주 목격하게 된다. 인용의 효과적인 처리와 반복을 피하기 위해 맨 처음 인용시엔 모든 출처를 상세히 밝힌 후, 이같은 말로 대신하여 (이후 인용시 쪽 번호를 괄호 안에 표시하겠고, 모든 번역은 저자의 것임을 말하는 위의 예문) 긴 인용 출처의 반복을 생략한다.

■ All volume and page references from Blok's poetry, unless otherwise specified, will be taken from Aleksandr Blok, *Polnoe sobranie sochinenii* (Leningrad: Nauka, 1965), vol. 4.

위의 예문과 유사한 표현으로 '이후 본 논문에서의 모든 인용의 출처는 특별한 다른 언급이 없는 한 다음의 책으로부터'가 있다. 다음의 표현도 참고해 보자.

Unless otherwise indicated, footnotes refer to this edition.

■ All biblical references are to the *Authorized Version* unless otherwise stated. Entries concerning liturgical customs of the Church of England refer to those associated with the *Book of Common Prayer*.

본 책에서 인용한 모든 성서 참고 구절은 특별한 언급이 없는 한 ~에서 한 것이다.

■ All references to Tolstoy's works are to the ~ edition ~.

문학 작품의 인용에서 가장 기본적이면서도 중요한 것은 판본의 선택이다. 즉, 어떤 판본으로 인용을 하느냐가 논문의 학술성의 여부를 판가름하는 중요한 기준이 된다. 이때 이러한 판본 인용의 표현이 이것이다.

■ All subsequent references to this story will be placed parenthetically within the text.

- In all references to the text of *Crime and Punishment*, the numbers in parentheses indicate, correspondingly, the section and chapter of the novel.

- Further references to this edition will be by page number within the text.

- Further citations from this text will be parenthetically referenced by page number.

- References to *The Brothers Karamazov* will be noted within the test of this article by volume and page numbers.

- Parenthetical references to citations from *Don Quixote* refer to the part and the chapter, respectively, from which the citations are drawn. The former are provided in roman numerals, the latter in Arabic numerals. Page numbers are those of the edition cited.

- Here and below all citations from Leskov's works refer to ~. The first number in parentheses is that of the volume, the second-the page.

- Henceforth all references to Gorky's work will be indicated by volume and page number.

- Quotations in English are from Nabokov's translation.
  영어를 제외한 다른 제3의 언어로 되어 있는 자료의 영어 해석을 인용할 때, 저자 자신보다 더 권위 있고 번역이 잘 된 것을 논문에 인용할 때 쓰는 표현이 바로 위와 같은 방법이다. 그러나 저자 자신이 직접 한 번역일 경우엔 다음과 같이 표현한다.
  - Translations are my own.
  - All translations are my own unless otherwise noted.
  자신이 누군가가 번역한 자료를 인용하면서도 마음에 들지 않아 부분적으로 자신의 번역을 삽입하거나 타인의 번역을 수정하면서 인용할 때에는 다음과 같은 표현을 이용한다.
  - I have used Brown's translations, but have made considerable changes.
  - All translations into English are mine and aim at a close rendition only.

- Throughout this article, page references after quotations from Gorky are to the most readily available English translations: ~.

03 반복되는 주요 텍스트 생략법과 저자의 특별한 언급

- All quotations from Pushkin's works are from ~, hereafter abbreviated as ~.
  '이하 혹은 이후부터는 ~로 생략한다'의 표현이다. 먼저 인용하는 출처를 완벽하게 밝힌 후 쓴다.

- *PSS from here on.*
  흔히 인용하는 책의 제목이 너무 길거나, 논문에서 반복적으로 사용되는 경우 이처럼 책 제목 전체를 한 번 언급해 주고 '이하 ~로 생략한다'는 표현을 많이 쓴다.

- Mandelshtam's *The Egyptian Stamp* (1928; henceforth: *ES*)

- Here and further on this section I use **bold face type** for my own emphasis.
  때에 따라서는 논문을 쓰다가 저자가 원본에서도 없는 강조를 할 때가 있다. 이럴 때 '인용 시 굵은 글씨체 강조는 원본의 것이 아닌 저자 자신이 한 것'이란 표현이 위와 같은 문장이다.

- (emphasis added)
  인용 시 원본에는 없는 강조 표시를 할 때, 혹은 특별한 강조를 추가로 삽입한 경우 이렇게 표현한다.

- (*my italics*, S. H. K.)
  저자가 따로 강조를 한 경우 '이탤릭체 강조는 저자의 것'이라고 한 후 자신의 이니셜을 부기한다.

- In order to keep the specific gravity of scholarly substance as high as possible in these references, a number of technical economics have been made. Full references are given only on the first usage; all titles are given only in the original language; only the first initial of an author is generally given.
  이 말은 각주나 미주를 달 때, 어떤 책이 처음으로 인용될 때에만 정확한 모든 사항(저자, 서명, 출판사 등)을 표기하고, 그 다음부터는 간단하게 적겠다는 말이다.

- The literature on both topics is very extensive, and no attempt at comprehensive listings will be attempted here. But readers interested in ~ could start their research with some of the following: ~
  여기서(참고 문헌에서) 모든 자료를 다 기입하지는 않을 것이다. 하지만 관심 있는 독자들은 아래의 리스트를 참고하라.

04 다른 논문에 대한 언급

■ V. Erlich accurately articulated this approach, ~.

■ The strength of Fellman's approach came from his sophisticated weaving of historical events with the diverse and complex sociological undercurrents of the guerrilla war. 접근 방법의 강점은 ~에 나타난다.

한편, weave A with B는 '~과 ~을 연결시키다'란 뜻이며, interweave A with B와도 유사하다. 다음 문장과 비교해 보자.

Lincoln's religious transformation was closely interwoven with his policies regarding emancipation and war. The political economy arguments changes are closely interwoven with the socio-structural considerations. An extensive discussion of Marx and Engels is interwoven with an analysis of social theory in the 19th century novel. The histories of museums and archeology are closely intertwined. The structure and urban design are intertwined with historical evolution. If ethics is not woven into the fabric of business education, the business academy runs the risk of encouraging telepathy in its hidden curriculum.

■ Lincoln's wartime rhetoric drew on ancient traditions that remained popular in American religious culture.

동사 draw on은 '~에 의존하다'란 뜻으로 rely on과 같은 말로 자주 쓰인다.

■ Drawing from the macrocomparative method, I analyze variation across more than five hundred labor markets in the United States in 1990 to determine whether ~.

~한 방법론에 의거하여(기초하여) 저자는 ~을 분석하고자 한다.

■ Wolfgang is correct / wrong in claiming that ~.

다른 사람의 논문을 얘기하면서 '~는 ~하는 점에서 옳다 / 잘못이다' 등의 표현을 이렇게 한다. 만약 그 사람의 논문이 아주 매력적이어서 ~로부터, 어떠한 점에 영향을 받았다는 등의 논평을 말하고자 할 때는 다음과 같은 비유적 표현도 적절해 보인다.

I am much persuaded by Anderson's idea of the ~.

- Richard Peace seems **right in** his **contention that** ~.
  ~라고 주장하는 점에 있어서 ~는 옳아 보인다.

- **The key to** Anderson's **arguments** is the invention of the ~
  ~의 논의의 중심, 핵심은 ~이다. 즉, ~가 주장하는 논점의 핵심은 ~이다.
  The desire to manage the body is the key to producing the social body. = A well-educated labor force is another key to economic success in an information age. = Understanding the interplay of geography, technology, and institutions is fundamental to understanding human history. (~의 핵심은 ~이다, ~을 하기 위해서는 ~이 핵심이다)

- McKeown's argument **is weak on** two points. First, he does not explain why ~.
  '~의 논증은 두 가지 점에서 미약하다'란 뜻으로 자주 쓰이는 표현이다.

- William Commer is **probably right to see** it as ~.

- Witchell's work **offers useful** insights into Dostoevsky's methods of presenting the personal perspectives of his characters.

- Kuprin **offers the fullest account of** this odd event in the history of Russian modernism.
  ~에 대해 가장 완벽하게, 빠짐 없이 모두 설명하고 있다.

- Epshtein's discussion of neo-paganism **offers a good example of** his overall approach to culture studies.

- None of these approaches, I believe, **offers** an adequate solution.

- Unbegaum **gives a fully justified critique of** the ~.

- Vinokur **hints at** this connection in her article on ~.

- The basic **tenet** in William's **reasoning** about ~ **rests on** ~.
  tenet은 principle, dogma, doctrine 등과 같은 말로 사용된다.

- **At the heart of** Hayek's political philosophy **lies** the conception of the ~.
  ~의 사고, 이론의 중심에 ~이 있다 즉, ~은 ~의 이론적 중심이다.

유사한 다음의 표현을 참고해 보자. At the center of Schulz's approach lies an attempt to understand the problem of the social distribution of knowledge. Ian Hacking employs the concept of dynamic nominalism to accentuate the interplay between experience and classification. Two approaches are employed to examine ~. In surveying various modes of the narration, Jakobson observes that ~.

위 예문에서 "~의 중심 ~가 있다"라는 표현을 배웠는데, 이번에는 비유적인 의미에서 중심지, 본거지에 해당하는 두 단어를 알아보자. 바로 '진앙지'에 해당하는 epicenter라는 단어와 '본거지, 고향'에 해당하는 단어 home이 있다. In 2010, China was home to the two largest and four of the ten largest banks in the world. = Tropical climates are home to rain forests and savannas, the ancestral homes of humanity in Africa.

■ Vladimir Propin **puts forward** the very interesting **hypothesis** that ~.
~한 가설을 내놓다.

■ This **assumption** is **supported** not only **by** the mention of ~.

■ Proffer **reads** Makar's speeches **as** direct expressions of Dostoevsky's opinions.
~을 ~로 받아들이다, 이해하다.

■ Perhaps **it would be informative to** cite Felix Oinas's comments on ~.
~하는 것이 정보가 될 만하다 즉, ~하는 것이 도움이 되어 보인다.

■ Conrad's study is very **informative** and **wide-ranging**.

■ As scholars across the social sciences have become interested again in the problem of inequality, **research on the issue has become increasingly wide-ranging**.

■ Sidney Monas's book may be **the first in-depth discussion of** the Biblical myth.
~에 대한 최초의 심층 있는 연구, 토론

■ The most **authoritative account of** the ~ is still ~.
~에 대한 가장 권위 있는 설명, 언급은 ~이다.
반면, 말 그대로 '비중 있는'이란 뜻을 표현하고자 할 때는 weighty란 형용사를 쓰도록 하자.
Despite its slim size, ~ is a weighty and welcome contribution to the study of ~.

■ To date the **most authoritative version** seems to be published in the journal *Neva*, No. 6, 1985, although other versions should be consulted, such as ~.
가장 권위 있는 판본 인용

- Hughe's new book can be recommended without hesitation to anyone looking for **an authoritative account of** its subject of ~.

- **Major contributions to** the study of Russian cultural poetics in the early 19th century **have been made by** Donald Fanger.

- Linsey Watton has already **done** some very interesting **works on** Kuzmin.

- Interesting **observations on** the meaning of ~ **can be found in** Bethea's recent study, *Modern Russian Culture*.
  ~에 대한 흥미 있는 관찰은 ~에 나와 있다.

- Meyer has some interesting **remarks on** the ~.

- **In** Ewha Thompson's **discussion of** ~, one detail turns out to be of particular interest; he tries to ~.
  '~의 논증, 토론 속에서 매우 흥미 있는 ~이 들어있다'는 표현으로 자주 쓰이는 예이다.

- **Even more positively**, Lotman suggested that ~.

- Tynianov **succinctly** expressed the nature of ~ and he aptly ~. 간결하게

- Like Proffer, Gasparov **is inclined to** see ~ as ~. ~하는 경향이 있다.

- There are some indications that historians **are** more **inclined to** seek generalization than they used to be.

- In civilized countries, we **are inclined to** associate literature with writing.

- Nabokov **made** a great many **statements about** reading, and **there is not space here to give them an adequate discussion**.
  간혹 이같은 주를 우리는 발견하는데, 이는 주로 한정된 논문의 지면을 이유로 추가 설명을 생략한다는 의미이거나 혹은 논지의 흐름상 논의의 설명이 불가피하게 들어가는 것을 방지하기 위한 설명으로 보면 좋겠다.

- She **made** a number of clear **theoretical statements**, each with important political implications for feminism.

■ *Philosophy of Art* is a classic statement on general hermeneutics.
'~에 대한 고전적인 설명' 즉, '~을 논한 아주 중요하고, 대표적인 설명'이라는 뜻

■ However, his studies do not sustain scrutiny.
위의 문장을 직역하면 '~의 연구는 자세한, 주위 깊은 관찰을 유지하지 않고 있다'란 뜻으로 즉, '~을 자세하게 분석하고 있지 않다'정도로 이해하면 좋을 것이다. 이 명사가 들어간 예문을 알아보자. The link between culture and psychology first came under close scrutiny in the 19th century.

■ The amount of research ~ poses some provocative questions on ~.
pose a question on은 '~에 대한 문제를 다루다, 취급하다, 야기시키다'란 의미로 '~에 대한 문제 제기를 하다'로 보면 무난하겠다. 다음 문장을 비교해 보자.
This suggestion poses interesting and meaningful challenges ~.

■ To this question Conrad offers no reply.
'~에 대해 응수, 응답이 없다'는 뜻으로 '~을 다루지 않고 있다'로 보면 된다.

■ This approach to market embeddedness suffers from no theoretical logic.
동사 suffer from은 '~로, ~ 때문에 고통받다'란 뜻이다. 따라서 이 문장은 '~한 접근법은 이론적 논리가 부족하다'로 의역하면 좋겠다.

■ Fuller's account suffers from many shortcomings and mistakes.
'~의 설명은 결점과 과실 태반이다.' 즉, '결점과 실수들이 너무 많아 ~의 설명은 설득력이 없다, 명쾌하지 못하다.'는 뜻까지 유추해 볼 수 있다. 다음 문장과 비교해 보자.
At this point, Kierkeggard runs into difficulties with which he cannot conclusively deal.

■ This new concept currently suffers from a number of fundamental flaws.

■ For decades, India suffered from what some called the "Hindu rate of economic growth" of a little more than 1 percent *per capita*.

■ Our theories about the world can suffer in other ways as well.
'이런 접근 방법이 위험에 직면하다'의 의미를 나타내고자 할 때는 다음의 문장을 알아 두자.
This approach runs two risks.

■ For all of these positive achievements, Soviet librarianship suffers from weakness, some of which the Soviet themselves acknowledge.

- **To** Proudhon's **claim** that the woman had no other function but the domestic one, Marx **answered that** if so, she was unfit for the care of children.
  '~라는 주장에 대해 ~는 뭐라고 답하다'란 의미로 아주 많이 쓰이는 문장이다. 이와 비슷한 유형으로 다음을 참고하자. <u>To the argument</u> that woman had always been subservient, Mill <u>answered that</u> new knowledge and conditions necessitated change and the mere description of the status quo was not sufficient to justify it. 또는 In regard to woman's role beyond the family, Mikhailov was in the favor of maximum development.

- Each of these approaches has its **drawbacks**, and there is the additional problem of establishing ~.
  접근 방법들이 한결같이 단점들을 보여 주기 때문에, ~을 제기해야 하는 문제가 더 남아있다.

- There are several **deficiencies** in these statistics that should be noted at the outset.

- This type of media effects theory has **been widely criticized** as textual determinism which robs readers of their social context and critical agency.
  많은 부분에서 비판 당한, 여기저기서 비판 당한

- **Against the charge that** ~ Bech invokes the argument of ~.
  ~라는 비난에 대해(~에 대한 맞대응으로) ~는 ~하다.

- **Against claims that** postmodernism dissolves hierarchial gender dichotomies, this account implies that ~.
  ~라는 주장에 대해 ~은 ~하다.

- Boris Uspensky **was the first** critic **to** use the term.

- Wertz **was the first** scholar **to** treat in detail the issue of the experience in Russian of words which ~.

- Andrew Barratt **is** apparently **the only** writer **to** have discussed ~.

- William's thesis, while elegant, **has by no means been universally accepted.**
  ~의 이론이 아주 훌륭함에도 불구하고 보편적으로 인정되고 있지는 않다.

- Although the claim **has been championed by** Mideast specialists, it is difficult to test by examining only cases from the Middle East.
  이 밖에도 '~에 의해서 옹호되다' 즉, '누가 ~라고 주장하다'란 의미로 동사 champion이 많이 쓰인다.

- The concept of market price efficiency **has been widely applied in** domestic commodity markets.

  동사 apply는 '~을 어디에 적용하다'라는 뜻으로 가장 일반적으로 쓰이는 동사이다. 다음 예문을 통해 그 쓰임새를 잘 알아 두자. In recent years, scientists have <u>applied</u> the tools of public health and medicine <u>to</u> better understand the incidence of injuries and the risk factors. Collective action is a term that has been broadly <u>applied to</u> a wide range of phenomena in the social sciences. Postmodernism is a term <u>applied to</u> a general shift in progressive cultural politics.

- In a discussion of ~, Dan Slobin **suggests that** ~.

- This interpretation **is given by** Lonard Babby's ~.

  ~에 의해서 해석된 즉, ~가 해석한

- Many excellent suggestions for the usage of ~ **are offered by** Joseph Lake.

- This article does not **provide** an **exhaustive analysis** of romantic irony in the novel.

  매우 전체적인, 포괄적인, 철저한(thorough, comprehensive) 분석을 보여 준다.

- E. Driessen **provides a very helpful summary of** the scholarship surrounding the mystery of the work.

- He **holds the view that** ~. ~한 견해를 지니다, 갖다.

  hold가 들어간 또 다른 예를 알아보자. This confirmation <u>holds true</u>, in any case, <u>for the</u> ~. 이 예문에서 '우리는 for 이하의 문장에서도 이같은 확정적인 내용이 여전히 사실이다, 즉 이같은 분명한 것이 어떤 경우에 있어서건 for 이하의 내용에도 들어맞는다'로 이해하면 좋을 것이다. 또는 다음의 문장도 비슷한 범주 내에서 이해될 수 있다. This <u>holds good for</u> all periods; ~ (즉, 이것은 모든 기간에 걸쳐 유효하다, 어느 시기에도 들어맞는다).

- Yet elsewhere Kollontai **made it clear that** ~. ~을 분명히 하다, 입장을 드러내다.

- These ideas **leave no doubt of** what Lenin's intentions were.

  아무런 의심을 남겨 놓지 않는다. 즉, ~임이 분명하다.

- References in this work **leave little room to doubt that** ~.

  ~라고 의심할 여지(기회)를 거의 남겨 놓지 않았다, 즉, 아주 분명, 확실하다.

- The more recent studies of congressional voters **leave no doubt that** ~.

- Later historians **have cast doubt on** the Masonic origins of iconography of the Great Seal of the United States.
  ~에 의문을 던지다, 표하다, ~을 의문시하다

- The author's interests are **by no means exhaustively theoretical**.
  아주 철저할 정도로 이론적이지는 않다.

- Two points in Mellor's paper **calls for further investigation**.
  연구가 더 필요하다.

- In an interesting article Diana Burgin **elucidates** the connection between ~.
  명료하게, 명확하게 설명하다.

- A similar **assertion is made** in Paul's excellent chapter of *The Queen of Spades*.

- **A similar trend is observable in the** ~. 유사한 경향이 ~에서 관찰된다.

- The "master plot" **is discussed in detail** in Section I of my introduction to *Russian women's writing*, ~, **to be published by** Oxford University Press in 1997.
  '~에서 자세하게 다루어져 있다'는 뜻. 뒤의 굵은 글씨 부분은 '~에서 출판될 예정인'이란 의미이다.

- **Until relatively recently**, Soviet literature **was** very much **dominated by** normative definition of realism which dictated, among other things, the mimetic depiction of reality.
  비교적 최근까지 ~은 ~에 의해서 지배되어 왔다.

- The **bibliography is enormous. For a start**: ~.
  위의 예문은 '참고 문헌이 방대하며, 그 초보적인 책으로는 ~을 참고해 볼 것'이라는 의미이다. 흔히 참고 문헌은 bibliography 혹은 reference라는 말이 있다. 여기에서 이 단어를 이용한 문장의 예를 살펴보자. For a useful bibliography in ~, as well as ~, see ~. For further reference to material dealing with ~.

- On this point, **see** V. Frank, *Russian Folk Arts* (Indiana University Press, 1996), pp. 34-80.
  '~ 점에 있어서는 다음의 책을 참고하라'는 가장 전형적인 표현이다. 이때 동사 see를 이용하면 된다.

- **For** an account of the ~, **see** ~.

  이 표현 역시 가장 일반적인 예문으로서 '~한 설명, 해석을 위해서는 ~을 참고하라'는 의미이다. 물론 전치사 for 다음엔 설명하고자 하는 내용 즉, discussion, explanation, survey 등이 다양하게 올 수 있다.

- **For** the most thorough study of ~ **to date**, **see** ~.

  지금까지 ~에 대한 가장 꼼꼼한(철저한) 연구를 위해서는 ~을 보라.

- **For** a more extensive treatment of ~, **see** ~.

- **For** a comprehensive discussion of the novel's structure, **see** ~.

  ~에 대한 보다 포괄적인 논의는 ~을 참고하라.

- **For** a detailed examination of ~, **see** ~.

- **For** a more detailed discussion of this, **see** ~.

- **For** a fuller discussion of these issues, **see** ~.

  ~에 대한 보다 자세한 논의는 ~을 보라.

- **For** an overview of popular and critical responses to the novel, **see** ~.

- **For** an informative and balanced assessment of the problem, **see** ~.

- **See** in particular the work of Roger's study. ~의 연구를 특히 참고하라.

- **See** the excellent illustration of these relations provided by ~ R. Symes, *The Roman Revolution* (Oxford, 1939). ~이 보여 주는 훌륭한 설명을 참고하라.

- DuMouchel **provides** some useful additional **evidence on** ~.

  ~에 대한 유용한 증거를 보여 준다.

- Another recent study, conducted by Smith et al. (1998), also **provides supportive evidence** for this element of the theory. ~을 뒷받침해 주는 증거를 제공한다.

  '~한 실험, 연구를 하다(실시하다)'를 의미하는 동사에는 주로 conduct와 perform을 사용한다. et al은 보통 논문이나 저서의 저자가 4인 이상인 경우 많은 지면을 차지하는 것을 피하기 위해, 첫 번째의 main author 이름만 기재한 후 이렇게 간략하게 표시를 해 준다.

- These findings **strongly support** his theory's line of reasoning: ~.

- As can **be inferred from** Carver's (1995) definition of ~. ~의 정의로부터 유추할 수 있듯이

- The first obvious **inference to** be drawn from this table is the ~.
  이 도표에서 찾아질 수 있는 첫 번째 유추는, 본 도표에서 우리가 유추할 수 있는 첫 번째의 것은 ~이다.

- In a more recent study, Kim and Mauborgne (1996) **took things one step further by arguing** that ~.
  ~을 논증함으로써 ~의 연구는 한 발짝 진일보하였다.

- **Based on this finding**, Goldhaber ultimately concluded that ~.
  '이같은 결과에 기초하여 ~는 ~한 결론을 내리다'라는 뜻. 여기에서 finding은 사회과학 혹은 자연과학 계통에서 어떤 실험 등의 연구 결과물을 지칭하는 단어로 가장 널리 쓰이는 말이다.

- Dahl's new paradigm for political studies **is based upon** three concerns: ~.
  ~의 새 패러다임이 ~한 관심 사항들에 기초해 있다.

05 연구 현황에 대한 언급

- **Much has been written**, of course, **about** Pasternak's artistic conception, and I cannot here even begin to list relevant titles or to cite pertinent references. However, I would like to point to two particular treatments of the subject which I have found unusually insightful: ~.
  ~에 대한 연구가 많다.

- **A great number of** articles concerning ~ have been published in Germany.

- There is a **vast literature on** ~.
  literature는 문학을 뜻하기도 하지만 문헌, 자료, 참고 문헌 모두를 두루 일컫는 말로도 사용된다는 점을 상기해 두자. 이 문장에서는 '~에 대한 방대한 문헌이 있다'가 된다.

- **A vast literature is dedicated to** the history of the relationship of Georgia and Jerusalem.
  엄청나게 많은 문헌이 ~에 바쳐져 있다. 즉, ~에 대한 연구 문헌이 많다.

- **The existing literature on** national identity provides little guidance in exploring ~.
  ~에 대한 현존 문헌은

- **The literature on** nationalism and national identity **has been dominated by a focus on** the historical origins of ~.
  ~에 대한 문헌은 ~에 대해 주로 초점이 맞추어져 왔다. 즉, ~에 대한 초점이 ~의 문헌에 지배적이었다.

- While **there has been a great deal of research on** the ~, the ~ remain underrsearched.
  위 문장은 '~에 대한 연구는 상당히 많이 있어 왔으나 그에 대한 ~은 여전히 연구되지 않고 있다'는 대구 내용의 표현이다.

- **Amidst the stream of** Pushkin-related publications of recent years, arrives an excellent three-volume collection of critical and investigative articles.
  최근 ~ 관련 출판물의 홍수 속에서

- **There has been quite a bit of recent scholarly effort aiming to** understand territorial disputes.

- These debates **have provided a substantial body of theory upon which** ~ social scientists have subsequently been able to draw.
  이같은 논의들은 이후 ~들이 기초로 삼을 수 있었던 광범위한 논리의 구심체를 선보였다.

- Despite the prominence of evaluations of statistics texts, there is surprisingly little **literature on** ~.
  ~에 대한 평가는 상당함에도 불구하고 ~에 대한 문헌은 놀라울 정도로 없다.

- **Enough has been said to** demonstrate that ~.

- **There is currently much discussion about** which is the correct way to practice Feng Shui in the West.
  풍수를 실행할 올바른 방법에 대한 논의가 현재 서구에서 활발하게 진행되고 있다.

- **There is increasing awareness** that ~.
  ~에 대한 인식(~라는 인식)이 날로 늘어가고 있다.

- **Many attempts have been made to** cope with ~.
  ~하기 위해 수많은 시도들이 있어 왔다.
  반대로, '~한 시도가 없었다'는 표현은 No attempt has been made to ~.

- In the past decade, Halina Stephan **has attracted considerable attention from** the emigre community by a number of controversial books of non-fiction.
  ~로부터 상당한 관심을 끌어 왔다.

- Dulle Griet (1562), perhaps Bruegel's most puzzling painting, **has attracted the attention of scholars.**

- The question of Heidegger's mysticism **has attracted a certain amount of attention.**

■ The question of how to characterize the ~ **has engaged current scholarship across a range of fields.**
~에 대한 문제는 다양한 분야에 걸쳐 현재의 학계에 관련되어 왔다.

■ Charles Peirce's writings **have had immense appeal for** analysis of visual culture in recent decades.
~에 막대한 영향을 행사하였다, 매력을 끌어 왔다.

■ To date **no single monograph yet surpasses** the seminal contribution made more than fifty years ago by G. T. Robinson, whose ~ **remains best study** in English on the Russian peasantry.
지금까지 그 어떤 단행본도 ~의 연구를 앞지르지 못했으며, ~의 연구는 가장 훌륭한 연구(업적)으로 남아 있다.

■ The "YBA"(Young British Artist) **came to international attention** in the early 1990s with a combination of elaborate construction, lame jokes, and apathetic shock.

■ For a long time, the lack of English translations of early Russian literature was a great obstacle for teachers and students of Russian literature as well as general European literature at the universities in the United States and in other English speaking countries. **Luckily in recent years, this situation has started to change for the better.** This is partly **a result of the growing awareness of** the richly diversified area of early Russian culture which for a long time had been closed to the West.
~에 대한 점증하는, 늘어나는 인식의 결과

■ **In recent years** the historiography of Spain has made small but perceptive **strides toward** discussing women as historical subjects outside the specific context of the household.
최근 들어, ~에 대한 연구에 있어 규모는 작지만 눈에 띌 정도의 두드러진 발전이 있어 왔다.

■ Recent scholarship **has been inclined to** consider Anglo-American relations during the first two decades of the 20th century in terms of an enhancement of American power.
최근의 학계는 ~하는 경향을 보인다.

■ Despite cultural differences, the focus of Japanese politics today **tends to** be centered on universal political issues regarding sources of state authority.

■ In recent years, with popularity of whole language, literacy researchers **have become increasingly interested in studying** ~.
~에 대한 연구에 점점 관심을 보여 주고 있다.

■ The issue of the social status of women during the Middle Age, especially that of German women, **has been raised with increasing frequency** at international scholarly forums of the recent decade.

■ In recent studies, communication researchers **have indeed become interested** in explicating communication traits in terms of biology, ~. The twenty years following Warren's book (1978), subsequent legislation and codes of practice **saw (witnessed) a plethora of debate and research on** the ~.
~에 대한 논쟁과 연구가 엄청나게 증가되었다.

interest가 들어간 문장을 하나 살펴보자. Sociologists have a long-standing interest in the study of social deviance. 여기에서 당연히 long-standing interest란 '오랜 동안 관심을 두어 온, 즉 시간적으로 오래된'이란 의미가 내포된 것이다.

■ **Much interest has been aroused in** Russian books among the English speaking public since the appearance of such excellent translations of the works of Tolstoy and Turgenev.
~의 분야에서 상당한 관심이 고조되고 있다.

arise와 같은 의미로 '생겨나다'란 뜻을 지니고 있는 come into being을 알아 두자. Likewise the idea of the family came into being to serve the needs of a newly recognized childhood.

■ **Recent years have seen an increasing discussion about** the way in which the legal system deals with children and the issue of children's rights.

■ The democratic deficit in the EU **has been of increasing importance for** the political agenda of the EU, after the signing of the Maastricht Treaty.

■ The impact of book reading in the home on children's language and literacy development **has been a topic of active interest** since at least the 1960s.

■ The new historiography **has become a leading force** in French historical science.

■ **The focus on** improving worker and workplace competence accelerated in the UK during the 1980s, driven by concerns that ~.

- The chapters in this volume **have gone through several rounds of commenting**.
  많은 코멘트를 받은

- The role of state policies in shaping new worker and carer practices is **a much debated issue**.
  많이 토론된(논쟁의 대상이 많이 된) 이슈

- This chronological definition of the Middle Ages **has been under attack for decades**, and in recent years with particular intensity.
  ~은 수 년간 공격을 받아 왔다.

- The central platform of these criticisms **concerns an attack on** the coherence of the general understanding of the ~.
  이같은 비판의 중심은 ~에 대한 공격이다, ~에 대한 공격이 비판의 핵심이다.

- This type of media effects theory has **been widely criticized** as textual determinism which robs readers of their social context and critical agency.
  ~는 ~때문에 (~로) 광범위하게 비판받아 왔다.

- Policy interest in the nation's early education and child-care enterprise **has risen dramatically** over the past decade.
  ~에 대한 관심이 눈에 띄게 성장했다.

- Historians in recent years **have begun to take an interest in** the body.
  ~은 ~에 관심을 갖기 시작했다.

- Point of view has **taken on renewed importance** in the past few years.
  ~의 중요성이 새롭게 인식되고 있다.

- Recent scholarship on third-wave democracies **has come to focus on** ~.
  제 3세계 민주주의의 최근 연구 경향은 ~을 중심으로(~에 초점을 맞추고) 이루어지고 있다.

- In the earliest years of the field, the majority of historical field workers **focused their attention on** the ~, using traditional and conservative field methodologies to analyze the material culture of the recent past.

- Multidisciplinary studies **are currently receiving new emphasis among** scholars in a wide variety of ~.
  ~은 현재 ~들 사이에서 새로운 강조(주목)를 받고 있다.

■ Since the 1990s the topic of rhetoric **has assumed increasing significance** not only **in** ~ but even in ~.

~의 주제가 ~에서 점점 의미를 갖게 되었다.

■ Interest in international business **is** understandably **gaining visibility in** the curricula of many business schools.

~은 ~에서 점점 눈에 띄게 나타나고 있다.

■ Most recent research **has been preoccupied with** the macro and meso (institutional) changes, resulting in an emphasis on the functioning of collective bargaining.

동사 be preoccupied with는 '~에 완전히 몰입한, 오로지 ~에만 신경 쓰는'(completely engrossed in, absorbed in) 이란 의미로 자주 사용된다. Urban water supply planning <u>has been preoccupied</u> historically <u>with</u> how to increase supplies to meet growing demand. French romances <u>occupy</u> a central position in the development of medieval European literature.

■ There has been **a general tendency to** hypothesize ~.

~을 하는 일반적인 경향이 있다.

■ **There are currently two main approaches in** the psychology perceptions: one argues that ~; the other opts for ~.

~의 분야에는 현재 두 가지 주요 접근 방법이 있다.

■ The material in this study **comes from the work of the following authors**: ~.

각주나 미주에서 저자가 주로 사용한 참고 문헌을 개략적으로 언급할 때 이렇게 표현하면 좋겠다.

■ **Much of the material presented here is drawn from** research on the ~.

■ Kinship has long **constituted** an important **domain of research** in sociocultural anthropology.

~한 분야가 연구의 중요한 영역을 차지해 오고 있다.

중요 영역(important domain)의 개념으로 유사하게 쓰인 예문을 살펴보자.

This is encouraging not only because the PS hypothesis becomes part of the <u>public domain</u> and is consequently ~.

■ Historians considering this issue **have generally fallen into one of two camps**: (1) those who believe that ~, and (2) those who argue that ~.

이같은 이슈를 논하는 사학자들은 다음의 두 진영으로 나뉘어졌다.

- Since 1989, the question of public values has been one of the most critical and the most controversial in the study of postcommunist politics.

- Social movements have become a privileged arena for Latin American social inquiry today.

- Health and welfare services are an integral part of human societies and cultures.
  ~의 아주 중요한 부분이다.

  be integral to란 표현을 더 배워 보자. Ultimately, refinement is integral to the entire writing process. 또는 Freud's more literary engagements are integral to the writing and practices of psychoanalysis but ~. 한편, be central to, be essential to 모두 비슷한 의미로 쓰인다. The confrontation of body and soul and of earth and heaven was central to medieval aesthetics and was expressed especially in the grotesque, in both art and literature.
  지금처럼 술부를 후치시켜도 좋고, 아래의 예문과 같이 전치시켜 문두로 내보내어 사용할 수도 있다. Essential to the public health of the modern European city was the ability to bring clean water into the city and to expel sewage from it. (~에 본질적인 것은 ~ 이다)

- In fact, nowadays, it is commonplace to describe economic restructuring and the new economy as essentially about the spatially defined process of "globalization"– the worldwide spread and integration of capital, goods, and service markets.

- Reading aloud to children has been a commonplace activity in homes and schools for centuries.
  commonplace는 ordinary, uninteresting의 의미로, '~은 이미 진부하고 식상하다'란 뜻으로 해석하면 좋다. 달리 말해서 이 표현은 '~은 (~을 말하는 것은) 이제 이미 진부한 얘기이다, 이미 많이 알려져 있다'는 뜻이다. 다음 문장과 비교해 보자. It has become commonplace to speak of crisis and transformation as one phenomenon. commonplace와 유사한 표현으로 '~한 것이 일반적이다, 다반사이다, 상당히 보편화되어있다'란 뜻으로 customary를 넣은 문장을 확인해 두자. More recently, it has become customary to characterize business cycles by means of the statistical properties of observed time series. 또는 It is conventional to assume that modern social theory is a post-Enlightenment phenomenon.
  It is commonplace to say that science concerns "is," not "ought."

- Interdisciplinary has long been a familiar word in discussion of education and pedagogy, but recently it has acquired a new force and urgency.
  학제 간 연구는 ~에 대한 토론의 장에서 이미 친숙한 말이 되어 왔다.

- Several historians have **pointed out that** ~. ~을 지적한다.

- A number of scholars have **expressed** in various ways the idea of double visions.

- **It has been suggested** that ~.

- **It has been claimed** that ~.
  '~을 주장하다'란 동사는 많이 있다. 다음의 예들은 특히 논문에서 자주 사용되는 것들이니 알아 두자. 참고로, 유사한 동사에는 contend, assert, insist, maintain, ascertain 등이 있다.
  A central proposition of this study <u>contends</u> that changes within capitalist social relations will result in changes in the spatial organization of production.
  Classical economic theories <u>maintain</u> that humans are rational calculating machines.
  Religion <u>asserts</u> that we humans are subject to a system of moral laws that we did not invent and that we cannot change.

- Central idea of Marx is the **claim** that ~.

- Many **claims** have been advanced concerning talk show experts.

- Certainly **there is no dearth of relevant sources on** this topic; ~.
  ~과의 관련 자료가 적지 않다.

- Kelly's study **has been largely ignored by** ~.
  대체로 무시되어 왔다, 관심을 끌지 못했다.

- Surprisingly, the poem **has rarely studied** in the vast literature on Pushkin.
  부사 rarely는 seldom, hardly 등과 같이 '거의 ~하지 않다'는 뜻으로 (이미 이 속에 부정의 의미가 들어가 있기 때문에) 그 다음에 부정의 표현이 오지 않고 긍정의 표현이 와야 문법적으로 옳은 문장이 된다. 즉, 위의 문장은 '~에 대한 엄청나게 많은 참고 문헌에서 ~은 거의 연구되어 있지 않다'란 의미이다.

- Surprisingly **few studies have examined** ~.

- Chekhov **is underrepresented**, while Pushkin is overrepresented.
  미비하게 다루어진, 반면 과도하게 비춰진

- Despite the **plethora** of humor research, **little is understood about** the ~.
  plethora는 overabundance 또는 excess를 의미한다. 즉, '연구된 바는 많아도 ~에 대해서는 인식이 부족하다'로 보면 좋겠다.

- **There is**, however, **little research yet on** the ~.

- There are no statistics available to confirm the ~. ~을 확증해 줄 통계 자료가 없다.

- In contrast to the voluminous scholarship on ~, there have been **few general studies on** ~.
  ~에 대한 엄청나게 두터운 학계(학문적 결실이 많다는 의미에서)에 비해 ~에 대한 일반적인 연구는 매우 적었다, 거의 없었다.

- Feminist perspectives on international relations **have proliferated in the last ten years**, **yet** they **remain marginal to** the discipline as a whole.
  여전히 지엽적이다. 즉, ~의 연구 분야는 여전히 사각지대이다.

- **The field of** tourism studies **is relatively young** and, as such, is still establishing its basic tenets. In addition, gender analysis within tourism studies is even younger and the integration of the two bodies of tourism and gender research is, in fact, almost never seen.
  ~의 영역, 연구 분야는 아직 초보 상태이다.

- There is a **paucity of research on** the history of women in social work in Canada, particularly for those who provided leadership in social work education.
  ~에 대한 연구가 적다, 소량이다.

- **Given the paucity of material on** Chinese culture written by non-Chinese scholars, this collection is essentially welcome.
  ~에 대한 자료가 매우 적은 것을 감안해 볼 때

- **On the question of** Turkish membership in the European Union, however, **no meaningful progress has been made**, nor appears likely in the near future.
  ~의 문제에 대해서는, 관련해서 어떤 가시적인, 의미 있는 (연구) 진척은 없었다.

- In my view, **there is no up-to-date**, **clear**, **short history of** Spain that gives approximately equal attention to earlier Spanish history and to the modern period since 1800.
  저자가 아는 한 지금까지 명쾌하고 간결한 ~에 대한 ~은 없다.

■ **On the subject of** ~, students should begin with Joseph Conrad's book.
~에 관한 주제에 관련해서

■ This view **is dismissed by** a number of French historians who insist that ~.
위 예문은 "이 견해는 일단의 프랑스 사학자들에 의해서 묵살, 무시되었다"란 의미이다. 즉, 동사 dismiss는 "어떤 생각을 일축하다, 묵살하다"란 뜻으로, 보통 수동태로 사용되지만, 아래와 같이 능동태로도 역시 많이 사용된다.
1) Many thinkers <u>dismiss</u> the idea of superintelligence as science fiction, because they view intelligence as something mysterious that can exist only in biological organisms.
2) The controversial position on AI safety research is no longer to advocate for it but to <u>dismiss</u> it. 3) The signaling role of sanctions has often <u>been dismissed</u> as "merely symbolic." 4) Many others have <u>dismissed</u> privacy as a normative value.
반대로 "주장하다, 목소리를 내다"와 같은 의미로는 argue, voice, hold와 같은 동사를 사용한다.
1) Conventional wisdom has always <u>held</u> that the state with the largest military prevails, but in an information age it may be the state(or nonstates) with the best story that wins.
2) Animal-welfare activists have <u>voiced concerned about</u> the suffering such experiments inflict on the rats.(~에 대한 입장을 표명하다, 목소리를 내다) 3) You may <u>counter-argue</u> that the ability to silence or enhance the voices in your head will actually strengthen rather than undermine your free will.(반대론을 주장하다, 반대 입장을 주장하다)

■ Much Soviet work **has** also **been marred by** a thick ideological emphasis on the Russian peasants supposedly progressive influence on non-Russian groups.
be marred by는 '~로 인해서 손상되다, 훼손되다, 가치를 잃다'란 의미이다. 즉, 이 문장에서는 '두터운 이데올로기로 인해 소비에트의 많은 연구들 본래의 가치가 손상되고 있다'로 보면 좋겠다.

■ Standard approaches **have failed to reveal** the unity of ~.

■ None of these theories under consideration **provides satisfactory criteria for** identifying the boundaries of the Middle East regional system.
어떠한 이론도 ~에 대해(~을 위한) 만족스런 판단 기준을 보여 주지 않는다.
위 문장에서 criteria for와 거의 동일한 의미(~의 기준, 척도)로 사용되는 숙어 중에 다음의 것이 있다. In the twentieth century per capita GDP was perhaps the supreme <u>yardstick for</u> evaluating national success.

■ Adherents of this approach **tend to** believe ~.

■ **Evidence of** ~ is the highly readable and densely compact study **by** Leonov, who has managed to capture some of the facets ~.
~에 대한 증거는 ~의 연구에 잘 나와 있다.

■ While there appears to be no definitive **evidence** that ~, it is clear that ~.
비록 ~에 대한 명백한 증거는 없어 보여도 ~은 확실하다.

■ The key to Morson's theoretical model **is supplied by** Mikhail Bakhtin, especially his notion of ~.
~의 이론적 모델의 핵심은 애초에 ~의 것이다.

■ The terms **have gradually gained currency in** all kinds of non-Western cultural **milieu.**
여기에서 동사 gain이 들어간 예문을 더 알아보자. ~한 주제 혹은 용어가 점차 토론의 중심이 되면서 학계에서 빈번하게 논의될 때 이 동사를 많이 쓴다. The battle over lesbian and gay rights has gained increased prominence in the political arena. 또는 occupy를 써도 무방하다. Debates over methodology have long occupied a prominent role in political science and its various empirical subfields.

■ The relationship of outside-school learning with higher school levels of achievement across students **has been a recurring theme in** policy discussions ~.
recurring은 recurrent와 같은 말로 '~에 있어서 반복되는, 되풀이하여 나타나는'이란 말이다. 여기에서는 '~의 분야에서 자주 나타나는 주제가 되고 있다'는 의미로 '연구 대상으로 자주 나타나고 있다'는 말로 보면 좋겠다.

■ Democracy and human rights in Canada **have been a prominent subject of discussion** in many international forums over the past ten years.
~ 토론의 두드러진 주제가 되어 왔다. 즉, ~이 어떤 토론의 주제로 자주 상정되고 있다.

■ Other important feminist issues **have surfaced** within the American Library Association since 1985.

■ Concern about becoming a magnet for the high-level nuclear waste of other nations **has** not **surfaced as a serious issue** in the United States.
동사 surface는 '표면으로 드러나다, 가시화 되다, 나타나다'(bring to the surface; cause to appear openly)란 의미를 모두 포함한다. 즉, '~한 이슈가 공론화 되고, 논쟁의 대상이 되기 시작했다'는 의미이다. 동사 emerge로 대체해도 위의 문장은 의미 전달에 문제가 없을 것이다. 다음 예문을 참고해 보자. The second wave of feminism emerged in the late 1950s in the

form of a sustained women's movements. Communibiology has emerged recently as a new paradigm for study of communication. The environment has recently emerged as an important dimension of the public debate over international trade. Korean emerged as one of the fastest-growing foreign languages in the world.

■ Intense criticism of the auditing standards-setting process **has surfaced** periodically over the last 20 years.

■ The symbolic relationship between central cities and suburbs is **a frequent topic for** social **research.**
~은 ~ 연구에 주제 대상이 자주 된다. ~의 잦은 연구 대상은 ~이다.

■ Sex discrimination is a **paramount issue** for liberal feminists.
여기에서 paramount는 major와 대체될 수 있다. 즉, '~에게 있어 주요 이슈'로 해석하면 좋겠다. 비슷한 표현을 소개하면 다음과 같다. Lesbianism is another major concern of radical feminists. Homosexuality and lesbianism have been an active topic within ~.

■ Causation **has become a promising area of research** over the last five to ten years due to progress on the three fronts: ~.
~의 연구는 전도유망한(비전이 있고, 장래가 밝은) 영역이 되어 왔다.

■ During the 1990s, the related issues of citizenship and identity **have become two of the most widely debated topics** in the social science.
~ 분야에서 가장 활발하게 토론된 주제가 되어 왔다.

■ The Gothic stained glass in the choir clerestory of the cathedral of ~ **has come to scholarly purview only recently.**
'극히 최근에 와서야 ~은 학자들의 연구 영역이 되었다'는 뜻으로, 여기에서 purview는 the range of concern, understanding, or insight의 뜻을 포함한다. purview가 사용된 또 다른 예를 알아보자. None of this rich and diverse material falls within the purview of our discussion here(본 논문에서 우리가 살피고 있는 토론의 범위, 영역). 즉, 이 문장에서처럼 purview는 scope 혹은 range와 동의어로 사용되고 있다는 것을 알아 두자.

■ Relational satisfaction is one of the **most researched areas** of interpersonal communication.
~은 가장 연구가 많이 된 분야이다.

■ Identity politics **is an increasingly central focus of** theories of global politics.

■ The controversy **created a minor stir in** Russian circles before appearance of Turgenev's major articles.
~에 대해 반응을 불러일으키다.
다음 문장들도 함께 확인해 두자. Deming Brown's own articles and his translation of Mill <u>met with immediate response</u>(즉각적인, 신속한 반응을 얻었다). Kim's articles and his views of ~ <u>met with immediate response</u>.

■ Kollontai's views **have won** her some **celebrity** in the West.
to win someone celebrity는 '~에게 ~한 위세, 유명, 명성을 안겨주다'로 이해하면 좋겠다.
비슷한 표현을 더 알아 두자. Her views <u>enjoyed</u> more or less <u>the full respectability of</u> a government white paper.

■ The *Annales* school **left its most controversial imprint** and **met with** the most opposition abroad.
가장 논쟁적인 흔적, 인상을 남겨 놓았고 가장 강한 반대에 직면하였다.

■ Lately, these ideas **have enjoyed enthusiastic reception from** ~.
~로부터 대대적인, 열정적인 환영을 받아오고 있다.

■ One scholar **has argued** that ~.

■ Some pro-Soviet thinkers **made the radical arguments** that ~.
급진적인, 혁신적인 논쟁(언쟁)을 했다.

■ Scholars and critics today **are quick to** question such cultural constructions and to seek to ~.
~에 민감한, 예민한

■ **There has been a general recognition of** the superiority of markets relating to short-term responsiveness to shifting economic conditions.
'~에 대한 일반적인 인식이 있어 왔다' 즉, '~이 일반적으로 인정되어 왔다'로 의역해서 이해하면 가장 좋을 것이다.

■ This new focus **entails** a shift in the meaning of ~.
동사 entail은 '필연적으로 ~을 수반하다' 즉, involve by necessity or as a consequence란 의미로 강한 메시지를 전달할 때 쓰인다. 다른 동사로는 contain을 쓸 수 있다.

- The process of linguistic creolization **entails** grammatical and lexical expansion.

  동사 entail과 비슷한 의미로 embrace 또는 engage가 있는데, 다음의 예문을 통해 용례를 확실하게 알아 두자.

  The humanities have increasingly <u>embraced</u> interdisciplinary practice-not without fights and struggles. The interdisciplinary modes of the humanities <u>engage</u> questions of meaning and significance, of value and virtue in practices and products. The humanities <u>engage</u> three broad sets of questions: those of meaning, value, and significance. His failure to <u>engage</u> western sources helps to make ~. If there is a shortcoming in the book reviewed, it is that they do not <u>engage</u> recent work in textual criticism in any significant way. James Billinton's latest book <u>is an engaging look at</u> Russian identity formation through the lens of intellectual history, particularly the writings of figures in the 19th century. Sang Hyun Kim's article <u>engages in a detailed study of</u> very particular ritual-the lament.

- **On the grounds that** women were actual or potential mothers, this legislation banned them from certain types of work which might damage their health.

  on the grounds that은 '~과 같은 입장에서, ~을 근거로'란 의미이다.

- Arguments over the Soviet cannon **have spawned** a debate over the function of writers.

  동사 spawn은 원래 '알, 새끼를 낳다'라는 의미로 은유적으로는 '~을 야기시키다' (give rise to), '~을 대량으로 만들어 내다, 양산하다' (produce in large number)란 뜻에서 cause, bring about과 동의어로 사용된다. 다음 문장을 참고해 보자.

  In the United States, the federal structure <u>spawned</u> a series of industrial politics, under the umbrella of antitrust, that made the state a referee in the market.

- This naive image **spawned** the belief that the United States enjoyed a special relationship with China as a kindred spirit.

06 감사의 표현

- I **wish to express my gratitude to** Hugh McLean **for** his helpful suggestions.
  가장 일반적인 표현으로 먼저 감사의 마음을 전하고자 하는 사람 앞에 전치사 to를 쓴 후 그 이유 즉, 친절한 조언, 아낌없는 제안 등의 내용은 전치사 for 다음에 표현한다.

- I **wish to thank** Mary Halpin **for** her helpful advices and comments.

- **My thanks** also to David Ransel and Jane Burbank **for** their helpful comments on an earlier version of this article.

- **My deepest debts of gratitude goes to those people** who helped to shape this project from its earliest stages-before it was ever to be a book?to its present form.

- I **am indebted to** John Bailey's technical assistance.
  be indebted to란 표현을 알아 두자. 말 그대로 '~에게 빚지고 있다'는 뜻으로 '~로부터 영향을 받은, 도움을 받은, ~ 때문에 ~하게 된'의 뜻으로 이해하면 좋겠다. 다음의 문장을 하나 더 알아 두자. This study builds upon and is greatly indebted to the past twenty-five years path-breaking work on the Western European family by the Cambridge Group. 따라서 be indebted to는 '영향을 주다'란 뜻의 influence와 대체될 수 있다. The accounts I have in mind have been partly influenced by the claim of historians like Jacques Le Goff(저자가 염두에 두고 있는 설명은 [프랑스 아날 학파의 대가] 쟈크 르 고프 같은 사학자들의 주장에 일정 부분 영향을 받아 왔다.).
  이와 유사한 표현으로 be fueled by는 '~로부터 연료를 받은' 즉, '~에 의해서 촉발, 시작된' (to be encouraged by, to be stimulated by)의 아주 고급한 의미로 쓰인다. 다음 예문을 통해서 그 쓰임새를 잘 알아 두자. Fueled by the growing influence of social history and development studies in the sixties, the field has made significant advances ~(1960년대 사회사와 사회 발달 연구의 점증적인 영향들에 자극 받은 이 연구 분야는 그간 의미 있는(상당한) 진전을 이루어 왔다.). 유사한 의미의 또 다른 문장을 살펴보자. 모두 어떤 연구 성과를 개괄할 때 많이 쓰이는 것들이다. Mulvey's essays gave fresh impetus to the debate about the male gaze and

voyeurism, power and subordination(~의 에세이가 ~에 대한 토론에 신선한 자극제를 부여했다, 즉 ~로 인해서 연구의 신선한 바람을 불러일으켰다.). (=Lacan's ideas <u>opened up the field</u> for ~.)

■ The author is most indebted to J. Thomas who noticed that ~.

■ I remain deeply indebted to the many friends and colleagues who have guided and stimulated my thinking about ~.
~에 진정으로 감사한다.

■ I am greatly indebted to the libraries in which I have been privileged to work: ~.
~에 깊이 감사하며(빚진 것이 많다), ~을 연구하는 데 특전을 받았다.

■ I feel a special debt to the Congress of the United States, a number of whose official delegations I have accompanied to Russia and many of whose members have encouraged me to produce a work something like this.

■ I wish to acknowledge the helpful comments and advice of Stephen Beller.
~의 도움될 만한 조언에 감사를 표하고 싶다.

■ I am grateful to Prof. Maia Kipp for her useful comments on an early version of the paper.

■ I am grateful to Saladin Peterson and Diane Koenker, who read several drafts of this article and offered me the benefits of their comments and suggestions.
이 논문의 초고를 여러 번 읽어 주고 코멘트와 조언을 해 주신 ~에게 감사드린다.

■ The author gratefully acknowledges Prof. Fanger's indebtedness to the following teachers and colleagues for their advice and encouragement at various stages of ~.

■ I would like to express my deep gratitude to the Center for the Advancement and Study of Peace for the fund necessary to conduct the research that led to this article.

■ The author wishes to thank Stephen Baehr and the readers from *SEEJ* for (perceptive) commenting on the earlier drafts of this article.

■ The author would like to thank all those who have commented on the subsequent paper.

■ **For critical readings of earlier drafts of this paper** I wish to thank Boris Annenkov **for** his conductive suggestions.

■ **For helpful comments on previous drafts of this article,** I am grateful to Irina Baehr, and an anonymous referee for the journal.

■ **For support in the preparation of this paper, my thanks to** the Kennan Institute **for** a Research Scholarship in the summer of 1997, where I was fortunate to work in close proximity to Prof. Paul Werth.

■ **I benefited from comments on** a version of this paper presented at the conference, "Between Past and Future: The Struggle for Democracy in Russia," organized by Vladimir Sorin and held at Central European University, 27-29 March 1999.
~에 대한 코멘트에 감사드린다(~의 은혜를 입었다).

■ I **received critical research support from** the International Research and Exchange Board.

■ I **owe many thanks to** my colleagues **for** their assistance with this project.

■ I **owe a special debt to** Professor Sir Isaiah Berlin of Oxford.

■ **For the book, I owe special thanks to** the Cambridge Corporation of New York and its past and present presidents, Drs. David Hamburg and Vartan Gregorian.

■ I certainly **owe a debt of gratitude to** Lona Valamo, whose understanding and flexibility permitted me to orchestrate an undertaking of such daunting size.

■ **Special thanks are due to** my research colleague Geoffrey Hosking.

■ The author **thanks** Herb Eagle and anonymous reviewers **for** their helpful criticism of earlier versions of this paper.

■ I **appreciate** the enthusiasm and good counsel of the publisher Peter Kaufman.

- Much of the research for this article was assisted by generous support from the Social Science Research Council and the American Council of Learned Societies and the Center for Soviet and East European Studies at the University of Chicago.

- Research for this article was supported (assisted) by a grant from the International Research and Exchange Board, with funds provided by the US Department of State (Title VIII program).

- Research for this article was made possible in part by funding from the Social Science Research Council and the University of Florida Scholarship Enhancement Fund.

- Support for the research was provided by the International Research and Exchange Board, with funds provided by the National Endowment for the Humanities ~.

- The research on which this article is based was facilitated in part by a faculty research grant from the University of Massachusetts at Boston.
  동사 facilitate는 '조장, 촉진시키다'란 뜻으로 '~에 의해서 촉발, 야기, 시작되었다'는 의미로 이해하면 좋겠다. 다음 문장을 통해서 확실하게 알아 두자. This task can be facilitated by the criterion of the system and by consideration of its various levels: (1) ~ and (2). 또는 To facilitate understanding of this book, and thus as an introduction to the questions themselves, it seems necessary to examine the different meanings and evaluations assigned to the concept of civilization in Germany. 이와 유사한 단어로 launch 역시 빈번하게 사용된다. The study of Russia in the United States, as in England, was launched not by universities or by the government, but by gifted amateur scholars and journalists.

- The research and travel undergirding this lengthy project have been funded at times by grants from the Davis Postdoctoral Fund of Princeton University.

- This article is based on research financed by a grant from the Economic and Social Research Council.

- Grants from the Kennan Institute for Advanced Russian Studies and from the West Chester University supported the research and writing of this paper.

- I gratefully acknowledge a grant from the International Research and Exchanges Board(IREX) in the Fall of 1983.

■ Research for this article was made possible by grants from the International Research and Exchange Board and the American Council of Teachers of Russian.

■ Funding for this article was provided by a World Bank project investigating the state of interest groups in Ukraine.

07 학회 Conference 등에서 발표된 논문에 대한 언급과 박사학위 논문에 대한 언급

- A slightly revised version of this article was delivered at the Kentucky Foreign Language Conference in Lexington, Kentucky (April, 1998).

- An earlier version of this paper was presented at the 1980 annual meeting of the American Association of Teachers of Slavic and East European Languages (AATSEEL) Huston, then included as the second chapter of my dissertation.
  '디서테이션'은 박사학위 논문을 말한다. 다음 문장을 참고해 보자.
  The present paper is the first of four projected chapters of a monograph on the trial in Dostoevsky's works.

- An earlier draft of this article was read at the AATSEEL meeting in San Francisco on 30 December 1987.

- A previous version of this paper was read at the AATSEEL meeting in New York, December 28, 1974.

- A previous version of this article was presented at the AATSEEL Conference in San Francisco, 1998.

- The first essay in this collection was originally presented as a paper at a conference on The Strange and Marvelous in Medieval Islam.

- This text was presented in 1980 at a colloquy held at Cornell University on problems in intellectual history.

- This article was presented as a paper at the 1975 Annual Convention of the South Atlantic Modern Language Association in Atlanta, GA.

- A preliminary version was delivered at the Wilson Center, and a variation on it was presented at the annual meeting of the American Historical Association in Chicago, January 2000.

- An abbreviated version of the paper was delivered in July 1993 at a conference hosted by the University of Liverpool in England on "Literary Theory and the Practice of Editing," which I attended with a grant from the University of Arizona.

- I presented a preliminary version of this paper at a panel on language and ideology at the 1998 annual meeting of the AATSEEL in Chicago.

- This article was written while in residence at the Kennan Institute for Advanced Russian Studies and the Hurriman Institute at Columbia University.

- This paper was written while I was a Visiting Faculty Fellow at the Center for Ideas and Society, University of California at Riverside, in the Spring Quarter of 1993.

- It was delivered as a lecture to the Classics Department of UCLA in March 1993.

- The preparation of this article was supported in part by a grant from the University Research Committee of Emory University.

- This paper has been given at seminars in Cambridge, London and elsewhere.

- This volume represents the fruits of papers and discussions from the 32nd National Conventions of the American Association for the Advancement of Slavic Studies (St. Louis, 18-21 November, 1999).

VII 서평에 자주 등장하는 표현

1. 애정 / 열정의 소산 / 관심의 성장 / 결실
2. 책의 내용에 대한 구체적인 언급
3. 책의 구성과 편집에 대한 언급
4. 책의 장단점에 대한 언급

01 애정 / 열정의 소산 / 관심의 성장 / 결실

- This two-volume set is a labor of love which presents some twenty years of painstaking work.

- Pamira's anthology is a labor of love which accomplishes many things.

- The compiler of the volume is to be congratulated warmly for his labors.

- Duganov's research is the result of his endeavor.

- The collection is an outgrowth of interest in the criticism of Russian literature.

- This book is an outgrowth of the great intellectual support I have received over the years from colleagues around the country who study foreign policy analysis.

- This monumental fruit of the translator's labor ~.

02 책의 내용에 대한 구체적인 언급

■ Graffy **provides** a well-ordered and well-reasoned **analysis of** ~.

■ Barbara Helt **provides** some fascinating **observations on** ~.

■ In her introductory essay, Tamira has **provided ample information about** Russian cultural life.
~에 대한 충분한 정보를 제공한다, 보여 준다.

■ The cinema section **provides a superb overview of** the film output, noting the difficulties the industry faced after the fall of the Soviet Union.
각 장이 ~에 대한 총체적인 조망을 보여 주는

■ It **presents an adroit mixture of** literary and popular forms ~.
~의 훌륭한 복합, 결합을 보여 준다.

■ Overall, throughout the work the author **makes a considerable effort to provide** the reader **with a detailed analysis of** the socio-political and economic context in which films were produced.
독자들에게 ~에 대한 자세한 분석을 보여 주려고 상당한 노력을 하고 있다.
동사 provide는 언제나 with와 함께 '~에게 ~을 제공, 공급, 보여 준다'는 의미로 많이 쓰인다.

■ Roger Key **offers** a discerning **analysis of** the deep connections and affinities.
discerning은 '통찰력 있는, 분별력 있는'이란 뜻이다.

■ Volfgang Kasek **offers** the reader **an analysis of** the work of the lesser-known writer.
잘 알려지지 않은 작가에 대한 분석을 선보이고 있다.

- The book **offers** a useful **compendium of** Leskov's extensive writings on the subject of satire.
  ~에 대한 개요, 요약을 보여 준다.

- The introduction **offers a wealth of information.**
  풍부한 정보를 제공한다.

- Fusso's masterful commentary **offers an indispensable key to** the understanding of ~.

- This book **offers** some trenchant **guidelines for** approaching the writer's literary work.
  작가의 작품에 대한 접근 방법을 위한 지침서 역할을 한다.

- Bogert's book **offers a sophisticated examination of** the aesthetic, political and philosophical significance of Dostoevsky.
  ~에 대한 매우 정교하고 치밀한 연구를 선보이고 있다.

- Belknap **offers** a structural **method for boiling** literary plots **down** to a series of binarily linked events.
  숙어 boil down은 '~을 요약하다'라는 의미이다.

- Baehr's book **is** sufficiently **sophisticated to appeal to** a professional audience of literature specialists.

- This book **pulls together a great deal of useful information about** the lore of Slavic vampire.

- The book should **prove useful to** students of French and allied studies as well as to the general reader.

- Karlinsky **gives an overview of** Gogol's satirical works.
  ~에 대한 전반적인, 총체적인 설명을 한다.

- The aim of this book is to **give the reader** a logically organized, lucid, unembellished **account of** the main events and developments in the history of Mexico from its origins to today.
  본 저서의 목적은 독자들에게 ~에 대한 논리적이며 간결하고 윤색되지 않은 설명을 제공하는 것이다.

- The book contains a number of interesting observations on ~.

- This book contains a wealth of survey and statistical data on ~.
  ~에 대한 조사와 통계 데이터가 풍부한 책

- Jebb Husik makes the correct observation that ~. ~을 올바로 보고 있다.

- No folktale, ritual, or work of literature is analyzed in depth.
  ~이 깊게 논의된다, 분석된다.

- In his book, Pronin undertakes a detailed analysis of ~.
  ~에 대한 자세한 분석을 하고 있다, 분석을 실행, 단행하고 있다.

- The author presents here a comprehensive review of Bulgakov's usage of biographical and thematic structure.
  comprehensive는 '포괄적인, 종합적인'이란 의미이다.

- The collection presents a great range of material on popular culture in focused, incisive analyses of specific phenomenon.
  ~에 대한 광범위한 범위를 보여 준다.
  이와 유사한 의미의 다른 문장을 더 알아보자.
  The book provides the most broad-ranging coverage of major domestic and international political shifts in the Balkans over the last fifteen years.

- Making Sense of Social Movements offers a clear and comprehensive overview of the key sociological approaches to the study of social movements.

- Alexandrov, with great lucidity, presents parallels and connection ~.
  알기 쉽게, 명쾌하게 보여 준다, 제시한다.

- Hubbs made an explicit statement on how ~. ~에 대해 함축적인 설명을 했다.

- In the treatment of Pasternak's text, the author follows and verifies the assumption that ~.

- Most of what he says in this essay was carefully thought out, lucidly delineated, and tested by poetic text.

- Otto has **marshaled a wide range of** sources, including publications from the beginning of the century and documents from the ~.

  동사 marshal은 '~을 인도하다, 안내하다, 소개하다'란 의미로 이 문장은 '광범위한 자료들의 출처를 소개하고 있다'로 이해하면 좋다.

- Barker's book **employed a wide range of sources** for this study of Ivanov.

  바커의 저서는 ~의 연구를 위한 출처의 광범한 범위를 이용했다, 보여 주었다.

- Owell's study **sketches out** the important relationship with ~.

  ~의 연구는 ~을 일별, 조망하고 있다.

- Petunin's research **sheds new light on** the problem of ~. ~을 새롭게 조명한다.

  '새롭게 조명하다, 밝히다'란 뜻의 다른 표현에는 throw new light on이 있다.

  Hosking's article on Tolstoy's critique of art <u>throws new light on</u> Tolstoy's attitude toward ~.

- Robert Martin **brings new insight to** the same problem of ~.

- Gail Lehnhoff's book **has advocated a new approach to** the study of ~.

  ~에 대한 새로운 접근 방법들을 제창, 주장한다.

- The author **exhibits** a fairly high degree of unity in his **approach**.

  저자는 자신의 접근 방법에서 ~을 보여 주고 있다, 펼쳐 보인다.

  위의 문장에서 동사 exhibit은 display, present, employ 등의 다른 단어로 대체될 수 있다.

- **New approaches to** classic works **are taken by** Gerald Mikkelson, who argues compellingly against the widely-held view of the ~.

  ~는 새로운 접근 방법을 선보이고 있다.

- Daniel's careful survey of the popular genres in terms of subjects and plots **opens the way for further** analysis of the value system.

  ~의 연구가 향후 ~의 길을 열어 놓다.

- Dolez's paper **sets up** the innovative **theme of** ~. ~한 주제를 선택하다.

- In this book, the author **traces the roots of** the distrust to the ~.

  ~의 근원을 찾다, 추적하다.

- The book **touches on** the ~ issues, but brings in a new perspective.   ~한 주제를 다루다.

- This issue has been several years **in the making**.   최근 수년에 걸쳐 형성되고 있는 이슈

- **Heavy emphasis is given** in this volume **to** the Jewish question.
  이 책에서 중요한 강조점이 ~에 있다, ~의 문제에 많은 비중을 두고 있다.

- In her conclusion to the book, Marina **sets out a new framework for** postmodernism in cinema.

- Belknap, like any others, **focuses much attention on** Tolstoy's usage of language in his works.
  ~에 상당한 많은 중점을 두고 있다, ~에 초점을 많이 맞추고 있다.

- Considerable documentation **is produced to show** ~.
  상당한 양의 문서들이 ~을 보여 주기 위해 제시되어 있다.

- Inna Broude, in her recent book, **detects** various aspects of nostalgia in the poetry of Vladislav Khodasevich.
  동사 detect는 '~을 찾아 내다, 발견해 내다'를 뜻하는 것으로 find out과 같은 표현으로 많이 사용된다.

- Having obtained access to a mass of **archival material**, Boyd has provided the most complete and accurate record of Nabokov's life.
  영어로 알카이브(archive)는 고문서 기록으로 통하는 단어이다. 즉, 역사적으로 중요한 인물, 작가 등의 생애 필사본 서한문이나, 정부의 주요 기록 등을 일컫는 것으로 이에 대한 치밀한 연구는 기존 연구 결과에 새로운 답을 제시하거나, 연구 경향의 새 흐름을 만들어 낼 정도로 아주 중요한 연구 출처가 된다. 위의 문장은 'Boyd는 상당한 분량의 고문서 기록을 확보함으로써 (작가) 나보코프 생애에 대한 가장 완벽하고 정확한 기록을 보여 주고 있다'로 해석하면 좋겠다.

- Peter Barta's work **challenges** some basic tenets in Soviet research on Turgenev.
  ~에 반기를 들다. 즉, 기존의 비평에 도전하다.

- Siniavsky **challenges** an accepted interpretation of ~.

- Frederic Deyo **offers an ambitious challenge** prevailing theories of ~.
  ~의 지배적인 이론들에 과감한 도전을 보여 주고 있다.

- These remarks **challenge an entire set of postulates** implicit in contemporary socio-cultural history in France.
  이같은 언급들은 ~ 일련의 가정 전체에 반기를 들고 있다.

- As its title suggests, Agriculture in the United States is **an ambitious work**, and there are few scholars as qualified to undertake such a project as Dell Upton.
  ~는 야심작이다.

- Raymond William's Culture and Society, 1780-1950 **remains a masterful summing-up of** this "culture and society" tradition~.
  어떤 분야에서 ~를 가장 잘 요약하고 있는

- This paper **represents a challenge to these kinds of assumptions**, asking what ~.

- It is unclear **on what basis** the author of this book made his selection of Tolstoy's novels, and **with what criteria in mind** he prepared his bibliography, which is insufficient.
  '저자가 어떠한 바탕에서 자신의 참고 문헌을 작성하였으며, 또 어떠한 기준을 잣대로 삼고 있는지 명확하게 제시되어 있지 않다'는 의미이다.

- **The overall argument of the book** is sufficiently broad and interesting to recommend it to both Slavists and comparativists.
  본 저서의 전반적인 토론(점)은 ~이다.

- The volume is **timely and useful in its concerns with** a whole range of phenomenon associated with modernism.
  ~한 점에서 시의 적절하고 유용하다.

- In her conclusion Reyfman **sums up** matters as follows: "~."
  다음과 같은 결론을 내린다.

- **The translations** are both **accurate** and **fluid**, clearly **the labor of the informed love of** the individuals responsible for each translation as well as the scrutiny of knowledgeable editors.
  번역이 정확하고, 수려하고, ~한 애정의 소산이다.

- Cornwell's **translation** is **quite solid** and **reliable**.
  번역이 믿을 수 있다.

solid가 들어간 다른 문장을 예로 들어 보자.

The author's study of Turgenev and his literary criticism is also a <u>solid</u> piece of research.

■ The author's **translations** are **thoroughly annotated**, providing the reader with information on the secondary literature on a given historical and literary problem.
저자의 번역에는 철저하게 주가 달려 있다. 즉, 독자들의 이해를 위해 상세한 주가 달려 있다.

■ This monograph is **a richly detailed study of** the nature of evil in Dostoevskii's major works.

■ Its appearance **will be a welcome addition to the body of translations of** recent Soviet Russian literature, as is the current volume.

■ Medieval texts are notoriously difficult to translate, and Dr. Heppell **has produced a translation that is far superior to the excerpts previously available** in English.

■ Tony Anemone **deserves our admiration for** the clarity and verve of his writing, as well as the rigor of his thinking.
~ 때문에 독자들의 환영을 받아 마땅하다.

■ This assumption **deserves** scrutiny in light of the unusual, even unique, example of the Italian peninsula in the Middle Age.

■ The author **delves into** how Gogol has his characters misread.
동사 delve는 '~ 속으로 파고들다'란 뜻으로 학술적인 우리말로는 '~을 천착하다'로 보면 좋겠다.

■ Hilton **grapples with** the question of how Dostoevsky's thinking about.
'~와 씨름하다' 즉, '~로 고심하다'란 뜻으로 '~의 문제를 놓고 열심히 해결하려 노력하다'란 의미로 이해하면 좋겠다.

■ Each of these essays is an attempt to **grapple with** some aspect of imaginative universe of Sholokhov.

■ American art educators have been **grappling with** concepts of multicultural art education for a number of years.

- It would be impossible to quibble with ~.
  숙어 quibble with는 '억지스런 변명을 하다'란 의미이다.

- Rather than quibble with specific points of view and interpretations in the work, I will end by reemphasizing the importance of this book for Russian intellectual history and Russian literature. It is a must for any medieval age scholar.

- For reporting on Soviet participation in the World War II, readers should consult Alexander Werth, *Russia at War* (New York: Carroll and Graf, 1984).
  ~의 분야에 대해서는 ~의 책을 꼭 보아야 한다.

- Philippe Sherry has provided one magisterial interpretation of the way death has been perceived in European history.
  ~에 대한 기념비적(두루 기억에 남을, 훌륭한) 해석을 보여 준다.

03 책의 구성과 편집에 대한 언급

■ This two-part monograph **is devoted to** the detailed discussion of ~.
책의 내용이 주로 '~한 것을 다룬다' 혹은 '~에 할애되어 있다'는 표현인 경우 지금처럼 be devoted to를 가장 많이 사용한다.

■ The author **owes** his last observation **to** Nabokov's narrative.
위의 예에서처럼 '~을 ~에 바치다'란 의미로 결국 '이 저자의 마지막 장은 ~에 대해서 쓰고 있다, 다루고 있다'는 말로 이해해야 할 것이다.

■ In Chapter III, the author **devotes considerable discussion to** Tolstoy's *War and Peace.* He then examines ~.

■ **Particular attention is devoted to** the interaction between ~.

■ Marwitz's **main intension is to** correct certain subjective critical errors by appealing to ~.
이 경우처럼 '~하기 위한 것'이란 표현에서 주로 be to-용법을 많이 쓴다. 이러한 예는 논문의 도입 부분인 서론에서도 빈번하게 이용되는 것으로 이 책의 PART 1 (II-3)을 참고해 보자.

■ Chapter 3 is a **cornucopia** of information on Leskov.
상당히 비유적인 단어로서 본래 '풍요의 뿔'이란 신화적 배경을 지닌 말이다. 이로부터 풍부란 말이 파생된다.

■ Chapter I **provides a useful overview** and **evaluation of** criticism of Blok.
~에 대한 유익한 요약(개요)과 평가

■ Chapter III **makes perceptive observation about** ~.

■ Chapter VI **treats various topics ranging from** style **to** translation.

- The chapters **are ordered as follows**: ~.
  모든 장들은 다음과 같이(다음과 같은 방식으로) 구성되어 있다, 짜여져 있다.

- Each chapter **follows the same outline**: ~.

- The rest of the volume **is divided into sections** on: ~.

- The present volume **consists of** four parts: ~.

- Part I **is concerned with** the portrayal of women and their new roles from the first issues of the 1920s. Chapter 2 **discusses the ways in which** changes in the law marriage were presented to women. Chapter 3 explores writings on gender relations. Chapter 4 **looks at** attitudes towards beauty. Part II **looks in** general terms at writings on women's experiences of collectivization. Chapter 5 **focuses mores specifically on** representations of women and work. Chapter 6 turns to the domestic sphere. Chapter 7 **draws out** the gender confusion in the law. Chapter 8 **is devoted to** representations of women in the magazine of the 1930s.

- **Most welcome is the chapter on** Ivan Bunin.
  가장 환영받을 만한 것은 ~에 대한 장이다. 즉, ~을 논한 장이 가장 훌륭하다.

- This book is divided into ten chapters, **in accordance with major historical-literary periods**.
  문학사의 시기 구분대로 나뉘어진 책에 대한 설명이다.

- The findings of this study were **in accordance with** my expectation that ~.

- **Each chapter is preceded by an abstract, written by the general editor and focusing on important literary and historical events of the period**–a useful feature for undergraduate and graduate survey courses.
  각 장이 짧은 요약과 역사적으로 주요한 사건들에 대해 편집자가 설명을 달아 놓은 형식의 책을 소개할 때 대표적으로 나타나는 문장이다.

- The present volume **is a most welcome contribution** since it makes available virtually all Pushkin's known early verse.

- All in all, this book **is most welcome** and **should be of great interest to a broad audience**.

- This book is the highest priority reading for anyone interested in modernism.

- The best pages of the book are devoted to 19th century European novels.

- Of the book's five chapters, the first is the best.
  다섯 개의 장으로 된 책 중에서 첫 장이 가장 훌륭하다.

- Section III includes some of the author's best work on ~.

- The book is organized into seven thematic parts with nineteen chapters.

- The book is arranged as a set of case studies of well-known controversies surrounding evolutionary topics.
  ~의 사례 연구로 이루어진 책

- Susan Amert's excellent study operates on an elementary division of Anna Akhmatova's poetry into two major periods.
  동사 operate on은 '~한 효과를 나타내다'란 의미로, 이 문장에서는 '~을 논하는 장에서 저자의 탁월한 연구가 돋보인다'로 이해하면 좋겠다.

- The book purports to be a study of Chekhov's attitude toward women.
  동사 purport는 '~을 취지로 한다, 목적으로 한다'의 의미이다.

- The overall direction of this volume is clearly stated in the introduction.

- The 15 different papers in this collection reflect ~ in their variety the wide range of approaches to German literature.

- The range of topic in this collection is wide, reflecting the varied scholarly interests of Prof. Maia Kipp.

- The author displays a vast knowledge of world literature.

- Fleishman's book deepens our knowledge of the history of Japanese literature.
  우리의 지식을 넓혀 준다.

- William Veder's **profound knowledge of** the subject is evident in the detailed bibliography at the end of the book which alerts the reader to recent studies in the field.

- Propp's articles are very **knowledgeable** and **give the reader an imaginative and subtle analysis**.

- The list is supplemented with **extensive annotations** giving information on ~.
  ~에 대한 정보를 제공하고 있는 광범위한 자료 목록이 딸려 있다.

- An accurate **index is provided** and the **bibliography is extensive**, **helpful** and easy to use.

- The book concludes with an **extensive bibliography** of sources cited and a **detailed index**.

- The work is **copiously annotated** in general. 엄청난 양의 주석이 달려 있다.

- Paul's work provides the reader with a clear and **thoroughly annotated bibliography**.

- Each division **is arranged** chronologically.

- The book's **organization is chronological**, with a periodization according to cultural and political time spans. 시대 순서로 책이 구성되어 있다.

- Each section **provides a bibliography for further research**.
  각 장이 추천 도서 목록으로 끝나는 챕터 형식 언급

- This book has a **meticulously documented** and **informative introduction regarding** ~.

- The essays in the book **are diverse in scope** and theoretical **approach**.

- The present book **brings together a wide selection of articles on** ~.

- This edition **has undergone substantial revision** and now contains much important material not found in earlier translations.
  여러 번의 개작이 있었다.

- The main section **is divided into** eleven chapters, some of which are in turn subdivided. Almost all of the sections are of excellent quality.

- The book **is shaped into** four major sections: ~.

- The book **is structured into** five themes: ~.

- The six main chapters of Luke's study contain mostly **papers previously published in** various places.
  이전에 저널 등에서 이미 발표된 논문들의 모음집에 대한 언급에서 대표적으로 나타나는 문장이다. 또는 다음과 같이 표현할 수도 있다. A number of tables in this book, as well as sections of chapters, have previously appeared in print.

- The book, **reproduced directly from the dissertation manuscript**, needed better proofreading and copyediting.
  종종 우리 독자들은 이런 형식의 책을 보게 되는데, 이는 박사학위 논문의 원고가 곧바로 단행본으로 이어지는 경우로 먼저 학위 논문으로 인쇄됐다가 나중에 직접 책으로 나오는 책을 일컫는다.

- This is the **companion volume to** the PBS television series which I have written and narrated under the same title. **This book is designed for a broad readership and can be read independently**, but it will be best appreciated if read in conjunction with viewing as the series–and with the same five basic units treated in the same chronological order.
  TV시리즈물이 후에 책으로 묶여져 나온 경우를 말하는 내용이다.

- This book **is designed to give readers a picture of** the nation as it exists in the contemporary world.

- This volume, **a published version of a doctoral dissertation** completed in 1984, centers on a discussion of what is often referred to as ~.

- Harber's provocative work is an **outgrowth of his doctoral dissertation**.
  이 경우에서처럼 종종 우수한 박사학위 논문이 잘 다듬어져 단행본 책으로 출판되는 경우가 많다.

- To some extent, this book is **the outgrowth of my career** as a student and teacher of French sociology for almost thirty years.

  이 책은 상당 부분 저자의 ~ 활동으로부터(경력으로부터) 기인한다.

- The research **was conducted in preparation for a doctoral thesis on** the theme of ~.

  본 연구는 ~의 주제에 대한 박사학위 논문을 위한 준비 작업에서 이루어졌다.

- This essay **is adapted from the final chapter** of my unpublished doctoral dissertation.

- The book **follows two earlier studies by the same author on** the medieval literature of the Slavs, ~ 책이름.

  이 표현은 동일 저자가 펴낸 이전의 책에 이어 새로 나온 책을 일컬을 때 사용하는 예이다.

- This book (A) **is a sequel to** N. Shneidman's earlier study of contemporary Russian literature and literary criticism, (B) and (C).

  A책은 동일 저자가 펴낸 기존의 B와 C에 이은 세 번째 책이다. 즉, 연속 시리즈 중 하나이다.

- This book is part of a much larger work **in progress**.

  in progress는 '현재 진행 중인, 작업 중인' 책이란 뜻이다.

  참고로, in press는 조만간 나오게 될 article 혹은 paper를 말한다.

- Bogomil's volume **serves as a supplement to** the well-known four-volume compendium by Rogozhin.

  선행하는 어떤 책의 보충물, 추가로 이용될 수 있는 책이다.

- The book **presents a collection of articles from** the first international **symposium on** "Transitional Language" in Russian culture of the 20th century.

  심포지엄에서 발표된 논문들의 묶음집 성격을 띤 책이다.

  비슷한 예문으로 다음을 참고하자.

  This book is based on transcripts of addresses and discussions featured at the conference.

- This stimulating volume **grew out of** the 1990 Summer **Workshop on** Medieval East European Studies held at UCLA. 하계 워크숍에서 있었던 결과물의 묶음집

- This book is basically the **outcome of a conference** that was held in Melbourne in September 1994 on the theme of "Citizenship and National Identity in Europe."

- The papers in this volume were chosen from those presented at the Thirteenth Annual Conference of the International Association for Philosophy and Literature.

- The genesis of this particular book can be traced to the early 1980s and the present author's interest in the politics of the outer space commons.

- This is one of eighteen volumes of papers culled from the Third Congress for Soviet and East European Studies held in Washington in 1986, and one of four devoted mainly to literary topics.
  동사 cull from은 '~로부터 발췌하다, 추려내다'란 의미로 select와 동의어이다.

- The broad title of this volume introduces a series of seminar lectures held in 1985, presumably at the University of London.
  연속 강의물이 후에 책으로 출판되어 나오는 경우이다.

- This book was forerunner of a series of the ~.
  ~ 연구 시리즈물의 선구자격인, ~의 연구 가운데 가장 처음 나온 성과이다.

- Wolf Schmid's latest book has grown out of a series of articles on the theory of narrative prose in general and on Pushkin's *The Tale of Belkin in particular*.
  위 예문의 경우에서처럼, '~에 대한 논문들이 모여 이룬 집대성, 결실'로 이해하면 좋겠다.

- The book is based on the author's paper at the Sixth Colloquium on Russian literature in Kansas in 1990.

- We owe a debt to the French Bicentennial that the two volumes came out at all.
  이 두 권의 책을 출판한 ~에게 많은 감사를 보낸다, ~에게 빚지고 있다.

- Terras is generally guided by the insights of Slonim's famous early study.
  ~로부터 영향 받고 있다, 가르침을 받고 있다.

- The Russian original of this English translation was reviewed in *The Russian Review* 32 (Spring, 1995).
  영역판의 러시아 원본은 이미 한 저널에서 서평으로 소개된 바 있다.

- Following Solov'ev, Terras argues that ~.

- After following Hoover's exposition, the reader will have an appreciable and appreciative understanding of Malevich the artist.
  저자 ~가 밝혀놓고 있는 점들을 따라 읽다 보면, 독자들은 ~하게 될 것이다.

- The book is evidently aimed at scholars and advanced students because it presupposes a wide familiarity with the subject.
  책이 ~을 겨냥한, 대상으로 한

- The primary aim of the book is to define the ~.
  책의 중요한, 기본적으로 삼고 있는 목표는 ~이다.

- In the introduction, the author presents the aim of the work as being "to demonstrate that ~."

- The book is primarily about Nabokov's Russian fiction.

- The underlying goal of the collection as spelled out in the introduction is to explore the contradictory situation in which ~.

- The primary value of this collection lies in inclusion of stories which have never before been translated into English, and it should prove an invaluable resource to those students who are mainly aware of the writer.
  책의 귀중한 가치가 ~에 있다.

- This book is designed as a guide to Soviet cinema.

- This study of Turgenev's fiction seeks to redefine the writer's relationship to 19th century literature. 본 책은, 본 연구는 ~을 추구한다.

- The book's scope is perhaps too ambitious for a volume of 125 pages, the length of which impedes analysis that is both rigorous and comprehensive.
  125페이지의 분량의 소규모 책이 소화하기엔 너무 커서 다룰 수 없는 범위

- The book has brought out the immense scope of the author's erudition.
  저자의 박식함을 보여 주는 책
  All these topics, and many more, have been illuminated by his erudition and incisive judgments.

■ Birnbaum's **encyclopedic knowledge of** the sources and the secondary literature is everywhere apparent.

~에 대한 백과사전적 지식, 방대한 지식

■ Forrester **uses a wide of range of secondary literature** and indicates more than once the range of positions ~.

광범위한 2차 자료를 사용하고 있는

'~에 대한 참고 문헌이 방대하다'란 의미로 다음의 문장을 알아 두자.

There is a vast literature on finding information, only a small part of which we can list.

■ The book **fills a serious gap in** the corpus of scholarly translations of the literary culture of medieval Balkan.

~의 간극을 메우는 책

■ **Apart from** scholars of Dostoevsky and 19th century Russian literature, Murav's book is important for those interested in modes of characterization.

~에 상관없이, ~은 둘째 치고라도

■ The volume **is a useful starting point for** those interest in studying Gorky's highly sophisticated writings in the ~.

~에 관심 있는 사람들을 위한 초보적인 책, 출발점으로 사용될 수 있는 책

■ Tara Welsh's introduction **provides a good starting point for study of** the works.

■ For folklorists, this volume **provides a snapshot of** where the interdisciplinary endeavor of vernacular architecture scholarship finds itself. For a general reader, the volume presents a few problems: ~.

~에 대한 단상을 보여 준다.

■ The volume will be **a valuable starting point for** all future students of Bulgakov's novel.

■ Epshtein's essay is valuable not only **because it acquaints the reader with little-known trends in** modern Russian poetry, but also **because it provides a theoretical base for** discerning them.

■ Overall, the author's study **is a useful addition to studies of** Nabokov's artistic development.

- Harm's edition **provides thorough documentation** so that even a reader completely unfamiliar with Russian history can benefit from it.
  ~에 대해 잘 알고 있지 못한 독자들조차도 도움을 받을 수 있는

- The new collection **comprises** twenty articles on a range of medieval Russian tales, broad historical and cultural surveys.
  동사 comprise는 '~을 포함하다, 구성하다'란 뜻으로 consist of 혹은 수동태로 be composed of 로 달리 쓸 수 있다. It <u>consists of</u> a remarkably fruitful application of the tools of formalist analysis to some Ukrainian folk songs. 혹은 The main body of the book <u>consists of</u> the author's translation of V. Propp's important articles.

- This admirable book is **a compact monographic study of** the novel which combines two approaches: ~. ~에 대한 압축적인, 치밀한 연구
  같은 의미에서 형용사 exhaustive가 동의어로 사용될 수 있다.

- The book is the **first book-length exposition** in the English language of the life and work of the Russian artist-philosopher Alexander Ivanov.

04 책의 장단점에 대한 언급

■ Particularly **rewarding** are the stylized and richly colored illustrations of ~.
특별히 가치가 있는 것은 ~이다.
'유사한, 견줄 수 있는 연구가 없는 경우의 표현'으로 다음의 문장을 확인해 두자.
We have written a book which, so far as we know, <u>lacks any close parallel</u>.

■ The book will provide stimulating materials for Korean studies classrooms and will offer **rewarding** and **fascinating reading for** all those interested in Korean culture and civilization.

■ Indeed, the book **deserves** both recognition and **sound scholarly treatment**.
'~할 만하다'란 의미로 아주 많이 사용되는 표현이다. 즉, 위의 문장은 이 책이 독자로부터 인식을 받아야 함은 물론 순전히 학술(문)적인 목적에서도 활용되어야 함을 말하고 있다.

■ The subject treated in this book **deserves a further study**.
이 책에서 다루어진 주제는 차후의 연구를 필요로 한다, 이후의 연구를 할 만하다.

■ Like any serious work, Hackel's study requires and **deserves attentive reading**.
주의 깊게, 조심해서 읽을 필요가 있다.

■ The writer's ideas and views **deserve our full attention**.
우리 (독자)들 모두가 충분한 주의를 할 만하다, 주의를 기울일 만하다.

■ Professor Parker's latest book **deserves attention for its** originality, treating a genuinely little-known area of 19th century Russian literature.

■ Parker's book **will deservedly serve as** the benchmark for future inquires into Nabokov's metaphysics.

■ **All in all**, Thompson's book is an enlightening one, and **deserves to be noticed by** the community of Turgenev's scholars.

여기에서 all in all은 '전체적으로, 전반적으로'란 뜻이다. 아울러 또 다른 예문을 읽혀두자. Taken as a whole은 '전체적으로 보아서, 전반적으로 고려해 볼 때'란 의미로 위와 동일한 뜻으로 쓰인다. <u>Taken as a whole</u>, the book is exhilarating. <u>Taken as a whole</u>, the various chapters of this book raise and address many of the most contested and important issues in contemporary political and social theory. <u>Taking these findings together</u>, it is now possible to correct some common misconceptions about the ~(이 모든 결과들을 하나도 종합해 볼 때). When <u>these elements are taken together</u>, it looks like there is ~.

■ It is a book that **deserves to be read and debated by** every serious student of Russian and Soviet literature.

■ The study **takes a major step in** the development of ~.

본 연구는 ~에서 진일보하고 있다, 중요한 단계를 밟고 있다.

■ Franklin's book can **serve as a convenient first step for** specialists.

~의 저서는 ~을 위한 편리한, 용이한 첫 번째 단계 역할을 한다.

■ This book, which represents the proceedings of a 1989 conference at Amherst College, **takes an important initial step in** exploring the problem of postmodernism.

본 연구는 ~에서(~라는 점에서) 중요한 주도권을 잡고 있다.

■ Blumfield's book is **a major addition to** the field, the best study to date of Dostoevsky's early works.

~의 저서는 ~에 주요한 업적을 덧붙였다. 즉, 또 하나의 주요 업적이다.

■ Foley has brought us another **significant step forward in our understanding of** ~.

~는 ~에 대한 우리의 이해에 있어 상당히 의미 있는 진일보, 전진이다.

■ Galina's study **represents an important contribution to** the study of ~.

■ There are two important theoretical **contributions** which Robert Feuer makes to our thinking about Dostoevsky.

■ Gillian's book is **a major contribution to** scholarship and deserves the closest scrutiny and the fullest response.

~의 책은 ~학계에 보여 준 주요 공헌, 업적이다.

■ Eve Levin's substantial book **is a welcome addition to the growing number of** Russian women's writings available in English translation.

■ This book is an **excellent introduction to** the primary subject of ~.
~에 대한, ~을 위한 훌륭한 입문서

■ **This translation makes available to** the English-reading **audience** a wide array of current analytical approaches to the ~.
이 책의 번역은 ~한 독자들에게 ~을 알 수 있도록 해 준다, 가능케 해 준다.

■ Grenoble's book **represents a solid contribution to the field of** Slavic literature and Balkan culture.
~ 분야에 대한 확고한 공헌이다, 부동의 공헌이다.

■ The book is **noteworthy** as a perspective and **innovative contribution to** Turgenev studies.
~ 연구에 혁신적인 공헌, 기여를 하는 책

■ The book is a **treasure-trove of** linguistic information relevant to the origins of the Slavs.
~의 정보를 전해 주는 귀중한 보물과도 같은 책

■ The book **should be regarded as a milestone** in any historical survey of French cultural patterns.
획기적인 일, 이정표로 받아들여져야 한다.

■ Tom's volume **opens new perspectives for studying** folk poetry and points the way toward ~.

■ The book **supplies** the reader **with** valuable references and sources for further research.
숙어 supply A with B는 'A에게 B를 제공하다'란 의미이다. 같은 뜻의 동사에는 offer, provide 가 있다.

■ The book **provides** useful and interesting material both for specialists and for those with little knowledge of the man.

- Edward Brown's book provides a rare up-to-date analysis of the current state of Polish drama.
  오늘날까지도 보기 드문 ~의 분석을 시도하였다, 보여 주고 있다.

- The monograph provides information for those who know nothing virtually about ~.
  ~에 대해 전혀 모르는 초심자들을 위해 ~한 정보를 제공해 준다.

- The book provides an authoritative and very readable history of ~.
  본 저서는 ~에 대한 권위 있는 역사를 보여 주고 있다.

- Bert Beyen's book offers a satisfying account of the conception of ~ and provides a theoretical frame for much of what came before.
  ~에 대해 매우 만족한 설명을 보여 준다.

- Bethea has brought an impressive critical ~ to ~ and the results will serve as a standard to which future studies of ~ should aspire.

- It is useful to watch the dusting off of the traditional image.
  구태의연한 이미지를 떨쳐버리다, 구식의 틀을 벗어 버리다.

- In considering the role of this book, we have to acknowledge that it fills in some significant lacunae in scholarship on the third wave.
  lacunae는 lacuna의 복수로, '지식 등의 빈틈, 공백'을 의미한다. 즉, 위 문장에서는 '제 3의 물결에 대한 연구에서 나타난 학문적 연구의 공백을 이 책이 메우고 있다'는 의미로 쓰였다.

- All the above considered, Shrayer's new book can be of some valuable for scholars and students of Chinese literature.

- What makes this book most valuable is not only ~, but also ~.
  이 책을 가장 값지게 만드는 것은 ~이다. 즉, ~ 때문에 이 책이 귀중하다.

- The scholarly introduction and painstaking annotation make this book a pleasure to read and to use.

- The volume's introduction and notes render it a major contribution to the study of the ~.
  Richard makes another significant contribution to cultural and social history.

한편, '~의 분야에서 누구는 ~한 이름으로 명성을 날리고 있다'란 표현을 하고자 할 때는 다음의 예문을 참고해 보자.

In the world of Russian Studies, Richard Stites <u>is renowned for his scholarship on</u> culture and society, or more precisely, culture in society. 연구자의 명성이나 이력을 표현하는 이와 같은 용법을 잘 알아 두자.

Paul has <u>proven himself to be</u> a remarkable translator as well as a superb Pushkinist (~임을 스스로 증명해 보이는, ~함으로써 ~를 입증해 보이는). 또는 This analysis of ~ is clearly one of the high points of Paul's interpretative skills (~ 해석 실력이 탁월한 면을 보여 주는).

- Jakobson's remarkably authoritative book is **an invaluable work of** reference not only Pasternak student but also for literary critics and theorists, regardless of their specialty.
  ~에 대한 매우 가치 있는 ~이다.

- Murav's excellent book is **first and foremost** a study of the cultural phenomenon of holy foolishness.
  처음이자 마지막의, 초유의

- The collection of essays in this book was generated by the first international conference held on the history of the Russian peasantry. The conference itself **represented an important breakthrough in the field of peasant studies.**
  ~ 연구 분야에 선도적 결실

- Huizinga's thoughts on the relationships between history and aesthetics **came to fruition in his best known work**, *The Waning of the Middle Ages.*
  저자의 성숙된 결실의 표현

- Michael Miko's anthology is without doubt a **considerable achievement** which will become an indispensable book for teachers and students of Italian history.
  위대한 업적, 결실

- The author of the book **should be congratulated for** an **accomplishment** that is remarkable and long overdue.
  ~한 이유 때문에 환영받아, 축하받아 마땅한 책

- Cathy Frierson is to be **congratulated** not only **for** her inspired choice of theme but also for her accomplished execution of the task.

■ This collection of stories **should be widely appreciated by** those who wish to broaden their understanding of Russian romantic fiction.
~에 의해서(~로부터) 광범위하게 평가받을 만하다, 가치를 인정받을 만하다.

■ The editor **is to be applauded for** successfully coping with the difficulties of the multilingual edition.
~때문에 찬사를 받아 마땅한

■ Michael Stevenson's paper **should be singled out for** the originality and breath of his method in tackling Victor Shklovsky's criticism.

■ His narrative is **masterful and moving**.
문체가 매우 훌륭하다고 할 때, 주로 형용사 masterful을 쓴다는 것을 알아 두자. 다음의 문장을 통해 masterful의 쓰임새를 알아 두자.
Boym's topic is <u>vast</u> and the assimilation of these diverse elements is <u>masterful</u>.

■ **It is worth mentioning that** this book represents probably **the first study that devotes considerable attention to** popular films.
~을 다룬 최초의 책

■ One of the many **merits of** Serman's book is its focus on ~.
~ 책의 여러 장점들 가운데 하나는 ~이다.

■ **The greatest merit of this volume is** its extensive coverage of the ~.
이 책의 가장 큰 장점이라면 ~이다.

■ **The greatest merits of the book are the discussion on** ~.

■ As a reader, this book certainly has **merit and appeal**.

■ **The book's strongest contributions** are in its descriptions of Lermontov's early years.
이 저서의 가장 강력한 공헌은 ~이다.

■ One of the **beneficial aspects** of this collection is that ~.

■ The analytical **strength of** the book is ~. 책의 분석상의 강점은

■ One of the book's greatest strengths is its rich grasp of the multifarious dualisms which pervades the novel.

■ The book's greatest strength lies in the fact that ~.

■ Erlich's forte is to deepen the meaning of texts we already know well.
~의 강점

■ Kerenz is also at his best when presenting the socio-political context ~.
~함에 있어, 저자는 혹은 책은 가장 탁월하다. 즉, ~할 때 분석이 가장 돋보인다.

■ Comire's book will be on the shelf of everyone in the filed of Japanese economics.

■ The volume surely belongs to the bookshelf of every serious student of French sociology.

■ In many ways this is an excellent book which will be useful reading to student and scholar alike.
학생, 학자 모두에게 유용한 필독서

■ This book is indispensable to a student of French modernism because of its historical range and thematic focus.
~에 필수 불가결한, 꼭 필요한, 빼놓아서는 안 될

■ This book is a must for those who are interest in the theme explored in the author's monograph and also for those who would like to undertake further studies of the ~.
~을 위한 분들께 꼭 필요한, 필독서이다.

■ Shneidman's book is unquestionably obligatory reading for Pasternak specialists and other interested in Russian literature.
의심할 나위 없이(매우 분명하게) ~을 위한 필수 도서 목록이다.

■ The book is most useful for its ~ and for its background and bibliographical material.
~라는 점에서(~ 때문에) 본 저서는 가장 유용하다.

■ This book would probably be the most useful either as a reference work for linguists or for scholars who are investigating the ~.
~한 독자층에게 가장 유용한 책

■ **With these points in mind, this collection** is particularly well suited for those Slavic linguists of Russian teachers who are just embarking on their careers.
~에게 특별히 필요한 책

■ **In sum,** Terras's book **has done a remarkable job in** synthesizing ~.

■ **In sum,** the book is a deeply serious, energetically researched, and engagingly executed treatment of its subject.

■ **In sum,** the book **serves as useful introduction to** French symbolism and its trends for English-language students of French art and culture.
~에 있어 유용한 기본, 초보적 단계의 도서 역할을 한다.

■ The book **is very well researched and clearly and cogently written.**

■ Tony's latest book **should be of interest to anybody** working with the theory of intertextuality. The author shows a commendable erudition both in the area of Pushkin criticism and Pushkin's possible sources.

■ **The book is noteworthy** for its extraordinary **evenhanded approach to** the topic which can **provoke** intense emotions among either the admirers or enemies of the ~.
~에 대한 공정한 접근 방법
동사 provoke는 bring about과 같은 의미로 '~을 야기시키다'란 뜻으로 쓰인다. 다음을 참고하자. Baeher's book will doubtless provoke lively interest and productive discussion among linguists.
Malthus made a provocative and important point, but unfortunately for us, his conclusions were far too pessimistic. 동사 '유발하다, 야기하다(provoke)'가 들어간 예문을 하나 더 살펴보자. COVID-19 similarly provokes the reckoning of the balance sheet of globalization, and the policy challenge of promoting the positive sides while limiting the negative consequences. = 동사 wreak(유발하다, 자초하다, 일으키다)는 보통 수동태 형태 (즉, 과거분사 형태인 wrought)로 주로 사용된다. 다음의 예문을 보자. To be sure, we are still struggling with many of the problems wrought by industrialization, like climate change, economic inequality, and the increased risk of pandemics wrought by international air travel. 능동태로 사용된 예문은 다음과 같다. Religious wars recurrently wreaked havoc within and between kingdoms from 1524 until 1648. (havoc은 '대혼란' 혹은 '파괴'를 의미하 므로, 위 문장은 "종교 전쟁은 반복적으로 대혼란을 야기하였다"로 해석하면 된다.)
형용사 provocative는 논문의 아이디어가 기본적으로 매우 선도적이고 놀랄 만하다는 의미로 주로 사용된다. 어감이 아주 강한 단어이니 사용에 주의를 기울여야 한다. 다음을 참고하자.

Susanne Fusso has <u>put together</u> this volume of <u>provocative</u> and illuminating essays. 또는 Overall, Fiszman's book offers provocative and rich observations about this prolific and often contradictory writer. Unfortunately, this provocative thesis is not demonstrated throughout an otherwise first-rate monograph.

- **I am happy to report that** Karlinsky's latest book is **a reliable scholarly edition** of such legends which I can heartily recommend as a basic source book.
  참고로, 반대의 부정을 나타내고자 할 때는 <u>I am unhappy and disagree with</u> many things in Greenwood's book.

- The book can, thus, **be recommended without reservation** both to college students and all those with an abiding interest in ~.
  반대로, 결점으로 인해 추천할 만한 책이 아닌 경우에는 다음 문장을 참고하자. Ultimately then, the book <u>cannot be recommended</u> either as an illuminating study of the authors discussed or as a text in itself. Its only <u>saving grace</u> is that it points to a real need in American Slavic studies. 여기에서 saving grace는 결점을 보완하는 장점이란 의미이다.

- Prof. Maia Kipp's recent book **is highly recommended for** those who care passionately about literature and drama, and for those who enjoy thought-provoking, conscientious, and truly intellectual scholarship.
  ~한 독자들을 위해 매우 추천할 만한 책이다.

- **It is to be hoped that** this new edition will contribute to the rereading of a novel that, in my view, has been unjustifiably neglected.
  '~이 기대된다, ~을 바란다'란 의미로 서평의 마지막 결론에서 가장 빈번하게 쓰이는 표현 중의 하나이다.

- **It is to be hoped that** the second book will avoid the shortcomings of the first.

- We **hope** this book is able to **provide an impetus** for strengthening the ~.
  우리는 ~하도록 자극을 줄 수 있는 책이길 희망한다.

- These minor qualifications aside, the collection **is an important contribution to** the critical literature on Sokolov.

- In all, this book **succeeds in stimulating a range of important questions** in the study of ~.

■ In general, the other views put forward in this collection of papers, although diverse in their origins, can be seen as remarkably **compatible with each other**, complementary rather than in conflict.

이 논문집에 나타나 있는 서로 다른 견해들은 서로 상충된다기보다는 상보적이다.

■ For those interested in early Russian history, Janet Martin's book is a **highly detailed, excellent study, but it may be a bit difficult for the lay reader.**

~의 책은 매우 자세하고 우수한 책이지만 일반 독자들이 이해하기에는 어렵다.

■ This book is an excellent resource and a good means for a quick overview of a huge body of ~, **but it could be rather difficult for the nonspecialist.**

하지만 비전공자에겐 다소 어렵다.

■ This technical **cavil** does not, however, **spoil** the overall positive evaluation earned by the volume.

cavil은 동사로 쓰일 때 '~을 흠잡다'란 뜻이 되며 이 문장에서는 '흠, 단점'이란 의미의 명사로 사용되었다. spoil은 동사 mar와 같이 '~을 훼손시키다, 손상시키다'란 표현으로 자주 쓰인다.

■ My only **cavil with** the interpretation of the work ~.

여기에서 cavil with는 complaint about로 대체될 수 있다. My only complaint about this masterful work is that it neglects one facet of ~. 필자가 보는 (찾은) 유일한 단점/불만인 점은 ~이다.

■ The main **defect of** the book as a biography is that too little attention is paid to Tolstoy's character.

~의 결점, 단점

■ **Minor flaws** may be found. 몇 가지 단점들이 발견된다.

■ However, such **glitches** are minor and rare indeed.

그 같은 미흡한 점은 소수에 불과하고 사실 매우 드물다.

■ The great majority of the factual information is accurate, **but there are still a few more mistakes**

■ Two relatively **minor inaccuracies** should be mentioned. First, ~.

소소한, 별로 심각하지 않은 부정확한 것들(실수들)

- Three **printing errors**, beyond the author's control, are noticeable.
  프린트 상의 실수들

- The book **is not entirely free of errors**.
  이 책은 오류(실수)로부터 전적으로 자유롭지 않다. 즉, 몇몇 실수가 눈에 보인다.

- The main **weakness of** the book is a disregard of some basic assumptions of literary criticism.

- The **weaknesses** of Marinov's analysis, though, far outweigh its strengths.

- The book's **main weakness** results from **the absence of a commonly accepted methodology and terminology**.
  공인된 접근 방법과 전문 용어를 사용하지 않는 점이 이 책의 큰 결점이다.

- The book has **no footnotes to document** or support the editor's own assertion.

- The **principal weakness of the book** is the author's persistent abstinence from analysis.
  책의 원칙적 결점은 분석의 결여

- At first glance, only two important components seem to **be lacking**.

- Another **serious problem with the book** is the absence of a bibliography.
  이 책의 심각한 문제점은 참고 문헌이 없다는 것이다.

- There are, however, two somewhat **troublesome points that must be mentioned**.
  몇몇 문제점들은 언급되어야겠다.

- There are some qualities that **detract from the merits of the volume**.
  책의 장점에서 벗어나는 몇몇 요소들 즉, 장점의 빛을 발하게 하는 단점들이 있다.

- A **grave shortcoming**, which makes the book very heavy reading is its repetitiveness.
  엄청난 실수, 최악의 결점

- There are many excellent aspects of this book, but there are also **some irritating shortcomings**, mostly of an editorial nature.
  몇몇 짜증나게 하는 단점들, 결점들

- **While** Lina's book appears to have undertaken painstaking research in dating and attributing certain letters, **the many inaccuracies and inconsistencies that mar Lina's own text is all the more regrettable.**
  ~을 훌륭하게 수행하고 있는 반면에, 부정확성과 비일관성 때문에 이 책은 매우 유감이다.

- **The only regrettable aspect of the author's study** is that <u>it examines only</u> a small section of larger picture of the field of semiotics.

- Perhaps **the only regrettable feature of the book** is its author's tendency to ~.
  아마도 이 책의 유일한 결점은 ~이다. 이 책의 한 가지 유감스러운 점은 ~이다.

- I, for one, **regret that**, for whatever reason, he did not put his enormous talents to work and attempt a full-scale and thoroughly researched reassessment of the Soviet century.
  ~이 아니라서 유감이다.

- **The primary shortcoming is that** the book is not always adequately footnoted and the vocabulary list is not complete.

- **Rather less satisfactory**, in my eye, although very informative, is the treatment of the ~.
  다소 불만족스런 부분은 ~이다.

- This book **is marred somewhat by** a distracting and inconsistent use of transliterations.
  동사 mar는 '~을 훼손시키다'란 의미로 이 문장은 '~때문에 책의 가치가 손상되고 있다'고 보면 좋을 듯 하다.

- The book **is marred by** numerous misprints.

- These objections are in no way meant to **belittle** the reader's supreme utility.

- Unfortunately, this book **offers very little new on** Chekhov's relation ~.
  ~에 대해 새로운 것을 거의 보여 주지 않는다.

- The author's attempt to combine ~ in this book **met with little success**.

- The reader **is still left to** wonder about ~.

'독자는 ~한 점에 대해 여전히 모른 채로 남는다' 즉, '저자는 ~한 내용을 설명하지 않거나, 잘못 전달하고 있다'는 말로 이해하면 좋을 듯 싶다.

■ The reader **is left to wonder why**, for instance, a novel such as Belyi's *Petersburg* is listed as ~.

■ To sum up, the author **leaves the reader uncertain about** his argument and intentions.

■ Unfortunately, the book **leaves unanswered** the question why ~.

■ The author's attempt to combine ~ in this book **met with little success**.

■ Klein's application to these ~, while largely successful, **leaves the reader with some unanswered questions**.
대체로 성공적이지만 명쾌한 대답 없는 결론.
여기에서 leave가 들어간 다른 예문을 알아보자.
This volume <u>leaves a reviewer both cheering and slightly frustrated</u>. Cheering, because most of the contributions are exquisitely researched, original and fine additions to the ongoing scholarship in feminist discourse. 새롭게 조명해 보려는 시도가 실패하다 (His attempt to recast Dostoevskii <u>in a new mold leaves us grappling with</u> abstract and schematized statements ~.)

■ Whether territorial changes bring peace is **an open and rarely explored question**.
~연구되지 않은.
반대의 경우, 즉 '연구가 엄청나게 많이 된'이란 뜻은 다음의 예문을 통해 알아보자.
This topic <u>is seriously understudied</u> even thought the world is currently facing several possible unifications.

■ The book **has no index**, and thus it is hard for a casual reader to locate information readily.

■ **The book's final name index comes as a useful surprise, given** the absence of all other **scholarly apparatus**.

■ The **textual apparatus is exceptionally helpful**. The introduction reviews the historical context, manuscript history, and literary features of the oral tradition. The text is followed by a series of appendices on related scholarly issues.
텍스트 상의 구성, 외관 등은 예외적으로(상당히) 도움이 된다, 매우 도움이 될 만하다.

- The scholarly apparatus of the book will be helpful in leading to further research and study.

- Free-standing quotations muddy an argument.
  마음대로 한 인용이 논쟁을 흐림, 망치고 있음.

- The original serious drawback to this collection is that no indication is given as to the original place of publication of each of these essays, making it difficult to track down the Russian originals.
  유일한 단점은 ~이다.

- Despite its technical shortcomings, the book has some value for its reasonable introduction and its bibliography.
  ~한 결점에도 불구하고, ~한 점에서 가치를 지닌다.

- But whatever the shortcomings of this glossary, it is undoubtedly an important contribution to one of the most interesting dialects of present-day Russian culture.
  결점이 있다 해도 ~에 상당히 중요한 공헌을 하고 있다.

- Such shortcomings notwithstanding, the book is well worth reading for its wealth of linguistic explication and for its sensitive critical insights into larger questions of Bakhtin's worldview and poetic process.

- Although, inevitably, questions remain, the book should be congratulated for producing a fine study which challenges us to think many of ~.

- There is one question I would like to put to the author of the book: ~?

- In spite of these minor defects, McLean's book is a welcome contribution to the growing stock of German politics.

- With the caveats enumerated above I would like to recommend this book both to those interest in folksong as well as those concerned with folklore in general.
  위에서 언급한 (책의 결점에 대한) 경고에도 불구하고 저자는 다음의 책을 추천하는 바이다.

- Despite such superficial shortcomings, the book is a mine of careful, detailed and insightful scholarship that can be highly recommended.

- **Despite these apparent drawbacks, this book is still very worthwhile** within the constraints of its stated goal: to provide an exhaustive list of Russian affixes.

- **Even with these reservation, the book is a challenging and provocative contribution to the study of** the Chinese economy, and is highly recommended to anyone interested in, or indeed ~.
  ~한 결점에도 불구하고, ~ 분야의 연구에 있어 획기적이고 고무적인 기여, 공헌을 하는 책이다.

- **Reservations about** the book's criteria for selecting the text **aside**, the book contains a fascinating set of readings.
  ~ 같은 단점들은 차치하더라도
  한편, '이 책에서 한 가지 문젯거리가 있다. 즉, 논의하고 싶은 구석이 있다'는 표현을 하고자 할 때는 다음과 같은 예문을 알아 두자. I have only one quarrel with the book.

- **My reservations** may have been prompted by a merely infelicitous choice of words on the editor's part.

- Kim's analysis of ~ **is outstanding on all accounts and withstands the one minor reservation I have.**
  대체로 좋지만 한 가지 반대하고 싶은, 마음에 들지 않는 구석

- **These errors and omissions aside,** this book represents an excellent synthesis of the complex nature of Croatian national identity.
  이같은 실수와 누락만 없다면, 빼고 나면

- **These weaknesses aside,** Shneidman's book **provides a useful guide to** literary trends and controversies of the past decades.
  이러한 결점들은 별문제로 하고, 제쳐놓고

- The above **flaws notwithstanding,** Nollan **is to be recommended for** producing a much-needed study of Soviet film and the masses.
  위에서 열거한 결점들에도 불구하고, ~는 ~을 위해 추천할 만하다.

- However, **such mistakes are minor compared to the pleasure the reader will find in** these largely unknown and forgotten writings.

- Readers of this volume will find it **fascinating to read and useful in** understanding the ~.

- Still, further reworking and careful editing would have made this volume more reliable and more authoritative source.

- Why did Knapp commit such an obvious logical misdemeanor?
  명백한 논리적 결함, 또는 논리적 박약

- Its idiosyncratic structure, episodic treatment of topics, and failure to offer a liner narrative will render it inaccessible to general readers, while specialists will rightly expect the author to know what others have to say about the topics he chooses to privilege.
  책의 허술한 구조와 중구난방인 문제점 때문에 독자에게 해가 되는

The Essential Guide to Writing Papers in English

VIII Acknowledgement

1. 연구를 하게 된 동기 / 세월
2. 연구비 / 장학금 / 도서관 시설 등 각종 혜택 언급
3. 특별한 감사의 표현
4. 가족과 부모 / 지인 / 스승에 대한 감사의 표현
5. 독자 제현에 대한 언급

01 연구를 하게 된 동기 / 세월

■ This book had its **genesis** in the spring of 1986 in Finland, where I was spending the academic year as a Fulbright Research Fellow working at the University of Helsinki Library.
말 그대로 ' ~의 기원, 시초'란 뜻의 genesis가 들어간 문장의 예를 하나 더 들어 보자.
The conceptualization of folk sociology finds its <u>genesis</u> and development resting upon real situations and continuing needs in ~. ('민속 사회학'이란 개념화의 기원(시초, 발단)과 그 용어의 발달은 ~에서 찾아진다, 나타난다.)
genesis란 단어 이외에 genealogy란 고급한 말을 사용하는 경우도 많으며, 그 의미는 같다.
The <u>genealogy</u> of this book begins with Andrew Dubill. Even before the idea of publication was broached, Andrew threw himself unabashedly into the task of creating an invaluable speechwriting resource. It is due to the quality of his efforts that this published work even exists.

■ **Twelve years of** working on this book have **engendered** many doubts.
12년 간에 걸친 본 저서에 대한 연구는 ~을 낳았다

■ Sometimes attraction and the resulting soft power it **engenders** require little effort.

■ Over the past decade, a new term has **entered discussions** of men and clothing—the New Man.
~의 토론, 논의를 야기하다

■ **This book has been a long time in the making** – almost twenty years, if one goes back to its first incarnation.

■ My long preoccupation with the church music of the Eastern Churches has **convinced me that** ~. The narrative of the subsequent pages is conducted in this light.
저자의 오랜 연구(천착)로 ~한 믿음을 갖게 되었다. 본 저서의 이후 내용들은 바로 이같은 점에서 이루어졌다.

- **The present** book was written over a period **of** ten years, and during that time many people aided and encouraged me in ways to numerous and varied to mention.
본 저서는 10여 년이란 세월에 걸쳐 쓰여졌다.

- Materials were first gathered for this collection **as part of a seminar on ~**.

- Versions of some parts of this book's chapters **have been previously published**, in somewhat different forms. Permission to reprint my article, "Myth," was granted by Random House.
위 예문은 이미 다른 저널 등에 실린 논문들을 모아 단행본 책으로 낸 경우의 표현이다.
다른 예문도 참고하자.
My thanks for <u>permission to use this material</u> go to the editors of *History of Education Quarterly* ("The Myth of the Zemstvo School," 24, no. Winter 1994).

- I have been fortunate to know many of ~, and **I have been privileged to** interview ~.
도서관 혹은 어떤 프로그램 등의 편의 시설을 이용할 수 있었다는 감사의 표현을 하고자 할 때 가장 대표적으로 사용하는 말이 지금과 같은 have been privileged이다.

- Discussions with these colleagues have helped inform this work.

- This book is the result of a longstanding curiosity about ~. The problems and issues engaged here **were first formulated for a dissertation chapter**, ~.
박사학위 논문을 dissertation이라고 한다.
위의 표현은 '이 책에서 논의되고 있는 문제점들은 실은 저자의 박사학위 논문의 한 장을 위해 만들어졌었다'는 점을 밝히고 있다.

- This article is **dedicated to the memory of** ~.
이같은 표현은 '작고한 ~를 기린다'는 표현으로 흔히 저자의 돌아가신 스승이나, 어느 유명한 학자에게 바치는 글을 나타내고자 할 때 사용하는 표현이다.

- This volume <u>owes its origin to</u> the seventh meeting of the Japan Anthropology Workshop which was held in April 1993 in Banff, Alberta, Canada.
이 책의 기원은, 즉 이 책은 어떠한 것이 계기가 되어 쓰여졌음. origin을 이용해 쓰여진 다른 문장을 살펴 보자.
<u>The origin of this book goes back to</u> the mid-1990s, when the China threat scenario became popularized in the media and seemed on the rise in Washington policy circles.

- This book **is written in the spirit of** this passage above from William James.

■ It is **in this spirit that** this chapter presents a remarkably comprehensive yet comparatively brief primer on architects and ethics.

■ The second edition is **substantially a reprint of** the first except that, in the text, we have made a few corrections and clarifications, and have added some links in the arguments and a few references to new developments in literary theory.
재판 이후 수정과 첨부 설명

■ The book **is a real instance of a collaboration** in which the author is the shared agreement between two writers.
−공동 저작의 경우 설명

■ Since this book is **the culmination of several decades of thinking about** power, I owe more intellectual debts than I can possibly remember.
다년간 ~에 대해 생각해 온 결과, 축적된 것

■ This book **originated as a series of** three **lectures hosted by** professor Gordon Clark at the Oxford School of Geography and the Environment in May 2017.

02 연구비 / 장학금 / 도서관 시설 등 각종 혜택 언급

- Funding and institutional support for research and writing were obtained from a variety of sources.

- Funds for research were provided by the International Research and Exchange Board.
  '연구비는 ~에서 지원받았다'라는 뜻의 가장 대표적인 표현이다.

- Research for this article was supported in part by a grant from the IREX, with funds provided by the NEH, which administers the Title VII Program.

- The research and writing of this article were made possible by funding from the IREX and the Social Science Research Council.
  본 연구와 집필은 ~로부터의 연구 지원비 때문에 가능한 것이었다.
  즉, ~의 지원비를 받아 본 논문 작업이 수행되었다.

- Research for this article was conducted with funds from the Philips Faculty Fellowship at Bates College, whose generosity and support I gratefully acknowledge.

- The staffs of the Academy of Sciences Library and The State Historical Museum were consistently helpful in uncovering previously unstudied manuscripts and in making available those already known.

- Without the rich resources of Houghton Library, this volume would have been far less vibrant and colorful, and I am grateful to the capable staff members there, both in the reading room and in imaging services.

'~이 없이는 ~은 불가능했었을 것이다'란 가정법 구문을 이용한 표현을 알아 두자.
<u>It would never have been completed without the help and encouragement of</u> my academic adviser, as well as my family.

- During my year in Cambridge I benefited greatly from discussions at the Harvard Feminist Theory Group, and I would like to thank the members of that seminar who commented on my work.
~의 토론으로부터 많은 도움을 받았다.

- I am also very grateful to Peter Cornell. As ever, I benefited from his vast knowledge and originality of mind.

- This research has been supported by University of Melbourne Special Initiatives Grant and the American Research Council Small Grants Scheme.
본 연구는 ~ 대학으로부터 재정 도움을 받았다.

- The research on which this article is based was supported by grants from ACTR.
본 논문이 기초해 있는 연구는 ~로부터 연구비를 받은 것이다.

- The research and travel undergirding this lengthy project have been funded at times by grants from the Davis Postdoctoral Fund of Princeton University.

- This article is based on research supported by IREX Individual Advanced Research Opportunities Program.
본 논문은 ~로부터 지원 받은 연구를 바탕으로 한 것이다.

- Some of the research was done at the New York Public Library (Slavic Division) to whose expert staff I am indebted.

- To Haverford College I owe special thanks for the help I have received with the copying of the various versions of the manuscript and other technical assistance.
~ 대학 측에 내가 받은 특별한 도움에 대해 감사를 표하고자 한다.

- Work on this dissertation has been supported over the years by Faculty Research Grants (1988-93) from the University of California, Davis.
이 박사학위 논문에 대한 연구는 ~의 연구비에 의해 작성된 것이다.

- **This book has been published with the help of grants from** the Social Science Federation of Canada, using funds provided by the Social Science and Humanities Research Council of Canada.

  본 저서는 ~로부터의 연구 지원비를 받아 출판된 것이다.

- I am **extremely grateful to** the British Academy **for the award of** a two-year Research Readerships in 1997-1999 and to the Arts and Humanities Research Board **for research leave** in 2000-2001 that enabled me to investigate this topic.

  ~의 연구 지원비에 깊이 감사한다.

- I have **greatly appreciated the strength and encouragement of** the ~.

- Santa Clara University and the National Endowment for the Humanities **provided some of time and resources needed to complete this project.**

- **This book would never have become what it now is without the experience** I had as a visiting scholar at the University of California, Berkeley. **My stay there was rendered possible by** the Fulbright Scholar Program, and I should like to express my most cordial thanks to the J. William Fulbright Foreign Scholarship Board.

  저자가 경험한 ~로부터의 도움 없이는 이 책의 출간은 불가능했었을 것이다.

03 특별한 감사의 표현

■ Bob Weil brought this project to life and **remained** intellectually engaged with it right to the end.

흔히 '언제나 ~했다'는 점을 말하고자 할 때, 이처럼 동사 remain을 쓴다.

다음 문장도 역시 같은 표현을 통해 감사의 마음을 전달하고 있다.

My parents remained benevolent even when pressed into active service: the study never have been produced without their labors and support.

■ I **especially wish to express my gratitude to** ~, who from the outset, encouraged me in my work, provided me with many details and suggestions for research and carefully read the manuscript.

■ I **wish** also **to record my appreciation to** the directors and staff of the following institutions: ~.

■ I **would like to record my gratitude to a number of individual** who have given me help and encouragement over the period in which this dissertation was written.

■ I **am** also **most grateful to** my husband, Robert Massie, who took the time to patiently read and edit my pages while working on his own book.

■ **It is a particular pleasure to acknowledge my debt to** the remarkable cohort of students of the University of Chicago.

■ **It is a pleasure to acknowledge debts** incurred over the years in the preparation of this book.

■ Many colleagues have **offered useful suggestions for** the content and format of the book, and I **would like to give particular thanks to** ~.

■ Finally, I **thank** Tom Nchinda **for proofreading the completed manuscript**, and **for** her **generous appraisal of** the book's potential application in policy and program development.

■ **Most of all**, I **wish to record my thanks to** ~, **for** his faith in this project and his patient encouragement over many years.
무엇보다도 ~에게 ~에 대한 감사의 변을 하고자 한다.

■ In acknowledging the various kinds of help and support I have received in the preparation of this book, **I would first of all like to mention with deep gratitude** the late Professor ~.
저자가 받은 도움과 재정 지원에 대한 감사의 변을 함에 있어 본인은 먼저 ~를 언급하고자 한다.

■ A number of people and institutions **have contributions to this study in a variety of ways**.
~는 물심양면으로 본 연구에 기여해 왔다.

■ Finally, **my most sincere thanks go to** Professor ~, whose perceptive criticism, kind encouragement, and willing assistance helped bring the project to a successful conclusion.
~에게 가장 깊은 감사를 보낸다.

■ Finally, **my special thanks go to** my wife Betty for selflessly encouraging my research and giving me technical assistance.

■ **A final word of thanks is due to all those** involved in the preparation of this book.

■ **Invaluable help was furnished by** Professor ~, a distinguished scholar of ~, who acted as my consultant and meticulous first reader. He not only caught many errors and awkward expressions but was willing to discuss with me points of ~.
~께서 아주 값진 도움을 주셨다.

■ And **a very special thanks to** Brends Silver who has generously read every page several times, offering detailed and invaluable comments.

■ There are other kinds of help that make this dissertation possible: ~.

- The conventions of the acknowledgement cannot **do justice to** the personal debts **incurred** throughout the work in a project such as this one.

- In writing this research monograph I have **incurred many debts** which I am glad to have this opportunity to acknowledge.

- This dissertation **has** also **been nurtured** in several academic communities ~.

- To properly thank everyone to whom I **am indebted in** this project would involve listing all of my friends and colleagues over the last 20 years or more.

- Over twenty years for making this book, I **acquired intellectual debts to** so many people that I cannot list them all.

- Many individuals have **offered constructive criticism of** my work as it progressed.

- The completion of this book involved the labor and support of many people.

- I **am** also **indebted to** ~, who reviewed earlier drafts of the manuscript and provided me with valuable observations.

- **It is a pleasure to acknowledge** the support, assistance, and guidance of numerous individuals who helped create this book. **Foremost among these people is** ~
  ~의 도움과 재정 지원에 감사드리는 바, 가장 으뜸은 ~이다.

- **First and foremost**, I want to acknowledge the early insights of ~, who suggested several key pieces on the first draft.
  무엇보다도(어느 모로 보나 가장 ~한 것은)

- **For offering valuable suggestions** on parts of an earlier draft, I thank William Newell of Miami University.

- I **would like to recognize** the creative and patient efforts of several individuals, including ~.

- **My highest appreciation goes to** ~.

- **Thanks are** also **due to** ~ for his assistance in preparing the illustrations.

- To all these immediate colleagues, **I here express my more than grateful recognition.** Lastly, **if it had not been for** Paule Braudel, who has been daily associated with my research, I should never have had the courage to write this book.

- Several people **have directly affected this book, but none more than** Gerald Mikkelson, who patiently read the manuscript at each juncture, always improving the prose and the sense.
  '이 책이 나오기까지 많은 분들의 영향이 있었지만 ~만큼 베풀어 주신 분은 없다'는 표현을 비교급으로 나타내고 있다.

- As I mentioned in the introduction, **I have learned an enormous amount from** the hundreds of people I have talked with about ~.

- **I am incredibly grateful to have been able to work with** amazing current and former colleagues at Washington University.

- This work has been shaped directly and indirectly by the dozens of scholars who are part of ~.

- Both the book as a whole and the individual chapters have **benefited from** invitations to give lectures and feedback I have received at workshops at a variety of institutions around the world.

- Two scholars in particular have **had an outsized influence on** the ideas in this book.

- Many of the ideas that **are advanced** in this book were first developed in earlier academic articles.

- I **am very lucky to have had** the same faculty **assistant** for the past fifteen years.

- I **owe a great debt of thanks to** my family and friends, some of whom I neglected to thank in my previous book.

04 가족과 부모 / 지인 / 스승에 대한 감사의 표현

- I also **want to take this opportunity to thank a few members of my family**, especially my parents, Nonda and Deb Kumar, and my aunt. **They instilled in me the belief that** intellectual pursuit is the highest calling, and that ideas do have the power to change people's lives.

- At one time or another, many individuals **have read and commented on parts of this manuscript**.
  많은 사람들이 저자의 원고를 읽고 평을 해 주었다.

- And most of all, **my gratitude goes to my wife/husband**, who **remained** encouraging and full of useful suggestions.

- Finally, I **would like to thank my family members** and loved ones for their patience and advice.

- Finally, I **send gratitude separately to** my daughter, Anna Etkind.

- As always, **my family** have been there, providing **all sorts of tangible and intangible support**.
  물심양면으로 온갖 도움을 베풀어 준 나의 가족

- **My parents**, Lotte and Carl, as well as other members have provided care, physical and emotional.

- **My wife**, Clarie Rigger, **has assisted me in innumerable ways**, whatever I might say here cannot do full justice to the extent and the value of her contribution.

- Finally, and most of all, I owe enormous thanks to the three people I live with and love the most and who had the great misfortune to be locked in a house with me for months while a pandemic upended our society and I finished this book.

- My own understanding of ~ grew slowly throughout my career, and I owe a huge debt of gratitude to the many people who brought me challenges which I slowly realized were ~.

- Prof. Gerald Mikkelson supervised my doctoral work in Kansas. He has overseen the planning of this project and has given my work minute consideration for over five years. In dedicating this dissertation to my dead mother, Rose Spitzer, I wish to recognize a bond that is unlike any other.
  ~가 나의 박사학위 논문 지도 교수이다. 즉, ~가 내 박사학위 논문을 읽고 도움을 주었다.

- In writing my dissertation, I have contracted many debts. First of all, I should like to thank Christopher Wheeler for encouraging me to think about the topic and then offering constant assistance while this dissertation was being written.
  박사학위 논문을 쓰면서 나는 많은 빚을 졌는데 그 중에서도 첫째로 ~에게 감사드린다.

- This book is dedicated to my children, who rekindled my interest in fairy tales and remained me how powerfully and deeply stories nurture imagination, spirit, and passion.
  내가 동화에 관심을 갖게 해 준 우리 아이들에게 이 책을 바친다.
  여기에서 kindle이란 동사는 '촉발시키다, 불을 지르다'란 의미이다.
  다음의 문장을 더 알아보자. My early interest in history was kindled and nurtured by professors Kim Steele and Nicholas Clifford.

- Some specific debts need to be acknowledged here.

- The period during which this dissertation was being translated will always remain associated with the birth of my son, Anton. I have dedicated my dissertation to him.
  저자의 박사학위 논문이 번역되는 동안 아들이 태어났다.

05 독자 제현에 대한 언급

■ To anyone I may have omitted, my apologies: I appreciated your efforts nonetheless.

■ Last but not least I **would like to express my thanks to the anonymous readers** of the typescript for Cambridge University Press, whose comments and suggestions were invaluable.

last but not least는 "마지막으로 덧붙일 중요한 말은"이라는 뜻이다.

■ Of course, any and all remaining errors **are solely my own**.

어떠한 오류도 전적으로 필자의 몫

IX 이력 Curriculum vitae 소개에 자주 등장하는 표현

RESUME (Sample-1~7)

이하의 예문들은 자신의 현재 소속, 학업 진척 정도, 관심 분야, 저널과 학회 등에서 발표했던 논문 소개, 각종 학술 경력 등을 어떻게 소개하는 지를 일목 요연하게 다루고 있다. 뿐만 아니라, 이 예문들은 저널의 논문 기고 자들을 소개하는 표현 등에서 흔히 찾아볼 수 있으며, 책에서는 주로 머리말 등에 많이 나타난다. 영어로 흔히 c.v. 혹은 vita로 간단히 불려지는 이력서에는 자신의 현재 지위(학교, 학위 정도, 주소 등)와 학술적 이력, 학회 논문 발표 경험, 연구 경력 등이 기본적으로 포함된다. 때문에 resume보다 학술적이며 보다 형식을 갖추고 있다고 보면 좋다.

저자가 찾아 낸 아래의 영어 원문 정보를 통해서 미국 사회에서 통용되는 vita vs. resume의 차이점을 먼저 익혀 두면서 자신의 이력 소개에 중요한 표현법을 알아 두자. 참고로, 이력서를 쓰는 요령과 직업 서치에 대한 모든 정보는 다음의 사이트에서 찾아 낸 것임을 밝혀 둔다 (http://www. ku.edu/~uces).

http://chronicle.com/jobs/archive/advice/talk.htm
http://www.careers.ucr.edu/Students/Graduates/CV.html
    University of California, Riverside 대학에서 제공하는 것으로, 샘플 비타와 지원 원서 예들이 많이 소개되어 있다. 아래의 사이트도 참고하자.
http://www.careers.ucr.edu/Students/Graduates/CV/cv_model.pdf
http://www.careers.ucr.edu/Students/Graduates/CV/coverlet.pdf
http://www.columbia.edu/cu/ccs/99website/99student/basics/cv.html
    Columbia 대학에서 만들어 낸 사이트로, 기본적으로 비타 작성에 필요한 것들을 잘 소개해 놓고 있다.
http://www.uncwil.edu/stuaff/career/Resumes&Vitas_files/frame.htm
    North Carolina at Wilmington 대학이 제공하는 사이트로, 비타 작성의 기본 요령과 주의 사항을 잘 설명해 놓고 있다.

또한 영문으로 쓰여진 이력서, 자기 소개서 등의 각종 전공별, 직업별 예문 sample을 이 장의 마지막 부분에 소개함으로써 독자들이 이력서를 작성할 때 실질적인 도움을 받을 수 있도록 꾸며 놓았다.

Vita vs. Resume

There is no standard definition of curriculum vita or resume, but generally the focus is more on academic preparations, research, and publications than in a resume. Another significant difference is that a vita is not limited by length. A master's level vita may be 3 or 4 pages, while persons with doctorates may have vitas of 10 or more pages in length. Content determines the length.

As with a resume, a vita should be written in concise language, perfectly typed, edited, and duplicated, logically organized, and tailored to each specific position. On pages other than the first, put the page number, your name, and your phone number. Begin descriptions with action verbs, emphasizing accomplishments and achievements. Names, dates, and titles should be consistently in the same place within entries. Always package a vita with a personalized letter.

Vita have no set format. Consult with professionals in your field about what to include and appropriate layout. Be complete but concise. The order of sections is determined by your strengths: experienced conditions may begin with experience, inexperienced candidates may begin with educational background.

학교 직위, 직함, 현재의 신분 소개

■ Lesile Pal is **chair** and **assistant professor in the Department of** Political Science **at** the College of St. Catherine in St. Paul, Minn.
학과 department 앞에서는 전치사 in을 쓰고, college 혹은 university 앞에서는 전치사 at을
쓰도록 한다.

■ Kent Weaver is a **professor** and a **director** at the School of Public Policy and Administration at Carleton University.

■ Richard Schultz was **coeditor** of Changing the Rules and the journal ~.

■ Raymond Donley is currently a vice president for policy development and associate **provost** of the University of Toronto.

■ Sylvia Huot is University **lecturer** in French and a Fellow of Pembroke College.

■ Thomas Hans teaches medieval literature and culture at the University of Rochester, and he is a **general editor** of the Chaucer Bibliographies.

■ Jacob Edmond is a **Ph.D. candidate** (= a doctoral candidate) in the Comparative Literature Program at the University of Auckland, New Zealand.
박사 후보, 즉 현재 박사학위 논문을 쓰고 있으면서 곧 학위를 받고 졸업을 하게 될 학생을 일컬어
캔디데이트라고 부른다. 다른 말로 '박사 종합 시험을 마치고, 박사학위 논문만 남겨 둔 사람'을
흔히 ABD(all but dissertation: 박사학위 논문만 제외하고 모든 것을 다 마친)라고 부른다.

■ Roman Kozlov is a **doctoral** candidate at Carleton University in Ottawa.

■ Linda Rae Bennett is Postdoctoral Research Fellow at the Australian Research Centre in Sex, Health and Society of La Trobe University.
흔히 우리가 '포닥'이라고 하는 것이 postdoctor이다. 박사학위를 받고 모교 혹은 다른 학교에서
이같은 박사 후 과정을 하는 경우가 많은데, 대체로 학교 당국의 정식 고용인으로서 정기적으로
연구비, 혹은 급료를 받을 뿐만 아니라 연구 경력에 있어서 아주 중요한 역할을 한다.

■ Roger Barta is a **full-time senior research fellow** at the Institute of ~.
~의 책임 연구원

- John Dingey is **Emeritus Professor** of Russian and Slavic Linguistics, University of Alberta.
  명예 교수

직책 역임

- He served as an adjunct professor of anthropology and visiting professor of American Indian and Native Studies at the University of Iowa from 1977 to 2002 and **as chair of** the American Indian Program.

- Starting in January 2003 Prof. Rifkin will **assume the presidency of** AATSEEL.

- Most recently, she **served as president of** the American Folklore Society (2000-2002).

학위 취득

- Prof. Zimmermann **received his doctorate in** anthropology **from** Boston University in 1988.
  학위 취득을 뜻하는 동사로는 위의 receive 외에 earn이 있다.

- Lilly Goren **holds a Ph.D. in** political science **from** Boston College.

- She **holds a B.A. from** (received bachelors' degree) ~ and **an M.A. and Ph.D in** political science **from** Yale University.

- Isaura Barrera **holds a doctoral degree in** education research and evaluation, **with concentration in** early childhood research.

~에서의 오랜 경험

- Dr. Sullivan has more than twenty years **experience in** making, researching, and curating archeological collections.

- Prof. Marc Greenburg **has extensive working experience in** maternal and child health projects in rural India.

- Dr. Maria Carlson **has worked** more than 36 years in economics **in** San Antonio, TX and was a visiting assistant professor in the Department of Business from the University of Illinois, where he coordinated several large-scale training and technical assistance projects.

  위의 모든 예문에서처럼 과거의 어느 순간에서부터 현재까지 계속 진행되는 경험 혹은 경력을 말해 주는 대목이므로, 문법적으로 현재완료시제를 많이 쓴다는 것을 잘 알아 두자.

- **Previously he taught** English and Comparative Literature for twenty years **at** the University of East Anglia.

  과거 20년 간 ~ 학교에서 ~을 가르친 바 있다.

- Dunrop is an energetic, ambitious scholar, with **unparalleled familiarity** with Japanese archives in educational history.

  ~에 있어(~ 분야에 있어) 타의 추종을 불허할 정도의 박식함

전공 분야

- Her **main area of expertise is** the late prehistory of the Southeast.

- Her **primary field research interest is** the Iron Age of Sub-Saharan Africa.

- Her **main research interests focus on** the development and spread of native agriculture.

- Her **research interests relate to** the ~.

- Her **area of research and teaching interest is** ~.

- An expert on medieval Russian history, Lawrence Langer **has focused his studies on** ~.

- Dr. Roger's **major area of** research continues to be the relationship between folklore and film studies, particularly with regards to contemporary legend and horror cinema.

  ~의 주요 연구 주제는 ~이며, ~에 특별한 관심을 기울이고 있다.

- Prof. Barre Toelken's **professional** focus has been primarily on ~.

■ He **specializes** in the history of early twentieth-century immigration from Russia to Canada.

책과 논문 다수 발표

■ Dr. Lynne **has published numerous books and articles on** ~.

■ He also **writes** and lectures **extensively on** the ~. Previous publications include ~.

■ He is **the author of** three recent books: ~.
위의 두 표현에서처럼 '~을 많이 썼다'는 뜻으로 동사를 직접 쓸 수도 있고, 지금처럼 '~의 저자이다'란 표현도 많이 쓰인다. 마찬가지로 다음과 같은 표현도 상당히 일반적이다.
Prof. Michael is <u>the author of many articles on</u> ~.

■ He is also **the author of numerous** journal articles and book chapters in the areas of ~.

■ She is **the author of** over fifty articles and **reviews on** various topics in ~.
수십 편의 논문과 다양한 주제의 서평을 쓴 바 있다.

■ She **has edited** *Reflections* in the Frame (1991). **Among his publications are** ~ (1998); ~ (1993), "Early Middle English" in the *Cambridge History of Medieval English Literature* (1999).

■ He has published **widely on** French Revolution and Napoleonic history.

■ His publications **include** ~ (1984) and ~ (1991).

■ His **publications on** Afro-Cuban religion **include** two books, ~ (2001) and (2002).

■ She **has published articles** on the problems of ~.
~에 대한 문제의 논문을 발표, 소개해 왔다, 또는 ~의 문제를 다룬 논문을 써 왔다.

■ **In addition to** her publications on ~, Merry Carlyn **has also written about** ~.
~에 대한 책과 더불어 (이외에), ~ 분야에 대해서도 쓴 바 있다.

최근 업적 소개

- His **recent work includes articles on** ~ and ~.
  최근 그의 연구는 ~을 포함한다. 즉, 그는 최근 ~에 대한 연구를 해 왔다.

- He recently **completed a book on** ~.
  최근 ~에 대한 책을 완성하였다, ~에 대한 책을 탈고하였다.

- Erb is a **recent recipient of** the Jack L. Walker Award for an outstanding contribution to the research of ~.
  ~는 최근 ~ 상을 받은 바 있다. 즉, ~ 수상자이다.

- He **has received grants** from the National Endowment of the Humanities (NEH) to develop new course curriculums in Western civilization at the University of Connecticut.

- Barbara Hochman is senior lecturer at ~ and **received** an NEH Fellowship **for** a project examining the relation between fiction and reading practices.
  위와 같이 장학금 혹은 연구비 지원 프로그램에서 당선된 경력을 나타낼 때 receive를 쓰는 것과, ~ 해당 분야, 즉 수상 내용 혹은 연구 분야를 뜻할 때는 전치사 for를 쓴다는 점을 알아 두자.

- Dr. Haring **received** a 1995 Ohioana Book Award **from** the Ohio Library Association and was a finalist for the Ralph J. Gleason Music Book Award.
  수상 경력을 얘기할 때 지금처럼 receive 동사를 사용하며, finalist는 말 그대로 당선 최종 주자를 말하는 것으로 최종 당선자는 아니지만 마지막 대상자 리스트에 오른 사람을 일컬을 때 쓰이는 말이다. runner-up은 차점자, 즉 2등으로 당선된 사람을 말한다.

- She has most currently **conducted fieldwork** on the German goddess tradition in the south in Germany, in which the focus of her research was ~.
  현지 답사를 동반한 fieldwork 혹은 field research를 한다고 할 때 언제나 위의 동사 conduct를 쓴다는 것을 알아 두자. carry out 역시 같은 의미로 쓰이는 대표적인 표현이다.

- As director of Kenyon's Rural Life Center, Sacks **conducts fieldwork and public projects** on subjects including family farming, foodways, and rural expressive culture.

- Julia **holds** a Social Sciences and Humanities Research Council of Canada postdoctoral fellowship at Northwestern University.

현재 작업 중인 저서 혹은 논문 소개

- He **is currently writing** an article **on** ~.

- He **is currently working on** another monograph investigating ~.

- Prof. Kelly **is working on a manuscript** that examines the ~.
  ~을 점검하는 원고 작업 중이다.

- Prof. Marietia Messmer **is at work on** a book-length study entitled *Rewriting the Postmodern.*

- His **current research explores** the ~.

- Prof. Andrew Rich's **current project** is "Contested Networks: The Politics of Telecommunications Restructuring in Canada, 1976-1993."

- Dr. John Rowe's **current scholarly projects are** ~.

- Her **latest project is a book on** the social history of language in Europe.
  가장 최근의 프로젝트는 ~에 대한 책이다.

- Her **current research elaborates on** her interests in gender studies and German Literature.

- Prof. Jeef Rider will soon publish *God's Scribe* from Cambridge University Press (2003).

- Linda Khan **is now completing** her Ph.D. and is also an active member of ~.

- She **is currently completing a study of** the politics of festival, entitled "The Naked Saint."
  현재 ~에 대한 연구를 진행 중이다, 끝내가고 있다.

- Anne **is currently working on questions related to** ~.
  현재 ~에 관련된 문제들을 연구 중이다.

- In retirement he **continues** his **research into** the sociolinguistics of the Slovenophone minority in Austria.

- Harvey's **researches into** the blood **prompted** other researchers **to** look at other body systems in similar ways.

- **Research into** prospective market niches may exceed the time taken to develop the cosmetic products.

향후 출간될 저서 소개

- **Forthcoming are** his book *Place and Dream: Japan and the Virtual* and "The I and the Thou: A Dialogue between Nishdia Kitaro and Mikhail Bakhtin" (*Japan Review*).
  '~에서 곧 출판될 것임'을 뜻하는 문장으로 가장 일반적인 것이 forthcoming from이다. 이때 from 뒤에는 출판사 이름이 오게 된다. 또 다른 것으로 in press는 현재 인쇄 중이란 뜻으로 앞의 예문보다 시간상으로 보다 빨리 이루어질 일에 대해서 쓰는 표현이다.

- Her book, *Not in My District*, **is forthcoming** from Peter Lang Publishing.

- **His article ~ will soon appear in** a collection of Turgenev's work ~.
  그의 논문은 ~에 조만간 나올 것이다.

Biology Major (생물학 전공)

Sharon L. Stevenson
1615 Ellis Dr. # 9
Seattle, Washington 92013
703/555-3298 [1]

Education

1995-1999 [2]   Bates College

Awarded [3] a Bachelor of Science degree in May 1999,

majoring in [4] Biology, minoring in Horticulture. Courses include [5]

Biochemistry, Anatomy & Physiology, Chemistry, Physics, Computer Science and Advanced Calculus. 3.77 grade point average. Awarded the Biological Sciences Society Award for Outstanding Students of Biology.

Experience

Summer 1998   Maine State Parks and Recreation

Volunteer for State for Maine Summer Clean-Up Program.

Removed trash and litter from state grounds, landscaped state and local parks, repaired and repainted state buildings, signs, and benches.

Part-time

1996-1999   Bates College Library

Front desk clerk. Processed books, restacked shelves, answered phones, and assorted other duties.

Personal

Background   Enjoying gardening, reading, and scuba diving. Published feature article in American Horticulture.

References   Personal references available upon request. [6]

---

1) 지금과 같이 전화번호를 기입하는 요령에는 슬래쉬를 쓰는 경우도 있고, 괄호를 하기도 하는 경우도 있다: "(703) 555-3298"

2) 이력서 작성의 가장 기본은 모든 인적 사항과 경력에 해당하는 정보를 기술할 때 가장 최근의 사실부터 나열한다는 점이다. 그리고 지금과 같이 현재 학생으로서 가장 중요한 것이 바로 자신의 교육 정도이기 때문에 education 정보가 가장 앞에 오는 것을 기억해 두자. 한편 표제어, 즉 각 항목의 타이틀은 지금과 같이 첫 글자만 대문자로 표기하기도 하지만 모든 글자를 대문자로 표기하고, 굵은 글씨체로 강조함으로써 눈에 보다 잘 들어오게 하는 방식도 많이 쓰인다. 예를 들어, EDUCATION.

3) '학위를 취득하다'라는 동사에는 award 혹은 receive, earn, take가 있지만 take 동사는 거의 사용되지 않는다는 것을 알아 두자. 같은 의미이긴 하지만 이력서와 같은 형식적인 문서에는 award, earn, receive 이렇게 세 동사들이 주로 사용된다.

4) '자신의 전공이 ~이다'란 표현이 바로 major in이며, 부전공은 minor in ~라고 사용한다.

5) 자신이 수강했던 교과목을 간략하게 기술하는 대목에서 지금과 같은 Courses include란 표현이 가장 일반적으로 사용된다.

6) 미국에서는 어떠한 종류의 이력서를 내더라도 지금과 같이 '자신을 잘 알고 있는 지인(지도 교수, 학과의 책임자, 이에 버금가는 추천인 또는 가까운 친구)'의 정보 일체를 반드시 제출하는 것이 통례이다. 따라서 reference는 지금의 이력서와는 별도의 종이에 자세한 인적 사항을 기술하게 되어 있으며, 일반적으로는 추천인의 이름, 주소, 연락처, 직위 등이 포함된다.

Business Administration Major (경영학 전공)

Michael J. Johnson
21 Stouffer Place # 12
Lawrence, Kansas 66047
785/812-3007

EDUCATION

1995-1999 University of Wisconsin

Candidate for the degree of[7] Bachelor of Science in May 1999, majoring in Business Administration. Courses include Marketing, Industrial Relations, Finance, Accounting, Business Law, and Computer Applications. 3.4 grade point average.

EXPERIENCE

Fall 1998 Gooddell & Hite Associates[8]

Data entry clerk for order department. responsibilities included order processing, customer service, inventory control, and some packing and shipping.

Summer 1997 Island Fitness Health Club

Aerobics instructor and choreographer. Voted "Best Instructor" by members and staff.

ACTIVITIES

Founder and Director of League of Women's Soccer in Madison. Recipient of Wisconsin Times Scholar Athlete Award, awarded to the most outstanding female student athlete in Green County.

---

7) '학위 취득 예정자' 혹은 '졸업 예정자'를 뜻하는 표현으로서, 위에서는 '학사 졸업 예정자'로 해석하면 좋을 것이다. 석사는 Master of Arts(M.A.)이고, 박사는 Doctor of Philosophy(Ph.D.)이다.

8) 지금과 같이 어떤 사업체 부서에서 일한 경우의 표현 가운데 참고할 만할 것들을 살펴보자: 1) Assistant to the Warehouse Manager. Responsible for supervising warehouse operations. Trained new summer staff. 2) Marketing Intern. Assistant the Marketing Director in promoting a new program designed to increase corporate interest and participants in the United Way. 3) Provided technical assistance to farmers, ranchers, and other concerned with the conservation of soil, water and related natural resources.

Economics Major (경제학 전공)

Nancy Allen
12 Island Road
Salinas, California 21131
(619) 555-3071

Education

1994-1998   Norte Dame College
Bachelor of Arts degree awarded in June 1998, majoring in Economics. Minor in German language. Courses included: International Relations, International Business Law, and Communications. Ranked 4 in a class of 53.

1990-1994   Bay City High School
Received High School Diploma in June in 1994. High honors list. Took advanced college-level courses in English, Mathematics, and Physics.

Languages   Able to speak fluently and write in German.

Interests   Enjoy photography and collecting antique books, particularly 19th century German novels. Have travelled extensively in Europe, Asia, and South America.[9]

References   Available upon request.

---

9) 지금과 같이 취미 항목 이외에 별도의 장기 혹은 특기 사항을 첨가하는 경우도 있다. 이 경우 주로 어떤 컴퓨터 소프트웨어 프로그램을 잘 다룬다는 것을 강조하는 것이 일반적이다. 다음의 예들을 참고해 보자.

COMPUTER
SKILLS   **Word Processing**: working knowledge of Word Perfect and Microsoft Word.
Spreadsheets: Familiar with all aspects of creating and using a spreadsheets using Lotus 1-2-3.
또는
SKILLS AND
ABILITIES   Procificient in the use of Lotus 1-2-3, Microsoft Excel, SASSE, and SPSSX.
Excellent communication and interpersonal skills.

International Relations Major (국제 관계 전공)

Lynne Ann Jordan
156 Newton Heights
301/494-9865

Education

1995-1998   George Washington University

Awarded the degree of Bachelor of Arts in June 1998, majoring in International Relations. Minor in French Language. Thesis concentration in International Law. Completed 4-year requirements in 3 years. Honors with Advanced Standing and Dean's List.[10]

1997   College of International Relations

Participant in summer International Studies Session. Studied French, International Politics, Comparative Government, and History of the United Nations. Received Bilingual Proficiency Certification.

Experience

Summer 1996   Interpreted for negotiation over film co-productions, translated agreements, film scripts, and foreign correspondence.

Part-time

1998   Deshabilles Associates

Worked as an Assistant to Parisian Correspondent. Duties included translation of documents and general clerical.

Personal

Interests   Enjoy modern French literature and film.

References   Available upon request.

---

10) Honors with Dean's List란 표현은 졸업 시 단대에서 최우수 졸업 학생이었다는 뜻이다. 수상 경력은 일반적으로 교육 (education)란에 들어간다. 앞의 예들에서 나온 대로 동사 award를 사용하기도 하고, 때로는 win을 쓰기도 한다(Won the Alfred Pinder Award for Outstanding Students of Pshychology in 1998).

Women's Studies Major (여성학 전공)

Linda McFarlane
756 Maple Street
Manchester, NH 03104
Phone: 603/555-0817

Education

1994-1998   University of Vermont

Awarded Bachelor of Arts degree in May 1998, majoring in Women's Studies, minoring in Art. courses included Economics, Politica Science, and Public speaking. Thesis topic: The Political Economy of Our Domestic Health Care System. 3.5 point average. Awarded the Bailey-Howe Scholarship in 1996.

Experience

Summer 1997   Office of the Public Defender

Summer Intern working with five attorneys. Performed extensive research to support court cases and attended court sessions. Handled confidential documents and paperwork.

Summer

1995-1996   Sweetwater's Restaurant

Began work as waitress, promoted to hostess. Also relief bartender.

Part-time

1994-1995   University Bookstore

Cashier/Clerk. Acted as cashier, stocked shelves, and miscellaneous other duties.

Personal

Background   Enjoy painting, aerobics, and camping. Member of the National Organization of Women.

References   Personal references available upon request.

Communication Major (커뮤니케이션 전공)

Joseph Larson

Present Address:
1234 Main Avenue
Lawrence, KS 66046
(785) 843-1025

Permanent Address:
East Street 6789
Omaha, NE 68044
(402) 334-1951

Professional	A full-time position leading to Branch Management/Operations
Objective	for a financial services organization.
Education	Bachelor of Arts, Communication Studies, May 2002 University of KansasLawrence, KS Major GPA: 3.5/4.0 Cumulative GPA: 3.2/4.0
Relevant Coursework	Business Communication Legal Communication Conflict Resolution Intercultural Communication Finance Operations Management
Supervision and Training	-Supervised staff of 35 people, maintaining the lowest turnover rate in five years -Developed and implemented a training program for new employees, resulting in increased productivity -Created company video used in orientation sessions -Part of interview and selection team
Communications	-Wrote an orientation handbook for new employees -Approved articles for inclusion in school newspaper -Interacted with customers and supervisors from 15 different departments of retail store -Effectively dealt with customer concerns while working in customer service department
Work History (8/00–5/01) (9/99–5/00)	Features Editor University of Kansas Lawrence, KS Assistant Manager Burger Bonanza Omaha, NE Sales Clerk Mays Department Store Lakewood, CO

English Major (영문학 전공)

Ima J. Hawk
1422 West Campus Road
Lawrence, KS 66045

(785) 842-1903
Email: ijhwak@ku.edu

Education

Bachelor of Arts, English, May 2002, University of Kansas, Lawrence, KS
- GPA in Major: 3.5/4.0
- Employed during college, earned 75% of college expenses
- Jayhawk scholarship recipient, complete award for leadership

Sales Experience

Sales Representative, University of Kansas, Lawrence, KS
8/23-Present
- Effectively managed 30 active accounts
- Responsible for sales, advertising budget and creative campaigns
- Exceeded sales guota by 65% during first time months

Other Experience

Waitress and Hostess, Silvercryst Resort, Wautoma, WI
Summers 1998 & 2001
- Trained and supervised new staff members
- Greeted and welcomed patrons to the restaurant
- Ensured that customers were pleased with food and service

Activities

University of Kansas Student Ambassador
Member, Association of Collegiate Enterpreneurs
Member, Alpha Chi Omega Sorority
- Scholarship Coordinator
- Chairperson of Rush committee
- Volunteer, Big Brothers/Big Sisters

The Essential Guide to Writing Papers in English

X 논문 투고와
요약문 작성의 실례

ABSTRACT (Sample-1~36)

이번 장의 내용은 일반 논문의 작성법과는 약간 다르다. 이하의 예들은 수업 시간을 통해 발표하거나 학기말에 흔히 제출하는 그런 페이퍼가 아니라, 주로 Conference 등의 학회 혹은 Workshop, Colloquium에서 발표되는 논문들과 같은 성격을 갖는다.

다음에 예로 든 36편의 요약문 abstract는 저자가 실제로 가입해서 정기적으로 받아 보는 학회 소식지 newsletter와 매년 정기적으로 열리는 전국 규모의 학회 national conference에서 발표된 논문들의 요약 모음집 proceeding, program book에서 발췌한 것들이다. 저자는 우선 독자들이 문체의 다양성을 맛볼 수 있도록 서로 다른 양식의 내용을 가려 뽑는 데 주안점을 두었다. 아울러 우리가 이미 이 책의 본론을 통해서 익힌 실질적인 표현들이 많이 사용된 글들을 주로 엄선하여 학습의 반복 효과를 높이도록 하였다. 그 예로 저자는 독자들의 이해를 돕고, 이 책에서 배운 것들을 반복하여 확인할 수 있도록 중요 표현들을 이탤릭체와 굵은 글씨체로 구분해 두었다.

참고로, 우리가 알아야 하는 것은 research paper나 모든 종류의 paper 혹은 essay를 쓸 때 반드시 2줄 간격 즉, double space로 작성해야 한다는 점이다. 물론 각주나 미주는 1줄 간격을 원칙으로 한다. Abstract는 논문을 받는 학회에 따라 약간의 차이는 있을 수 있으나 대체로 250~500자 내의 분량을 기준으로 한다. 미국 표준인 letter size (8.5×11 inch, 대략 가로 21.6×세로 28cm) 1~2장 내외로 요약문의 분량을 비교적 엄격하게 지키도록 요구하는 편이다. 하지만 예로 든 다음의 글들은 글쓴이에 따라서 그 양이 각기 다르다. 때문에 엄격한 의미에서 논문 작성의 규정에는 다소 어긋나는 것이 있음을 먼저 밝혀 둔다.

Abstract Sample-1

Political Science (162자)

Political Citizenship and Democratization: The Gender Paradox

This research challenges models of democratization that claim liberal principles affirming the equality of rights-bearing individuals equably enhance the political inclusion of groups marginalized by race, class, or gender. While such explanations may suffice for race and class, ***this study's quantitative*** cross-national ***analysis of*** women's contemporary officeholding patterns ***establishes that*** gender ***presents*** a counter case whereby women's political citizenship is enhanced, first, by government institutions that paradoxically affirm both individual equality and kinship group difference and, second, by state policies that paradoxically affirm both individual equality and women's group difference. ***These findings challenges assumptions about*** the relationship between political citizenship and democratization, ***demonstrate how*** women's political inclusion as voters and officeholders is strengthened not by either a sameness principle (asserting women's equality to men as individual) or a difference principle (asserting women's group difference from men) but rather by the paradoxical combination of both, and provide hew views for assessing multiculturalism prospects within democratic states.

Abstract Sample-2

Political Science (160자)

The Quest for Certainty and the Demise of Political Theory

In this paper, ***I contribute to the ongoing conversation*** in New Political Science ***regarding*** the status of political science in general, and political theory in particular. ***I argue that*** the quest for certainty and desire to quantify knowledge has not been limited to empiricist political scientist. ***The emphasis*** on quantification and deductive logic ***is found in*** many places within the political theory tradition itself. Time and again, mathematics and the physical sciences ***are held up as the model for*** all knowledge. I argue that this focus has ***led*** theorists ***to*** distance themselves from politics, either out of desire or disdain for the ambiguity and variability present in political life. While ***I do not suggest that*** Aristotle provides a magic remedy for the current problems in the discipline, ***I suggest that*** his combined interest in logic and the close examination of material detail ***provides a perennially viable framework for*** political theory.

Political Science (182자)

Determinants of Presidents Legislative Support in the House, 1949-1995

This paper has several purposes. First, **it illustrates** the changing nature of research on presidential-congressional relations. **In general**, scholarship has moved away from viewing the president as the dominant actor in the relationship, toward one of congressional influence, and ultimately toward emphasizing more equal power sharing between the two institutions. Second, **we discuss our use of** the most widely used measures of such relationships, presidents legislative support and success and our rationale for choosing the former. Third, **we introduce** three broad environments of presidential-congressional relations in order to explain such support from what we call a multiple perspectives approach. **We find that** variables from each of the three environments are important in explaining presidential support in the House. Fourth, we control for policy areas using the two presidencies typology and **observe** significant differences in support by domestic and foreign policy. Our multivariate two stage least squares (2SLS) analysis explains considerable variance in support across all three models. Finally, **we explicate how our approach improves** our understanding of this important presidential-congressional interaction.

Political Science (200자)

Cold War in the Kitchen: Gender and the De-Stalinization of Consumer Taste
in the Soviet Union under Khrushchev

Consumption, **key issue in the study of** post-Soviet culture, **was** already **a central concern** during the Cold War. In the late 1950s and early 1960s, the Khrushchev regime staked its legitimacy at home, and its credibility abroad, on its ability to **provide** its population **with** consumer goods and a decent standard of living. Despite promising "abundance for all" as the precondition for the imminent transition to communism, the regime could not afford to leave abundance undefined. **In this article, I examine the way** discourses of consumption, fashion, and the ideal Soviet home sought to remake consumers' conceptions of culturedness, good taste, and comfort in rational, modern terms that **took into account** the regime's ideological commitment and economic capacity. Such efforts to shape and regulate desire **were directed** above all at women. **I propose that** the study of consumption **provides insight into the ways in which** post-Stalinist regimes manipulates and regulated people through regimes of personal conduct, taste, and consumption habits, **as opposed to** coercion. Indeed, the management of consumption was an significant for the Soviet system's longevity as for its ultimate collapse.

Sociology (191자)

The Truly Disadvantaged and the structural Covariates of Fire Death Rates

The present paper study investigates the social demographic correlates of fire death rates for large metropolitan countries (N=199). ***Date were derived from*** the 1990 census and the Centers for Disease Control (CDC). Multiple regression ***analyses revealed that*** age of housing, prevalence of mobile homes, and the proportion of the population renting had significant independent effects on fire death rates. Furthermore, ***the results indicated*** a significant interaction between the proportion of the population that is African American and median family income. The combination of low income and a high proportion of African Americans ***was related to*** fire death rates in a multiplicative rather than additive view. That is, the combination of low income and high proportion of African Americans appears to ***be associated with*** extremely high fire death rates, much more so than would be predicted by simply summing the two risk factors together. ***The results are discussed in relation to*** cumulative disadvantage theory. ***It is argued that*** the relationship between race and fire death is the product of both racial disparities in income and the geographic concentration of multiple disadvantages.

Sociology (184자)

Mythscapes: Memory, Mythology, and National Identity

In this paper I seek to challenge the dominant modes of conceiving the relationship between memory and national identity, ***and in so doing offer analysis of*** nationalism an improved understanding of the dynamics of national identity formation. The concept of collective memory is invoked regularity in attempts to explain the pervasiveness and power of nationalism. ***I argue that*** the concept is misused routinely in this context, and instead ***I employ*** a social agency ***approach to*** theorizing, whereby memory is conceived in a more limited and cogent manner. ***I argue that*** it is important to distinguish clearly between memory and mythology, both of which ***are essential to*** understanding national identity, for not only are the two concepts distinct, they can also act in opposition to each other. ***Following from this I introduce the notion of*** a mythscape, the temporally and spatially extended discursive realm in which the myths of the nation are forged, transmitted, negotiated, and reconstructed constantly. Through employing the idea of a mythscape I can ***relate*** memory and mythology ***to*** each other in a theoretically profitable way.

Sociology (82자)

Preference Discrimination and Faculty Diversity

Drawing upon Becker's theory of preference discrimination, *this paper proposes a theoretical framework that* analyzes the effect of employer discrimination, employee discrimination and customer discrimination on faculty diversity. *The authors then consider* institutional features of the U.S. academic workplace in order to discuss the extent to which each source of discrimination can explain faculty diversity across universities. *This discussion suggests that* customer discrimination is a particularly convincing argument to explain differences in faculty diversity across U.S. universities. Finally, research directions are suggested.

International Affairs (186자)

Another Century of Conflict? War and the International System in the 21st Century

This article examines the major factors likely to affect sources and methods of armed conflict in the coming century. First, it considers the role of changing military technology, concentrating on the Revolution in Military Affairs. Second, *it then turns to the issue of* possible balances between economic conflict and cooperation and their effects on war, including whether the current extreme economic inequality within and between nations will be reduced by widespread industrialization and the prospects for China becoming an economic equal of and military rival to the USA. Third, *it considers how* climate change may affect the role of states and the sources of conflict between them. Finally, *it raises the question of whether* international norms will be extended and consolidated, *leading to* greater cosmopolitan governance. *It concludes that* this is unlikely in an environment where states are facing confrontational non-state actors and where the major powers are forced to intervene in collapsing states. The article *envisages* a century of conflict, different from the 20th century but in many ways no less brutal.

International Affairs (137자)

NGOs and the Advancement of Economic and Social Rights:
Philosophical and Practical Controversies

This article explores controversies surrounding economic and social rights in the context of recent moves by non-governmental organizations, notably Amnesty International, to strengthen their commitment to these second-generation rights. Although this move is long overdue, *the article argues that* these efforts will fail if we simply attempt to add economic and social rights to the existing liberal human rights discourse. *This article focuses in* the contribution that feminist ethics has made to the reconceptualization of rights in theory and practice. Specifically, *it argues that*, in order to make sense of both the moral imperative of so-called welfare rights, and the political work required to realize them, *we must rethink* rights *in terms of* relationships and the patterns of responsibility that emerges out of them.

Child Education (159자)

Gender and Political Orientation in Childhood

This study explores whether boys and girls differ in their levels of political orientation and the extent to which race/ethnic heritage mediates such an association. *We analyze survey data for* 14,855 children across 20 states *using a fixed-effects analytical technique that* confines the children to their immediate environments. *We find that* girls surpass boys in political interest and activity, and this persists without a significant drop in teen years as might be expected. This pattern *is evident* whether political orientation is measured as a composite indicator or as discrete items tapping specific activities and opinions. *Within* subgroups, White and Native American girls consistently displayed higher levels of orientation than comparable boys. Among Black, Hispanic, and Asian Americans, observed advantages for girls attenuate with full specification of control variables; at worst, Black, Hispanic, and Asian girls are equally as political as comparable boys. *These findings have implications for theorizing about* political orientation in childhood.

Education (171자)

Race, Poverty, and the Student Curriculum:
Implications for Standard Policy

The purpose of this article is to examine the links between the minority and poverty status of public secondary schools and course-taking patterns within those schools. ***This analysis looks at*** the 1984 Regents Action Plan in New York State to explore the role of standards-based politics in altering the connections between schooling context and curriculum. ***The finding show that***, on average, schools increased student participation in traditional and advanced courses in the six years immediately following the plan, ***in compassion with*** the four years preceding it. ***It is significant to note that*** in the ten-years period studied (1980-1990) the links between course-taking patterns and the minority and poverty status of schools in the rest of New York State. However, school size plays an increasingly important role for schools in all locations. The magnitude of the associations between size and course-taking patterns increased in the years after standards-based reform, ***suggesting that*** standards are not a cure-all for the ills of high schools.

Education (107자)

Serving Too Many Master

In this article, the author illustrates how teacher educators are caught in a world of ill-conceived and often contradictory policies and practices. They provide exemplars of the contradictory demands that emanate from both outside and inside of the academy, including unilateral legislative mandates for curriculum coverage, restrictive university regulations, and the growing consumer orientation of the higher education marketplace. ***The author then focuses on the issue of*** professional standards and ***discusses how*** extreme teacher shortages influence how equality-control practices in teacher preparation are conceptualized and implemented. Finally, ***with exemplars from the field of*** special education, ***they conclude with several suggestions for*** next steps.

Special Education (155자)

Toward an Understanding of Developmental Coordination Disorder

We consider three issues concerning unexpected difficulty in the acquisition of motor skills: terminology, diagnosis, and intervention. Our preference for label Developmental Coordination Disorder (DCD) receives justification. Problems in diagnosis are discussed, especially ***in relation to*** the aetiology-dominated medical model. The high degree of overlap between DCD and other child disorders appears to militate against its acceptance as a distinct syndrome. In this context, ***we emphasize the need to*** determine whether incoordination takes different forms when it occurs alone is combined with general development delay or with other specific disorders in children of normal intelligence. ***Studies of*** intervention ***have mostly shown*** positive effects but do not, as yet, allow adjudication between different sorts of content. ***We suggest that*** the study of DCD and its remediation would benefit greatly from the employment of the simple but rich paradigms developed for the experimental analysis of fully formed adult movement skills.

International Education (82자)

Globalizing Classroom Resources

This paper documents and analyzes a yearlong Cultural Ambassadors program at California State University, San Bernardino in which 22 international students established intercultural dialogs with teaches and students in two elementary schools and one high school. After ***providing a brief review of*** other programs of this type and an institutional profile of CSUSB, ***this report will describe*** the rationale, objectives, unique features, evaluation methodology and data for a yearlong Cultural Ambassadors program, ***as well as suggestions for*** future projects.

Business (152자)

Team Incentives and Worker Heterogeneity: An Empirical Analysis of the Impact
of
Teams on Productivity and Participation

This paper identifies and evaluates rationales for team participation and for the effects of team composition on productivity using novel data from a garment plant that shifted from individual piece rate to group piece rate production over three years. The adoption of team at the plant improved worker productivity by 14 percent on average. Productivity improvement was greatest for the earliest teams and diminished as more workers engaged in team production, **providing support for** the view that teams utilize collaborative skills, which are less valuable in individual production. High-productivity workers tended to join teams first, despite a loss in earnings in many cases, suggesting nonpecuniary benefits **associated with** teamwork. Finally, more heterogeneous teams were more productive, with average ability held constant, which **is consistent with** explanations emphasizing mutual team learning and intrateam bargaining.

Business (152자)

A Study of MBA Student Attitudes and Their Causes

This paper examines the results of a survey that solicited the views of a group of MBA students from two countries. **The purpose of the survey was to determine if** cultural difference did exist among these two groups of students and do identify exactly what these differences were, if in fact they were found. **The survey instrument was designed to discover if** national cultural differences would in any way be reflected in the respondents' conception of the "ideal" job, their internalized values, their opinions on which career benefits might **result from** obtaining an MBA degree, the importance of various skills acquired during the MBA program, and in the demographic fences would permit global organizations that eventually employ these graduates of MBA programs an opportunity to develop a proactive program for preparing organization members from diverse cultures to operate effectively in just such circumstances.

Business (209자)

An Empirical Assessment of the Loose-tight Leadership Model:
Quantitative and Qualitative Analyses

Using questionnaire and interview data, this study attempted to find out whether the organizational loose (participative) and tight (directive) practices are compatible with or contradict each other. Using the theoretical framework of Sagies (1997) loose-tight leadership approach, ***our hypotheses concerned*** the effects of both practices on the employees work-related attitudes, and the mediating role of two variables, cognitive (information sharing) and motivational (exerting effort), in these effects. ***Data were analyzed using two methodological approaches***, quantitative and qualitative. ***Based on a quantitative analysis of the questionnaires*** given to 101 professional employees of a textile company, partial support was ***provided*** for the study hypotheses. A quantitative analysis of in-depth, semi-structured interviews with all the employees (n=20) in one of the company divisions led to similar conclusions. Specifically, ***we found that*** although the loose and tight practices affected work attitudes, the interviewees attributed more impact to the tight practice. ***In addition***, none of the study variables mediated the loose impact on attitudes, whereas information sharing (but not exerting effort) mediated the influence of tight practice. Finally, ***the qualitative analysis revealed a deeper insight into*** the nature of both leader practices and their possible integration in the decision-making processes in organizations.

Economics (129자)

Long Run Growth and Investment in Education:
Does Unemployment Matter?

In this paper we propose a model of endogenous growth with inefficiencies in the production of human capital caused by unemployment. ***The rationale underlying this assumption can be found in*** the observation that educated youngsters need to ***acquire*** firm-specific knowledge by working activities for schooling human capital to become productive. ***The model implies*** a negative long tin relationship between growth and equilibrium employment. Data on a panel of 19 OECD countries covering the period 1960-1990 support our model predictions. Unemployment significantly lowers the output growth. ***In addition***, despite previous results in the literature, once controlling for unemployment also the traditional measures of human capital accumulation turns out to be significant and to positively affect the long run output growth.

Economics (139자)

Modeling and Forecasting Realized Volatility

I provide a framework for integration of high-frequency intraday into the measurement, modeling, and forecasting of daily and lower frequency return volatilities and return distributions. *Building on the theory of* continuous-time arbitrage-free price processes and the theory of quadratic variation, I *develop formal links between* realized volatility and the conditional covariance matrix. Next, *using continuously recorded observations for* the Deutschemak/ Dollar and Yen/Dollar spot exchange rates, *I find that* forecasts from a simple long-memory Gaussian vector autoregression for the logarithmic daily realized volatilities perform admirably. Moreover, the vector autoregressive volatility forecast, *coupled with* a parametric longnormal-normal mixture distribution produces well-calibrated density forecasts of future returns, and correspondingly accurate quantile predictions. *My results hold promise for* practical modeling and forecasting of the large covariance matrices relevant in asset pricing, asset allocation, and financial risk management applications.

Economics (170자)

A Spatial Analysis of Sectoral Complementarity

This paper presents a spatial economic method for characterizing productivity comovement across sectors of the U.S. economy. Input-output relations provide an economic distance measure that is used to characterize interactions between sectors, as well as conduct estimation and inference. *I construct* two different economic distance measures. One metric implies that two sectors are close to one another if they use inputs of other industrial sectors in nearly the same proportion, and the other metric *implies* that sectors are close if their outputs are used by the same sectors. *Our model holds that* covariance in productivity growth across sectors is a function of economic distance. *I find that (1)* positive cross-sector covariance of productivity growth generates a substantial fraction of the variance in aggregate productivity; *(2)* cross-sector productivity covariance tends to be greatest between sectors with similar input relations, and *(3)* there are constant to modest increasing returns to scale. *I test and reject the hypothesis that* these correlations are due to a common shock.

Statistics (134자)

Markov Random-Field Models for Estimating Local Labor Markets

This work is motivated by data on daily travel-to-work flows observed between pairs of elemental territorial units of an Italian region. The data were collected during the 1991 population census. **The aim of the analysis is to** partition the region into local labor markets. **I present a new method for** this which is inspired by the Bayesian texture segmentation approach. I introduce a novel Markov random-field model for the distribution of the variables that label the local labor markets for each territorial unit. Interference is performed by means of Markov chain Monte Carlo methods. The issue of model hyperparameter estimation **is** also **addressed**. **I compare the results with** those obtained applying a classical method. **The methodology can be applied with** minor modifications to other date sets.

Accounting (198자)

Oil and Gas Reserve Value Disclosures and Bid-ask Spread

My paper presents empirical evidence to suggest that the initial disclosure of the discounted **present** value of oil and gas reserves, mandated by the United States Securities and Exchange Commission (SEC) in Accounting Series Release No. 253 (ASR 253) (SEC, 1978) **was associated with** a decline in the bid-ask spread of disclosing firms common stock that appears to have perished for twelve month period following the initial reserve disclosures. **This finding is important because** it **implies** that ASR 253 equalized access to information across classes of inventors, thereby enhancing the equality of opportunity in financial markets. The objective of decreasing information asymmetry and increasing equality of opportunity in financial markets is an operational **criterion for** disclosure regulation which also **provides** accounting researchers with a means to study the effectiveness of accounting policy. **The results of this study suggest that** ASR 253 (SEC, 1978) constituted effective public policy because it helped mitigate information asymmetry. **The question of whether or not** firms should be required to disclose value-based measures of assets and liabilities is important and timely because regulators appear to be moving toward a policy of expanding fair value disclosures.

History (199자)

The Antislavery Rank-and-File in Michigan

Ever since the publication of David Donald's 1956 essay, "Toward a Reconsideration of Abolitionists," a number of historians have endeavored to identify those segments of the population who were most likely to be attracted to this reform. Presently, most scholars do not accept Donald's thesis that abolitionists were dying white elite struggling to retain social authority in American life, and they generally agree that abolitionists in both the Northeast and Northwest had a strong New England background, and that many were influenced by evangelical Protestantism. However, beyond this *consensus* there is some confusion. *This paper analyzes over* 800 of the anti-slavery rank-and-file who lived in a large, contiguous, geographical unit-the state of Michigan-and thus looks at the constituency of abolition in the setting of city, town and countryside. The majority of these men were farmers, although a significant minority were artisans, professionals, and merchants. *This paper will argue that* besides sharing a conviction regarding the immorality of slavery, Michigan abolitionists demonstrates greater optimism *with respect to* the growth of the American market economy than the population at large, and that this belief in economic progress *was congruent with* their desire to see slavery eradicated.

Library and Information Science (174자)

Cataloging of Internet Resources: How Much is Enough?

The proliferation of information on the Internet *provides a wealth of information* for the researcher and causes a dilemma for catalog librarians seeking to provide access to the most valuable information available. Whether to catalog Internet sites, and, if so, which sites to include in the library's catalog has become a major question in most academic institutions. Electronic books and journals also abound and are a part of the issue of providing access to items not physically present on the library's shelves. *This paper will analyze the literature regarding the question* and *offer an answer* from the point of view of a small library's cataloging department. Included will be example of cataloging records, online catalog displays and a practical approach to making the decision. *In an effort to* help collage the vast array of information available, in addition, *this paper will include* a link to a site, created by another author, which collects, organizes and annotates national land international Internet sites useful all technical services librarians.

Asian Studies (194자)

Tracing the Indian Heritage: Adolescence and Its Implications for Education
in Rabindranath Tagore's Works

Rabindranath Tagore (1861-1941), the first Indian Nobel Laureate for literature in 1913 and the founder of Vishva-Bharati University, *is* also *regarded as* the poet of youth. In his poems, songs, short stories, dramas, novels, essays, letters, and speeches he addressed adolescence as a critic of child marriage, the dowry system, social class, and caste. *In this paper, I have three objectives*: (1) *I organize Tagore's concept of* adolescence from his collected works; (2) *I analyze why* he borrowed the Hindu idea that adolescence begins at about age 12 when the young receives the sacred thread and devotes himself to a course of study and service in the ashram (school) guided by a gun; and (3) *I discuss how* he reintroduced, in scientific form, the ancient practice of brahmachriyya in his own school, founded in 1901. The brahmachriyya refers to wearing simple clothes, eating natural food, and "early to bed and early to rise" to foster emotional, social, cognitive, moral, and artistic growth of students. *In this context, I also supplement* the presentation with Indian and Western art works on adolescence.

Anthropology (198자)

Concordance of Two Methods of Assessing Sex and Race of Human Crania

The objective of this research was to assess the concordance of two methods for identifying the sex and race of human crania. The first method was morphological observation. The second was metric measurement as prescribed by the software program Fordisc 2. The collection of 24 undocumented crania in the Mathur anthropology laboratory at Princeton University *originated from* supplies drawing upon sources in America, India, and China. The degree of concordance of the two methods is 50%. Out of 20% crania with complete data there are 10 that agree in classification and 10 that disagree. *Included in this paper is discussion of* potential problems with the various methods used to determine sex and ancestry. *It is important to state that* while the concept of biological race has been criticized and rejected by many anthropologists still *employ the methods* used in this research to determine "race." The legal system, in which some forensic anthropologists work, requires the determination of "race." of human remains. *My findings*, if replicated, *will support the idea that* the concept of "biological races" as distinct homeogenous populations is not supported by the methods available.

Sports (146자)

Empowerment through the Sport Context:
A Model to Guide Research for Individuals with Disability

Our purpose is to propose a model of Empowerment through the sport context to guide psychological research in disability sport. *We discuss the concept of* empowerment *in relation to* sport for individuals with disabilities. Expanding upon the work of Hutzler (1990), *we include three levels of* empowerment (societal group, and individual level) in our approach. Important moderators are age of onset of disability, gender, and type of disability. Important mediators are *(a) at the individual level*, achievement goals, identity, and self-efficacy; *(b) at the group level*, motivational climate, group identity, and collective efficacy; and finally, *(c) at the societal level*, the cultural context and political efficacy. *Several methodological considerations are discussed*, and *various solutions are suggested*. *We also discuss* the critiques that have emerged *in relation to* the use of empowerment concept.

Sports (156자)

Altruistic Cooperation during Foraging by the Ache,
and the Evolved Human Predisposition to Cooperate

This paper presents quantitative data in altruistic cooperation during food acquisition by Ache foragers. Cooperative activities are defined as those that entail a cost of time and energy to the donor but primarily *lead to* an increase in the foraging success of the recipient. *Data show that* Ache men and women spend about 10% of all foraging time engaged in altruistic cooperation on average, and that on some days they may spend more than 50% of their foraging time in such activities. The most time-consuming cooperative activity for both sexes is helping during the pursuit of game animals, a pattern that *is* probably *linked to* the widespread sharing of game by Ache foragers. Cooperative food acquisition and subsequent food redistribution in hunter-gatherer societies are critical behaviors that probably helped shape universal, evolved, cooperative tendencies that are well illustrated in modern experimental economics.

Philosophy (122자)

Herder, Gadamer, and the Twenty-First Century Humanities

We cannot **address the central questions of** philosophy such as the problems of human life, civilization, and residence on the Earth by insisting upon the means and prescriptions of any one tradition. **This paper addresses** a philosophy of education **by considering the views of** Johann Gottfried Herder and Hans-Georg Gadamer on education and history. In spite of attacks on his religious loyalty, Herder supported what may today be called pluralism. Having studied history and having watched history in the making in one of its darkest moments, Gadamer also sees the future of the humanities in the global conversation. To educate humanity, **the paper concludes**, first philosophy should try to understand the existential conditions of humanity.

Science Philosophy (146자)

A Framework for Analyzing Dialogues over the Acceptability of Controversial Technologies

This article asks under what circumstances controversial technologies would be considered seriously remediation instead of being rejected out of hand. **To address this question, the author developed a conceptual framework** called public acceptability of controversial technologies (PACT). PACT considers site-specific, decision-oriented dialogues among the individuals and groups involved in selecting or recommending hazardous waste remediation technologies. It distinguishes technology acceptability; that is, a willingness to consider seriously, from technology acceptance, the decision to deploy. **The framework integrates four dimensions: (1)** an acceptability continuum that underlies decision-oriented dialogues among individuals and constituency groups, **(2)** the attributes of these individuals and groups, **(3)** the attributes of the technology at issue, and **(4)** the community context-social, institutional, and physical. **This article describes and explores** PACT as a tool for understanding and better predicting the acceptability of controversial technologies.

Literature (183자)

Portrayal of the Jew: Use and Abuse of Stereotype
in Dickens and Thackeray

While the Victorian period experiences a liberalization of attitudes and legislation, the literary portrayal of Jews by Dickens and Thackery **remains basically unchanged**, with the Jew as Other depicted by traditional stereotypes. With conventional images already ***ingrained within*** the cultural imagination, the literary device acts to enhance characterization, theme, and plot within the discourse of ***Oliver Twist, Our Mutual Friend***, and ***Vanity Fair***. While Dickens ***makes an attempt*** in Our Mutual Friend to revise previous prejudicial representations, his use of stereotypes is thinly disguised and projected onto other characters. The stereotypes of the varied Jews are developed by references to physiognomy, attire, demeanor, occupation, hygienic codes, and illustrations. Although Thackery undertakes some inclusion of his Jews into society, albeit a superficial, materialistic institution, Dickens' Jews persist as outcasts, existing either in self-imposed seclusion or in socially mandated isolation. Thackery also expands his portrayal by the addition of gender and race issues. Ultimately, the portrayal of the Jew encompasses monetary concerns, ***regardless of*** the character's virtue or vice, gender or class.

Urban Planning (146자)

Estimation of Housing Needs amid Population Growth and Change

This article proposes a theoretical framework and more accurate methods for projecting the household growth component of estimates of housing needs. These estimate combine ***empirical evidence*** with normative assumptions about the quantity of housing expected with population growth. Recent California experience illustrates the theoretical and practical issues involved. Alternative empirical methods are used to model changes in per capita household formation and homeownership rates over time. ***The results show*** great instability between 1960 and 2000 in the linkage between population and housing needs, casting doubt on which linkage to use for future projections. Past changes in housing growth ***are attributed to*** changing population composition and occupancy patterns for subgroups. Estimates ***based on*** a cohort method are lower than recent experience, but it may not be desirable to lock in the deficiencies of the past when projecting needs.

Psychology (192자)

Our Changing Views of Homosexuality in Psychoanalysis

Historically, our culture has stigmatized homosexuality as being profoundly deviant. In recent years, health professionals have sought to redefine homosexuality patients: (a) reparative therapy, and (b) "Gay Affirmative Therapy." They have divergent views in etymology, treatment, and outcome of therapy. Often sex is considered the only socially acceptable way in which a man can seek closeness. Homosexuality are both implicitly and explicitly denied social support, and then they are stigmatized when this is reflected in their behavior. Masculinity and femininity **are characteristics central to** our self-concepts and are the ways of relating in our lives. These distinctions **are central to** the misconception that homosexuality is the failure to act in the ways that meet societal expectations or our perspective gender roles. Conflict often arises when one identifies and lives **in accordance with** a particular gender and splits off their sexual self to confirm to societal norms. The clinical task, therefore, is to free the homosexual patient from conflicts that cause self-destructive behavior. This will enable the patient to live as gratifying a life as possible, become well adjusted, and maintain stable and long-lasting love relationships.

Psychology (176자)

Who Gets Caught at Maturity Gap?
A Study of Pseudomature, Immature, and Mature Adolescents

This research examines links among adolescents maturity status, their biological, social, and psychological characteristics, and parents perceptions of their adolescents maturity. The participants were 430 Canadian adolescents in the sixth and ninth grades, and a subsample of their parents. Pattern-centered analyses **confirmed** the existence of three clusters of adolescents differing in maturity status: pseudomature (25%), immature (30%), and mature (40%). Further analyses found differences among the clusters in adolescents pubertal status, the social context (presence of older siblings and friends), and their age, involvement in pop culture, school and peer involvement, and close friendships. **Analysis of** mother and father reports **revealed some differences in** how parents of pseudomature, immature, and mature adolescents perceived their adolescents maturity, and in how they felt about their adolescents maturity. There were few grade differences in the findings. **The results suggest that** pseudomature adolescents, and to a smaller extent, immature adolescents, are caught in a maturity gap, which could have longer-term implications for their transition to adulthood.

Ecology (199자)

Environmental Organizations in New Forms of Political Participation:
Ecological Modernization and the Making of Voluntary Rules

Environmental organizations have been active since the early 1960s in putting environmental ***issues on*** the political agenda and in strengthening the environmental consciousness of the public. The struggle has been successful ***in the sense that*** there is now a strong demand for practical solutions among all kinds of actors. It is, however, difficult for states and political actors to manage environmental problems by traditional forms and instruments, due to the complex character of the problems. Therefore, environmental organizations take their own initiatives to participate in policy-making by developing new forms, within new arenas, with the help of new instruments (voluntary rules or standards). ***Special attention is paid to*** the possibilities of identifying and developing constructive roles ***in relation to*** other actors and institutions as well as the capacity to organize standardization projects and to mobilize and make use of powerful resources such as symbolic capital and knowledge. ***In order to interpret characteristics and implications*** (possibilities and limitations) of standardization strategies, I ***draw*** in the ecological modernization perspective. Empirically, I ***refer to*** the role of Swedish environmental organizations in standardization projects such as eco-labeling.

Biology (203자)

Expansion of the Neocerebellum in Hominoidea

Technological and conceptual breakthroughs have **led to** more serous consideration of the cerebellum as an essential element in cognition. Recent studies show the lateral cerebellum, seat of the neocerebellum, to be most active in cognitive tasks. An examination of the relative volumes of the cerebellar hemispheres in anthropoids would reveal whether some groups show greater neocerebellar development through hemispheric expansion beyond expected allometry, *implying* a greater contribution of the lateral hemispheres to recognition. ***This study expands the exiting data on*** primate brain and brain part volumes by incorporating data from both magnetic resonance scans and historical sections for a total sample size of 97 specimens, including 42 apes, 14 humans and 41 monkeys. The resulting volumes of whole brain, cerebellum, vermis, and hemisphere enable a reliable linear regression contrast between hominoids and monkeys, and demonstrate a striking increase in the lateral cerebellum in hominoids. The uniformity of the grade shift suggests that this increase took place in the common ancestor to the hominoids. The importance of the neocerebellum in visual-spatial skills, planning of complex movements, procedural learning, attention switching, and sensory discrimination in manipulation would facilitate the adaptation of these early hominoids to frugivory and suspensory feeding.

PART 2

I 논문의 기본 형식

I 논문의 기본 형식

1. 기본 서식
2. 기본 구성
3. 장 chapter의 구성
4. 구두법 Punctuation

01 기본 서식

논문 용지

미국 표준은 레터 사이즈 (Letter Size: 8.5×11 inch)이다.
한국에서 사용하고 있는 규격으로는 가로 21.6×세로 28 cm 크기에 해당한다.

글자체와 크기

모든 논문에서 가장 권장되는 글자체 font는 Times New Roman체이다. 이 글자체는 미국 내에서 사용되고 있는 각종 행정서류와 학위 논문에서 가장 널리 쓰인다. 간혹 석·박사 학위 논문에서 Times New Roman체 외에 Arial과 Courier체가 사용되기도 하는데, 이 경우 해당 학과의 논문 작성 지침을 따르는 것이 좋다. 크기는 12포인트가 표준이며 인용문에서도 동일하다. 단, 각주와 미주에서는 10포인트로 다소 작게 설정되어 있다. 뿐만 아니라, 글자체마다 크기가 약간씩 차이가 나니 아래의 예를 참고해 두자.

Research Papers(Times New Roman): 12포인트
Research Papers(Arial): 12포인트
Research Papers (Courier): 12포인트

줄 간격

2줄 간격, 더블 스페이스 double space를 원칙으로 한다. 논문 첫 장 맨 위의 제출자 성명, 담당 교수와 학과목, 날짜를 쓰는 곳에서부터, 논문 제목과 본문의 모든 행간은 이처럼 2줄 간격을 기본으로 한다. 인용문 passage인 경우엔 2줄과 1줄 간격 두 방식이 다 쓰이기 때문에 담당 교수에게 사전 문의를 구하는 것이 좋다.

문단 정렬

아마 이 부분이 한국에서 사용하는 양쪽 정렬과 가장 눈에 띄게 다른 방식이 아닌가 생각한다. 미국식 문서 작성법에서 모든 문단은 '왼쪽 정렬' 즉, 단어가 시작되는 왼쪽에 세로열을 맞추게 되어 있다. 때문에 맨 오른쪽에 공간이 남아도 커서가 다음 열로 넘어가게 되어 있다. 언뜻 보면 한국식처럼 양쪽으로 고르게 정렬이 되어 있지 않아 어수선해 보이지만, 규정인 이상 따라야 하겠다. 왼쪽 정렬 작성법은 모든 관공서의 서류 및 학위 논문 모두에 폭 넓게 적용되고 있다.

문단 들여쓰기

영어로 indent라고 한다. 이 역시 MS Word 프로그램을 사용하면 tap으로 자동 설정되어 있어 따로 신경을 쓰지 않아도 된다. 새 문단이 시작될 때마다 지켜야 하는 들여쓰기는 1/2인치 안쪽이다. 단, 인용문인 경우에는 첫 줄에서만 2배 즉, 1인치를 들여쓰기하고 다음 줄부터는 1/2인치로 해 준다.

쪽수 매기기

일반적으로 아라비아 숫자로 한다. Term Paper의 경우 오른쪽 상단에 위치시키며 숫자 왼편에는 필자의 영문 이름 중에서 성 last name만을 기입한다 (예: Kim 1). 단, 숫자 양옆으로 하이픈을 넣은 형태 (예: - 5 -)는 권장하지 않는다. MS Word의 아이콘 View로 들어가 Header and Footer를 클릭하면 눈금으로 된 박스가 나오면서 쪽수와 이름을 달 수 있도록 되어 있다. 그러나 학위 논문 혹은 각종 저널의 경우에는 쪽수 매기기 방식이 다를 수 있다. 쪽수 번호를 하단의 정 가운데 혹은 오른쪽에 위치시키기도 하며, 일반적으로 숫자 옆에 성을 넣지도 않기 때문에 이용에 주의하자.

02 기본 구성

I. Introduction: 서론
         A. Purpose
         B. Literature Review / Previous Research

II. Body: 본론
         A. Research Questions
         B. Methodology / Approach
              1. Source Texts
              2. Hypotheses
              3. Limitation of the Study
         C. Results / Findings
         D. Discussion

III. Conclusion: 결론
         A. Conclusion and Implications / Summary
         B. Further Research / Future Work

Appendix

Reference / Bibliography / Works Cited

앞의 도식은 전통적으로 지켜지고 있는 리서치 페이퍼의 기본 형식이다. 석·박사학위 논문뿐만 아니라, 저널에 게재되는 각종 논문들도 이와 거의 흡사한 틀을 갖고 있다. 그러나 앞서 이미 얘기했듯이 이 구성은 인문과학에서 관행적으로 사용하고 있는 것과 많이 다르다. 실험이나 통계 분석을 다루지 않는 계열(문학, 어학, 철학, 역사학 등)의 논문에서는 위와 같이 세분화된 장 구분이 없고, 글의 처음부터 끝까지 하나의 흐름으로 연결되어 있다.

논문에 사용된 참고 문헌을 기재하기 전에는 흔히 appendix 즉, 부록이라고 하는 별도의 장이 첨가된다. 각종 도표, 그림, 그래프, 설문 조사 내용 등이 주로 들어가는데, 때에 따라서는 지금같이 독립되어 있는 장 대신에 본론 속에 들어가기도 한다. 여기에서 조심할 것은 부록과 참고 문헌의 표제어에는 로마 숫자로 장 구분을 하지 않고 그냥 제목만 달아 준다는 점이다.

아울러 앞에서 사선(/)을 이용한 이유는 사선 앞뒤의 용어가 같은 비중으로 쓰이고 있음을 말하기 위해서이다. 즉, Reference / Bibliography / Works Cited는 모두 논문의 결론 뒤에 붙는 참고 문헌을 지칭하는 말이다. 그러나 이렇게 세 개의 다른 표현이 있는 것은 학문의 각 영역마다 선호하는 것이 다르기 때문이다.

03 장 chapter의 구성

각 chapter와 그 밑의 소 chapter를 나열하는 방식은 다음과 같이 두 가지 방식이 있다.

로마자를 장 chapter 구분의 가장 큰 원칙으로 하는 방식

> I.
>> A.
>>> 1.
>>>> 1)
>>>>> a.
>>>>> b.
>>>> 2)
>>> 2.
>> B.
> II.

아라비아 숫자를 이용하는 방식

> 1.
>> 1.1
>>> 1.1.1
>>>> 1.1.1.1
>>>>> 1.1.1.1.1.

04 구두법
Punctuation

기본적으로 구두법엔 마침표 period, 쉼표 comma, 물음표 question mark, 느낌표 exclamation point, 따옴표 quotation mark, 세미콜론 semicolon, 콜론 colon, 대시 dash, 어파스트로피 apostrophe, 괄호 parentheses, 꺾음쇠 brackets, 슬래시 slash, 하이픈 hyphen이 포함된다. 이 자리에서는 논문을 작성하는 과정에서 가장 틀리기 쉬울 뿐만 아니라, 그 쓰임새를 반드시 알아 두어야 할 것들만 소개하고자 한다.

마침표 period

1 기본적으로 모든 문장의 종료를 나타내고자 할 때 사용한다. 단, 느낌표나 의문 부호로 끝난 문장에서는 사용하지 않는다.

2 축약어를 사용할 때
- Feb. (February)
- R. S. V. P. (in French: Replay, if you please)
- e.g. (*exempli gratia*: for example)
- i.e. (*id est*: that is)
- cf. (*confer*: compare)

3 긴 내용을 짧게 생략할 때 보통 마침표 3개를 찍는다.
- He said, "Please pass the ... potatoes."
- In surveying various responses to plagues in the Middle Ages, Barbara W. Tuchman writes, "Medical thinking ... stressed air as the communicator of disease, ignoring sanitation or visible carriers."

4 그러나 문장 전체나 혹은 한 문단 이상을 생략하는 경우에 한해서 점을 4개 찍기도 한다.
- In discussing the historical relation between politics and the press, William L. Rivers notes, "Presidential control reached its zenith under Andrew Jackson .... For a time, the United States Telegraph and the Washington Globe were almost equally favored as party organs, and there were fifty-seven journalists on the government payroll."

5 특히 시를 인용하는 경우, 한 행 혹은 그 이상을 생략할 때 마침표는 앞 행의 길이만큼 마지막까지 찍어 준다.

In Worcester, Massachusetts,
I went with Aunt Consuelo
to keep her dentist's appointment
....

It was winter. It got dark
early.

쉼표 comma

1 복합 문장에서 절 clause들을 서로 구분하기 위해 사용한다. 즉, 한 문장 안에서 연결 접속사 (and, but, for, nor, or, yet, so)를 동반한 독립절이 오기 전에 쉼표를 사용한다.

- A woman drove me to drink, and I never even had the courtesy to thank her.
- Congress passed the bill, and the president signed it into law.
- Take along a tape recorder, or you risk misquoting your interviewee.
- Other wars were longer, but few were as costly in human lives.
- The poem is ironic, for the poet's meaning contrasts with her words.

2 그러나 독립절이 너무 짧은 경우엔 되도록이면 생략하기도 한다.

- Who is up and who is down?

3 문두에서 도입의 의미를 지니는 단어, 부사구, 전치사구가 올 경우에 사용한다.

- Hey, cut it out!
- Well, move the ball or move the body.
- Yes, I bought my tickets yesterday.
- On the whole, holistic medicine is a wholly new subject.
- In particular, commas are important.
- Furthermore, the person responsible for breaking or damaging university equipment will be fined.
- When you write, you make a sound in the reader's head.
- From the deck, I could not see my father, but I could see my mother facing the ship, her eyes searching to pick me out.

따옴표 quotation mark

1 논문 작성 시 다른 저작의 내용을 직접 인용할 때 쌍따옴표를 사용한다. 이때 마침표는 쌍따옴표 안에 찍어 준다.

- As Lotman puts it, "Medieval Russian literature had several religious colorings in its writings."

2 문장의 중간에 단어 혹은 짧은 구를 인용할 때도 쌍따옴표를 쓰고, 일부 단어를 강조하는 경우에는 따옴표를 사용한다. 이때 역시 콤마는 쌍따옴표나 따옴표 안에 넣어 주는 것이 일반적이다. 이 예는 마침표를 쌍따옴표나 따옴표 밖에 찍는 한국의 경우와 다르니 주의해야 한다.

- In his recently published book, Edward Brown uses some important terms such as "theurgy," "sophia" and "mysticism."

3 대화를 인용할 때 이용한다.

- Through an interpreter, I spoke with a Bedouin man tending nearly olive trees. "Do you own this land?" I asked him.

He shook his head, "The land belongs to Allha," he said.

"What about the trees?" I asked. He had just harvested a basket of green olives, and I assumed that at least the trees were his.

4 마치 서술되고 있는 것은 같은 어떤 생각을 나타내고자 할 때에도 이용한다.

- "I won't make that mistake again," I thought.

세미콜론 semicolon

1 쉼표처럼 복합 문장 안에서 독립절을 구분하여 쓰기 위해 사용한다. 즉, 접속사로 연결되지 않는 독립절들 사이에 위치한다. 이때 조심할 점은 앞뒤 모두 한 칸씩을 띄우는 한국의 경우와는 달리, 세미콜론을 사용한 다음에만 한 칸을 띄어 준다는 점이다.

- The coat is tattered beyond repair; *still*, Akaky hopes the tailor can mend it.
- Rain had fallen steadily for sixteen hours; many basements were flooded.
- The examination was finally over; Kim felt free to enjoy himself once more.
- The house was for sale; the price was reasonable.
- Lead me not into temptation; I can find the way myself.
- In this world of sin and sorrow there is always something to be thankful for; as for me, I rejoice that I am not a Republican.
- Tolstoy's *War and Peac*e offers a panoramic portrait of the Tsarist feudal nobility during the Napoleonic period; it is a thoroughgoing depiction of the life of a whole social class.
- Some french fries are greasy; others are not; I like them all.

(= Some french fries are greasy, and others are not, but I like them all.)
- One man at the auction bid prudently; another did not.
- The clock of history does not wind itself; its hands are moved by the sweat and blood of men and women who choose to be fully present on the stage of time.
- This book represents a portion of a co-operative attempt to understand the people of China; to isolate and analyse the principal motives which can be discerned as informing and underlying their typical behavior.
- Our foreign policy is not well defined; it confuses many countries.
- Teleopathy is not a theory; it is a condition.

- The key to survival in Africa lies in the ritualization of physical powers; that is, the spiritual and, in turn, sociopolitical fabric ~.
- It is unfortunate how many architects are eager to do competitions without a fee; this is harmful to the profession as well as to the architects themselves.
- Injustice and oppression obviously existed; the masses just needed to be shown how to fight.
- Typically, two of the six issues per year are special issues on specific topics; submissions for special issues are largely by invitation of the special issue editor.
- Finally, the advent of standards has contributed to expanded national early childhood policy; indeed, in some countries such accelerated commitments to early education are actually written into national legislation.
- People continue to worry about the future; our failure to conserve resources has put the world at risk.
- In all forms of logos, however, the speaker is identified with his words; they belong to him and he is responsible for them.
- Our identities are not just messy; they are also fluid.
- The "rise of China" is misnomer; recovery is more accurate. ("중국의 부활"이란 표현은 부적절한 호칭이다, 회복이란 말이 보다 맞는 말일 게다.)
- The Renaissance was not a popular movement; it was a movement of a small number of scholars and artists, encouraged by liberal patrons, especially the Medici and the humanist popes.
- These misconceptions are not only widespread; several of them are seductive, persistent, and dangerous, meaning that they can be used to obscure or mislead from the critically important issues that are at stake.
- Early educators should know they are not alone; elementary school teachers also report feeling less prepared and competent to teach science than other content areas.
- The math subtest of the PSAT contains a wide variety of mathematical problems that range in difficulty; it consists of 38 questions including word problems, geometry, algebraic equations, and complex arithmetic.
- A significant negative relationship was found between math achievement and the size of the symbolic NDE; however, this relationship did not hold for the nonsymbolic NDE.
- I reflected and amended my practice while in action and afterward on numerous occasions, such as when journaling; when conversing with the teacher and the children; when planning the next workshop; and when transcribing, analyzing, and writing up the study.
- School-sponsored extracurricular activities include a choir and a band; both perform at school, district, and local community.

2 두 독립절 간의 의미가 너무도 분명하게 다르고 연결부사가 이어서 올 때에도 세미콜론을 사용한다.

- Politician may refrain from negative campaigning for a time; but when the race gets close, they can't seem to resist trying to dredge up personal dirt to use on their opponents.

위와 같은 경우 대체로 연결부사가 세미콜론 다음에 위치한다.

- Television is a popular medium; *however*, I would define it as the bland leading the bland.
- Blue jeans have become fashionable all over the world; *however*, the Americans originators still wear more jeans than anyone else.
- The Labor Department lawyers will be here in a month; *therefore*, the grievance committee should meet as soon as possible.

이같은 연결부사 conjunctive adverbs에는 다음과 같은 것들이 있다.

also	however	next	anyhow
incidently	nonetheless	anyway	indeed
otherwise	besides	instead	similarly
consequently	likewise	still	finally
meanwhile	then	furthermore	moreover
therefore	hence	nevertheless	thus

3 때로는 전환어구 transitional phrases가 세미콜론 다음에 오기도 한다.

- Sexual harassment is not just a women's issue; *after all*, men can be sexually harassed too.

이같은 전환어구에는 다음과 같은 것들이 있다.

after all	even so	in the second place	at the same time
for example	on the contrary	at any rate	on the other hand
as a result	in fact	by the way	in other words
in addition			

4 하나 또는 그 이상의 쉼표가 들어가 있는 긴 문장 안에서 연속되는 단어 열거를 분리하고자 할 때 사용한다.

- On the table were orange from Florida; pears from Washington, Oregon, and California; and apples from Oregon.
- I subscribe to several computer magazines that include reviews of new, better-designed hardware; descriptions of inexpensive commercial software programs; advice from experts; and actual utility programs that make keeping track of my files easier.

콜론 colon

1 단어, 구, 절, 혹은 문장을 도입할 때 사용한다. 세미콜론과 마찬가지로 사용 후 한 칸을 띄우고 다음 문장을 이어 쓴다.

- There was only one appropriate color: pink.
- Chastity: the most unnatural of the sexual perversions.
- The price includes the following: travel to London, flight to Venice, accommodation, and excursions.
- There's only one person old enough to remember that wedding: grandma.
- The soft power of a country rests heavily on three basic resources: its culture, its political values, and its foreign policies.
- Two types of power shifts are occuring in this century: power transition and power diffusion.
- First, consistent with previous research, both cognitive ability and parenting behavior displayed significant longitudinal stability: Parent behavior at 2 years predicted parent behavior at 4 years, and Bayley scores at 2 years predicted reading skills at 4 years.
- A number of models have been put forth to explain the numerical distance effect and its underlying cognitive processes of numerical representation: the ''accumulator'' model, the ''number line'' model, and the ''numerosity code'' model.
- According to theorists, play is characterized by one or more of these features: (a) active engagement, (b) intrinsic motivation, (c) attention to means rather than ends, (d) nonliteral behavior, (e) and freedom from external rules.
- Institutionally, Lower Richmond provides students with a variety of valuable resources: There are a computer laboratory and a computer teachers, as well as speciality teachers for art, music, and gym.
- There are two issues to be addressed: the impact of industrial policy on the initiation of growth, and its effect after the initial stage.
- External hegemonic forces have interacted with different domestic societies in Korea and Taiwan to produce rather different political outcomes: this, too, has been characteristic through the century.
- Both Liberal and Marxist theories postulate a utopia to end the struggle: a world of free trade and the greatest good for the greatest number, or societies submitted to a rational plan under a world socialist government.
- American policy in the mid 20th century resonated with Jacob Viner's description of British policy in the 18th century: it was governed "by joint and harmonized considerations of power economics."
- Philosophers have encapsulated this riddle in a trick question: what happens in the mind that does not happen in the brain?
- Ask yourself: what was the most influential discovery, invention or creation of the twentieth century?

- We see a contemporary example of this when companies offer us "privacy choices": we can choose only the ones that they offer and build into their systems.

2 어떤 품목 즉, 리스트를 나열할 때 사용한다. 이때 이어질 리스트가 어떤 것들인지 미리 독자들에게 상기시키는 역할을 하는, '다음과 같은' the following이란 말을 넣어 주기도 한다.

- My shopping list included: apples and oranges.
- My shopping list included the following: apples and oranges.
- The hiker's equipment should consist of: a flashlight, a small ax, and a waterproof tarpaulin.
- There are two issues to be addressed: the impact of industrial policy on the initiation of growth, and its effect after the initial stage.
- The mass media are of two types: print and electronic.
- In this book we provide four different perspectives on the development of mobile media: technology, content, business, and policy.

3 어떤 규칙 같은 것을 상세하게 설명하는 대목에서 많이 사용한다. 또는 선행하는 독립절을 보다 자세하게 설명하거나 어떤 예를 들고자 할 때에도 사용한다.

- The plot is founded on deception: the three main characters have secret identities.
- Many books would be briefer if their authors followed the logical principles known as Occam's razor: Exclamations should not be multiplied unnecessarily.
- This chapter is concerned with the high view of married love that is evident in English society and its relation to the literary tradition: particularly with whether it brought into being a counter-tradition to that which saw love and marriage in contest.
- Surprisingly enough, my first impression of Nairobi was that it was just like any American city: skyscrapers, movie theaters, discos, and crime.
- The sorrow was laced with violence: In the first week of demolition, vandals struck every night.
- The relation between leisure and income is as follows: the equality of play depends on the equality of pay.
- Despite these differences, Canada medicare and U.S. Medicare have one final important similarity: They have been extraordinarily popular social programs.
- The question to ask now is: is there a future of agency for women in cyberspace, or will cyberfeminism prove to be an empty promise?
- One overarching question that should be kept in mind is: "What is the teacher trying to accomplish?"
- The present research question emerged from the question: "Did you experience feelings of being treated differently from others in either school/outside in America?"
- The 2000 election reminded Americans of a fact they learned in high school civics classes: the President is not directly elected.

- The question is therefore: "How can content providers make money delivering their wares via a wireless process that goes beyond their known business models?"
- The answer to the above question is: Because it should be part of the architect°Øs job to dwell on ethics.

이때 마지막 예문에서 콜론 다음에 이어지는 독립절의 시작은 MLA와 APA 작성 방식에 차이가 있다. MLA에서는 소문자로, APA에서는 대문자로 새 문장을 시작하도록 규정하고 있다. 그러나 인용된 문장 passage이 이어질 때는 반드시 쌍따옴표와 함께 대문자로 시작해 준다.
Claire Safran points out two of the things that cannot be explained: "One of them is poltergeists. Another is teenagers."

4 중심 되는 문장의 구조와는 다소 동떨어진 인용구 quotation를 소개할 때 사용한다.
- In *The Awakening*, Mme Ratignole exhorts Robert Lebrun to stop flirting with Edna: She is not one of us; she is not like us.

5 시간 혹은 부제를 명시할 때에도 콜론을 사용한다.
- We are to be there by 11:30 a.m.
- I just read *Women's Ways of Knowing: The Development of Self, Voice, and Mind.*

6 성서의 한 장을 인용할 때 사용한다.
Isaiah 28: 1-6
1 Kings 2:1
1 Corinthians 3: 6-7

7 공식적인 문서, 편지 등을 쓰는 경우 칭호 혹은 수신자 이름 다음에 써 준다.
Dear Dr. Joseph Conrad:
Dear Faustine:

대시 dash

1 동격의 의미 혹은 대조되는 내용을 서로 구별해 나타내고자 할 때 사용한다.
- There was one important man in her life–her father.
- In the game of life, there are no winners–only losers.
- Mobility–a magic word in the 1950s.
- This moves us to another point–the political nature of spontaneous shrines.
- One thing's for sure–he does not want to face the truth.
- Things have changed a lot in the last year–mainly for the better.
- Britain, the first mover of the industrial era, also became the world's first superpower – indeed, the world's first hegemonic power.

- For our vacation–which was much too short–we went to Florida and basked in the sun.
- They must be allowed occasionally to experiment with their own way–possibly even a wrong way.
- I should be able to train an avatar, an AI, that will do what I can do–perhaps better than I could.
- This strongly suggests that our two key manipulations–a longer delay and constrained retention test–had a substantial impact on infants' ability to retain or correctly retrieve the novel name-object mapping.
- Compared to many subjects–especially science–design and technology in England have long been relatively process oriented.
- Over time, some of these rule systems–encoded in bureaucracies, legal proceedings, and bureaucratic regulations–coalesce into institutions.
- Fashion pieces–mostly for women, but occasionally for men–were multipage themed photo layouts with brief captions.
- Data were collected for this study using two approaches–a comprehensive questionnaire for parents and teachers and a series of focus group interviews for children.
- Data were collected for this study using two approaches–a comprehensive questionnaire for parents and teachers and a series of focus group interviews for children.
- Most current projections of a shift in the global balance of power are based primarily on one factor–projections of growth in the gross national product of different countries.
- New surroundings, new friends, a challenging new job–all these helped Eugene overcome his grief.
- Cyberspace is indeed inhabited by harmful program, but these primarily take the form of malware–viruses notable for their malign mindlessness, not for their superintelligence.
- Humankind was salvaged not by the law of supply and demand, but rather by the rise of a revolutionary new religion–humanism.
- Seen in this perspective, the things we today call art have characteristics not fully comprehended in the term–namely, functions within the material culture of a society; and these functions set the parameters in which the demand for art operates.
- Within the CIRL framework, one can formulate and solve the off-switch problem–that is, the problem of how to prevent a robot from disabling its off switch.
- Data science is a science only to the extent that it facilitates the interpretation of data–a two-body problem, connecting data to reality.
- The Foreign Policy Association's mission today–as it has been throughout its 95-year history–is to contribute to a more vibrant democracy through citizen participation in the foreign policy process.

- Although the United States has many social problems–and always has–they do not seem to be getting worse in any linear manner.
- Culture–in the form of resistance to the transformation of certain traditional values to those of democracy–thus can constitute an obstacle to democratization.
- But whatever their religion–whether they are Catholics, Jews, or Muslims–these families share one quality.
- The Portuguese government–which had little desire to accept any of these refugees–sent agents to escort the disobedient consul back home.
- Computer science has a long history–going back to before there even was the computer science–of implementing neural networks.
- And yet, while the most successful modern economies may be capitalist, not all capitalist economies are successful–or, at any rate, as successful as others.
- We can–and should–debate the appropriate level of regulations on microtargeting given the dangers of regulation of political activity.
- We wrote it to create a spark of hope–and to see what might happen if we together blow that spark into a flame.
- There is a dip in the global life expectancy curve in 1960 because 15 to 40 million people–nobody knows the exact number–starved to death that year in China, in what was probably the world's largest ever man-made famine.
- The moral component, the cultural component, and the element of free will–all make the task of creating an AGI is fundamentally different from any other programming task.

2 도입에 해당하는 일련의 품목, 목록 혹은 시리즈가 이어진 후에 사용한다.
- Keen, calculating, perspicacious, acute, and astute–I was all of these.
- New surroundings, new friends, a challenging new job–all these helped Eugene overcome his grief.

3 어떤 예를 요약하거나 보여 주는 단어를 구별하고자 할 때 사용한다. 또는 의미를 분명히 하기 위해 추가 설명을 삽입하고자 할 때에도 사용한다.
- From reading this book, you are learning material–grammar, spelling, punctuation–that will always be useful to you.
- We packed our camping gear–tent, sleeping backs, and stove.
- The sound of harpsichord–two skeletons copulating on a tin roof in a thunderstorm.
- Local government–with the encouragement of cable operators–have thrown up nearly insurmountable barriers to the entry of more than one firm into each market.
- I argue that the original core human social institutions–economy, kinship, religion, policy, and education–are the outcome of macro level forces that have generated selection pressures on human populations.

- It is difficult to sustain the synthesis of these views–namely, that the industrial policies were the source of superior macroeconomic performance.
- Second, autonomy requires individual to possess particular attributes–for example, the capacity to reason, to determine the adequacy and appropriateness of criteria of evaluation.
- Application of the principles includes–and in several cases goes beyond–the accommodations of the Clinton administration documents.
- Knowledge that gives us real estate must turn all its subjects–including nature and human beings–into objective things.
- Linton noted the acceptability of release-time policies allowing students to be dismissed for off-campus religious instruction, and–of particular interest to religious conservative–made clear that students have the right to express their religious beliefs in homework, artwork, and other assignments.
- Steve Brown's study is rich in ideas–far too many to summarize in a short review.
- The writing of the ethnography–as separate from the field research–might be experimental, creative, or quite "traditional."
- Cultural landscapes–as opposed to natural landscapes–are formed by human land uses.
- Political contexts–such as rights to assemble, and free and fair elections–encourage some types of activities and discourage others.
- George W. Bush and his advisers–perhaps knowingly–adopted policies closer to the ones Machiavelli might have advocated.
- The nation faced difficult choices by the 1980s–or so it seemed.
- Creating a sustainable–or renewable–energy future as a goal gained credibility among those who were dissatisfied with the old notion of America the Abundant.

4 콜론 혹은 세미콜론과 같이 두 독립절을 연결시킬 때 사용한다. 특히, 두 번째 절이 놀라움이나 반대의 대조를 의미할 때 매우 유용하게 쓸 수 있다. 또는 생각의 단절, 서사톤의 갑작스런 변화, 중얼거리는 말투를 표현하고자 할 때 사용한다.

- He smiled when the thief ran off with her handbag
- It was empty!–I don't know anything about music–in my line you don't have to.
- Superior students–notice that I said *superior*–will not have to take the test.
- A hypocrite is a person who–but who isn't it?
- When I was six I made my mother a little hat–out of her new blouse.
- If she found out–he did not think what she would do.
- But perhaps Miss–Miss–oh, I can't remember her name–she taught English, I think–Miss Milross? She was one of them.

주의할 점은 한국에서의 사용법과 달리 영문에서는 대시를 2번 그어 사용해 준다는 점이다. 한글에는 없는 기능으로서, **MS Word** 프로그램을 사용할 경우 대시 키를 2번 연속으로 사용한 다음에 다음 단어를 친 후 스페이스바를 누르면 2개로 분리된 대시가 하나의 줄로 이어 붙는다.

괄호 parentheses

부수적인 정보를 첨가하는 문장 전체 혹은 이같은 단어들 주변에서 사용된다.

- Some people (Einstein, for example) are smarter than others.
- He went into the bar before a quick one (which became a quick one).
- He went into the bar for a quick one. (She did a show burn.)
- The population of Philadelphia (now about 1.7 million) has declined since 1950.
- Unlike the creatures (some insects, for instance) that have been unchanged for five, ten, even fifty million years, man has changed over this time-scale out of all recognition.

꺾음쇠 brackets

이미 괄호가 들어간 한 문장 안에서 추가로 어떤 정보를 넣고자 할 때 사용한다. 또는 독자의 이해를 돕기 위해 역자가 임의로 원저자의 것이 아닌 것을 추가로 부기하는 경우에 사용한다.

- (The cost was 3 pounds [about 6 dollars].)
- "That Texaco station [just outside Chicago] is one of the busiest in the nation," said a company spokesperson.
- But when he [George Washington] was elected President, we forgot the cherry tree.

슬래시 slash

반대 혹은 양자택일의 의미가 한 쌍으로 연결된 두 용어 사이에 집어넣는다.

- The writer discussed how fundamental oppositions like good/evil, East/West, and aged/young affect the way cultures view historical events.
- The options and/or and he/she should be avoided.
- I don't know why some teachers oppose pass/fall courses.

하이픈 hyphen

이하 모든 예문에 쓰인 하이픈은 dash의 길이보다 반 정도 짧다.

1 두 낱말이 결합된 복합어에서 사용하며, better, best, ill, lower, little, well 등과 같은 부사로 시작하는 복합 형용사 내에서 사용한다.

better-prepared student	best-known work
ill-formed reporter	lower-priced tickets
well-dressed announcer	well-kept lawn

2 복합어로서 형용사 역할을 하게 되는 경우에 사용한다.

hate-filled speech	second-semester courses

fear-inspired loyalty
twelfth-floor apartment

a roll of twenty-dollar bills
her doll-like face

3 동등한 명사들을 결합시킬 때 사용한다.
writer-critic
author-chef
scholar-athlete

부록

1. 논문 작성 방식 소개
2. 기본 약어 Common Scholarly Abbreviations
3. 기본 용어 정의 Glossary
4. 이탤릭체로 표현되는 외래어
5. ', with ~' 전치사 구문
6. 대학원생들을 위한 조언

01 논문 작성 방식 소개

논문 작성 방식을 소개하기에 앞서 저자는 우선 다음과 같은 사실을 강조하고 싶다. 첫째는, 영어로 논문을 쓸 때 (물론 한글로 쓸 경우에도 마찬가지로 생각되지만), 논문 작성 방식을 잘 지키고 있는지의 여부가 매우 중요시된다는 점이다. 논문 작성 방식은 한 마디로 학술 논문을 쓰는 사람들에게 공통으로 지켜져야 할 약속과도 같은 것이기 때문에 세세한 것 까지도 소홀히 하지 말고 반드시 익혀 두어야 하는 것들이다. 둘째는, plagiarism 즉, 표절의 문제이다. 특히 문학같이 작품을 비평하고, 모든 지면을 통해서 자기 견해를 많이 보여 주어야 하는 글의 논문에서 표절의 문제는 조심스럽고도 한편으로는 유혹적인 것이기도 하다. 왜냐하면 어느 다른 비평가의 비평이 자기 견해와 비슷하거나 꼭 인용하고 싶은 생각에 글의 전문을 쌍따옴표(" ")없이 인용하는 것은 절대로 금물이며 모든 것이 표절로 간주되기 때문이다. 더욱이 우리와 같은 외국인 입장에서는 인용 과정에서 가장 어려운 작업이 생기기 마련이다. 같은 말이라도 자기식대로 소화하여 다시 풀어 쓰는 이른바 paraphrase를 우리가 해야 하기 때문이다. 부득이하게 원문의 많은 부분을 그대로 인용하고자 할 때는 4줄을 넘어서는 안 된다. 그렇지 않고 남의 글 가운데 일부분을 따오고자 할 땐 다음과 같이 전형적으로 사용되는 표현을 읽혀 두기 바란다.

- As Lotman says, "~~~~."
- "~~~~," as Lotman points out, "~~~~."
- According to Lotman, "~~~~."
- As Lotman puts it, "~~~~."
- At this point Lotman states as follow: "~~~~."
- In this regard, Lotman suggests that "~~~~."

논문 작성 방식 소개

논문 작성 방식에는 대표적으로 다음과 같은 것들이 있다. 인문과학 분야에서 주로 사용되는 것으로, 미국 현대 언어학회(Modern Language Association: MLA)에서 지정 배포하는 MLA 방식, Chicago University에서 사용하기 시작하면서 또 다른 논문 작성 방식으로 정착된 일명 시카고 스타일 CMS(Chicago Manual of Style) 방식과, 미국 심리학회에서 지정해 보급된 APA(American

Psychological Association) 방식, 그 외엔 자연과학 특히 물리학, 화학, 생물학 등에서 보편적으로 사용하는 CBE(The Council of Biology Editors), 인쇄 출판물의 자료보다는 인터넷상의 전자 문서 electronic sources를 주로 인용할 때 쓰는 COS(The Columbia Guide to Online Style) 등이 있다. 다음 장에서는 이들 가운데 가장 널리 쓰이는 MLA, APA, CMS 방식을 간단하게 소개하고 있다. 보다 구체적인 것들에 대해서는 다음의 책과 인터넷 사이트를 참고하기 바란다.

- Joseph Gibaldi, *MLA Handbook of Writers of Research Papers*, 4th ed. (1995)
- John Ruszkiewicz and Janice R. Walker, Bookmarks: *A Guide to Research and Writing* (2000)
- *Publication Manual of the American Psychological Association*, 4th ed. (1994).
- American Chemical Society. *The ACS Style Guide: A Manual for Authors and Editors*. 2d ed. (1997).

- *American Medical Association Manual of Style*, 9th ed. (1997)
- http://www.awoline.com/researchcentral
- http://longman.awl.com/englishpages
- http://owl.english.purdue.edu/files/33.html
- http://www.mla.org/main_mla-nf.htm
- http://www.press.uchicago.edu/Misc/Chicago/cmosfaq.html

각주 / 미주, 참고 문헌 기재 방법의 기본 원칙

이하의 내용은 MLA, APA, CMS 세 방식의 특징에 관계없이 공통적으로 지켜지는 가장 기본적인 원칙들이다.

▶ **저자명**

각주/미주에서는 저자 이름을 '이름 + 성'의 순으로 쓰지만, 참고 문헌에서는 성 last name을 먼저 쓴 후, 이름을 뒤로 돌린다. 참고 문헌의 저자명 기재 방식은 미국을 포함한 전 세계에서 통용되고 있다. 뿐만 아니라, 도서관의 소장 도서 분류 방식에서 모든 학술 자료의 정보 처리에 이르기까지 '성 + 이름'순의 원칙을 따른다. 따라서 어떤 자료를 찾기 위해서는 저자의 성을 정확히 알고 있어야 한다.

각주/미주	Sang Hyun Kim
참고 문헌	Kim, Sang Hyun

▶ **출판사와 출판년도 표기**

각주/미주에서는 출판사와 출판년도 표시를 괄호 속에 넣는데 반해 참고 문헌에서는 괄호를 없앤다.

각주/미주	⟨Cambridge University Press, 1999⟩
참고 문헌	Cambridge University Press, 1999.

▶ **쉼표와 마침표**

각주/미주에서는 저자명, 서명, 쪽수 사이사이에 모두 쉼표로 구분을 해 주는 것에 비해 참고 문헌에서는 모두 마침표로 해 준다.

각주/미주	Sang Hyun Kim, A Seminar on Contemporary
	Russian Culture, 4th ed. ⟨Seoul: Micro, 2000⟩
참고 문헌	Kim, Sang Hyun. A Seminar on Contemporary
	Russian Culture. 4th ed. Seoul: Micro, 2000

각주/미주, 참고 문헌 기재 방법의 차이점

이하의 내용은 MLA, APA, CMS 방식간에 나타나는 중요한 차이점들을 간단히 정리하였다.

▶ **저자명 표기법상의 차이점 (각주/미주/참고 문헌에서 공통 적용)**

MLA/CMS: 저자명 모두 기재 (full name 원칙)

각주/미주	Stephen J. Parker
참고 문헌	Parker, Stephen J.

APA: 저자의 성만 기재하고, 나머지 이름은 이니셜로 써 준다.

각주/미주	S. J. Parker
참고 문헌	Parker, S. J.

▶ **서명 표기법상의 차이점 (각주/미주/참고 문헌에서 공통 적용)**

MLA/APA: 밑줄 표기

Napoleon in Russian Cultural Mythology

CMS: 이탤릭체 표기

> *Napoleon in Russian Cultural Mythology*

▶ 출판사 표기법상의 차이점 (각주/미주/참고 문헌에서 공통 적용)

APA/CMS: 모든 정보처 기재 원칙

> Princeton University Press

MLA: 축약 형태 원칙

> Princeton UP

▶ 들여쓰기상의 차이점 (참고 문헌 인용시에만 적용)

MLA/CMS: 한 줄이 넘어가는 긴 문헌을 인용할 때 두 번째 줄부터 1/2인치 들여쓰기 적용

> **MLA**
> Kranz, Rachel and Judy Bock. <u>Scholastic Encyclopedia of the United States.</u>
>   New York: Bascom Communications, 1997.
>
> **CMS**
> Kranz, Rachel and Judy Bock. *Scholastic Encyclopedia of the United States.*
>   New York: Bascom Communications, 1997.

APA: 한 줄이 넘어가는 긴 문헌을 인용할 때 첫 줄만 1/2인치 들여쓰기 적용

> **APA**
>   Kranz, Rachel and Judy Bock. <u>Scholastic encyclopedia of the United states.</u>
> New York: Bascom Communications, 1997.

지금까지 설명한 모든 것을 아래의 세 가지 예를 통해서 일목요연하게 비교해 보자.

MLA

Wigzell, Faith. <u>Reading Russian Fortune: Print Culture and Divination in Russia from 1765</u>. Cambridge UP, 1998.

APA

  Wigzell, F. (1998). <u>Reading Russian fortune: print culture and divination in Russia from 1765</u>. United Kingdom: Cambridge University Press.

CMS

Wigzell, Faith. *Reading Russian Fortune: Print Culture and Divination in Russia from 1765*. Cambridge University Press, 1998.

---

02 기본 약어
Common Scholarly Abbreviations

abbr.	abbreviation, abbreviated	coll.	college
acad.	academy	colloq.	colloquial
anon.	anonymous	comp.	compiler (plural, comps.)
app.	appendix	cond.	conductor, conducted by
arch.	archaic	conf.	conference
art.	article (plural, arts.)	Cong.	Congress
assn.	association	cont.	contents; continued
assoc.	associate, associated	d.	died
b.	born	DA	doctor of arts
BA	bachelor of arts	DA,	Dissertation Abstracts,
bib.	biblical	DAI	Dissertation Abstracts International
bk.	books (plural, bks.)		
BS	bachelor of science	dept.	department
bull.	bulletin	diss.	dissertation
c.	copyright	div.	division
ca.	circa, about, approximately. Used with approximate dates, e.g., "ca. 1984."	doc.	document
		ed.	edition, editor (plural, eds.)
		e.g.	exempli gratia, for example
cf.	confer, compare. Used with when the writer wishes the reader to compare two or more works.	enl.	enlarged
		et al.	et alia, and others
		et seq.	et sequens, and the following
ch. or chap.	chapter (plural, chaps.)	fac.	faculty
chor.	choreographer, choreographed by	fig.	figure (plural, figs.)
col.	column (plural, cols.)	fr.	from

fwd.	foreword, foreword by	passim	here and there (throughout the work cited)
ibid.	ibidem, in the same place	Ph. D	doctor of philosophy
id.	idem, the same (person)	pref.	preface
i.e.	id est, that is	proc.	proceedings
ill.	illustrated, illustration	pseud.	pseudonym
infra	below (referring to a later point in the work)	pt.	part (plural, pts.)
inst.	institute, institution	qtd.	quoted
intl.	international	q.v.	quod vide, which see
i. or ll	line(s)	rev.	revised by; review, reviewed by
lang.	language	rpt.	reprint, reprinted by
lib.	library	sc.	scene
lit.	literally; literature, literary	sec.	section
loc.cit.	loco citato, in the place cited (referring to the same passage cited in an immediately previous footnote)	ser.	series
		sess.	session
		sic	so, thus (enclosed in brackets to indicate an error or unusual statement is a quotation)
ltd.	limited		
MA	master of arts		
misc.	miscellaneous	st.	stanza
MS	manuscript (plural, MSS)	supp.	supplement (plural, supps.)
n.	note, footnote (plural, nn.)	supra	above (referring to an earlier point in the work)
narr.	narrator		
n.d.	no date (of publication is given)	trans.	translator
		usu.	usually
n.p.	no place (of publication) or no publisher (is given)	var.	variant
		viz.	videlicet, namely
n.s.	new series	v. or vol.	volume (plural, vols.)
numb.	numbered	vs.	versus, against
o.p.	out of print		
op.cit.	opere citato, in the work		
o.s.	old series		
p.	page (plural, pp.)		
par.	paragraph (plural, pars.)		

03 기본 용어 정의
Glossary

Archive

a place in which public records or historical documents are preserved

Call number

a combination of characters assigned to a library book to indicate its place on a shelf

Draft

a preliminary sketch, outline, or version of an essay or paper

Interlibrary Loan

the loaning of a book by one library to another

Microfiche

a sheet of microfilm containing pages of printed matter in reduced form

Monograph

a scholarly study of a specific topic

Plagiarism

to steal and present the ideas of words of another as one's own; to use material without crediting its source; to present as new and original an idea or product derived from an existing source. Plagiarism is a serious act of academic dishonesty

Primary Sources

firsthand evidence that records the words of someone who participated in a witnessed the events described or of someone who received his or her information from direct participants.

Reference Book

a work, such as a dictionary or encyclopedia, containing useful facts or information

Research Paper

a formal writing assignment on a specific theme that requires the reading and synthesis of primary and secondary sources; also requires documentation such as footnotes/endnotes and a bibliography

Secondary Sources

records the findings of someone who did not observe a historical event but investigated primary evidence

Subject Bibliographies Theme

lists of books, articles, and other material according to subject
a narrow part of a topic that you have chosen or been assigned for research. A theme sets limits on the area to be investigated and also suggests the kinds of questions that will be answered and the points that will be made

Topic

a subject chosen or assigned for research

04 이탤릭체로 표현되는 외래어

ad hoc 특별한, 임시의

_ for this particular purpose; special(ly)

_ In 1899, government ministries were relatively small affairs, but the *ad hoc* jumble of Georgian buildings that housed them in Whitehall was deemed neither to be efficient, not to reflect the dignity of the largest empire the world had ever seen.

ad hominem (이성보다) 감정, 편견에 호소하는, 인신공격적인

_ appealing to an opponent's known personal views rather than reason; directed to the individual, personal

_ The writer's use of the dream device in his novel facilitates a rather cutting (but nevertheless very funny) *ad hominem* attack.

agon 희곡 등에서 인물간의 갈등

_ In effect, the two-part tale depicts an *agon* between nineteenth century conceptions of male and female power.

alma mater 모교

bete noire 혐오, 징그러운 것 (literally, black beast)

bric-à-brac 골동품, 고물

_ miscellaneous old ornaments, trinkets, small pieces of furniture, etc.

_ For many years the great auction houses of London sold only fine art in all its forms. If you wanted to dispose of the *bric-à-brac* of life you had to look for others to sell it for you.

commedia dell'arte 16세기 이탈리아의 즉흥 가면 희곡

comme il faut 우아하게, 격식에 맞게

_ literally, as it should be; proper(ly), correct(ly), especially of behavior

cul-de-sac 막다른 길, 곤경
  _ closed at the end; a blind alley
  _ Life-saving research could then become stuck in a *cul-de-sac*.

de facto 사실, 사실상의
  _ in fact, in reality, in actual existence
  _ Old Compton Street on a Saturday night has become a *de facto* pedestrian precinct.
  _ Since Dostoevsky was the *de facto* editor of Vremia, we can probably assume that ~.

de rigueur 예식상 필요한
  _ literally of strictness. Required by custom or etiquette
  _ In the case Tomas Mann, such an approach is almost *de rigueur*, since primary sources are scarce and the nature of the subject resists coherent analysis.

deus ex machina 작가들이 작품을 창작할 때, 인위적이고 부자연스럽게 보여 주는 미봉의 해결책
  _ a power, event, or person arriving in the nick of time to solve a difficulty; a providential (often rather contrived) interposition, especially in a novel or play
  _ This is not a *deus ex machina* ending which would signal real divine compulsion in human affairs.
  _ The *deus ex machina* resolution of the drama may provide one of the most feeble denouements in all opera.

ex cathedra 권위 있는
  _ In the style of 19th century the mode acquired *ex cathedra* sanction by use of the rubric.

ex nihilo 무에서, 무로부터

ex post facto 사후에, 과거로 소급한(하여)
  _ Nabokov's revealing *ex post facto* justification notwithstanding: "~."

en suite 연달아, ~과 조화를 이루어
  _ in agreement or harmony with; as a part of the same set of objects

fin de siècle 불문학과 러시아문학에서 (특히 19세기 말~20세기 초에) 생성된 세기말적인 사유체계, 세계관 등을 통칭하는 말
  _ the final years of a century; especially the nineteenth century; decadent

haut monde 상류 사회
  _ literally high world; upper class

idée fixe 강박 관념
_ an idea that dominates the mind, an obsession

ignis fatuus 사람을 현혹시키는 것, 헛된 소망
_ a delusive guiding principle, hope, or aim

incognito 익명으로
_ under a disguised or assumed identity

in extenso 상세히, 생략하지 않고
_ in full, at length

in extremis 임종 시에, 죽음에 이르러, 극단적 상황에서
_ at the point of death; in great difficulty; in a painful or awkward situation
_ As one thoughtful recent discussion put the bleak *in extremis* position ~.

in medias res 사건의 핵심에서
_ into the middle of a narrative, without preamble
_ He expressed admiration for the bold way in which the writer started, *in medias res*, and Tolstoy was promptly inspired to begin his novel in this manner.
_ The almost nightmarish rapidity of the action and its lack of resolution (broken off as it is *in medias res*) contribute to the comparatively dark satiric tonality of the passage.

in situ 본래의 장소에, 원위치에서
_ in its (original) place, in position
_ We thus have a unique opportunity to examine the creative process *in situ*.

inter alia 그 중에서도 특히
_ among other things
_ For a discussion about the theme of the novel, see *inter alia* Bundaev's interpretation in which he ~.
_ Prof. Kasack is, *inter alia*, the author and/or compiler of numerous publications on Russian literature.

in toto 전체로서, 완전히
_ completely, without exception, altogether, in all
_ Grosmann had no experience of revolutionary idealism and thus rejected the regime *in toto*.

ipso facto 사실상, 그 사실에 의하여

_ by the very fact or act; by the fact itself; thereby

_ Also significant is the preface by Andrei Bitov which *ipso facto* places Granin within the string of discursive ironism that Bitov himself established in his novel.

magnum opus 작가나 예술가의 대역작, 걸작, 대표작

_ a great and usually large work of art, literature, etc; especially the most important work of an artist, writer, etc.

modus operandi 일의 처리 방식

_ the way in which a person sets about a task

_ The author aims to summarize the artistic *modus operandi*, providing the reader with some essential guides for each writer.

_ A theoretical model which explain the *modus operandi* of online textual deviant activity forms the beginning of this chapter.

mutatis mutandis 필요한 변경을 가하여

_ making the necessary changes; with due alteration of details

_ Recently, the connection has been restated in terms that again–albeit *mutatis mutandis*–come down harshly on Mandel' shtam.

oeuvre 전(모든) 작품

_ a work of art, music, literature, etc.; the whole body of work produced by an artist, composer, etc.

_ Dostoevsky's entire *oeuvre* was translated into English.

par excellence 가장 뛰어난

_ pre-eminently; supremely, above-all

_ In Pushkin, we find a romantic ironist *par excellence*.

per se 그 자체로

_ by or in itself; intrinsically

_ Catharsis *per se* takes place at the cosmic level during the dawn at the novel's finale.

_ Apart from colloquialisms *per se* authors frequently use syntactic or intentional devices to approximate the quality of oral narration.

poetes maudits 저주받은 시인

_ a poet or other creative artist who is insufficient appreciated by his or her contemporaries

_ Macha displays many of the attitudes of modern writers as we know them, beginning with Baudelaire and the *poetes maudits*.

raison d'être 존재 이유

  _ a purpose or reason accounting for or justifying the existence of a thing
  _ The novel in particular undermined the whole *raison d'être* of the Soviet regime.

rara avis 보기 드문 사람, 진품

  _ a kind of person rarely encountered; an unusual or exceptional person
  _ Among the many varieties of critical theorists extant in the contemporary world, Mikhail Epshtein figures as a Russian *rara avis* who has yet to be sighted on the pages of any English or American guidebook to the global phenomenon of postmodernism.

savoir vivre 처세술, 사교술

  _ literally, know how to live. Knowledge of the world and the ways of society, ability to conduct oneself well

sine qua non 꼭 필요한 것(사람), 필수 조건

  _ indispensable, absolutely essential; an indispensable person or thing
  _ Phillip's other *sine qua non* for literary bilingualism–the evidence of a writer's works enjoying "a certain celebrity as well as critical attention in the different languages and countries concerned"–is even more problematical.

tabula rasa 글자가 적혀 있지 않은, 정신적 백지상태

  _ a tablet which the writing has been erased, ready to be written on again; a blank tablet; figurative a clean slate; a mind having no innate ideas

tour de force 묘기, 놀라운 솜씨, 예술상의 역작

  _ a feat of strength or skill; an impressive achievement or performance
  _ *tour de force* of Pushkin's prose.
  _ The article is a *tour de force* survey of the major scholarly approach to Pushkin's work.
  _ The author's answer to this problem is a *tour de force* of historical imagination and good detective work.

über alles 무엇보다도 먼저

  _ above all else
  _ Generally used with implicit reference to the opening words of the German national anthem Deutschland *über alles*, misunderstood to mean Germany supreme.

verbatim 축어적으로, 말 그대로

  _ word for word; in exactly the same words; corresponding with or following an original word for word
  _ The authoritative voice sounds like an old script, repeating the cannon *verbatim*.

vis-à-vis ~과 비교하여, ~에 대하여, ~을 마주보고 있는

  _ a counterpart, an opposite number; regarding, in relation to; opposite to, face to face with
  _ The avant-garde on the one hand is similar to that of his autographical narrator *vis-à-vis* the bourgeois and the proletariat.
  _ They have begun to position the other Europe *vis-à-vis* its Western audience.
  _ The complex interaction between the two dimensions serves to position the reader *vis-à-vis* the text so as to manipulate and control her/him.
  _ Lachman sets up a binary model which accounts for the response text displays *vis-à-vis* the latter calamity.

Weltanschauung 세계관(독일어에서 차용)

  _ a particular philosophy or view of life; the world-view of an individual of group

Zeitgeist 시대정신, 시대사조(독일어에서 차용)

05 ', with ~' 전치사 구문

영어로 글을 쓸 때, 가장 어렵게 느껴지는 부분이 아래의 예문들일 것이다. 전치사가 들어간 표현, 이른바 ', with ~' 전치사 구문이다. 이 표현이 사용된 문장을 실제로 읽다 보면 해석은 가능해 보이는데, 막상 국문 내용을 먼저 읽고 이것을 영어로 번역할 때 우리는 이 표현을 거의 사용하지 못한다. 아래의 다양한 유형을 잘 숙지하여, 쓰임새를 분명하게 알아 두자. 주로 '~한 상태, 조건, 부대상황'을 설명할 때, 관계대명사 혹은 대쉬의 기능과 동일하게 사용되는 것을 알 수 있다. 단, with가 문두로 나가면 그 의미가 전혀 달라진다는 것도 알아 두자. 이 경우는 "~함에 따라"라는 뜻으로 'As ~ 절'로 대체가 가능하다.

- **With** their appearance, Russian literature takes its rightful place in European literary history, but with works in verse, not prose fiction.
  러시아 문학이 등장함에 따라

- **With** the onset of industrialization, a decisive turn upward, with annual growth between 1820 and 2000 at 1.3 percent.
  산업화가 시작하면서

- **With** the Ocean and Industrial Ages, the global population soared.
  해양 및 산업시대가 도래하자, 도래함으로써

- **With** the spread of social equality, came important changes in the economics of war as well.
  사회 평등의 확산과 더불어

- **With** the dramatic increase in literacy after 1871, came the rise of mass-circulation newspapers.
  1871년 이후 비문맹에서 괄목할 만한 성장이 발생하면서

- **With** the collapse of the Soviet Union, the United States was the only military power with global capabilities.
  소련이 붕괴되면서, 붕괴되자

- With such a vast territory to govern, Russia evolved into a state ruled from its center and organized along paramilitary lines.
  그 같은 광대한 통치 영토를 가진 러시아는

- With a population of 1.2 billion people, India is four times larger than the United States, and likely to surpass China in population by 2025.
  12억의 인구를 보유하고 있는 인도는

- With 5 percent of the world's population, the United States accounted for about a quarter of the world's product, nearly half of global military expenditures, and the world's most extensive cultural and educational soft power resources.
  세계 인구의 5%를 차지하는 미국은

- With nearly 8 billion people on the planet, and with population projected to rise to around 9.7 billion by 2050, and the massive environmental dangers ahead–climate change, loss of diversity, mega-pollution–we have not yet shown that we can sustain the progress to date.
  지구상의 인구가 거의 80억에 달하고, 2050년 경에는 그 인구가 97억에 육박할 것으로 추정될 뿐만 아니라, 대규모 환경 위험을 앞에 목격하고 있는 우리는

- This market triumphalism continued in the 1990s, with the market-friendly liberalism of Bill Clinton and Tony Blair, who moderated but consolidated the faith that markets are the primary means for achieving the public good. Today, that faith is in doubt.
  빌 클린턴과 토니 블레어의 시장친화적인 자유주의 성향을 띤

- By the late 1830s, two parties had already formed, with opposing views of the historical-cultural differences between Russia and the West.
  ~역사 문화적 차이점들에 대한 상반된 견해를 가진

- In France, the academic and official art of the July Monarchy (1830-1848) and the Second Empire (1851-1870) put forward a version of Classicism, with emphasis on clear contours and smoothly brushed surfaces, tempered with a colorism associated with Romanticism.
  선명한 외곽선과 부드럽게 손질된 표면을 강조하고 있는

- Divorce was a frequent topic after the war, with many postwar marriages dissolving, and again in the 1960s, as marital breakups began to rise significantly.
  수많은 전후 시대의 결혼이 파경에 이르면서

- The new form of dress was called a sack, a comfortable, rather shapeless garment, with small box pleats behind.
  뒷편에 작은 상자형 겹주름이 잡힌

- The commodious streets, with their appealing shops and cafes, were perfect for leisurely strolls.
  매력적인 상점과 카페가 있는

- Japan is a global leader, with a life expectancy of eight-four years.
  평균 수명이 84세인

- In terms of military expenditure, Europe is second only to the United States, with 15 percent of the world total.
  세계 전체의 15%를 자치하는

- The former included the West and Japan, with about 15 percent of the world's population, the latter everyone else.
  세계 인구의 약 15%를 차지하는

- In my proposed reform, the Security Council would expand to twenty-one members, with Asia holding six seats, or around 30 percent.
  아시아 국가가 6석 혹은 약 30퍼센트를 차지하는

- India has significant military power resources, with an estimated 60-70 nuclear weapons.
  60-70기의 핵무기를 보유한

- Japan faces severe demographic problems, with its population projected to shrink from today's 127 million to under 100 million by 2050, and its culture is resistant to accepting immigrants.
  2050년에 이르면 지금의 1억 2천 7백 만인 인구가 1억명으로 감소할 것으로 추측되는

- Muslims are the largest minority, with estimates ranging from 14 to 23 million, comprising up to perhaps 15 percent of the population.
  1,400만에서 2,300만에 이르는 것으로 추정되는

- The biggest culprit is carbon dioxide(CO2), emitted by burning fossil fuels. The second is the massive loss of biodiversity, with an estimated 1 million species under threat of extinction.
  100만 종의 생물이 멸종될 것으로 추정되는

- India's economy grew fast but less dynamically, at around 6.3 percent *per annum*, with cumulative GDP growth of around 7.6 percent per year has been slightly higher than China's.
  연 7.6% 가량의 누적 국내총생산 성장률이 중국보다 살짝 상회하는

- The science of discovery was global, with new scientific knowledge moving rapidly across all continents.
  새로운 과학 지식이 모든 대륙에 빠르게 전파되는 경향을 보이면서

- It remained the official language of a great power, with the capacity for further development.
  향후 발전 능력을 지닌

- Those agricultural communes, with their equalitarian lifestyle and distribution of material benefits, were seen by Russian intellectuals as necessary to protect the peasants from the harsh competition of Western individualism.
  평등주의에 입각한 생활방식과 물질적 이익의 배분을 하고 있는

- Advertising expanded apace, with advertisers spending $15 millions to promote 483 products in 1949.
  광고주들이 150만 달러를 쏟아부을 정도로 신속하게

- American multinational companies expanded their operations in both Europe and Asia, with the United States the hub of new technology, global finance, and military security.
  신기술과 세계금융, 그리고 군사안보에서 미국을 주축으로 한

- The Romanov Empire was brought down by the war, with the Bolsheviks seizing power in 1917, winning a brutal civil war, and establishing the Soviet Union in 1923.
  1917년 볼세비키가 권력을 장악한

- Political ideas and ideologies can act as a form of social cement, providing social group, and indeed whole societies, with a set of unifying beliefs and values.
  일련의 일관된 신념과 가치들을 갖고 있는

- Protestants of various denominations are the second largest group of Christians, with more than two million followers.
  2백만 명 이상의 추종자들을 보유하고 있는

- Winter starts in October and continues through March, with November to January the darkest months.
  11월에서 1월 사이가 가장 어두운

- Most clergy and laity continued to see the Tsar as God's Anointed, ruling in harmony or "symphony" with the church, but the state was pursuing a totally different agenda, with the church as an instrument for secular policies.
  세속적 정책 이행을 위한 도구 교회를 간주하는

- After 1800, the technological dynamism was mostly in Western Europe, with technological innovations flowing from Europe to Asia.
  기술 혁신이 유럽에서 아시아로 흘러간

- Each farm family struggled to feed itself, with only a tiny margin of surplus, if any, sold in the marketplace or used to pay taxes.
  아주 소량의 흑자만 내면서

- I cite from the following translations of Tolstoy's works, with occasional changes in wording.
  일부 표현에서 변화를 가한 것 외에

- American leaders held that America was different, ultimately exceptional, with the inherent right to make and break the international rules of the game.
  게임의 국제규범을 만들고, 깨려는 생득권을 가진

- From 1945 to 1991, the global balance of power was described as bipolar, with two superpowers standing well above the rest.
  두 초강대국이 나머지 국가들 위에 군림하는

- It is useful to think about epochal transformation as a slow process, with each tiny change bringing us closer to a paradigm shift when everything is different.
  각각의 작은 변화가 어떤 패러다임 전환으로 우리를 이끄는

- Companies will have no choice but to follow market trends in that part of the world, with most new products and services reflecting the preferences of Asian consumers.
  대부분의 신상품과 서비스가 아시아 소비자들의 선호를 반영하고 있는

- It is also clear that venture capital (VC) funds are moving into Chinese companies at a greatly increased rate, with VC investments in China overtaking VC investments in the European Union.
  중국에서의 벤처 자금이 현재 유럽연합에서의 벤처 자금을 따라잡고 있는

- A bell curve illustrates the range of what is considered appropriate and acceptable business behavior on the scheduling scale in Germany, with a hump where the majority of responses fall.
대부분의 대응이 하락하는 변곡점을 지닌

- Table 1.1 summarizes the seven ages, with their time intervals, major technological changes, and scale of governance.
시대 간극과 주요 기술 변화와 거버넌스의 규모를 동반한

06 대학원생들을 위한 조언

다음 내용은 저자가 독자 – 특히 미국 유학 중이거나 유학을 준비중인 모든 분들 – 에게 개인적으로 꼭 드리고 싶은 얘기를 적어본 것으로, 저자가 지금까지 유학 생활 중에 지켜 오고 있는 공부 방법에 대한 것이다. 내용에 따라 나름대로 소제목을 달고 순서를 매겨 두었다. 그 이유는 저자가 보기에 낮은 번호에서 가장 높은 번호에 이르는 과정이 순차적인 단계이면서 동시에 학습에 꼭 필요한 기본 사항들이기 때문이다. 이는 깊이 있는 학습을 하기 위한 중요한 단계이자, 자기 논문의 저널 게재나 학술대회 발표와 같은 학문적 결실을 이루기 위한 하나의 방편이기도 하다.

계속해서 이어지는 영어 전문은 인터넷 사이트에서 발췌한 것으로, 한 대학원 지도교수가 학계에 몸담고자 하는 대학원생들에게 들려주는 조언이다. 지도교수 선정, 진로 선택, 전문학회 가입과 논문 발표, 박사학위 논문 테마의 선택 등과 같은 문제들이 잘 소개되어 있다. 이 가운데 일부 내용이 저자 본인의 경험담과 상당히 일치하기에, 저자가 강조하고 싶은 내용이나 공감하는 부분은 이탤릭체로 표기하여 다른 것과 구별되게 하였다. 참고로, 독자의 이해를 돕기 위해 원문에 약간의 수정을 가했음을 알려 둔다. 학문의 큰 그릇을 빚고자 하는 모든 독자들에게 아래의 내용이 실질적인 도움이 되었으면 하는 마음 그지없다.

1 도서관과 Interlibrary Loan Service : ILS 장악하기

저자가 보기에 한국의 일반적인 도서관이 안고 있는 숙제는 이용자들이 사방에 널려 있는 귀중한 학술 자료들을 편리하고 신속하게 이용할 수 없다는 점이다. 도서관의 책 소장량에서 뿐만 아니라, 기존에 보유하고 있는 도서관 이용 시스템 역시 세계적인 수준에 비하면 아직까지도 많이 낙후되어 있는 것이 사실이다. 그런 점에서 최첨단의 도서 관리 시스템을 운영하고 있는 미국에서 공부하는 사람들은 상대적으로 다행스러운 일이라 생각한다. 풍부한 자료를 편리하게 이용하고 이에 접근할 수 있는 기회가 많음은 물론이요, 이들을 활용함에 있어서 기술적인 제약을 거의 받지 않기 때문이다. 이러한 여건에서 미국 유학생들이 열심히 공부해야 함은 당연한 결론이자 의무라고 저자는 생각한다.

처음 시작하는 유학 생활 중에서 가장 중요한 것 가운데 하나가 바로 자기 학교 도서관의 운영 시스템과 시설을 빨리 파악해서 이용에 불편함이 없도록 하는 일이다. 수업 준비에서부터 리서치 페이퍼 자료 찾기에 이르기까지 학생들은 많은 시간을 도서관에서 보내게 될 것이다. 이곳에서 우리들은 세계 각국에서 들어오는 온갖 종류의 학술 잡지들을 거의 다 볼 수 있을 뿐만 아니라, 찾고자 하는 책도 거의 대부분 쉽게 찾을 수 있다. 이용자들이 원하는 자료를 편하게 찾을 수 있도록 도와 주는 온라인 컴

퓨터 도서 관리 시스템이 먼저 우리의 시선을 끈다. 자기 학교 인근의 도서관에서부터 다른 주에 있는 원거리 자료에 이르기까지 모든 것을 확인하고 대출할 수 있는 다양한 서비스가 학생들의 공부 욕구를 자극한다. 그리고 가장 매력적인 것은 아마도 학문 분야별로 체계적으로 구축된 데이터 베이스가 아닐까 한다. 저자가 자주 이용하는 어문학의 Proguest와 MLA Bibliography 1963-2003의 경우 박사학위 논문에서부터 최근에 발표된 논문과 단행본까지 거의 모든 자료가 빠짐없이 구비되어 있다. 이러한 좋은 공부 환경에서 자신이 얻고자 하는 리서치 페이퍼 자료를 정확하고 신속하게 찾아 자기 공부에 효과적으로 이용할 수 있는 길은 결국 도서관의 모든 것을 누가 먼저 빨리 정복하느냐의 문제와 마찬가지이다.

학술적인 자료를 이용할 때, 여러 가지 편리한 방법들이야 많겠지만 이 자리에서 쉽고 비용도 들지 않는 것을 한 가지 제안한다. 타 도서관 연결 대여 서비스 Interlibrary Loan Service는 말 그대로 자신이 다니는 학교에서 이용자가 찾는 자료(책이나, 저널의 논문, 박사학위 논문)가 없을 때 이것을 소장하고 있는 타 학교에서 빌려와 이용자에게 대출해 주는 시스템이다. 최근에는 메타 검색과 Web DB를 통한 논문 다운로드가 일반화되어 우리가 생각하는 연구의 절벽을 느끼지 못하게 하고 있다. 얼마나 좋은 기회인가! 그래서 이 편의시설을 이용하려면 먼저 자신이 찾는 자료가 자기 학교 도서관에 있는지, 그 소장 여부를 확인 후 없으면 신청하는 것으로 모든 과정이 끝난다. 저자의 경우 유학 온 첫해 1년 만에 모은 이러한 논문들만 해도 850편이 넘는다. 좋은 기회를 십분 활용했으면 하는 바람이다.

참고로, 아래의 내용은 도서관에 소장되어 있는 책의 분류 방식에 대한 소개이다. 듀이의 십진 분류법은 현재 가장 널리 이용되고 있는 미 국회 도서관 Library of Congress 분류법으로 대체되는 추세이다. 도서관에서 책이 어떤 방식으로 배열되어 있는지를 알고 있을 때, 우리는 손쉽게 원하는 자료를 찾을 수 있을 것이다. 도서관의 모든 책은 이처럼 고유한 소장 도서 번호 (일명, 콜넘버 call number)가 붙어 있어 도서관 이용자들이 책을 빌리고 반납할 때에 불편이 없도록 편의를 도모하고 있다. 예를 들어, 미국의 국회 도서관 분류 방식으로 어떤 책 한 권을 찾아보도록 하자. 외국어를 사용할 때 가장 많이 볼 수밖에 없는 영어 사전류가 어디에 위치해 있을까? 다음의 표를 보면, 언어 language 혹은 문학 literature 분야가 알파벳 P로 시작되는 번호로 분류되어 있다는 것을 알 수 있다. 따라서 *Random House Webster's College Dictionary* (New York, 2000)의 겉표지 안쪽의 왼편을 들여다보면 다음과 같은 번호를 보게 된다 "PE 1628. R 28 1999." 역사 분야의 책은 알파벳 C나 D로 시작되는 번호에서 찾을 수 있다는 것을 알 수 있다. 구체적으로 러시아 역사의 한 책을 더 찾아보자. Svetlana Boyam이 저자이고 (여기에서 Boyam은 last name 즉, 저자의 성이다), 서명이 *Common Places: Mythologies of Everyday Life in Russia*란 책은 "DK 266.4 B69 1994"란 번호가 달려 있는데, D가 역사 분야이고, B는 저자 성의 이니셜이란 것을 쉽게 알 수 있다. 그 외의 보다 자세한 분류 체계와 규약은 문헌정보학을 전공하는 분들의 몫일 것이다. 하지만 이 자리에서 우리는 이 두 방식만이라도 알아 두는 것이 도서관을 보다 쉽게 이용할 수 있는 수단이 된다는 것을 알아 두자.

The Dewey Decimal System (듀이 십진법 분류)

000 General Works
100 Philosophy and Psychology
200 Religion
300 Social Sciences
400 Language
500 Natural Sciences and Mathematics
600 Technology and Applied Sciences
700 Fine Arts
800 Literature
900 Geography and History

The Library of Congress System (미 국회 도서관 분류법)

A   General Works
B   Philosophy, Psychology, and Religion
C   General History
D   World History
E-F American History
G   Geography and Anthropology
H   Social Sciences
J   Political Science
K   Law
L   Education
M   Music
N   Fine Arts
P   Language and Literature
Q   Science
R   Medicine
S   Agriculture
T   Technology
U   Military Science
V   Naval Science
Z   Bibliography and Library Science

2 논문 정리와 도서 구입

사람마다 저마다의 공부 요령이 다양하고 선호하는 방식이 다 다를 것이다. 자신에게 맞는 공부 방법을 알고 있다는 것만으로도 학습에 좋은 출발이라 생각한다. 저자는 어떤 새로운 주제를 알고 싶어 자료를 찾을 때, 두껍고 내용이 쉽게 파악되지 않는 단행본보다는 해당 주제에 관련된 저자와 이 저자가 쓴 짧은 논문을 먼저 찾아 읽는 습관이 있다. 도서관에는 저자명이나 서명 둘 중에 하나만이라도 알고 있으면 그 분야의 모든 자료를 데이터 베이스로 검색할 수 있는 프로그램이 있기 때문에 이 문제는 그리 어렵지 않게 해결된다. 자료를 확보한 다음에는 논문을 먼저 읽고 단행본으로 넘어간다. 이 방법의 장점은 자신이 알고자 하는 주제, 혹은 전혀 알지 못했던 내용들을 가장 빨리, 정확하게 알 수 있다는 점이다. 아무리 길어야 30쪽을 넘지 않는 이런 소논문 article을 읽으며 알게 된 내용들을 정리해 두면 자신의 연구 주제에 좋은 밑거름이 된다.

또 하나 우리가 알아 두어야 할 것은 사고자 하는 책을 어떤 방법으로 사느냐의 문제이다. 매 학기 학과 수업에서 지정해 주는 교재를 빠짐없이 사는 것은 학생 신분에서는 당연해 보여도 금전적으로 상당히 부담되는 것이 사실이다. 기본적인 교재비에 자신이 읽을 기타 논문 복사비 등을 합하면 많은 돈이 지출되기 마련이다. 한국에 비해서 턱없이 비싼 책값과 복사비는 그야말로 용돈이 궁한 학생에게는 고민거리가 아닐 수 없다. 그렇다고 도서관에서 빌려 볼 생각을 하지만 다른 학생들이 많이 빌려 보는 중요한 책이거나 주교재로 이용되는 도서일 경우 그 사정은 더욱 어려워진다. 결국 큰 마음을 먹고 비싸게 책을 사지만 언제나 마음 한 구석엔 비싼 책값 때문에 생길 생활고가 눈 앞에 아른거린다. 저자 또한 마찬가지의 경험을 하던 중 우연한 기회에 자주 드나들던 책방 주인이 일러준 중고책방 인터넷 사이트를 이용한 후부터는 이런 걱정을 말끔히 씻어낼 수 있었다.

지금 소개하는 인터넷 중고책방은 기본적으로 새 책은 취급하지 않는다. 모두 중고책만을 다루며, 매력적인 것은 절판된 책 out-of-print을 거의 다 구할 수 있다는 점이다. 전세계적으로 잘 알려진 amazon. com이나 barnesandnoble.com에서는 구할 수 없는 낡은 책(그러나 자신에게 꼭 필요한, 오래 전에 출판된 도서)을 이곳에서는 아주 쉽게 찾을 수 있다. 가장 특기할 만한 것을 꼽아 보라면 위에서 말한 절판 도서의 구입과 지금 얘기할 엄청나게 저렴한 책값, 이렇게 두 가지를 말하고 싶다.

먼저 가장 규모가 크고 정보량이 많은 사이트부터 소개하면,

① http://www. addall.com이 으뜸이고, 그 다음

② http://www.bibliofind.com

③ http://www.abebooks.com

④ http://www.alibris.com의 순서이다.

위 사이트에 들어가 검색란 search box에서 자신이 찾고자 하는 도서명, 저자명 둘 중에 하나만이라도 입력하여 검색하면 이 책을 소장하고 있는 미국, 캐나다, 호주의 책방까지 온라인 on-line으로 연결된 모든 중고책방의 리스트가 나타난다. 또 하나의 강점이라면 책방마다 고시하는 책값이 제각각이라 자기가 가장 마음에 들어 하는 최저가의 책을 고를 수 있다는 점이다. 그리고 중고책이라고는 하지만 흠집이 거의 없어 새책이나 다름 없다. 지불 방식은 주로 신용카드 credit card로 하며 더러는 미국에서 사용되는 개인수표 personal check로 결제해 줄 것을 요구하기도 한다. 물론 인터넷상의 대금 결제에 있어서 절대 안전하다는 것을 말하고 싶다. 저자는 지난 5년 동안 이용해 오면서 단 한 차례의 사고도 없었다.

3 Journal을 내 손 안에

도서관 이용에 불편함이 없고 서서히 자신의 공부 방식에 익숙해지면 전문 학술잡지 즉, 주로 전문학회에서 출간되는 정기 간행물 periodical journal을 꼼꼼하게 점검하는 훈련을 해야 한다. 자신이 공부하는 분야에서 가장 인정받는, 저명한 학술잡지가 어떤 것들이 있는지 조사해야 한다. 처음부터 큰 욕심에 잡다한 모든 잡지의 글들을 빠짐없이 검색하겠다는 자세로 나가지 말고 가장 중요한 저널을 중심으로 5개 정도를 누락되는 호수 없이 규칙적으로 읽으면서 자신의 관심 영역을 넓혀 가는 것이 좋을 것이다. 저널을 구독하는 문제는 반드시 자신의 지도교수 academic advisor와 상의하기 바란다. 저널이 너무 다양하여 선정에 어려움이 있을 수도 있고, 각 학회 저널마다 표방하는 방향성과 색깔이 조금씩 다르기 때문에 저널 선택에 신중을 기해야 한다.

위에서 언급했듯이, 저널에 실린 소논문을 규칙적으로 읽는 습관은 여러모로 중요하다.

먼저, 자신이 잘 알고 있지 못해 막연하게만 이해하고 있는 분야를 빠른 시간 안에 파악할 수 있다.

둘째, 논문을 읽으면서 저널에서 채택하고 있는 논문 작성 방식(MLA이나 APA, CMS 중의 하나)을 자연스럽게 소화할 수 있게 된다.

셋째, 서평을 빼 놓을 수 없다. 흔히 논문이 저널의 앞부분에 실리고 뒷부분엔 신간 서적에 대한 전문가들의 서평이 게재된다. 신간 목록과 이에 대한 비평은 자신이 관심 있게 보고자 하는 분야의 책을 어떤 기준에서 평가할 수 있는가, 연구 동향은 어떠한가, 책의 장단점은 무엇인가 등의 문제를 일목요연하게 파악해 볼 수 있도록 해 준다.

4 전문학회 Professional Academic Association에 가입하기

전문 학술 단체, 흔히 Association이란 명칭이 들어간 학회에 정식으로 가입해서 얻을 수 있는 각종 혜택과 제공받는 정보의 효과적인 활용은 매우 중요하다. 학회에 따라서 약간씩의 차이는 있지만 우리 같은 학생 신분인 경우, 대체로 연회비 $25~30선이다. 이 비용은 보통 1년에 4회 발간되는 계간지 quarterly에, 비슷한 시기에 발송되는 학회 소식지 newsletter를 포함하는 가격이다. 한국에 비해서 무척 저렴하다고 생각한다. 전문학회에 가입하기 위해서는 자신이 직접 인터넷이나 학술 잡지의 동향을 통해서 선정할 수도 있겠으나 되도록이면 자신의 지도교수에게 자문을 구하는 것이 좋다. 또한 하나 이상의 단체에 가입하여 다양한 정보를 얻는 것이 중요하다.

이러한 저널과 학회 소식지에서 알게 되는 귀중한 정보는 이루 말로 다 표현할 수가 없다. 언제나 그렇지만 자신의 현재 주안점이 어디에 있느냐에 따라 이러한 정보들이 휴지가 될 수도 있고, 자신의 학문적 결실에 결정적인 동기 부여와 좋은 기회를 제공할 수도 있다. 저자의 경우 저널과 소식지의 정보를 통해서 짧은 시간동안 참 많은 것을 이루었다고 생각한다. 물론 자신이 전공하는 분야에서 성취감을 얻고 전문적으로 성장하기 위해서는 피나는 노력이 뒷받침되어야 함은 독자 여러분 모두가 잘 알고 있을 것이다. 어떤 정보를 현실적인 가치로 전환시키기 위해서는 언제든 자신의 창조적인 아이디어를 발산시킬 만반의 준비가 되어 있어야 할 것이다. 예를 들어, 10월 15일까지 원고를 마감하는 어떤 Conference 공고가 소식지에 실렸다고 했을 때, 이 기간까지 제출할 자신의 essay, proposal, paper가 하나도 없다면 소용이 없다는 얘기이다. 그렇기에 자신의 학문적 발전을 위해 언제 찾아올지 모를 좋은 기회를 십분 이용하기 위해서는 평소에 많은 준비를 해 두어야 함은 너무도 자명한 일이다.

전문학회에 가입하는 일은 사실 학계에 본격적으로 들어서기 위한 최소한의 통과의례이자 가장 기본이 되는 것이기도 하다. 자신의 전문적인 경력과 현재까지의 학력 모두를 보여 주는 커리큘럼 비타(영어로 curriculum vitae 간단히 C. V.로 표현)에는 자신의 학회 가입 여부를 반드시 기입하여야 한다. 학교의 이수 학점을 통해서 나타나는 졸업 평점 GPA(Grade Point Average)도 중요하지만 이같이 자신의 전문 관심 분야에서 보여 주는 특별 활동 professional and extra work interests은 특히 미국과 같은 사회에서 인재를 평가할 때 매우 중요한 기준으로 고려되고 있다.

학회 가입의 효과

(1) 인터넷 자료의 활용

학회 가입이 가져다 줄 수 있는 또 다른 좋은 기회는 인터넷상에서 이용할 수 있는 자료들을 받는 것이다. 인터넷 서치 엔진에서 당장 찾을 수 있는 자료들은 저자가 보기엔 학술적인 깊이에 있어 높은 점수를 주고 싶지 않다. 아쉬운 마음에 빨리 얻을 수 있는 정보는 많아도 막상 심도 있는 정보를 원할 땐 찾아지지 않는 것이 인터넷 이용의 허실이라고 생각한다. 이런 문제를 해결해 주고 양질의 인터넷 정보를 제공하는 곳이 바로 학술 단체의 웹 사이트이다. 저명한 학술 단체일수록 인터넷상의 학회 관리를 소홀히 하지 않으며 그 서비스도 매우 훌륭한 편이라 이용에 많은 도움이 될 것이다. 때문에 시간이 날 때마다 인터넷 접속을 통해서 자료를 찾아놓고, 이것들의 파일 file 관리를 잘 해두면 자신의 공부에 큰 기여를 할 수 있을 것이다.

(2) 자기 분야 전문가들과의 E-mail Discussion 및 Consult

위에서 말한 학회 가입을 통해서, 혹은 인터넷상으로 학회에 접속해서 얻는 정보 중에서 우리가 무시할 수 없는 것이 바로 학회원들의 이메일 연락처 즉, directory of members 정보이다. 물론 힘겹게 자기가 알고 있는 타 대학 홈페이지에 들어가서 교수진의 연구 활동을 일일이 확인하고 기억해 두었다가 개인적으로 접촉할 수도 있겠지만 지금 얘기하고자 하는 내용은 그 시간과 효과적인 방면에 있어서 비교가 되지 않는다.

첫째, 학회에서 1년에 한 차례씩 배부하는 학회원 주소록을 적극 활용해 보자. 학회마다 차이가 나지만 대개 주소록에는 학회원의 기본적인 인적 사항 – 관심 주제, 현재 진행중인 연구과제 혹은 프로젝트, 집주소, 이메일 주소, 학회 가입 여부 즉, affiliate – 이 모두 상세하게 수록되어 있을 것이다. 이것을 이용해서 자신의 질문이나 의견을 공유할 수 있는 기회를 가질 수 있다. 예를 들어, 주소록을 통해 타 대학 교수가 자신이 묻고 싶은 분야에서 명성이 있다고 하자. 일단 처음부터 단도직입적으로 이메일만 보내 물어보는 불손한 자세를 취하지 말고, 자신에 대한 간단한 소개와 함께 알고 싶은 내용을 상세히 설명하고 귀하의 고견을 듣고 싶다는 것을 잘 표현해 이메일로든, 자택 주소로든 문의를 해 보자. 그 결과는 대부분 만족스러울 것이다.

아울러, 학회원들간에 인테넷상에서 이메일로 정보를 공유하는 회원 공유 기능 listserve을 활용해 보는 것도 좋은 방법이 된다. 학회에 연회비를 내고 정식으로 가입해야만 이용할 수 있는 곳도 있지만 대개는 학회 홈페이지에 로그인 log in하여 가입하면 〈자유 토론방〉 같은 창구를 운영하여 학회원들이 자신의 의견을 다같이 볼 수 있도록 웹에 올릴 수 있는 서비스를 이용할 수 있다. 꼭 자신의 글을 올리지 않는다 하더라도 타인이 내놓은 의견이나 질문을 보는 것만으로도 좋은 아이디어를 얻을 수 있다는 점에서 저자는 이 방법을 권유한다.

5 자신의 논문을 교정 봐 줄 수 있는 Native Speaker의 확보

이 단계를 혹자는 앞쪽에다 위치시킬 수도 있을 것이다. 꼭 이렇게 맨 마지막에 놓여질 특별한 이유는 없다고 보는 이도 있을 줄로 안다. 그러나 여기서 저자가 말하고 싶은 것은 다음과 같다. 앞에서 저자가 예로 든 4단계를 찬찬히 밟아 가면서 본인이 생각하기에 학회에 내놓아도 좋은 결과가 있을 것 같은, 충분히 승산이 있는 리서치 페이퍼를 썼다고 가정해 보자. 지금까지 다른 교수들에게 이메일로 문의하고 간단히 정리한 노트 정도 수준의 내용도 아니고, 오랜 시간을 들여 갈고 닦은 좋은 글이라고 상상해 보자. 정말이지 어딘가에 발표를 해서 멋지게 학계 데뷔를 해 보고 싶을 만큼 잘 쓴 글이 있다고 생각해 보자.

가장 먼저 걸리는 문제가 바로 자신이 쓴 영어가 설득력 있게 쓰여졌는지, well written, convincingly demonstrated의 여부일 것이다. 한두 장 짜리 에세이도 아니고 전문적인 내용을 다룬 학술 논문이기 때문에 글을 쓴 본인은 당연히 긴장하기 마련이다. 그렇다고 누구에게 쉽게 보일 성격의 글도 아니기 때문에 문제는 더욱 어려워지기도 한다. 아쉬운 대로, 자신이 쓴 논문에 대해 전혀 모르는 사람에게 교정 부탁을 했다가 오히려 뒤죽박죽 엉망이 되어 낭패를 볼 수도 있을 것이다. 그 사람에게 영어가 모국어라는 이유 하나만으로 그같은 문외한에게 자신이 쓴 영어 문장의 교정을 내맡길 수도 있겠지만, 되도록이면 자기 글의 내용을 잘 아는 자신의 지도교수에게 먼저 부탁을 시도해 보는 것이 올바른 방법이라고 생각한다. 시간상의 이유로 자신의 부탁이 받아들여지지 않았을 때 가장 필요한 사람은 자기 영어의 문제점을 잘 지적해 줄 수 있는 같은 과 친구이다.

자신의 아이디어가 아무리 훌륭해도 영어로 표현되어 있는 것이 어색하고 독자에게 납득이 되지 않을 때 그 글은 무용지물이나 마찬가지이다. 저자 또한, 공들여 쓴 논문을 native speaker의 교정 없이 저널의 논문 의뢰 심사에 제출했다가 영어의 어색한 문장을 이유로 게재 불가 판정을 받은 아픈 기억이 있다. 당시 저자는 '내용은 일급 대학원생 수준을 갖추고 있으나 표현이 서툴러 게재할 정도의 영어 수준이 아니다'라는 심사인의 평가를 받았다. 그때까지도 저자는 자신의 글이 타인의 교정의 도마 위에 올려지는 것이 무척이나 싫었고, 자신의 영어가 그토록 난도질당할 정도로 심각한 지경이었는지 상상도 못하고 있었다. 그러던 중에 진정으로 꼼꼼하게 교정과 조언을 아끼지 않은 같은 과 친구의 도움을 받은 적이 있었다. 절망감과 오기의 발동으로 저자는 똑같은 주제와 내용의 같은 논문을 같은 과 친구에게 교정 proofreading, error correction을 부탁하였다. 눈에 띄는 실수가 적게 나오기도 했지만, 이 친구의 적극적인 도움으로 저자는 학회의 논문 응모에서 당당하게 선정되어 내 자신 미국 유학 생활 최초로 학회에서 발표 presentation를 할 수 있었다.

돌이켜 보면 저자의 논문 작성 writing paper에 많은 발전을 가져다 준 것은 이런 native speaker의 역할이 컸다는 것을 새삼 느끼게 된다. 숱한 자기 반성과 노력도 중요하겠지만 저자는 자신의 영어를 기꺼이 고쳐 주고 충고도 해 줄 수 있는 같은 과 친구가 반드시 필요하다고 생각한다.

Practical Tips for Planning a Career:
Mostly for Ph.D Students Who Intend to Enter the Academic Market

Graduate study is multifaceted and aimed at making the student a uniquely qualified scholar, teacher or general expert in a discipline or set of related disciplines. The time spent in graduate school, at least for those continuing on for the Ph.D., should be viewed as the first step in a lifetime commitment to a field. This is the time to test one's interests and proclivities as one embarks on an arduous, but rewarding path. To this end, the faculty offer adevice, classroom teaching and, at advanced levels, individual guidance in matters related to theses and career preparation in general. Nevertheless, the graduate career should not be seen as a guided tour each student must take responsibility and make an effort to take advantage of opportunities in the Department, in the University (e.g., interdisciplinary courses, workshops, lecture, advising), and in the field in general.

Much of what is outlined below is aimed at the graduate student on the Ph.D. track. However, much of the advice is applicable at the M.A. candidate as well. It is not unusual to enter a graduate program and able uncertain whether graduate study beyond the M.A. is for you. At some point before the M.A., you should decide whether you wish to try for a Ph.D. or not, but there is nothing wrong with being undecided during the first year of study. Many people decide that the M.A. degree is sufficient for their needs and goals. Indeed, the M.A. program is designed to give the student a broad background in appropriate areas that the student is interested, so that the degree is a meaningful indication of achievement in the field. *Work beyond the M.A. entails specialization and special long-term commitment to a particular discipline.* Consequently, it is not for everyone.

Among those things that a student should attend to both inside and outside of the Department are:

1. Give Thought to the Direction of Your Professional Career Now
2. Find the Right Mentor
3. Study in the Target Countries
4. Join Professional Organizations
5. Seek Support in the University at Large and Outside of the University
6. Choose the Right Minor Field
7. Develop a Paper from Course Projects into a Conference Presentation and, perhaps, Publishable Paper

1. Give Thought to the Direction of Your Professional Career Now

If you know that you plan to continue to the Ph.D., start building your career path now. The courses you take depend on the curriculum, faculty availability to give those courses, and your choice from among the courses offered. Demonstrably successful students see their course work not as a smorgasbord of unrelated dishes, but as stepping stones to what will eventually become their dissertation on lifetime research plan. Properly selected, your courses should first give you a broad understanding of the entire field you are studying, and then allow you to focus on the specific problems that will lead eventually to your dissertation work.

This is another reason why the selection of an appropriate minor is so important. In the choices you make (of course, of minors, of second languages, etc.) you are crating a defined professional profile that will form the foundation of your future work.

If you plan to continue to the Ph.D., give thought early to what your dissertation might generally be about (time period, genre, author, problem, theory). Take courses that will support this future research. Choose paper topics that will introduce you to the literature and sources of area in which you will able specializing. By the time you get through the exams and to the dissertation, you will have already done a great deal of preliminary bibliographic and research work and will shorten your dissertation writing time. You will also have built up sufficient expertise in an area to revise a paper for publication.

Take control of your own intellectual and professional development. Consult with your mentor and other faculty as often as you need to, but take personal responsibility for planning and implementing your graduate program.

2. Find the Right Mentor

Every academic program has a unique set of strengths that derives from its mix of faculty interests and the resources of the institution. Presumably, you have chosen to engage in graduate study at the University of _____ in order to take advantage of the unique program offered here. As you advance in the studies toward the Ph.D., you should become increasingly aware of the need to find a mentor or mentors with whom you will work closely and eventually write your dissertation. It is assumed that your dissertation work will be in an area that is closely related to an area of expertise of one or more of the faculty members of the Department. You would not want it any other way the best advice comes an expert. *It stands to reason that you should educate yourself on the interests of the faculty members who are potential mentors. A good way to start is to read their published works and talk with them.* It may be possible to assist them in a research project, allowing you to try out an area and determine whether the area is appropriate for you, i.e., it holds your interest and has derivative possibilities for future pursuit in your own career. Although you will naturally seek a mentor with whom you have rapport, you should find a mentor whose area of interest is in accord with your own.

3. Study in the Target Countries

It is now standard practice for graduate students to stay for an extended time in one or more other countries as a means of gaining language proficiency, acculturation, and acquaintance with professional partners in those countries. There is no set for formula, but is common to spend a semester or an academic year in the country of primary interest and, minimally, a summer in a country of secondary interest. If you foresee yourself as a teacher of Russian and, say, Polish, the professional nowadays expects that you will have spent a substantive amount of time in Russia and Poland engaged in some meaningful academic pursuit. Often there is funding available outside of the University to pursue education goals or work on projects abroad.

In some cases there will be opportunities to serve as a group leader or director of a study group, for which you will receive remuneration along with essential in-country experience. Information on opportunities is available on the continuous basis through posters in the Department as well as on the Internet, through organizations such as the International Research and Exchanges Board(IREX), as well as through individual faculty members.

4. Join Professional Organizations

Professional organizations foster a sense of community across a discipline. The sooner you join and participate in the organization, the sooner you will feel a part of it. Through these organizations you can widen your net of contacts in the profession, help you to seek advice or collaboration on projects, arrange to deliver papers and, ultimately, look for employment through standard search procedures.

5. Seek Support in the University at Large and Outside of the University

Advancement in the profession is in part linked to one's success as obtaining outside support for one's work. Because peer review is involved in the selection of candidates for support, this process serves as a referendum on the candidate's ability to succeed in the profession. *The sooner one can establish a track record of success, the better.* Moreover, it is not bad to have money to pursue one's interests. Although there are relatively smaller amounts of money available for humanities discipline than in the sciences, there is still a surprising number of opportunities available to those who seek them. Information about support can be found on posters in the Department, the Grants Book in the library, through the Humanities Research Center, on the Internet, and through individual faculty member. Individual faculty members can and should be consulted in identifying appropriate sources of funding and applying for them, but one should also take advantage of Graduate School's GFOG database and the Humanities Center.

6. Choose the Right Minor Field

Your ability to obtain gainful employment will depend not only on assembling a coherent set of a academic accomplishments on your vita, but also on the particular combination of areas of expertise that you bring with you. *The minor field has been designed to give you a special, unique academic profile.* When a choosing a minor, ask yourself what area you think would help you to become employed in the kind of job that you envision. For instance, if you are interested in developing your profile as a teacher (including a teacher of teachers), you may with to choose the pedagogy option offered in the Department. If you see yourself as a literature specialist who would like to work in a comparative literature program, you may wish to choose a minor in another cultural area. If you are interested in culture, you might consider philosophy, history, or even anthropology. *No one can predict the future, but everyone can go into it well informed. Once you have selected an advisor, meet regularly with him or her and keep them informed of your progress.*

7. Develop a Paper from Course Projects into a Conference Presentation and, perhaps, Publishable Paper

It has become the norm to have presented a paper at a national conference and, in some cases, to have a paper or two published before on enters the job market. Whether this is a good thing or not is debatable (it can be argued that time spent on the basics in graduate school is more important than time spent on jumping the publishing hurdle; in some cases this may also extend the time to completion of the terminal degree), but the fact remains that the field has come virtually to expect this. Also, preparing a paper to this level of sophistication may be very helpful in preparing for dissertation work. For these reasons, as well as others, it is good idea to try to develop a course project beyond the requirements of a course. A sensible approach would be to revisit the topic with the instructor and work independently under his or her guidance. The instructor can then give advice on when and whether the paper is ready for publication or presentation and, if so, suggest appropriate outlets. But note that not everyone is ready for this at the same time, so do not become overly discouraged if the first attempt does not result in publication. Periodicals have their own refereeing process and may turn down papers or ask for substantial revisions. If you do have a rejection on the first attempt, you should not feel that you are being singled out the same criteria apply both to established professionals as well as graduate students. A good solution for many people will be to try to place their first effort in a graduate essay collection.

General Advice for Job Seekers [12]

How to Begin

As soon as you begin specializing in an area of study with the intention of making a career in that field, you also begin establishing a record of your abilities and accomplishments. The earlier you start planning how to use your time and efforts to best advantage, the better prepared you will be for the rigors of the job search. If you have several years left in graduate school, you can do things right away to make your vita or résumé more impressive and thereby improve your chances of getting the job you want.

Consult the appropriate faculty members: your instructors, your thesis advisers, the graduate director, the placement officer, the department chair. Colleagues who are or have recently been job candidates themselves are good sources of information. Seek their advice on making yourself a better candidate; ask for their help on specific tasks like identifying an appropriate journal to which you might submit an article. Try to get a fuller sense of the profession from them, and solicit their aid in learning about careers outside the academic world. One way to do this is to ask them about their own careers. Consultation not only gets you expert advice but also makes you known to members of the faculty and interests them in your situation and progress. But remember that they are busy people; do not make excessive demands on their time or waste it with pointless meetings. Learn as much as you can about the variety of institutions in the humanities and about professions other than college teaching. You cannot choose a career intelligently without some knowledge of the range of opportunities open to you. Moreover, many of the principles that apply to job hunting in business also apply in the academic world. Talk with your friends enrolled in other graduate programs and with as many other people as you can about their work in business, government, non-profit organizations, and other kinds of employment.

Most graduate students in English and foreign languages expect an academic career in which teaching is crucial. More and more institutions, including research universities, now emphasize the importance of good teaching in their job advertisements. Gain some teaching experience well before you seek a position—as early as your school year or second semester of graduate study. Consciously develop your skills as a classroom teacher, and document these skills in a teaching portfolio. Most departments in American higher education need faculty members who can work effectively with the wide range of students in the introductory language, literature, and writing courses that form a staple of the curriculum. If your department has no systematic provision for supervising and evaluating graduate students' teaching, invite the appropriate faculty members to visit your classes and advise you.

Develop more than one area of expertise. An academic can be pigeonholed for life by the choice if a thesis topic. Even if you are a candidate for a teaching position in your specialty, the ability to take on a variety of teaching assignments will help distinguish you from other candidates. Become knowledgeable about both general areas of teaching in introductory courses and your areas of scholarly specialization.

While graduate study is primarily intended for attaining and deepening knowledge, it is a good idea to keep your professional future in mind as long as you don't curtail your opportunity for exploration and reflection–the long process of intellectual growth. Treat your term papers as possible articles. Conceive of them as the original work of an academic addressing an audience of peers. Write them in the style and format of journal articles. If they seem to have promise, revise them according to the criticism of the professor and send them to appropriate journals. Your first submission may not be accepted, but you will be learning the styles and the procedures. You may receive valuable critiques from the journal editors. If you think your idea is good, do not be discouraged by an initial rejection; revise again, and submit the essay somewhere else. If all goes well, you will have some publications to list on your vita before you complete your degree; at the least, you will have a sample of your work to show to prospective employers, you can list papers on your vita as "submitted for publication," and you will have gained valuable experience.

Class work not suitable for publication may still form the basis for a conference paper. A typical conference paper takes twenty minutes to read; for most people, that means a maximum of ten double-spaced pages. As with an article, if your paper is accepted, you have a significant accomplishment to add to your vita; if not, you will still have acquired experience and gained the attention of colleagues outside your campus. It is through such exposure that you build a network of professional colleagues and find new mentors.

If there is a graduate students' association in your department, participate actively in it. If students give reports on their work in progress, volunteer to give one. Propose someone to be invited as a guest speaker, and take charge of organizing the event, arranging for the room, introducing the guest, and hosting a reception afterward. Some of the best speakers are young scholars who have just published their first books. Such a guest will be flattered by the invitation and grateful for the opportunity to build his or her reputation.

Whenever a scholarly conference in your field takes place on or near your campus, attend. These conferences range from one-time-only events commemorating anniversaries to regular meetings on fairly narrow themes to annual meetings of associations like the MLA and the regional MLAs. To get a feel for them, you may prefer to begin with a smaller one close to your campus; registration will probably cost less, and you will have lower transportation and lodging costs. Graduate students are usually offered lower rates. You may be able to gain valuable experience and to attend free by working on the arrangements. Once you have seen what conferences are like, you should try to give a paper somewhere.

Many graduate departments sponsor a journal or serve as the headquarters for a scholarly society. Inquire about working for them. You will learn something about editing and management and will have opportunities for meeting people at other institutions.

All these actions can be taken early, and they should grow naturally out for your course work and research interests. You will want to know what others are working on and thinking about. You may feel uncomfortable at first approaching scholars who are not your professors, but common intellectual interests provide a basis for such discussions, and scholarly activities are designed to provide opportunities for them.

Since all these activities are associated with graduate work, their most obvious relevance is to an academic career. Each one, however, affords some experience that will have value in nonteaching jobs as well. The efforts you make to broaden your range of abilities will supply evidence of initiative. In addition, meeting with people in business, government, and other fields can help you decide how to orient your career and at the same time help allay employers' fears that you have decided to look at jobs outside the academy only as a desperate last resort.

- Start now
- Consult
- Read about the teaching profession, about other professions, and about job hunting
- Get teaching experience and develop and document your teaching abilities
- Submit articles for publication
- Go to conferences and give papers
- Look for professional opportunities in your department
- Develop more than one specialty

Preparing for the First Job Search

When

At some point in your career it will be time to leave graduate school and find a job. Once—that is, for many people who are today senior members of the faculty—this moment often arrived soon after the comprehensive examination; the student by then had completed all residency and credit requirements, and passage of the exam signified readiness to write the dissertation. More recently, most PhD candidates have remained at their graduate institutions, often as part-time teachers, while completing their dissertations. You should try to stay on campus until work on the thesis is well under way, at least; afterward, as in ABD (that is, someone who has completed all requirements but the dissertation), you can presumably work independently most of the time and send chapters to your director at intervals for criticism and advice. Your thesis work may affect your freedom; someone doing expensive research or using primary sources would require access to a major library and might not be able to work effectively in a small college in a remote area.

You will need to plan ahead for the year when you actually expect to look for openings and submit applications. The academic hiring cycle in four-year colleges coincides roughly with the academic year, beginning in September and ending in May, June, or sometimes even later. In community colleges positions are usually filled more quickly. You should take some important steps in the spring preceding that year, so it is to your advantage to make a firm decision around January that you will begin looking systematically in the fall and to set up certain parts of your campaign right away.

Outside higher education, job hunting is less seasonal and less organized across the entire field. Hiring takes place whenever a vacancy occurs or a new position develops, and searching for a job candidate usually takes far less time than the academic year faculties devote to it. Although advance preparation is equally important in all areas of employment, the highly defined structure of the academic job market is easier to describe systematically.

The Vita

Whatever sort of job you look for, you will need a document containing a record of what you have done and a description of what you can do. In the academic world, this document is called a curriculum vitae, vita, or cv; the other fields of employment it is called a résumé. The formats vary according to the kind of job (the specific variations are explained in the following chapters), but it is always crucial to follow the customary format and to prepare the document flawlessly, with professional-quality world processing and photocopying. Even before this document is read, its appearance will make an impression. Take great care with its preparation and format. When printing or photocopying, use white or cream-colored 20-pound-weight paper.

Obviously, an attractive, letter-perfect presentation will not compensate for a lack of substance. If you have weak credentials, perhaps you ought to delay the job search another year. However, placement counselors can often bring to light items that candidates overlook; get some advice before you make your decision. If you assess your status in January, moreover, you will have time to improve your qualifications before September.

Under no circumstances should you pad the vita or résumé with trivial or irrelevant items. Length is no asset if your audience finds the content unimpressive. You must consider the reader's perspective: a personnel officer in a business firm will be interested in your writing and public-speaking skills but not your scholarly publications, whereas a college department chair will pay close attention to a record of teaching and publication. Your work advising a student newspaper might be important to a community college department, but probably not to a university department.

References

You will need letters of recommendation or at least the names of people willing to write letters if asked. It is difficult to offer general suggestions about whom to approach; to some extent, that decision must depend on the type of job you want, maybe even the specific job. A letter carries much more weight if the reader knows the author personality. Students tend to want letters from the most famous members of the faculty; if Professor Superstar writes on behalf of fifteen or twenty students every year, though, a less prominent colleague who writes for only two or three may serve you better. Someone who knows you well is certainly preferable to someone, however celebrated and powerful, who can write about only in vague generalities. And it is essential to have at least one letter from a person who can comment knowledgably and specifically on your abilities and accomplishment as a teacher.

One thing is certain: you cannot wait until the last minute to line up your references. During your years of graduate study, you must earn the support of at least four people with established reputations. Consult with your thesis advisers and the department chair about the choice of references. Courtesy requires that you ask the permission of those you list as references. Very few people will write negative letters, if they agree to write; at worst they will fill their letters with vague clichés. Someone who begs off, claiming to be too busy or not to know you well enough, should not be pressed, no matter how flimsy the excuse seems to you.

Under federal law, certain letters of recommendation cannot be kept confidential from their subjects unless the subject waives the right to see the letters. University placement offices often have a form for letters of recommendation with a waiver printed on it. Some experienced people in the field urge candidates to sign the waiver. They argue that students who insist on the right to see the letters may appear insecure and suspicious and may annoy their own supporters. Many people will simply refuse to write without the waiver, and those who write may resort to bland, cautious comments of little use. Others, however, think that it is never inappropriate to avail yourself of your legal rights. You should know that employers have the right to check references using the telephone. There is certainly no reason for you to raise the waiver, but you should think about it and make up your mind about what to do, in case it comes up.

Cover Letter

Whenever you send the vita of résumé to a prospective employer, you must accompany it with a letter. In the academic world, this letter is usually called a letter of application; in business it is called a cover letter. Here again, appearance is extremely important; the letter should be flawlessly typed on good stationery, institutional letterhead if appropriate (your chair or director of graduate studies will advise you). Although the vita or résumé may be photocopied, these letters should be prepared individually for each job. If you revise your letters on a word processor, be careful: some experienced chairs report receiving application letters with the addresses of another department still in the upper-left corner. The letter offers you your only chance to explain why your skills and interests make you a strong candidate for this particular job. Do not waste that chance by sending an imperfect letter.

As a rule, a letter of application should run a page and a half to two typewritten pages in length. It should describe your qualifications and interests as a teacher as well as your dissertation and developing scholarly interests. The description of the dissertation should be concise and should be accessible to prospective colleagues who may be working in fields distant from your own. Avoid vogue phrases or jargon. And remember: your readers will search your letter for evidence that you do or do not understand the specific demands and rewards of working in their department or type of department. Beware the all-too-common mistake of sending a cover letter emphasizing one's ambitions for a high-profile research career to a department in an institution that requires heavy teaching loads and values teaching nonmajors and service on campus more than national visibility through publication.

Departmental Services

Many departments offer services for students who are looking for jobs. Some possibilities include a late spring meeting at which prospective job hunters, veterans of the previous year's efforts, and younger faculty members talk together; an early fall meeting at which the department chair, graduate director, or placement officer goes over specifics; an individual conference with the faculty member heading the department's placement effort; and a meeting before the MLA convention to practice with mock interviews.

Above all, keep your advisers informed. Let them know as soon as you decide to look; ask them for help with any problem and advice on any questions; tell them about any response you get from a prospective employer; discuss any plans you have. If nothing seems to be happening, go over your situation with them. Throughout your career, success will depend on the support of colleagues and mentors.

- Allow plenty of time for the actual job search
- Prepare a budget and acquire a major credit card
- Prepare your vita of résumé in advance
- Pay attention to appearance
- Pay attention to the audience
- Line up your letters of recommendation
- Write letters of application or cover letter individually
- Make use of departmental services
- Keep your advisers informed

Letters of Application

You may hear of job openings in various ways. For academic jobs in language and literature departments, the MLA *Job Information List* gives the most convenient and reliable information, especially in the period from October to January. From January forward, be sure to consult listings in the *Chronicle of Higher Education* if you have not been doing so up to then. As soon as possible after the List appears, you should send letters of application in response to all the appropriate announcements. For jobs in academic administration, consult the Chronicle. For jobs in two-year colleges, consult local newspapers or the college personnel office. For jobs in not-profit organizations, government, or business, you may have to pursue leads from a variety of sources, including the placement office, classified ads, personal contacts, and visits to potential employers. Sooner or later, however, you will probably write a letter of application to some of them.

The letter of application is one of the most important documents you will ever write. Give it the thought and care it deserves. While you can work out the paragraphs describing your dissertation and teaching experience well in advance in consultation with your advisers, you should prepare every letter individually on a word processor in correct business format. If you are entitled to use a letterhead from your department, do so.

The letter is intended to present you and your qualifications crisply and attractively. It should address itself explicitly to the requirements stated in the announcement. It should be precise, well structured, and appropriately styled. Remember that its appearance, manner of expression, and tone will constitute the first personal impression you make.

In the heading of the letter, give the address at which you wish to receive mail; this address should also be on your vita. On the left, above the salutation, place the name and address of the person to whom you are writing. Whenever possible, address the letter to an individual, not simply to the office.

In the first paragraph, state what job announcement you are responding to; mention both the title of the job and the place where you saw the ad, or explain how you heard of the job. In the second paragraph, present yourself, mentioning your degree status and institution or your current job. Assert your eligibility for the job, and mention the aspects of your background that meet its specific requirements. Make every effort to show that you understand the character and needs of the department and institution—a small college in an isolated rural area, a regional state university with a diverse and nonselective admissions policy, a nationally recognized PhD-granting department, or a multi-campus two-year college in a major metropolitan area.

Avoid simply repeating the information on your vita. Highlight the strong points and elaborate on them. If, for example, the job calls for specialty in a century and your ideas falls within the period, describe what you are writing about. If the job calls for experience in teaching a certain area, give some details about the courses you have taught. You should apply for positions for which you are clearly not qualified, but the number of teaching jobs is too small to ignore those for which your qualifications are close but not perfect. For nonacademic jobs, discuss the value of your graduate education for the field you hope to enter. You should expect some skepticism about the suitability of graduate school as a preparation for other careers. Never lie or falsify your preparation, but put the best face on what you have done and avid self-deprecation. A positive, upbeat attitude will be especially important when you present graduate work to nonacademic employers. Before you write the letter, visit the library and consult your faculty advisers and friends to learn whatever you can about the employer. Anything you can cite that makes the job special to you will improve your chances.

In the closing paragraphs, take care of the practical matters. Mention the vita and any other enclosures. Explain where your dossier is on file and how it can be obtained; if you have to order it yourself, offer to do so. Have a chapter of your dissertation or some other substantial piece of writing ready to send; describe what you have, and offer to send it on request.

Enclose a stamped, self-addressed postcard with which your application can be acknowledged. Be sure to put some identification on the card so that you will know who has returned it, in the event it is simply dropped in the mail. Mention the card in your letter, and ask whether it could be used to tell you when you might have further word.

Show your letters of application to your adviser before you send them, and incorporate any recommended changes.

- Write various sections of your letter of application early and in consultation with your advisers
- Send letters of application promptly
- Write each letter individually
- Pay attention to the appearance of the letters
- Highlight your qualifications for the particular job
- Do not just repeat your vita; amplify, explain, give new information
- Tailor your letter to the job
- Do not apply for jobs for which you are not qualified
- Enclose a stamped, self-addressed card for acknowledgement
- Keep a copy of each letter
- Have your adviser check your letter of application before you send them

What Happens Next

Candidates for jobs in colleges and universities tend to hear of many openings at once, to apply for several at a time, and then to hear the results, good or bad, between October and April. Outside academe, cycles are more varied, if, indeed, hiring follows a cycle at all.

Within a couple of weeks, you should receive the acknowledgement card; if you do not, telephone to make sure your letter arrived. Some departments will give you specific dates for the further stages of the hiring procedures; others will simply return the card. Some, giving little or no explanation, may even notify you by return mail that you do not qualify as a candidate.

Do not become discouraged or depressed by early negative responses; remember that the rejections always come first. The competition is intense, and all but one of the applications for any given job must be turned down at some point. It is in fact a courtesy to the unsuccessful applicants to notify them as soon as possible. Departments usually try to communicate this disappointing news as tactfully as possible, but most will give only vague and general reasons, frequently in a form letter. Often the letter will say something like "Your qualifications do not fit our needs," which may seem quite untrue to you, but do not waste your time writing back. Occasionally you may get an intensively worded rejection; resist the impulse to dash off a rejoinder, try not to let it bother you, and console yourself with the thought that you would not have wanted to work with such people anyway.

The earliest favorable responses will probably be requests for your dossier. If you have to order it from the placement office or authorize its release, do so as promptly as possible. When you have done so, send the requesting department a note to inform them. Notify your department and your advisers about any dossier requests; your professors may be able to give you useful advice about the job and may be willing to send a supporting note to make a telephone call to a colleague on that campus. Meanwhile you should begin to prepare yourself by doing some additional research on the institution.

Requests for the dossier indicate some interest, but only at the most tentative level. You may hear nothing more for a long time, and you may then be notified that you are no longer a candidate. If you were given a timetable and you do not hear when you should, feel free to call and ask what your status is and when you can expect to hear something more. You may not improve your situation, but you can probably clarify it.

If your dossier confirms your qualifications for the jobs, the department may invite you to an interview. This invitation expresses real interest. When done with care, conducting interviews is expensive, time-consuming, and demanding; only those with a real chance at the job are likely to be invited. The interview is also one of the most important elements in the screening process. You should respond favorably to any invitations and—if the interview is to take place at the MLA convention or if the institution is not far from your own—should be willing to bear some inconvenience and expense to accommodate the search committee or the head of the hiring department.. as soon as you have scheduled an interview, you should learn more about the school and the members of the department. Outside the academic world almost all interviewing is done at the site of the job and usually at the candidate's expense; at least for entry-level positions. The significance of being interviewed may also vary widely from one situation to another.

Inevitably, much of your time will be spent waiting. The stress of living in uncertainty, of building up hopes and having them dashed, can wreck your morale. The best way to ward off depression is to use the time making yourself a better candidate. Don't cry to keep your anxiety to yourself; talk to your advisers, your colleagues, and your friends. Don't stake all your hopes on one kind of job; make some contingency plans. The research for the first job is in many ways the hardest, but you will find the pattern repeated many times in an academic career, as you look for other jobs, watch the mail for news of your manuscripts of the fellowship winners, and await decision on promotion and tenure. The search and the waiting are part of the career.

- Do not be discouraged by early negative responses
- Keep your morale up
- React promptly to positive responses
- Do not just wait; use the time constructively

Conventions

The conventions of professional associations and learned societies play an important role in the careers of most academics. Graduate students often attend primarily to participate in the job service, especially to be available for interviews. Many other useful activities take place at conventions, however, and you should not limit your attention to job hunting. In fact, the MLA convention is well worth attending whether or not you have interviews scheduled and whether or not you expect to look for a teaching job in the future. Conventions offer unique opportunities for professional networking, for establishing and consolidating with colleagues from other campuses the sort of personal contacts you have with your teachers, your fellow students, and eventually your departmental colleagues.

Two-year colleges usually hold interviews in their regions rather than at the convention. The MLA convention is one of the largest in the academic world, with an average attendance of seven to ten thousand people. Traditionally, it is held every year on the same dates, 27 to 30 December, but in different cities. You need not be an MLA member to attend, although members enjoy advantageous registration rates and are sure to receive the announcements in good time.

A typical MLA convention program, which appears as the November issue of *PMLA*, lists over seven hundred functions, most of which are literary or pedagogical sessions where scholars and teachers give papers. In addition, a number of sessions every year are devoted to advising job candidates, and many others deal with practical professional matters. The program also includes a large number of social functions that, although they may place limits on attendance, are open to all registrations on a first-come, first-served basis.

As a newcomer to the profession, you should pay special attention to the sessions on the profession itself. The MLA-sponsored Association of Departments of English (ADE) and Association of Departments of Foreign Languages (ADFL) conduct workshops at the start of the convention to counsel job candidates. Some other typical subjects for professional sessions include part-time teachers, independent scholars, translation as profession, book reviewing, leaving the academy, the reward system for faculty members, the first year of teaching, the public perception of academe, women in the profession, faculty members in two-year colleges, business careers for PhDs, pedagogy and curriculum, scholarly publishing, grants, fellowships, and publishing your first book. In all these sessions, you can get advice directly from experts on the practical questions you have to face as an academic or as a PhD in a nonacademic job.

The paper-reading sessions are organized around subjects. The typical session has a presider and three speakers; their names and the titles of their papers are given in the program. If you want to hear one of the papers, you simply wear your convention badge proving that you have registered, walk in, and sit down. Many people in the audience come and go between speakers.

If there is discussion afterward, it is a good idea to ask a question, but MLA convention sessions usually do not evoke the sort of give-and-take from the audience that arises in more cohesive groups on a campus, for example, or at a small colloquium on a single subject. It is frequently more productive to go up to the rostrum afterward, introduce yourself to the speakers and organizers, ask questions then, mention your own interests in the area, and—especially in sessions sponsored by a division?inquire about the next year's program, many sessions welcome submissions from anyone.

- Attend an MLA convention before you go as a job seeker
- Take advantage of the Preconvention Workshops for Job Seekers, the Mock Interviews for Job Seekers, and the individual counseling at the Job Information Center
- Go to the sessions on professional topics
- Consider giving a paper
- Look for ways to meet colleagues in your field